EVATT

JOHN MURPHY is a professor of politics in the school of Social aɪ Political Sciences at the University of Melbourne. His previo books include *Harvest of Fear: A History of Australia's Vietnam W* (1993), *Imagining the Fifties: Private Sentiment and Political Culture Menzies' Australia* (2000), and *A Decent Provision: Australian Welfɑ Policy 1870 to 1949* (2011).

EVATT

John Murphy   *a life*

NEWSOUTH

A NewSouth book

Published by
NewSouth Publishing
University of New South Wales Press Ltd
University of New South Wales
Sydney NSW 2052
AUSTRALIA
newsouthpublishing.com

© John Murphy 2016
First published 2016

10 9 8 7 6 5 4 3 2 1

National Library of Australia
Cataloguing-in-Publication entry
Creator: Murphy, John, 1954– author.
Title: Evatt : a life / John Murphy.
ISBN: 9781742234465 (hardback)
ISBN: 9781742247779 (epdf)
ISBN: 9781742242408 (ebook)
Notes: Includes bibliographical references and index.
Subjects: Evatt, H. V. (Herbert Vere), 1894–1965
Australian Labor Party—History—1945–1965.
Cabinet officers—Australia—Biography.
Foreign ministers—Australia—Biography.
Judges—Australia—Biography.
Politicians—Australia—Biography.
Australia--Foreign relations—20th century.
Australia—History—20th century.
Dewey Number: 324.29407092

Design Josephine Pajor-Markus
Cover design Xou Creative
Cover images Ralph Sallon, Flinders University Library no. 622.
© Phillip Sallon.
Printer Everbest Printing

Contents

Acknowledgements   *vi*

Author's notes   *viii*

Abbreviations   *x*

Introduction: The puzzle   *1*

1   The boy   *14*

2   The young Evatt   *33*

3   Love and the law   *51*

4   Politics and Jack Lang   *70*

5   The judge   *91*

6   The moderns   *113*

7   The historian as judge   *135*

8   The celebrity candidate   *157*

9   The minister   *183*

10   To San Francisco   *214*

11   'The president of the world'   *241*

12   The Labor leader   *267*

13   The Petrov affair   *297*

14   'The wrecker'   *323*

15   The wreckage   *344*

16   'Dropping the pilot'   *372*

Epilogue   *384*

The players   *386*

Notes   *393*

Sources   *426*

Bibliography   *432*

Index   *442*

Acknowledgements

I am very grateful to the Australian Research Council for a generous Discovery grant in 2012–2014 that enabled me to conduct the research for this book. Without their funding support, it would not have been possible.

For their permission to research records held in the National Library of Australia, I am grateful to Australian Labor Party national secretary George Wright, for the papers of the ALP federal secretariat; to ALP caucus secretary Tim Watts, for the minutes of the federal parliamentary Labor party caucus, and to federal director Brian Loughnane, for selected records of the Liberal Party of Australia federal secretariat.

People who have care of archives are essential to historical research; they help you find your way through the labyrinth, and their enthusiasm for research is often infectious. First among them for my fulsome thanks are Gillian Dooley and her staff at the Flinders University Library in Adelaide, where the voluminous Evatt collection is housed.

I am grateful to the staff in Canberra at the National Archives, the National Film and Sound Archive, and the National Library of Australia in the manuscripts reading room and oral history collections; in Sydney, at the National Archives; in Melbourne, at the State Library of Victoria and the University of Melbourne archives; in Maitland, at the Maitland Public Library; in London, at the UK National Archives; in Austin, Texas, at the Harry Ransom Humanities Research Center; in Washington, at the Library of Congress, and in Hyde Park, New York State, at the Franklin Delano Roosevelt Library.

I am very grateful to Janet McCalman for her advice on how to interpret Mary Alice's medical crisis in the early 1920s, and to Dennis Velakoulis, David Ames and Geoff Donnan for advice on how to interpret Evatt's personality and his medical condition leading to dementia in the early 1960s.

For their hospitality while on research trips, I am grateful to Della Rowley and Louise Fuller in Adelaide, Cassandra and David Morrow in Canberra, and Sean Kidney and Julie Bishop in London.

At NewSouth Publishing, for guiding the book to publication, my thanks to Phillipa McGuinness, Paul O'Beirne and Elizabeth Cowell.

I particularly thank Carla Pascoe and Bill Garner for their huge efforts in helping with research assistance, and for providing their insights into what it all meant. Colleagues at the University of Melbourne and the Australian National University have been among those who have listened to me talk about the research and provided their insights. I am grateful to Mark Considine and Adrian Little for their support.

For reading and commenting on the final draft I am very thankful for the help of Peter Beilharz, Judy Brett, Lynn Buchanan, Bill Garner and Jenny Lord. As usual, none of the above should be held responsible for my own mistakes or misinterpretations.

And as usual and once again, my thanks to Lynn for putting up with another book.

Author's notes

Currency

Australia used pounds until 1966, before changing to dollars with decimalisation, when one pound was worth two dollars. My calculations for the current value of amounts mentioned in the text are based on the calculator on the Reserve Bank of Australia's website, which translates a given value of pounds in a given year into an equivalent value in dollars today.

The Labor party and the labour movement

Given it is such an important part of Evatt's life but may be unfamiliar to some readers, it is worth describing the structure and terminology of the Australian Labor Party at the time.

The ALP is structured federally, with a federal party and state 'branches'. Both the federal and state branches hold 'conferences', which ostensibly determine the policies ('platform') of the party. Conferences elect administrative officials: the 'president' and 'secretary' and the members of the 'executive', for the federal and each state branch.

The executive had considerable power in the running of the party between conferences, especially in deciding policy, and in 'preselection' or 'endorsement' of candidates for parliament. The federal executive – with representatives from each state – also had significant power to intervene in the affairs of a state branch.

The executives at state and federal level did not formally include any members of parliament; it was only in the late 1960s that the leader and deputy leader of the federal parliamentary party were ex officio included on the federal executive. ALP members of the federal parliament met in 'caucus'. Caucus elected, or deposed its parliamentary leadership. This caucus arrangement was duplicated in each state.

The relationship between the union movement (or the 'industrial wing') and the Labor party (the 'political wing') is crucial to understanding the ALP in this period. The combination of both is the 'labour movement'. Unions formally 'affiliated' with the ALP paid membership fees and had votes at conferences in proportion to their size. Key figures in larger unions held a significant position in the party.

In each state, unions were also members of their separate organisation, with various titles – in New South Wales, the Trades and Labour Council, and in Victoria, the Trades Hall Council. From 1927, these state-level organisations also formed a federal body, the Australian Council of Trade Unions, though during Evatt's lifetime it was not the powerful body it later became.

Finally, the spelling of 'Labor' or 'Labour': people used both spellings in the early years, but in 1912 the federal ALP formally decided it was 'Labor'. Yet both spellings continued in use, with a good deal of inconsistency. The 'labour movement' has always had that spelling.

The Hansard records of parliamentary debates, major newspapers and many Liberal politicians usually used 'Labour', presumably disapproving of the Americanism.

I have adopted the practice of the ALP's centenary historian, Ross McMullin, who used 'Labor' whenever possible – even retrospectively, in cases where 'Labour' was more likely – except in direct quotations from printed sources.

Key players

A listing of key players at the back of the book is intended to help readers keep track of the large number of characters in the story of Evatt's life.

Abbreviations

ALP	Australian Labor Party
ASIO	Australian Security Intelligence Organisation
AWC	Advisory War Council
AWU	Australian Workers' Union
CPA	Communist Party of Australia
DLP	Democratic Labor Party
ILO	International Labour Organization
MP	Member of Parliament
NATO	North Atlantic Treaty Organization
UAP	United Australia Party
UN	United Nations
UNESCO	United Nations Educational, Scientific and Cultural Organization

In 1935, when Evatt was a High Court judge, he bustled into Arnold Shore's Melbourne studio and asked him to paint a portrait. Evatt is wearing the robe of his Doctor of Laws, awarded by the University of Sydney a decade before. From the mid-1930s, he became an enthusiastic champion of the modern art movement. The moderns gave him a nickname – 'Judgie' – and the vermillion colour of his robe was his favourite, which they called 'Jevattred', as in 'Judge Evatt red'.

'HV (Doc) Evatt', 1935 by Arnold Shore (1897–1963), oil on canvas, National Portrait Gallery, Canberra. Gift of Elizabeth Evatt and Penelope Seidler 1998. Reproduced with permission of Malcolm Shore.

Introduction

The puzzle

Herbert Vere Evatt often perplexed and sometimes intrigued those around him – both his friends and his foes. He has perplexed me for some years now, as I have tried to 'write him down'; he is a difficult subject for a biography, for reasons I will attempt to explain. And he is intriguing. He was often described as an enigma, full of puzzling contradictions. He had intellectual brilliance and reached extraordinary heights, yet was so clearly flawed and quite often foolish. He was intellectually complex but emotionally simple, and sometimes childish. He was one of the most important figures of the 1940s and 1950s, and a household name about whom everyone had an opinion; he drew controversy down upon himself, polarising opinion, particularly in the intense 'us and them' political climate of the Cold War. The puzzling things about him were not just his idiosyncratic habits, such as phoning colleagues at 3 am and not noticing they resented being woken, or wearing newspaper inside his clothes to keep out the cold and ward off vapours. His puzzles went much deeper, to baffling misjudgements, to strange fractures through his character and an apparent inability to read the social world around him.

The most glaring example occurred on the evening of 19 October 1955. Giving a speech in parliament on the tabling of the report of the Royal Commission on Espionage, Evatt fatally undermined his remaining political credibility with what some journalists called his 'Molotov cocktail'. To place this in context, we need to recall the intense emotional atmosphere of Cold War alarms and anxieties about Soviet espionage, about local communist subversion and about an imminent third world war. For years, the Labor party and especially Evatt himself as their idiosyncratic leader had been accused of being too sympathetic to communism. Continuous pressure from the Menzies government had driven a wedge into Labor's ranks, dividing its own vigorous anti-communists from others who increasingly worried the anti-communists were taking over the party.

In early 1954, Prime Minister Robert Menzies had announced gravely that Vladimir Petrov, a spy based in the Soviet embassy in Canberra, had defected, bringing with him documents that revealed the extent of espionage in Australia. In the election shortly after, the Menzies government won again, and Evatt was denied his chance at the prime ministership. Evatt's own interventions into the royal commission Menzies had established to investigate Petrov's documents and espionage in general had only increased tensions inside the Labor party. Seven months before Evatt stood up to make this speech, the party had formally and disastrously split, with the Catholic right-wing anti-communists expelled. The Democratic Labor Party that formed out of the wreckage directed its supporters to give their preferences to the conservatives and helped keep Labor out of power federally until 1972.

On this evening in October 1955, the parliamentary galleries were full of journalists, diplomats and interested citizens who had been queuing for hours. Evatt was by this time aged sixty-one and had grown rather portly; he was typically dishevelled; his leadership of a stricken party was embattled. He had been quite obsessed by the Petrov affair, which he and many others in Labor's ranks saw as a conspiracy to damage the ALP and himself. But his speech was expected to be a vindication, with Menzies thought to be embarrassed that the royal commission had apparently come to very little. Yet early in a very long and argumentative speech, Evatt surprised everyone by announcing he had written to Vyacheslav Molotov, the Soviet foreign minister, a senior member of the Politburo, and a dedicated follower of Stalin since the 1920s.

Incredibly, he had asked Molotov to confirm whether Petrov's documents detailing Soviet espionage were genuine; the reply duly came that the letters were fabrications. The idea that Molotov might admit to espionage was ludicrous. Labor parliamentarians were appalled and incredulous, while their opponents laughed, stamped their feet and shouted 'Molotov'. Stan Keon, one of the most able and vociferous of the anti-communists who had been recently expelled from the Labor party, interjected, asking whether Evatt's letter to Molotov had been headed 'Dear Boss'. Evatt had foolishly thrown away any advantage he had, deflecting attention towards his naivety. Kim Beazley senior recalled in his memoirs: 'The Liberals were roaring with laughter and Evatt couldn't see why. The Labor Party sat stunned'.

Frank Chamberlain, the political correspondent for Keith Murdoch's *Sun* newspaper in Melbourne, was sitting above in the press gallery. Evatt had phoned him at home, telling him not miss the occasion, saying, 'I will expose the Petrov ploy once and for all'. Chamberlain later recalled the scene; the parliament was restless and Menzies was looking glum. When Evatt started to talk about writing to Molotov, he saw Menzies pulling his chair forward, signalling his colleagues to be quiet and listening intently; Evatt held up the letter from Molotov triumphantly and declared he attached great important to it. Most accounts of this dramatic event focus on the pandemonium that then broke loose, but Chamberlain was watching Menzies who, he said 'rubbed his hands together', and said clearly, 'The Lord hath delivered him into my hands'.

Evatt had been warned by several colleagues not to send this letter to Molotov. His friend and political ally Les Haylen remembered seeing a draft in the typewriter and persuading Evatt it was unwise; Evatt conceded that he was 'a bit too emotional' about the whole Petrov issue. But he was also obstinate. At the end of January 1955, shortly before the Labor party split, Evatt took the dog for a walk in Canberra's streets and deposited the letter at the Swedish embassy; diplomatic relations with the Soviets had been suspended after Petrov's defection and the Swedes were handling communications. In early February, Evatt followed up with another letter to the Swedish ambassador, reminding him to forward the letter and saying it was a matter of 'grave urgency'.

Many felt the revelation of this 'Molotov letter' was the beginning of the end for Evatt, evidence of his erratic and wilful behaviour, or the decline of his mental capacities; for some, it is evidence of madness. Haylen said: 'It was a disaster. And as soon as that hit us we knew we were out of government for many years to come'. Beazley saw it as proof that Evatt's judgement had become 'more and more erratic'. The young historian Russel Ward had helped draft the speech, but listening on the radio was then bewildered to hear the reference to Molotov, which had not been there before. Evatt, he wrote, 'had always been prone to misjudge ordinary people's reactions in the realm of practical affairs, but the Molotov blunder was more than that: it was the first unmistakable sign of the degeneration of his formidable mental and physical powers'.

While obviously a political blunder, Evatt's speech may have been evidence of his mental deterioration; five years later he was declining into significant dementia, and some then and since have read backwards to say that he was unhinged, if not insane. But the sort of misjudgement he made with his Molotov letter was not out of character. As Ward said, he was prone to misjudgements; further, he was usually convinced that he was right. While part of the puzzle is the contrast between intelligence and foolishness, there is no reason to expect that Evatt's prodigious intellectual gifts should be combined with emotional intelligence, let alone common sense or political judgement; life is replete with proofs to the contrary. But it is not enough to say, as Kylie Tennant did in her biography of Evatt, that he was simply trying to be rational in a political atmosphere that was inherently irrational. The deeper puzzle is what Evatt thought he was doing on this as on other occasions, and how his own rationale might illuminate his obstinate and contrary character.

Writing biography

Evatt has been the subject of three full-scale biographies, as well as smaller studies focused on his role in foreign affairs, or his role during the Cold War. He is necessarily a player, sometimes a central figure, in biographies of others from his period, and of memoirs and histories of the times in which he acted. An enormous number of people have been interviewed about him – journalists, politicians, bureaucrats, family and friends – all reflecting on who he was and what he meant, and I have made extensive use of over forty of these oral histories. In one sense, Evatt has been voluminously interpreted and over-interpreted, and that might seem quite enough. Yet Evatt's complicated and puzzling character often stays out of focus, evading capture or only being captured in fragments.

Kylie Tennant's 1970 biography was preoccupied with defending Evatt against what she saw as calumnies thrown at him during the highly wrought tensions of the Cold War. She shared that context and motivation with Allan Dalziel, who published in 1967 a portrait of the man for whom he worked as private secretary. These books were too invested in the Cold War, which had laid down such a dense thicket of interpretation about Evatt that it can be hard to see a way through. But the simplified polarities of the Cold War can now be left in the past, even if they shape the relics of the past that come down to us. We no longer need to be for or against him.

A different sort of attempt was Peter Crockett's 1993 biography, based on a great deal of research and often antagonistic towards Evatt; it was badly marred by a complexity of psychological layering that obscured its subject. While Tennant's story of a Titan brought down by lesser mortals leaves us wondering about all that she left out, and in that sense was too coherent, Crockett's account ventured so far into the psychological exploration of contradictions that all coherence was lost. Yet another biography was published the following year by historians Ken Buckley, Barbara Dale and Wayne Reynolds. It was commissioned by the Evatt Foundation and while insightful it was also very uneven, being written by three different hands. Like Tennant's book, it had a similar though more sophisticated dedication to restoring Evatt's place in history and countering his critics; some of this partiality was signalled by the heroic subtitle: 'Patriot, Internationalist, Fighter and Scholar'.

In some ways, the most penetrating portraits of Evatt are not biographies. Paul Hasluck worked closely with him in the Department of External Affairs in the 1940s, before entering parliament as a Liberal and himself becoming foreign minister. He wrote about Evatt as a minister, as an intellectual and as a person, and his recollections are revealing, not at all blind to Evatt's flaws but often generous and psychologically insightful. Evatt's friend, the American writer and academic Hartley Grattan, wrote a long notebook, originally composed for Tennant and intended to be the beginning of a biography he never wrote. Grattan's is an outsider's view, enriched by his deep knowledge of Australia and its politics, and he saw Evatt warts and all and tried to understand his contradictions. In the narrative that follows, I draw on both Hasluck and Grattan for their judicious insights into a character they knew well.

Many who commented on Evatt saw him as a complicated and bewildering mix, especially the journalists of the time, who found him by far the most intriguing character in politics. Alan Reid, for example, described him as 'a wonderfully complex character'. Keith Brennan, who was Evatt's associate when he was a High Court judge, was interviewed by Peter Crockett, and said something about this complexity that is inherently dispiriting for a biographer to hear:

> No generalisation about Bert Evatt holds up ... He was such a
> complex character, and nobody is ever going to write him, no
> way. I don't want to discourage you, but ... particularly to try to
> reconstruct a man of his complexity from externals in the memory
> of other people, you know. Hopeless.

I found these words discouraging because Brennan was saying that this biography is impossible.

A biography needs to be more than just a description of a trajectory through life: it is also an attempt to make sense of the self who passes along that trajectory; in short, to describe both character and identity. This sort of self is what we all experience, and perhaps this is what continues to make biography a compelling genre; we experience and remember our own selves as an unfolding narrative, with beginning, middle and end, and see some of the same in the life of another. As the philosopher Alasdair MacIntyre wrote, narrative of this sort is 'the basic and essential genre' for understanding the actions of others because we experience our own lives in terms of a narrative. It need not be neatly integrated or free of contradiction, but our sense of self is reasonably coherent and unitary, and the biographer hopefully provides a similar insight into the character of their subject. But this is especially challenging when confronted by a character as contrary as Evatt, whose narrative and whose identity can be perplexing.

Nevertheless, it seems to me that several aspects of his personality are the key to unlocking the whole. They do not necessarily explain the foolishness of the Molotov letter, but they start to describe consistent character traits and flaws that explain him, and it is worth rehearsing them here so that the reader can assess them in the pages that follow. The first is Evatt's ambition, his drive to excel and to win the prize, on which almost everyone commented. There was never any doubting Evatt's vaulting ambition. Hasluck joked that he imagined if Evatt was ever stranded in a country town and found the local football team was holding its annual general meeting he would be there wanting to be elected president. 'Ambition was both a spur and an impediment to him.' Hasluck wrote in his journal a few days after Evatt's death: 'He could not stop striving for the prize, whatever it was, big or little, or pause to consider [if] the effort was well applied'. It was not simply ambition – something else drove him on – but Hasluck confessed he was uncertain what the 'tangle of impulse' was. Grattan wrote that

Evatt's desperate desire to succeed destroyed him: 'No matter how high he rose, his ambition was still unappeased – undisciplined or uncanalized ambition was Evatt's "disease"'. In a sense, this was more than mere ambition: it was an urgent need to win in whatever sphere of work he was in, an extreme form of competitiveness that was never satisfied.

Second there is Evatt's overweening self-regard. This was in part narcissism, a pattern of grandiosity and demand for admiration, though narcissism is usually seen as self-importance out of kilter with actual achievements. Evatt drove himself to win all the prizes, and he reached great heights through intellectual ability and extraordinarily hard work. His brilliance at university, his precocious skills as a young barrister, his appointment to the High Court and his impact on the drafting of the United Nations charter were all achievements that reinforced and validated his own sense of self-importance. Cartoonists often lampooned his self-regard, but it had some substance. Keith Brennan commented that Evatt genuinely believed he had talents to offer and he felt bound to place his abilities at the service of his country by re-entering politics in 1940 during the war. But his enormous confidence in his own abilities also meant that once he had come to a conclusion he could not understand why someone else might differ. He thought he was right and was unable to recognise contrary views, a disabling characteristic in the realm of politics.

Brennan connected this with a third trait, Evatt's suspicion of the motives of others; this was also often remarked on. If others differed from the view he had come to, they must have some ulterior motive, there must be some collusion going on. Although he liked an argument, he expected to win it. In this sense, he was a 'conspiracist' rather than a full-blown conspiracy theorist. Conspiracists can see patterns of deceit or collusion in everyday events and think that nothing is entirely innocent, while conspiracy theorists think nothing is entirely accidental, that there is a single explanation underwriting seemingly unconnected events. Some called this paranoia and there is something in that description. Evatt was acutely sensitive to slights and read threatening meanings into benign events; he trusted very few people and suspected disloyalty all around him. He lived in a world frighteningly devoid of trust and many noted this well before he became Labor leader in the Cold War, when he had ample reason to worry about loyalty in the party and was under consistent and often ferocious attack. His suspicion of others was a profound disability in the fraught politics of the period.

A fourth characteristic was a sense of self fundamentally shaped by the law. Evatt had thrived as an outstanding young barrister and later as a well-regarded High Court judge. He was convinced that legal reasoning could arrive at the truth and that it was, for example, much more reliable than the methods historians used to examine the same evidence. This belief in legal argument and procedure shaped his conduct in life and was reinforced by his undoubted talent for legal rationality. In his Molotov speech, when he said to those taunting him that they had to listen to his account 'because it is the truth of the affair', Evatt believed it. He was sure he could get to the truth through what he thought of as a legal mode of reasoning. That was the explanation he gave Russel Ward for his letter to Molotov; he said it was 'established judicial practice' to give the defence the right to give their version of events. Ward asked incredulously how Evatt could not see that 'correct legal protocol was suicidal political insanity', finally concluding: 'He couldn't and I'm not sure that he ever did'.

There were times when this legal skill and conviction worked in politics – in drafting the charter of the United Nations for example, or when opposing the referendum on banning the Communist party – but at other times his inability to distinguish between law and politics was a distinct weakness. By approaching the Petrov affair as though it were a legal case, as though examining the evidence could help to prove a conspiracy, he only succeeded in enmeshing himself further in a labyrinth. The Petrov affair was much more about politics than legal enquiry, but he struggled to understand the difference. While in some ways Menzies and Evatt were very alike, born in the same year and both talented scholarship boys who excelled at the law, one major difference was that Menzies was a much more adroit politician. He made an easy transition from law to politics while Evatt tended to stumble, perhaps because Evatt always assumed the law was the royal road to justice. Evatt was much more of an advocate than a persuader.

Fifth, and closely related to his belief in legal reasoning, was Evatt's liberalism. As a student he had been shaped by the progressive liberalism and state action of the Australian politicians and jurists Alfred Deakin, Bernhard Ringrose Wise, Isaac Isaacs and Henry Bournes Higgins, as well as the liberal theory of the English philosopher T.H. Green and the social liberals. He believed that this progressive strand of liberalism was now being carried on by the Labor party, and it was fundamentally a legal form of liberalism, one which emphasised the rule of law, with its foundation in the rights of citizens. That of course made him somewhat anomalous in the Labor party, for Evatt was much more concerned with fighting for justice against tyranny and privilege than he was with reforming social conditions. If he had been less of a legal rationalist, and less of a liberal, he might well not have fought so tenaciously against the attempts to ban the Communist party.

Finally, there was Evatt's distinct lack of self-awareness. He had little capacity for self-reflection, for being self-aware and for understanding others; in this he was unlike Chifley, for example, whose wry stance on leadership and capacity to inspire loyalty were based on these qualities. Menzies too had learnt from the mistakes of his first prime ministership; even if he could still not suffer fools, at least he had stopped saying so to their face. In retirement Menzies wrote memoirs that reveal a little about his sense of self and how he reflected on his life. But Evatt was a man singularly lacking in this sort of reflexivity. He was an enigma to others, but perhaps also to himself.

He lived his life in public, with a relatively high profile while on the High Court and then from 1940 to 1960 as a figure on the national and, at times, international stage. He was one of the most prominent and controversial Australians of the period, attracting censure and even hatred from some, and adulation from others who invested their hopes in his public self. Yet he left very few reflections on what he was doing, what his motivations were and how he saw the world around him. The sheer number of interpretations of Evatt, combined with this absence of his own view, has made me sometimes think of him as like the chalk outline of a body on the pavement, drawn by others, but with no information within the outline itself.

Is it, as Keith Brennan said, a hopeless task 'to try to reconstruct a man of his complexity from externals in the memory of other people'? There are no diaries among his papers and very few letters; his correspondence files are almost all incoming letters and he rarely replied; some of his regular correspondents chided him that they knew he would not respond. Grattan looked through Evatt's papers and remarked on how 'poor' they were in private records: 'It is as though he did not want posterity to know his thought processes, least of all the secrets of his personality.' This absence of private papers is revealing as a sign of his lack of reflexivity, which in turn contributed to his inability to understand others; and it is frustrating for a biographer.

Of course, he had a private life, with a solid and supportive marriage to Mary Alice for forty-five years, two adopted children, a zest for life and for argument over dinner tables, a passionate attachment to his country, a love of classical music from Beethoven through to Stravinsky, and an intense commitment to modernism in art, with a collection including Modigliani, Vlaminck, Léger and Picasso as well as many of the Australian modernists. This is not a story of a grim, driven man demanding to dominate the public stage, or at least not that alone; some who knew him also described a man enjoying life to the full, inquisitive and passionate and with a wide range of intellectual and cultural interests.

But many of Evatt's characteristics meant he was singularly unsuited to politics; he was poor at cooperation and out of his depth in a turbulent party that largely considered him an outsider; often too suspicious to place trust in others or engender their loyalty; too sure of his rational truths to deal with the contending values and compromises that are part of political leadership; and too much of a liberal for illiberal times. That he continued in politics seems to me part of Evatt's tragedy.

It may appear perverse to see tragedy in the life of a man who was a High Court judge, a successful foreign minister and a president of the United Nations General Assembly, but none of that was enough for Evatt. After these high points he flirted, in 1946 and 1950, with resigning to return to law and scholarship, but then he pushed himself on to political leadership. Grattan was, I think, right in his view that Evatt's desire to excel drove him into a sphere to which he was unsuited, where his inability to read others and his unwillingness to cooperate were flaws, and where his predisposition to suspect conspiracies warped his judgement.

He was driven forward by the desire to be prime minister, but instead found himself in an uneven struggle against Menzies, the culmination of a lifetime of rivalry between the two; and he was trying to manage explosive forces within the Labor party as the tensions leading up to the 1955 split inexorably unfolded. Menzies won that struggle comprehensively, and Evatt was blamed for splitting the party. He retired in humiliation in early 1960; his own party, unwilling to topple him openly, pushed him upstairs to the New South Wales Supreme Court, where his mental deterioration became more obvious. He left the parliament broken and discarded, but seemingly still unaware.

The distinctive feature of tragedy is not just a story that ends badly. Tragedy is not about the unfairness of life or an untimely death: it is about being in the grip of forces that we cannot understand or overcome. In, for example, *Oedipus* or *King Lear*, the tragedy involves an element of inevitable self-destruction; the protagonist's flaws are exposed under pressure and yet he cannot help himself. Self-knowledge or reflexivity in *Oedipus* and *Lear* means not redemption or salvation; it just means the tragic figure becomes awfully aware of the destruction the audience can already see unfolding. Evatt as Labor leader from 1951 was being swept along by forces that would destroy him and split the Labor party. The question to be considered is how much influence he had to avert the coming disaster. In the pages that follow, I think we see a tragic figure, impelled by his ambition, patriotism and an urgent desire to succeed, but singularly unsuited to cope with or understand the highly charged politics of the period. It was less a case of what Menzies had said – 'The Lord hath delivered him into my hands' – than a case of Evatt driving himself forward to his ruin.

1

The boy

When she was widowed in October 1901, Jeanie Evatt was aged thirty-eight and was left with six sons. Bert was the third oldest, aged seven; above him were George, the oldest at eighteen, who had already left school, and John, aged thirteen. So the gap between Bert and his next older brother was six years and it seems he was never close to them; they had moved away to work as he was growing up. Below him were Ray, aged five, Frank, aged three, and the baby, Clive, aged one. Kylie Tennant suggested he had a protective position as the oldest of these four boys, though there was also some competition between them.

Maitland

Evatt's father, John Ashmore Hamilton Evatt, had been born in India in 1851; his was an Anglo-Irish family with a long history of providing army officers for the empire. In the First World War, there were distant relatives active in the British military. As a boy, John Evatt had gone home from India to Ireland, and then migrated to Sydney at the age of fifteen. By the time of his marriage, he was working in Morpeth, inland and to the north of Newcastle on the Hunter River in New South Wales, as a providore, or steward, for the Hunter River Steam Navigation Company. The company worked the sea route between Sydney and Newcastle with cargo and passenger steamers, trading up the Hunter. The slow, meandering nature of the river made it navigable, though sometimes the steamers were blocked by cedar logs being floated downstream.

Morpeth, along with Maitland a little further up the river, was an entrepot for the produce of the hinterland, which was then transported to Newcastle and down the coast to Sydney. Bullock teams brought in wool and timber, and warehouses lined the riverbanks at Morpeth and West Maitland; coal was mined in fields to the south, and vineyards had been planted by early white settlers in the 1820s. For a time in the mid-nineteenth century, the two Maitlands – East and West, separated by a floodplain – constituted the second town of New South Wales and the hub of the northern districts of the colony. Alan Wood, a local historian, painted it as a relatively wild town in the early colonial period, with raids by local bushrangers, some of them ex-convicts who had gone bush. But by 1900, the town had 'mellowed to a quiet and poor respectability'.

Evatt's mother, Jane Sophia Gray – known as Jeanie – was born in Sydney in 1863, into an Irish Catholic family, but her mother changed to the Anglican faith after a dispute with a priest over Jeanie's baptism. When her family moved from Sydney to Morpeth, her father, John Thomas Gray, worked as a marine engineer for the steamship company, in effect as a mechanic maintaining the steam engines. For a time before her marriage, it seems Jeanie was a domestic servant in the household of H.D. Portus, the Morpeth-based manager of the company. So Jeanie, her father, and the man she would marry were all linked through the steamships.

Jeanie and John Evatt married at St James Anglican Church, Morpeth, in 1882 and three years later moved to East Maitland. Initially John was the licensee of the Hunter River Hotel; the largest hotel in East Maitland, it was a two-storey brick building with balconies, extensive accommodation, a large public dining room and at the back laundries, kitchens and a bakehouse. Nearby was the railway station connecting Maitland to Sydney, and on the other side of the railway line was the courthouse; when the court was in session, the hotel 'was enlivened by visits of Judges, legal men, and witnesses for luncheons and other refreshments'. But by 1891, the family had moved to a much smaller hotel, a hundred metres further up the street. The Evatts were perhaps coming down in the world.

It was there that Bert was born on 30 April 1894. The Bank Hotel was respectable but very modest; with no room for accommodation it relied on hospitality. Wood, the local historian, described it as 'a modest weatherboard structure' of one storey. Bamboo grew in the front, enclosed by a picket fence, with vegetable and flower gardens at the back. It provided meals, drink and a public space. The kitchens were at the back in 'a huge barn made of slabs with two large coal or wood-burning stoves'; the family lived in the weatherboard building itself, with the cook and housemaid in the basement. There was a yard-man, too, but as Wood noted, 'nobody remembers where he slept'. The women of the household never entered the bar, 'a strictly masculine reserve'. A former maid recalled Bert's parents as 'very well educated'; Jeanie 'lived more like a private woman' and was 'a very nice person to work for'. Tennant noted that they were 'church people', with 'the reputation of "refined" people with more gentle manners than their neighbours'. The impression is of a family holding onto the lower rungs of the middle class; there is no mention of any political affiliation.

Respectable and solid, the Bank Hotel was evidently a place aspiring to refinement. Hotels were very much public spaces, available for meetings, for selling off property and for coronial inquests; their cellars even served occasionally as temporary morgues. Chess players who were assembling for a competition at the nearby Mechanics' Institute started at the hotel for speeches and 'light refreshments'; locals 'interested in musical affairs' met and resolved 'to establish a *liedertafel* society'. In 1897, a civic meeting honoured the outgoing mayor, with speeches, toasts and more 'light refreshments'. The hotel was regularly used for public auctions; in 1900, the executors of a man named James Watson went there to sell his 'well-known line of buses' along with buggies, hansom cabs and sixty horses. As a little boy, Bert Evatt grew up in a convivial and quasi-public home, hearing the murmur of civic committees, the shouting of auctioneers and the celebration of toasts and speeches.

His father was keenly involved in the East Maitland cricket club, which held its committee meetings in his hotel and played on the ground immediately behind it. When he was giving up the lease of the Hunter River Hotel, it appeared likely the family would leave town, so the cricket club organised a testimonial for John Evatt; but by the time all was ready, he had taken on the lease of the Bank Hotel. The local paper reported its front bar then hosted 'one of the jolliest social gatherings ... for many years'. The club presented him with a memento to honour his participation, and the club chairman's speech compared a bartender with a barrister:

> It was about five years ago that Mr Evatt was first called to the 'Bar' in East Maitland (Laughter) ... during the time you have presided at and adorned the bar, you have pleaded many causes ... and you have opened upwards of 1000 cases (Laughter). ... Your characteristic address to your clients will be well remembered by many here tonight – your soft, persuasive language, your half commanding, half entreating plea, 'Gentlemen, it is past 11 o'clock; Sergeant Forrest is outside, and the law says', etc. (Laughter).

Evatt made a 'graceful speech' in reply, thanking them for their kindness. The jolly event went well into the evening, with toasts 'interspersed with songs and recitations'.

John's enthusiasm for cricket was transmitted to his son Bert, and the game was woven through the boy's life. He would go on to be an active board member of the Balmain Cricket Club, a trustee of the Sydney Cricket Ground and a leading member of the New South Wales Cricket Association. He was an enthusiastic spectator, heckling from the sidelines and on one occasion walking onto the field to resolve an umpiring dispute. His friend Les Haylen called him 'a statistical cricketer'; he exercised his prodigious memory recalling and reciting scores, averages, events – all the numerical minutiae that cricket obsessives love. And yet he remembered little of his father, or more precisely he recounted few memories of him. Mary Alice recalled that one of his rare stories of his father was that in 1900 he gave young Bert a cricket bat. A photograph of Evatt at the time shows a grave six-year-old boy holding the bat, hand on hip and dressed in knee-length shorts with a sash around his waist.

Only a year later, John Evatt died at the early age of forty-eight. The papers reported that he had rheumatic gout and had been seriously ill for two months. The family story was that he contracted rheumatic fever helping others in the March 1893 floods, but the whispers many years later from Bert Evatt's detractors suggested suicide. To defend her champion Tennant sought out a copy of the death certificate, which showed that on 9 October 1901 John Evatt, hotelkeeper, died of 'heart and kidney disease' of three month's duration. The funeral cortege left from the hotel, where his body had presumably lain in the cellar, as was customary. He had died without a will, but Jeanie was quickly granted administration of his estate.

Bert was aged seven and may have been at Maitland Public School. Peter Crockett spent some time trying to determine exactly where he went to school, but some of the records are lost. It is unlikely to have been Maitland High School for Boys, which was a selective school charging substantial fees. In 1987, the state Labor government's education minister, Rodney Cavalier, despite some opposition, changed the name of Maitland Public School to Evatt High School. The school archivist told Crockett how the good citizens had resisted, evidently hostile to any association with the controversial Evatt:

> The Old Boys, the citizenry, the then-present students fought the good fight … The name of Evatt is not as revered in East Maitland as Mr Cavalier seemed to think. The town might be

slow and easy, but when outsiders attempt to meddle with our history and traditions, I'm afraid they take on a battle which, in this case, turned very nasty indeed.

With a change of government, the school reverted to its traditional name.

After the death of her husband, Jeanie continued with the hotel, and the cricket club still met there. The licence was in her name, and in September 1903 she was summonsed for selling liquor on a Sunday to 'persons who were not travellers, bona fide lodgers or inmates'; the case was adjourned because the summons had been incorrectly served, but four local residents were fined for 'drinking during unlawful hours'. It was hardly a scandalous affair, though perhaps it stung the rather proper Jeanie to have been caught in such an offence. In October 1903 she signed a new ten-year lease, but less than two years later she had sold that lease, along with the furniture, bar fittings and stock. They were about to leave.

While John had been only an occasional attender at church, Jeanie was very active in the Women's Guild of St Peter's Anglican church, singing in the choir and arranging the church decorations. In June 1905, when they appear to have already moved to Sydney, she was back in Maitland, perhaps having returned to wrap up her affairs and attend a small ceremony at which the Women's Guild recorded their appreciation of her years in the choir, and the rector wished her 'prosperity and happiness'. She replied 'in a feeling manner', and said she was sad to be leaving.

Few who recollected Jeanie failed to comment on her determination that her children would do well and her ferocious commitment to education. Mary Alice Evatt recalled her mother-in-law as 'a profoundly religious person', adding, 'I think she gave them a very good upbringing.' Asked about her husband's capacity for hard work, she began with his mother:

She expected them to work hard ... she was determined that they should all do well at school first. Then she wanted them to go to the university ... she was very industrious, very skillful and she was a very wise woman and very well read ... she didn't stay in school a great deal herself, but she used to read all the books the boys had, as they went through their various classes.

Her drive to push her boys, and particularly Bert when it emerged that he was precociously talented, was clear; he internalised it, driven to prove himself to her, to his absent father and to all those who might thwart his progress.

There are few records of Evatt as a boy in Maitland. One is a poem, from 1910, on the theme 'Recollections of Childhood'. It was stilted and self-consciously refined. In one image, Evatt connected home and childhood with death:

Our natal homes to us were kings' abodes,
From which we viewed a cortege pass below –
A cortege never ending, though it changed
(From beggars poor to lord-majors robed, it ranged).

His father's cortege had started from the Bank Hotel, but it seems this is not what he was thinking of; instead it was the passing parade of life: 'The labourers setting out their fields to mow ... The weary horses with their heavy loads ...' The apparent absence of his father from Evatt's thoughts is another of his mysteries. It could suggest his father's death exerted no influence, or that the influence was so charged it could not be mentioned, or could not be recognised.

Having a father who died so early might mean the figure of the father was frozen for him, or overly idealised. Although he would have seen his two older brothers grow into young men, he did not see his own father grow into an old man. In later life, Evatt had some intense relationships with powerful men who may have been father figures;

certainly his headmaster at Fort Street in Sydney was one, and Alan Reid thought Evatt had a 'schoolboy's admiration' for Ben Chifley, 'like somebody in the first year with a captain of football and cricket,' though this was perhaps more as an older brother than a father. Grattan mentioned Evatt's 'father-heroes', the Labor leaders William Holman and Billy Hughes, and noted that both were Labor 'rats' who had deserted the party; they were dead to the labour movement, which may have made them more intriguing. Evatt wrote a biography of the former, and seriously considered writing the life of the latter. Yet with other, often older and conservative men of power, such as the British minister Lord Cranborne, the Australian high commissioner in London, Stanley Melbourne Bruce, and the chief justice of the High Court, John Latham, Evatt's relations were intensely antagonistic.

Les Haylen recounted how, many years later, as a prominent Labor leader, whenever Evatt returned to the Maitland area, he would go out to have a look at his mother's grave, and the old pub his father used to have. According to Haylen, he did those things in seclusion, and 'never made a thing about it'. For Evatt to have made his visits privately may have been a characteristic of the restrained masculinity of the time, and in any case Evatt was entitled to his privacy and reflection. Yet there is something even more distinctly closed about Evatt than the average man of that era, and we can know little of what he was thinking.

Another glance back towards childhood was when he was attorney-general and returned to Maitland in December 1942. He was attempting to settle industrial disputes holding up coal production. 'It was an obstruction to the war effort,' he said, and he was there 'to take counsel with the people in the industry'. He appealed to a meeting of miners at Cessnock, saying that strikes were disrupting industrial planning and distribution of munitions. Kylie Tennant's notes include an article from a local newspaper recollecting Evatt's speech in the Maitland Town Hall on this occasion; it was published shortly after he died. Evatt 'nonchalantly stuck his thumb in the armhole of his waistcoat and gazed around at the wall and ceiling', the *Coal Miner* reported, then observed:

> After quite an appreciable time he said: 'You know the first thing that strikes you on returning to a place after so many years is how small everything seems. When I went onto the cricket ground at East Maitland today, I was amazed to find how it had altered from my boyhood days … That cricket ground is really quite small but I used to think it a tremendous feat when someone threw a ball in from the boundary'.

This is no more than a fragment, and one mediated through the memory of the writer, but it connects us to Evatt's boyhood in a country town on the cusp of the twentieth century. The article went on to describe his distinctively Australian drawl, wondering if he might have 'clung to that boyhood Australian accent on purpose – as his sentimental link with the friends and mates of his early bush days'. Others noted that Evatt's voice was rougher than expected for someone with his education, and Kylie Tennant commented, in one of her rare moments of scepticism about her hero: 'Of course the accent, to a politician, could be useful in other ways'.

Do origins matter? Is it not more significant to focus on what the young Bert Evatt became, rather than where he came from? In one sense, this story of modest, lower-middle-class beginnings in a New South Wales country town tells us little. But it signals the start of something that would be important in Evatt's political life, his position as a middle-class professional somewhat askance to Labor's labourist traditions. The Labor party was just emerging during the decade Evatt was born, as a political wing of the union movement, and as a party with ideological roots in the conditions and aspirations of labour rather than the broader socialist transformation imagined by European social democracy. Having made the choice to seek parliamentary power, Labor was acutely wary of losing control of its political representatives, and origins, loyalty and betrayal were major preoccupations.

In the year that Evatt was born, the fledgling party in New South Wales held a bitter debate in Sydney about adopting 'the pledge', by which its representatives would be bound to adhere to the policy platform and to majority decisions made in caucus. Binding members in a web of loyalty was always a major point of difference with the non-Labor parties, which decried the pledge as an abdication of individual judgement and independence. Hughes and Holman, the 'father-heroes' who attracted Evatt's admiration, led the successful campaign to adopt the pledge, and both later defected to conservative politics. Labor's insistence on the pledge was a sign that the new party worried it could not command the loyalty of its representatives, and that they would be tempted to forget their roots; Labor's fetish about origins in turn shows something of the anomaly of Evatt's position. He was the first prominent Labor figure to come into the party via a middle-class route. In this, his position was similar to Whitlam's, though a generation earlier and significantly more anomalous. Particularly in the first half of the twentieth century, Labor mistrusted intellectuals and middle-class professionals. It hoped somewhat desperately that the sons of toil would remember their roots, and was much less receptive to intellectuals than the equivalent movements in Europe, where social democratic parties brought together union movements and left-wing intellectuals.

Young Evatt had been born into an Anglo-Irish family that had for generations provided officers for the Imperial Army, and he was the son of respectable, lower-middle-class hoteliers. When combined with his university degrees and his outstanding success in the law, his was not an obviously Labor pedigree. When he first entered Labor politics in 1925, his critics alleged he was bourgeois, a prosperous barrister with a comfortable house on Sydney's north shore who had only recently attached himself to the labour movement. In the 1950s, a large part of his fraught relationship with his deputy leader

Arthur Calwell was that Calwell despised his education; as the journalist Frank Chamberlain said, Calwell believed 'no man should be in a Labor ministry unless he's worked with horny hands'. This was not, of course, about Evatt's lower-middle-class origins in Maitland, but about what he had turned himself into through education and effort in the intervening years. Origins mattered a good deal to the Labor party.

Tennant had a significant investment in her image of Evatt as a Titan among sheep, and her biography became a form of hero-worship, of a great radical torn down by the envy of lesser mortals. Her rendering of his origins in Maitland reflected this commitment. She wanted to show he was grounded in the people. She wrote to Hartley Grattan of her 'burning novelist's desire' to understand Evatt, but this produced romanticised images of the original soil from which Evatt emerged. Newcastle had first been settled in 1804 to banish the leaders of the Castle Hill uprising, and some old Irish convicts had stayed in the area after emancipation. Tennant plainly liked the idea that the child Evatt imbibed political folklore from Irish political prisoners or their descendants. She integrated him into her own imagining of Australian history as a contest between established power and the people, between jailers and convicts, and between the empire and the Irish. She imagined him meeting 'old whiskery characters with kind, hard hands', who taught him 'the language of working men humorous and hard'. Tennant identified Evatt with the attitudes of the Irish poor resisting their landowners, sentiments brought to Australia to become part of a tradition of opposition to empire. She imagined young Evatt growing up 'linked with the dust and grief of people's troubles'. From early boyhood 'he was interested in the problems of poor farmers, coal-miners, working men'.

This imagery of Evatt absorbing rebellious Irish folklore is touching, but appears to be complete fiction. There is nothing in Tennant's papers to suggest where it came from; nor do the same stories appear in Crockett's encyclopaedic research notes, in Evatt's own papers, or in the many interviews conducted with those who knew him. But

Tennant wanted to position Evatt as a champion against the Establishment, and this was part of dispelling any doubts about his loyalty to Labor. She painted his childhood in Maitland as the formative years of a lifelong battle against privilege, engaged in a struggle against what she variously described as a 'disguised or open dictatorship by the rich', and as an 'all-powerful tyranny' that had 'crawled ashore and bred monstrosities'. Any doubts about Evatt as a liberal, or about his lower middle-class origins, let alone about his personal ambition, were dispersed.

She made his contest with Menzies part of this bigger story; with similar origins in the respectable lower middle class, and similar trajectories as scholarship boys educated into the law before politics, they took divergent paths. Evatt sided with the labour moment and the struggle against privilege, while Menzies sided with the Establishment, with the rule of property and privilege. She was positioning Evatt and Menzies using the sort of polarised imagery that historian Manning Clark liked, in which the party of initiative opposed the party of resistance. The lore of the 'old whiskery characters' she had conjured up was polarised, too: 'There were only workers and bosses', she wrote. 'You were one or the other.' She ignored the fact that Menzies' origins gave him an acute understanding of the political and cultural values of the middle class, and glossed over Evatt's lower-middle-class background. This was as much a form of romanticism as of politics, and it was much more Tennant's narrative than Evatt's. It was less about Maitland than about the Cold War.

Sydney

On the evening in 1954 that Petrov's defection was announced, Evatt, now aged sixty, was waiting at Canberra airport to fly to Sydney to give a speech to the Fort Street Old Boys' Association. Menzies had neglected to tell him he was about to announce in parliament the sensational news of a Soviet defector. Evatt's friend and ally Les Haylen had travelled out with him to the airport to continue a conversation. The plane was late, but Evatt was in a cheerful mood, chatting about Australian literature; Haylen recalled he was 'utterly charming and rested'. He was keen to go back to his old school, which had shaped him in the years between about 1904 and 1911, saying: 'This is not a chore … I like to go and address my old school. I owe a great deal to Kilgour, the old teacher, and my own mother'. As they paced the tarmac waiting for the plane, Haylen said, Evatt started to talk about his mother, telling Haylen about the occasion he sat his final school exams. Evatt told him, 'I went home and I said to mother I've got eight As', and she had replied, 'What's the matter with you, you sat for nine subjects'.

Haylen thought the story illustrated 'the iron drive of Mrs Evatt', who wanted to see that 'this bright boy' excelled. But perhaps, he thought, she 'overdid it', producing in her son 'this curious characteristic Evatt touch that can't be explained, but can be understood if you know the man'. An echo of this story is found in Mary Alice's account of how Bert had 'won everything except one'. She explained: 'I've forgotten what it was now but I remember his mother could never forget that this one he tied with another boy. You know, she wondered how this happened'. Several years later, Mary Alice said, when Clive was studying at Duntroon and graduated with every prize except French, he met with a similar reaction from Jeanie. 'She looked at him and said, "Yes, that's nice – what happened about the French prize?" That was really typical about her attitude towards work.'

This sounds like a mother withholding praise, making her love conditional on continuous improvement, and continually escalating her expectations. Allied with her 'iron will' that her children succeed, her reserve may be the original source of Evatt's relentless ambition to excel. Grattan had commented that 'no matter how high he rose, his ambition was still unappeased'. Missing out on one prize meant that his mother was never quite satisfied and he in turn was never quite content with his achievements. Jeanie had moved the family to Sydney and it may be that the principal reason was about educational opportunities; Fort Street selective school was an incubator of excellence, without the fees of a private school. Perhaps this effort was made especially to invest in Bert, who was identified as talented and always described as 'outstanding' by his teachers. But in addition, her parents and a brother, Tom, were in Sydney and provided support in her widowhood, along with her two oldest sons, who had already moved there. It made sense to be near extended family, as well as to tap into the opportunities of Fort Street school.

Jeanie had sold the hotel lease in July 1905, and had been fare-welled by the church guild about the same time, but it seems the family had moved to Sydney earlier than that. Among Evatt's books is a copy of Dickens' *Dombey and Son* awarded to his younger brother Frank in 1903, by St John's Sunday School, Milsons Point. In Tennant's notes of an interview with George Evatt she recorded: 'When the family came to Sydney after the father's death the mother bought a house which cost £1,000 … The grey house was handy at Kirribilli – a very big house'. But George evidently did not mean the 'grey house', a puzzling reference not otherwise explained, but the 'Gray house' of his maternal grandparents. Jeanie's parents lived within easy walking distance and may have helped with the costs of buying the house; her father, the marine engineer, had transferred from the Hunter River steamships to working on the Sydney ferries. They lived on the corner of Carabella and Bligh streets, and the latter was an appropriate name for the young Evatt to encounter, as he would later write a book about the rebellion against Governor Bligh.

Jeanie's house in Milsons Point was first listed in *Sands Directory* in 1907, at 8 Grantham Street. While it no longer exists, it would have been either a sandstone cottage or small Victorian terrace similar to others in the area. She had given the house a name: 'Bella Vista'. It accommodated her and the four younger boys, in 1907 aged between thirteen (Bert) and seven (Clive). The area where the house stood was demolished in the 1920s for roadworks leading up to the new Harbour Bridge, but the little red-brick Anglican church of St John the Baptist still stands on the corner of Broughton and Bligh streets. The Evatts worshipped there and Jeanie was choir-mistress, while the boys were in the choir. In 1909, one of the boys – perhaps Bert, the eldest of the four at home – was employed as bell-ringer for ten shillings a month. Ten years later, after the death in France of Ray and Frank, a brass tablet was erected in the church in their memory.

The Bank Hotel in Maitland had been a busy place to grow up, full of meetings and speeches, and so was Milsons Point. From the late nineteenth century, it had been 'the transport hub for all of the lower north shore'. In Evatt's childhood it was a bustling scene of transit, of ferries and trains, of wharfs and fish shops. A cable tram and the rail lines from the northern suburbs were connected to the ferry terminus on the point. By the end of 1929, ferries were carrying over forty million passengers per year, though this traffic fell dramatically with the opening of the bridge in 1932. All four boys were at Fort Street, just across the harbour. Probably from as soon as they moved to Sydney, young Bert was taking the ferry across to Circular Quay, followed by a short but strenuous walk up the hill to school.

Only a few fragments remain suggesting what he thought when he reflected back to boyhood in Milsons Point. Among his papers is an exercise book of essays written in 1909 and 1910. In 1911, he wrote on the inside cover that these were 'mostly mawkish and immature ... for which I now blush'. In one essay, he complained in a mock petition to the Sydney City Council about the arduous morning walk up the hill to the school. In another, he described the school as an 'institution' and as a 'state'. 'A fair walk from The Quay: a long climb up a steep hill ... and then ... you have entered another "state" with another atmosphere. ... This "state" is not a Utopia, is not a dream of a poet's fruitful mind; it is a solid fact.' He went on to some artificial musings on the peculiarities of the school as a 'country' without rivers, lakes or grass, and noted that this 'state' was famed 'for its man-producing quantities if not its butter produce, and its citizen and scholar producing power though not its wool'. It was all quite adolescent, but he was, at fifteen, an adolescent.

From its elevated position on Flagstaff Hill, the school, as a later enthusiast wrote, had 'watched the growth of Sydney'. The school was also watchful of its own place in history:

> The old building known as the Military Hospital has in sixty years sent forth innumerable lads, many of whom have left footprints in the sands of time; lads who have made their mark in every walk of life. In politics, at the Bar, on the bench, on the battlefield, in the pulpit – in peace and war the Fort-street boys have held their own.

Not, we might note, medicine, nor capitalism, nor letters; the priorities were politics, the law, the military and the church. Young Evatt certainly relished the challenges of the Fort Street Model Superior Public School, as it was known until 1910. It was 'superior' both in the sense that it was a selective state school, and in the imagination of its teachers. They were ambitious for both the school and its pupils. Ron Horan, its archivist and historian, noted that the school magazine, *The Fortian*, had frequent references to Bert, 'an outstanding scholar and first captain of the high school'. Going back to his primary school years, 'outstanding' was the term consistently used by those recalling their role in Evatt's education; it was testimony not only to his natural ability and hard work, but to his desire to be outstanding, to be noted, to win the prize.

Mary Alice recalled, doubtless passing on what Evatt had said to her, that 'he loved Fort Street, he enjoyed it very, very much'. Early in his time there, Jeanie decided that he was not being challenged enough, that 'he could work harder', and she went to see the headmaster, to 'tell him that she felt he should be in the next class up', and he agreed with her. This headmaster, Alexander James Kilgour, was tailor-made to encourage the young Evatt. Born in Edinburgh, he had himself been educated at Fort Street and in 1905, around the time Jeanie brought her family to Sydney, he took over as the school's head-master. His teaching was said to be excellent, 'though his standards were inflexible', and he had 'no tolerance for slackers and dullards'. The boys found him an imposing though benign presence: 'He wore spectacles whose lenses were sliced horizontally along the middle; and, being moderately tall, he looked down over these with a quiet dignified authority that made any resort to corporal punishment inconceivable'.

The combination of scholarly excellence, hard work and inter-nalised discipline made Kilgour and his school legendary; and they were values that resonated with Jeanie and her son. Long after, Kilgour maintained contact with Evatt. Mary Alice recalled that her husband's former headmaster 'used to write him letters giving him good advice from time to time over many years', continuing until the older man died in 1944. She thought it 'a wonderful thing to do' and said Evatt 'always paid a lot of attention' to Kilgour. Kilgour wrote encouragingly about each of Evatt's achievements, such as when he was appointed to the High Court or published another book, suggesting that for Evatt he continued to be a fatherly figure.

Excelling at everything, Evatt was dux of the school, and captain of the football and cricket teams. Among his books are his prizes: a set of Dickens' novels he was awarded in 1907 for 'general proficiency', a Joseph Addison collection from *The Spectator* in 1909 for English, and Arthur Hinks' *Astronomy* in 1911 for mathematics. In 1909, he was dux of the lower senior class; in 1910, he was dux of the senior class, and came top in trigonometry, mechanics, English, literature and ancient history. At the end of his time there he won the Bridges prize for 'the boy who brought the greatest honour to Fort Street School'.

Mary Alice recalled him saying that he had not really worked hard until he began to think ahead to university. The fees were expensive and 'he wouldn't be able to go unless he got a scholarship and so he started working for scholarships and he won them on each occasion'.

After sitting the Senior Public Examinations in 1912, he 'qualified for admission to one or other of the Departments of the University', meaning the only university in town, the University of Sydney. He had won a scholarship to live at St Andrew's, the university's Presbyterian college. He had gained first-class results in nine out of ten subjects (history of Europe, ancient history, English, algebra, geometry, plane trigonometry, conic sections, mechanics and physics). But – as he would tell Les Haylen many years later – he had disappointed his mother with only a second-class result in French.

He was a robust adolescent. Bodily, as an adult, he was large chested, with broad shoulders and short, spindly legs. At the end of the thirties, the Melbourne writer and socialist intellectual Nettie Palmer wrote in her diary after he had been for dinner: she was struck by his physical presence, 'the broad, powerful shoulders of a former footballer, the gusty voice and laugh'. Yet in his adult years, Evatt was often morbidly concerned about his health, especially his lungs; he worried about the cold, about pneumonia, and often in times of crisis he took ill. The fragments we have of his letters often refer to illnesses: when on the High Court, he wrote about his 'old enemy', tracheitis, and to his son Peter he mentioned a bout of influenza, saying that 'at one time it was touch and go' and might have been pneumonia. He wrote plaintively to Curtin in 1940 about being on his sickbed and unable to defend himself against those who refused to endorse him for the Advisory War Council. These are only three examples of many.

Yet he was clearly not a sickly child. Photographs of the Fort Street rugby teams show his wide shoulders. None of the family stories collected by previous biographers, or told in interviews with family members and friends, suggest his constitution as an adolescent was the least bit fragile. On the contrary, he was vigorous and active, playing handball and Australian Rules football, and captaining the cricket and rugby teams. This was not a boy being kept at home, reading while his schoolmates played, absorbed in books and growing pale, training to be an intellectual.

As he prepared to go to university in 1912, young Evatt was still only partly shaped. The wound of losing his father was either slight, or buried deep; he did not reflect on it, though it left him with a tendency to seek the approval of senior men, and to resist if they thwarted him. His mother's undoubted drive and ambition for her talented son, and what may have been a withholding of approval and love when he did not achieve everything she thought he should, contributed to his own drive to excel. He was intensely competitive, wanting to win academic prizes and be the captain of sporting teams. He emerged from a reasonably happy childhood as a dogged, hardworking youngster, energetic and forceful, always pushing his way forward and upward, but not inclined to look back, not inclined to look inward.

2

The young Evatt

In 1924, when he was seeking Labor preselection for the New South Wales parliament, Evatt boasted in a leaflet that he was 'by far the most brilliant student that our State Schools and University have developed'. That was immodest, and may not have been what the Labor League members expected to hear – but perhaps it was what they wanted to hear, for Mary Alice found when she met them that the working people of the Balmain electorate had strong views about education. 'They practically all wanted their children to have a good education…' Evatt's boast signalled his commitment to the progressive, developmental possibilities of a good state-funded education system. In his first speech in parliament he declared that he was 'proud to say that any opportunity I had in my life is due to the people of this State in connection with the public schools system'. His trajectory truly was an exemplar of natural talent nurtured by the opportunities of education.

University

Jeanie could not afford the high costs of an education designed for a tiny elite, and Evatt made his way through university by winning scholarships and prizes which covered his tuition and college fees. He often urged the merits of conscientious study on the young as a way of forging ahead in life and achieving the upward mobility his mother had always striven for, but this was not a path open to all. Given the entry criteria for a selective school such as Fort Street, and the difficulty of winning scholarships and prizes to fund university study, Evatt's success made it clear that, in the absence of wealth, only those of exceptional talent could succeed.

Evatt enjoyed university, even though his time there was over-shadowed by the war and by the deaths of two of his younger brothers, who enlisted. He participated enthusiastically in debating, committee work, the student magazine, cricket, rugby, handball and even baseball; he lived, and tutored, at the Presbyterian St Andrew's College, one of the four residential colleges on campus. He was a boisterous, active presence, even if some resented the ease with which he won all the prizes available. He excelled in philosophy and then law, and when he graduated in April 1918, he had accumulated degrees in arts, law and a master of arts by thesis. He remained connected to the university throughout his life, as a member of the university senate.

St Andrew's college, with its attached theological hall and divin-ity training school, is a gloomy, neo-Gothic three-storey construction, complete with spires. Inside were high stained-glass windows and dark wood panelling, with a dining hall, lecture hall, students' common room and library. The tone of life there can be seen in its magazine, kept in Evatt's papers. There were cricket games against the other colleges, and an annual fancy dress dinner; but it was considered 'deplorable' that so few had attended an annual commemoration, and the editors hoped in future 'more college men will make it their duty to attend'. The college debating society explicitly saw its function as preparation for public leadership, because 'every university man is one to whom others of less fortunate gifts or circumstances will in future look for leadership'. That, of course, was a presumption of authority the labour movement found galling, but Evatt threw himself into debates about capital punishment and politics. On the back cover of the magazine for 1912, he carefully listed all the honours he had already won and committees he had now joined. He lived in this atmosphere of venera-ble neo-Gothic buildings, common rooms of 'college men' and his own hard work for six years.

Evatt's progress through university was spectacular. The university he entered in 1912 as an eighteen-year-old was itself just sixty years old, the oldest in the country and tiny by today's standards. There were only 1500 students in total, with arts and medicine the largest faculties; law, science, economics and engineering were much smaller. Two years before Evatt began, there were 442 students enrolled in the bachelor of arts, almost one-third of them women. The arts faculty had a teaching complement of six professors, five other full-time staff and six part-time staff. In 1920, two years after Evatt graduated, there were still only 257 students studying law. Until the mid-1880s, the arts curriculum had been heavily dominated by classical studies, alongside the natural sciences. By 1905, the curriculum had been 'modernised'. Latin and Greek were no longer compulsory, and professorships had been created in modern literature, philosophy and history. Politics and sociology were not available, though Francis Anderson included both – along with economics – in his classes as professor of philosophy. Some study in the sciences was still compulsory at the time Evatt completed his degree. His bachelor of arts consisted of three years of English, philosophy and mathematics, with physics in first year. Mary Alice later recalled that the professor of mathematics had told her Evatt was the best mathematician he ever had in his classes: 'He said he could get a scholarship and go to England and do pure mathematics'. She said 'Bertie' was tempted 'because he loved mathematics'.

Seemingly good at everything, Evatt's transcript of results is full of prizes and scholarships. Some were 'private annual prizes' given by individual professors, such as Mungo MacCallum's prize for English (which Evatt won twice), and Anderson's prize for philosophy (which he won three times). Others were university prizes, such as the Norbert Quirk prize for mathematics, the Wentworth prize for an undergraduate English essay, as well as a total of four scholarships in philosophy, English and mathematics (twice). In 1915, he was awarded the University Medal in philosophy. These prizes and scholarships were not only a recognition of academic excellence; they were usually cash grants, which went towards a student's university fees and the costs of college accommodation. The Wentworth prize was worth £10, Francis Anderson's prize was £5. When he won the 1915 Beauchamp prize, it was worth £25, equivalent to the annual value of the old age pension.

At the end of 1914, Evatt was one of two candidates considered for a Rhodes scholarship to Oxford; he was proposing to study law, preferably at Balliol. A revealing assessment was made by a selection committee, meeting in the rooms of the New South Wales governor in Macquarie Street. The committee consisted of the governor, a judge of the Supreme Court and, from the university, the chancellor, vice-chancellor, and chair of the professorial board. In the eyes of such an august body, the young Evatt was clearly ahead in 'Literary and Scholastic Attainments', but the other candidate was superior in athletics, being 'more successful than Mr Evatt in the playing field'. Evatt, they judged, was 'much superior' when evaluated against the criterion of 'Qualities of Manhood, Truth, etc.', because he had been very active in the management of student organisations, while his rival, Mr Crawford, had not 'entered into the corporate life of the University to such a marked degree'. Measuring the candidates against the fourth criterion, 'Moral Force of Character', they detected little difference between them, though the testimony of Evatt's teachers put him marginally in front.

He was offered the Rhodes scholarship, but then wrote to withdraw his application. Walter Crawford was awarded the scholarship for 1915, but why did Evatt stay home? His two much older brothers were absent – by late 1915 both were married and working – and he was the senior of the four boys Jeanie was bringing up alone. Tennant wrote: 'In the Evatt family, as in thousands of Australian homes, the question had been discussed as to who should go and who should stay'. He attempted to enlist but was rejected due to poor eyesight; his younger brothers Ray and Frank were both accepted and sent to France. Throughout the war Evatt regularly wore the badge given out to rejected volunteers. Keith Brennan, his associate years later, recalled

Evatt showing him the certificate rejecting his enlistment; interestingly, he had both kept it and brought it out to show.

At first it appears from Evatt's transcript of university results that he was not studying in 1915, though he was on campus, and active in the Student Union and in the handball club, the Sports Union and the cricket club. He was elected president of the Undergraduates Association in March 1915, and president of the Sydney University Union in November, the first time an undergraduate had won this role. Through 1915 he was working on an extended essay, 'Liberalism in Australia', to enter, and inevitably win, the Beauchamp prize for 'the best essay on a literary or historical subject'. This may have been the basis for a later thesis called 'Social and Political Tendencies in Australia', for which he was awarded an MA in philosophy in 1917. (That thesis has disappeared, but in 1918, Evatt published a book on the same theme, discussed later in this chapter.)

From 1916, Evatt studied law while also working on his masters thesis. In that year, he shared the Wigram Allen scholarship in law, valued at £50. He was still living at St Andrew's, tutoring in philosophy and English, and in the following year English and law. Only Jeanie and Clive remained at home in Grantham Street. Frank wrote from England in late 1917, saying he worried the house was so big and that 'the Mater must often feel lonely there'. By April 1918, with the war in Europe in its final year, Evatt had graduated with first-class honours in law and a second University Medal. Along the way he had collected more prizes, sharing the Pitt Cobbett prize for constitutional law, and more scholarships.

The law school had always been in separate premises away from the university, in Phillip Street, the centre of the legal profession and the courts. The law buildings were described some years later as 'old and uncomfortable … a black hole of Calcutta where a hundred students smoked and shouted between lectures', with the 'rain stains of past winters for mural decorations'. Proximity to Phillip Street – and nearby Macquarie Street, home to the New South Wales parliament house – meant some isolation from the rest of university life, but made for a close relationship between the legal profession, the university and the state, with the profession having significant influence over university policy and within government. By the time Evatt finished law, one former lecturer, William Cullen, had gone on to be chief justice and lieutenant-governor of New South Wales, and had long been chancellor of the university; another lecturer, George Rich, had been appointed to the High Court in 1913, where Evatt would join him in 1930. Sir John Peden, professor of law since 1910, was a member – and later president – of the Legislative Council.

The first divisive debate over conscription took place in 1916, after Labor prime minister Billy Hughes proposed a plebiscite to endorse his policy of compulsory military service. The campaign exposed fault lines in Australian society, with contending and passionate accusations of disloyalty to the empire, of Irish Catholic sympathy for Sinn Fein, of Hughes' dictatorial inclinations and of capitalism growing fat on war profits. Divisions between nationalism and British imperialism, between Catholic and Protestant, between labour and capital, were emotionally charged with the intense grief of the mounting war losses. The labour movement opposed conscription furiously, but the university publicly supported it. The university history suggests the staff, students and graduates were actively in favour of conscription and that: 'This was probably the first time that the University body had come out solidly in public on a national issue'. The student magazine *Hermes*, of which Evatt was editor, was vigorously pro-conscription, arguing in May 1916 that conscription 'should have been adopted on the outbreak of war'.

The fierce divisions over the plebiscite in October 1916 split the Labor party when Hughes, along with his New South Wales equivalent, the ALP premier Holman, left the party they loved – the party they had been instrumental in creating. Along with their pro-conscription Labor colleagues, they defected to the non-Labor side of politics, which by 1917 was reconstructed as the Nationalist party.

When he later wrote about Holman, Evatt argued that conscription need not have split the party, and that both Hughes and Holman had allowed themselves to be led astray by exaggerated demands for more soldiers. At the time, in late 1916, Evatt apparently supported Hughes on conscription, or was at least wary about expressing a view out of kilter with the university's orthodox support for conscription; but by May 1917 he was intending to vote Labor in the coming elections, rather than for Hughes' Nationalists. Labor, he wrote, had 'some decent policies as opposed to nothing' and he thought that 'conscription is dead anyway'.

A more radical influence was Vere Gordon Childe, who had started an arts degree the year before Evatt. He too was living in St Andrew's College until 1914. Childe was significantly more interested in political theory than Evatt, and more serious about his study of Hegel, Marx and Engels; his education made him into a lifelong Marxist, though of what inflection – guild socialist, democratic, syndicalist – remains debatable. By contrast, Evatt's political development remained more fluid, less certain and less determined. Compared with Childe's serious study of the Marxist tradition, Evatt was more taken with the social liberal tradition. Childe left in 1914 to study archaeology at Oxford, and returned in late 1917; from early 1918, he was a senior resident tutor at St Andrew's, and actively involved in anti-conscription and anti-war politics. These got him into trouble with the college and university authorities, and by mid-1918 he was in effect forced to resign. When he then applied for a teaching position, he was blocked by those who objected to his politics, with the active support of Cullen, the chancellor. If his friendship with Childe led Evatt in more radical directions, he was less publicly vocal about it, perhaps learning the lesson that radicalism could compromise the approval and support of powerful men.

Evatt wrote to Childe at the end of 1918, proposing they write a book 'renouncing bourgeois radicalism', but Childe was already planning the book that would be published as *How Labour Governs* in

1923. It was a complex and influential book studying Labor governments, in particular those in New South Wales; it was often highly pessimistic about the chances the ALP could achieve radical results. It combined several different analyses. The first was that Labor was dominated by 'politicalism', the 'degeneration into a vast machine for capturing political power', and this focus on means rather than ends led to forgetting what to do with power; a second theme was that betrayal and defection were inevitable as Labor struggled, even despite the pledge, to restrain its representatives from succumbing to temptations and opportunism. Childe's third theme was a more sociological argument that placed the book in a broader literature dealing with mass parties; fundamentally Labor was, and had to be, a mass party representing both the unionised working class and middle-class interests, and 'from the first the Labour Party had the dual character of a trade union party and a social democratic party'. Childe's gloomy conclusion was that Labor governments were probably doomed to vacillate between their working-class and middle-class constituencies, to have parliamentary representatives succumb to temptations, and to forget why power was worth achieving. When he wrote his biography of Holman in the 1930s, Evatt revisited these issues, but refused to accept what he read as Childe's prognosis of inevitable betrayal.

Death

Two of Evatt's younger brothers had enlisted as soon as they turned eighteen, Ray in March 1915 and Frank in September 1916. Ray survived Gallipoli, was promoted to lieutenant and awarded the Military Cross 'for conspicuous gallantry'; he was adventurous and had looked forward to seeing action at the front. Frank, by contrast, was sensitive and studious – he had completed a year of a medical degree before enlisting – and his career as a soldier took a very different course. Wounded almost as soon as he arrived at the front, he was sent to

England to recover. He seems to have made the most of his time in England, going to the opera, classical concerts and the theatre, but he was torn by constant doubts and felt inadequate, comparing himself with the dashing, masculine figure of Ray, and the intellectual achievements of Bert. It was Frank to whom Evatt was close; Mary Alice described him as 'my husband's very precious favourite brother'.

In September 1917, while twenty-three-year-old Bert was at home studying law, Ray, still just twenty-one, was killed near Ypres. Nine days later, but before the news was confirmed, Frank wrote to Bert: 'I hope Ray is allright but I heard a very grave rumour which please God isn't true. It is a hellish front we have just left, and so many officers have been killed there in the last week or two'. Bert had already heard the news from an old Fortian, who wrote that Ray 'had advanced with his company and had taken the front line of the German trenches'. The letter went on: 'He was a brave and capable officer well liked and deeply mourned ... He is enrolled amongst the long list of Fortians who have nobly sacrificed their all for their country and their liberty'. Frank wrote to his mother, preparing her. 'If the worst has happened try and take it as bravely as possible.' A week later, he confirmed the rumour, writing to Jeanie again:

> It is so hard to realize – dear old Ray was looking so splendidly
> fit when I last saw him ... He was looking forward with eagerness
> to another 'stunt'. He was a real soldier – and the bravest of the
> brave ... Overwhelming as the news is, one can feel pride in the
> fact that he died the bravest and best of deaths that ever man
> could – and he himself would have been content with such a fate.

This was comfortingly conventional, drawing on the tropes through which thousands were expressing their grief. As Frank wrote, 'God has willed it so'.

Towards the end of 1917, he wrote to his mother again, telling her not to worry about him as he returned to the front. Although he thought he had not been 'a great success in the Army', he had resolved to 'try and lead a life like Ray's if it were possible, and to strive to gain the glorious success which was his'. His mother can surely not have been thrilled to hear that, when the sentence could just have easily read 'to gain the glorious death which was his'. The following day, Frank wrote to Bert with much less enthusiasm for military life. 'I think we've done more than sufficient seeing that George and Jack are married and that you are ineligible.' He hoped Clive, the youngest, would not be allowed 'to come away', to enlist; and in fact at the start of 1918 Clive instead enrolled in the officer training course at Duntroon, which exempted him from service.

Reflecting on Ray's death, Frank wrote that he had 'always looked to Ray for advice and comfort – and he never failed me'. It was a poignant comparison with what Frank saw as his own mediocrity. He had not risen through the ranks like his brother, as promotion could only be won 'in the field' and Frank had been safe in Britain, recuperating, while his brother served at the front. 'I'm still the same as I left home – a plain gunner', he said. 'I feel so unworthy – such a "dud" when I think of his glorious life.' Meanwhile, Bert had been trying to get Frank released from the army. He had written to a relative, Major General Sir George Hamilton Evatt, a retired surgeon general in the British army, for help. But the request was refused, and Frank was soon to return to the front.

Evatt was studying hard while his brothers were in France, and kept Frank informed of his successes. He sent a copy of what Frank described as 'a glowing tribute from the Fortian' to his achievements. 'The whole sketch of your career was eminently pleasing to me', Frank noted generously. In May 1918, just after Evatt's spectacular success in his final exams, winning another University Medal, Frank wrote to his mother about Bert's 'usual excellent results', commenting, 'He has certainly had some academic career and will go high in the world of law I trust … He certainly deserves all that comes his way … no one is more pleased than me'. In July 1918, Frank wrote again to his mother, that Bert was 'certainly mounting the ladder of fame'. Poor Frank's letters regularly expressed his own sense of inadequacy compared with his two older brothers; the contrast between Bert's circumstances and his own must have stung, no matter how pleased he was to see his brother succeed. In a letter just a month before he, too, was killed, Frank wrote that they had held a swimming carnival in a river, but with what he called his 'usual mediocrity', he had tied for third place. In late September 1918, Frank was dead, aged twenty; it was barely six weeks before the war ended.

Jeanie was understandably devastated at the loss of two sons; she shared in the grief pervading Australian society. The story in the family was that she never recovered from the loss of Ray and Frank. In Evatt's biography of Holman, written years later, there is a clear echo of the emotions of the time. Holman, who was pro-conscription, had been accused of insensitivity in a debate about recruitment. Looking back, Evatt concurred with those critics: 'Holman failed to realize the tremendous strain and anxiety in every family from which a member was absent at the front. The burden was far greater that that of any politician. It was almost too heavy to be borne'. He quoted a passage from the official war history about the suffering of women anticipating 'news of the death of son or husband'. It was necessary, Evatt argued, to live in such an atmosphere in order to understand why some criticised Holman's insensitivity.

The sort of inadequacy Frank felt was not something that ever troubled Bert, but it is hard not to wonder whether he urged himself on to greater efforts as compensation for not having participated in the war that took his brothers. Tennant wrote that he 'was tortured with a peculiar anguish', and was 'irrationally convinced' that if he had enlisted he could have protected his brothers. 'How he expected he could have saved them no one understood but he had been a sturdy shield to protect them when they were little boys. Now, because he had not been there, they were dead.' 'Peculiar' and 'irrational' hardly seem the most appropriate terms for the wounds of guilt and grief that a survivor would understandably feel. He had repaid his mother's fierce attention and high hopes with a stellar record at school and university, yet now he had lost two younger brothers in the war. Perhaps the memory of his younger brothers urged him on to greater achievements, to justify – to both his mother and himself – the fact that he had stayed behind to study.

In November 1918, Evatt published a poem in the student magazine *Hermes*. Entitled 'November 12, 1918', its first stanza evoked the end of the war, with pealing bells and anticipations of homecomings. But the second stanza turned to loss:

A little while! But, Oh! Dear God, I yearn
For those dear boys who never shall return.
Our sweet young boys who bravely went along
To meet the storm and pain and death, and yet,
Faced all these terrors with a snatch of song.
Oh! how I yearn for them and can't forget.

It was conventional in both its sentiments and composition; the 'sweet young boys' and the 'snatch of song' are signs of the poignant formulations of the time. But while it evoked some commonly felt truths, there was no recourse to God's will, nor to patriotism and valiant sacrifice, just an ache of loss. In formulating his grief Evatt took a distinctly secular tone. In later life, religion seemed a matter of no great importance to him; he attended Church of England services and Mary Alice recalled 'he loved the hymns, he loved the whole service of the Church of England', but this seems to have been more about aesthetic pleasure than faith. It is hard to see any signs of his mother's religious conviction in his intellectual framework, and by the end of his university studies his cast of mind could best be described as secular and rationalist.

The death of his brothers was one of the few parts of his past to which Evatt sometimes returned. The family had already donated the plaque in the church in Milsons Point, and in 1921, Evatt established an annual prize at Fort Street, the Raymond and Frank Evatt Memorial prize, to be awarded for an essay on an 'approved Australian topic'. It was funded by a bequest of £100 in Commonwealth bonds. The deaths of Ray and Frank surfaced at times in later conversations; during the 1930s when he was on the High Court both his associates heard stories about his brothers. Keith Brennan said that 'he felt that loss very, very deeply', and his brother, John, who was also Evatt's associate, said that it was 'tremendously important', but that Evatt was guarded about it: 'In order to discuss it he'd drop his guard, but he'd hastily raise it again'.

In 1940, when Evatt was stepping back into federal politics, the journalist Alan Reid recalled him telling how 'his family was a military family, that they'd always served and his stepping down from the High Court and his advocacy of a national government was part of this desire to serve'. Reid interpreted that as genuine patriotism. It is not clear whether Evatt was referring to the military officers who ornamented the family tree and had served the empire in India, or whether he was thinking of Ray and Frank. It could well have been both. And later, in 1945, when Evatt was in San Francisco, journalists commented that the loss of his brothers was one of his motivations to build a United Nations that could help the world to avoid war. He was evidently still talking about a wound suffered a quarter century earlier.

The awkward young liberal

Evatt's cast of mind was secular and also distinctly liberal. He had been only partially influenced by Gordon Childe's radicalism. A more important influence was Francis Anderson, professor of logic and mental philosophy, who had been schooled in the social liberalism of the turn of the century. Evatt studied philosophy under Anderson throughout his arts degree, and considered it his first love, before it was displaced by constitutional law. Anderson awarded his 'private prize' to Evatt in each of the three years he taught him.

Professor Anderson was 'a small, neat man ... and always dressed in a grey morning suit and tall grey hat'. One former student described how his was 'the first and only lecture room ... where questions were asked and discussion was encouraged'. His enthusiasm for the social liberalism associated with the Oxford philosopher T.H. Green could be traced back to his time studying under British philosopher Edward Caird at Glasgow University. Evatt's own 1913 edition of Green's *Lectures on the Principles of Political Obligation* is heavily underlined and annotated, and the influence shows clearly in Evatt's *Liberalism in Australia*, published in 1918.

Subtitled 'an historical sketch of Australian politics down to the year 1915', Evatt's first book was a short but densely argued work genuinely extolling the virtues of liberalism. His focus was on what progressive liberalism had achieved in Australia and what it must do next. From the early struggles for responsible government, to the state action on protectionism, factory acts and wage arbitration of Alfred Deakin's governments in both Victoria and the Commonwealth, Evatt was clearly on the side of the new or social liberalism of the late nineteenth and early twentieth centuries. He endorsed ideas about positive rather than negative liberty, the necessity of state intervention and the bankruptcy of laissez faire noninterventionist liberalism. The latter he declared, was 'discredited'. Its conception of freedom – that individuals be free from the state – meant too much 'detachment from social interests'. 'Liberalism has grown to see that democracy is founded not merely on the private interest of the individual, but also on the function of the individual as a member of the community; and so the common good is based on the common will.'

Liberty was still essential, but the newer liberalism was 'an advance upon the old', especially in its conception of the self and the common good. Hence state intervention was justified 'on the principles of equality of opportunity and social freedom'. He echoed the

Evatt is liberalism

arguments Henry Bournes Higgins had made in favour of regulating labour markets and setting a basic wage; Evatt wrote that 'every citizen should have full means of earning as much material support as experience proves to be the necessary basis of a healthy, civilized existence'. He was arguing the idealist case Green had developed, that the state represented all citizens, and should intervene to ensure decent living and working conditions, to provide education and in general to clear the way for the full development of individual potential. As Evatt described it, the purpose of liberalism was the 'provision of external means for inner moral development'. Liberalism, he said, 'does its best to provide the external conditions for more efficient and fuller lives'.

His bibliography showed he had drawn on the works of Green (*Political Obligation*), J.A. Hobson (*The Social Problem, The Crisis of Liberalism*), L.T. Hobhouse (*Liberalism*), the young Winston Churchill (*Liberalism and the Social Problem*), William Pember Reeves (*State Experiments in Australia and New Zealand*) and Bernhard Ringrose Wise (*The Making of the Australian Commonwealth*, and *The Commonwealth of Australia*). These men were all figures in the development of interventionist liberal ideas and policies, both in Britain and Australia. A list of books that included both Green and Wise formed a nicely closing circle. Wise had studied under Green at Oxford before migrating to Sydney; he was then influential as the New South Wales Liberal attorney-general who passed legislation for wage arbitration and aged pensions in 1900, with the active support of the fledgling Labor party. Evatt wrote warmly of key Australian liberals, including Deakin, Higgins and David Syme, proprietor of *The Age*.

He correctly saw this progressive form of liberalism and its endorsement of state intervention as predating the emergence of Labor, and then forming an alliance or 'understanding', especially under Deakin, to collaborate in passing progressive legislation. But, like Deakin's Liberals, he disapproved of Labor's policy of the pledge or 'the caucus system', believing that 'liberalism should be prepared to fight once again for freedom and liberty' and that it was wrong that 'ideals of political and social philosophy should be sacrificed on the altar of utility and party discipline'. He also expressed sardonic views about socialism, influenced by those of Anderson, whose early enthusiasm for state action was now moderating into a suspicion of the growth of the state. Socialism, Evatt wrote, was soullessly materialist, and placed too much importance on 'material and economic interests at the expense of intellectual, moral, and religious principles'. The purpose of state action was not so much material advance as what he had called 'inner moral development', and although the distinction was somewhat pedantic, it clearly positioned him as a liberal opposed to socialism.

The book was a significant achievement, especially for someone so young; he was aged only twenty-one when it was composed. It is an insightful analysis of the new form of liberalism that had been so influential in shaping policy and politics at the end of the nineteenth century and into the first decade of the Federation. But at the time of its publication in 1918 it was already somewhat anachronistic and nostalgic, because the new liberalism had fallen out of fashion. After earlier alliances with Labor, Deakin had, in the 'Fusion' of 1909, led his progressive liberals into a merger with the more robustly anti-Labor conservatives. After their subsequent merger with Hughes and some Labor colleagues in 1917 to form the Nationalists, the non-Labor side of politics was more reactionary than liberal. Few were any longer attached to the liberalism of Deakin, Higgins and Wise that Evatt extolled, and what remained was submerged into two streams of influence, one devoted to workers' education and building the good society, and the other focused on civil liberties and legal struggles against injustice. Evatt, as we will see, fell into the latter camp, using the law as his weapon.

Only a few years after it was first published, Evatt's book was used against him, when in 1924 he sought endorsement for a Labor seat. His opponents brandished it as proof that he was not descended of Labor stock. And nor was he at the age of twenty-one. His politics were those of a progressive liberal, sympathetic to but detached from Labor traditions. There was irony in these attacks: Evatt was accused of endorsing a form of social liberalism with which Labor had once been allied, but by the time he was championing it in print, Labor had forgotten, or preferred not to remember, that they had been nurtured under the wing of the new liberalism. Liberals were now Labor's opponents, not their allies. Evatt, however, insisted that Labor was now the chief proponent of the liberal ideals he had described. Though it might have sounded odd to some of his Labor colleagues, it made some sense: theirs was the party advocating positive state intervention to achieve social progress.

Liberalism in Australia is a sophisticated piece of work, far from being just the juvenilia of a youngster, best forgotten like much of his poetry. Yet it was understandable that he did not want it revived. Several years after his death, Mary Alice recalled there had been suggestions of a reprint in the 1950s, but he was not 'keen on this idea at all', saying that it had been 'a very immature effort of a very young man'. In hindsight, it can be seen as a reasonably mature effort of a very young man; but a revival during the years of his embattled leadership would obviously have caused problems.

***

Evatt had enjoyed university and the opportunities it offered, and the university had also been good to him. Following his graduation in April 1918, he was appointed associate to the new chief justice. This was Sir William Cullen, who as chancellor had assessed the applications four years before for the Rhodes scholarship, and who had a few months earlier helped to block Childe's appointment to the university. Being associate to the chief justice was conventionally a stepping stone by which a bright young graduate could make his way towards greater things in the law. In October 1918 he was admitted to the bar, and photographs from the time show his strong, clean-shaven face, atop his broad shoulders, butterfly collar and a flouncy bow tie, his calm eyes looking through wire-rimmed glasses. The career of this forceful, confident young man of twenty-four, highly trained in the specialised realms of social liberal philosophy and legal rationality, was about to take off. In February 1919 he resigned as Cullen's associate and joined Andy Watt, a prominent King's Counsel, in the practice of the law.

3

Love and the law

Two years after Evatt had died, the Marxist activist Guido Baracchi, an old friend of the Evatts, wrote to Mary Alice, saying he thought often of them. 'I don't know how to convey to you how thrilled I was when you told us of Bert's writing a sonnet to you every day, in earlier times. I was thrilled that you evoked it and he did it, bless you both!' The sentimental little poems Evatt wrote for his wife are one small indication of the affection between the two over their forty-five years together. Along with his love for the law, Mary Alice was a constant in his life and significantly shaped his adult character.

Love

Evatt first met Mary Alice Sheffer just after he graduated in April 1918, not long after she had started studying architecture at the university. She had grown up in Mosman and knew his younger brothers; in a diary she began in 1914, she wrote down lists of the girls and boys to be invited to a party, and Frank and Ray were included among them. (She was sixteen at the time, the same age as Frank, and described herself in the pages of the diary as 'a tall healthy girl with grey eyes and golden hair, loving above all things reading'.) She first met Bert not through his brothers but through family friends in Mosman. He asked her if she would like to go to a lecture about the author Robert Louis Stevenson. They were both interested in politics; at school, she had been stirred by the 1917 railway strike and was an enthusiast for William Morris, the English craft and guild socialist. They were engaged in 1918 when she was nineteen and he was twenty-three, but not married till late November 1920; the relatively long engagement suggests her parents felt she was too young to marry.

The wedding took place in the Mosman Congregational Church on a Saturday evening, followed by a reception at 'Wapello', the grand family home of the Sheffers in Mosman. Mary Alice's father, who had migrated with the family from America, was a manufacturing chemist with a major interest in the Sheldon Drug Company, which made products such as 'Dr Sheldon's Magnetic Liniment' and 'Gin Pills'. Samuel Fuller Sheffer was wealthy; in August 1929, shortly before his death, his assets were valued at £172,000, the equivalent of about $13 million today. About half this wealth was invested in government bonds, a quarter in property and the remainder in shares, including shares in his own drug company, in the *Bulletin* and in a range of major banks. In 1939, after her mother died, Mary Alice would inherit over a third of this wealth.

While initially sceptical of the radical young lawyer, Mary Alice's parents had come round; the bride was given away by her father and the garden at Wapello had been strung with coloured electric lights, with a hundred guests in a large marquee on the lawn. It was announced in the *Sydney Morning Herald* that the newly married couple would be leaving on the *Niagara* for a honeymoon in California. In fact, the honeymoon cruise was to Hawaii and California, aboard the steamer SS *Marama*. Very little remains to tell us of this time; we know they stayed for a while in Honolulu, and later they named their Mosman home 'Nuuanu', after the principal valley of the island of O'ahu. Photographs from their honeymoon album show Mary Alice as a slim woman wearing the shapeless dresses of the early 1920s 'flapper', while even aboard the steamer Evatt dressed formally in a dark suit with waistcoat and a large tie around a turned-down collar. On the voyage across the Pacific, he had himself appointed honorary secretary of the sport and entertainment committee of the first-class passengers.

In a small exercise book, he conscientiously recorded the minutes of their meetings, held in the smoke room. They arranged games tournaments, dances and theatrical events, decided on a scale of tips for the stewards and cabin boys, and organised a concert, to which, in a show of democratic spirit, they resolved to invite the second-class passengers.

In both Hawaii and California, Evatt took it upon himself to investigate questions of race and immigration. Both states had significant Asian populations, and Hawaii was popularly supposed to suffer 'mixed race' problems. When they returned in mid-February, he was interviewed by the *Sydney Morning Herald* and declared he had been convinced, if he was not already, of the benefit of racial restrictions on immigration. Australia's migration policy was 'a protection against problems of the very gravest kind', he claimed, but he did not say what he had seen to convince him. He supported an orthodox view of the White Australia policy, and also added a flourish of patriotic pride. He was 'grieved' Americans knew so little about Australia, claimed the Sydney beaches were superior, and asserted: 'It is surely time Australians commenced to at least let other peoples of the Pacific know something about their country'.

Upon their return they settled into married life. Evatt seems to have taken Mary Alice on as a project, urging her to read and study. She said he disliked seeing her sewing and darning, exclaiming, 'For God's sake, get a good book and read it'. Earlier, he had told her there was no point continuing with her degree, because they must get married. She later recalled:

> He felt we shouldn't wait too long to get married and I thought
> I would finish my course. He said, 'no, don't do architecture
> – change into arts and you can get some credit for subjects in
> architecture and then you can do constitutional law. We won't be
> able to talk about cases unless you do constitutional law', because
> this was his favourite part of law.

Though she did not finish her degree, Mary Alice did study some constitutional law. He and Gordon Childe would tease her about books she had not read and then produce the book the next day. On one occasion before their marriage, she wrote to Evatt saying, 'I have not had much time for Bosanquet – but will try and finish another chapter this afternoon', adding that she was finding Evatt's annotations more interesting than the work of the famous philosopher.

They first moved into a flat in a small house on the point above Little Sirius Cove in Mosman. They would sleep out on the verandah and have a swim before breakfast. 'We liked fresh air but we also liked to sit up and look down over the water', Mary Alice said. Evatt told her all he wanted was 'a good book-case, a comfortable chair, two desks, a good light to read by at night and ... you really don't need anything else in the house'. In the early 1920s, he gave law lectures at the university in the evenings, and when she complained they never went out and she was left alone, he suggested she read his set of the Everyman's Library:

N.B.
His
attitude
towards
learning /
knowledge.

> He said 'have you read every one of those books?' And I said, 'Well, no, I've read a lot of them.' And he said 'Well don't let me ever hear you say you're lonely again until you've read every single one'. So I settled down to read them. It took me 2½ years to read them all.

It sounds like excessive, all-enveloping bossiness, but it was not tyranny; she considered herself liberated and modern, enjoyed arguments with him and respected his learning. Years later, during the war, when she went with him on hazardous flights across the Pacific, he was fortunate that she was more intrepid and calm than he was.

Evatt kept no diaries and few private letters. Unusually, though, there still exist some letters they exchanged in the earliest years of their marriage, which provide an insight into their life together. She was staying in the Blue Mountains while he worked in Sydney. He visited on weekends, but it is not clear for how long she was away. The letters are usually undated, but sometimes it is possible from references within them to work out when they were written.

In one early letter – we can date it to October 1921 because Evatt mentions the third anniversary of his going to the bar – he wrote of being alone in Sydney:

> This Monday night I would fain be by your side … I do miss
> you and the toil of the day is not relieved by the sweet joy of
> coming home to you and your dear sweet gurgle of welcome, the
> joys of evening. Last night I felt so sad as I went out to our dear
> verandah rooms, and wished you were with me there so as I could
> tell you of my love and kiss your dear face …

He reported on his success in various legal cases, and said he had been out to her parents' house for tea. 'Darling I need you and want you, but you must stay and have a rest because Sydney is terribly hot indeed today.' At about the same time, from the Carrington Hotel in Katoomba, Mary Alice wrote self-consciously of her own feelings, with a touch of sentimentality:

> I am sitting on the verandah writing to my lover, with my specs
> on my nose, papers on my knee, inky fingers and a heart full of
> longing and love … It is a quarter past ten and I suppose you will
> be in court looking legal and learned so that nary a person could
> guess that you are a dear passionate lover, full of Romance and
> glory and tenderness.

She asked him to send some books, a 'good life of George Eliot, also Victor Hugo or James', and urged him not to stay up late and to get plenty of exercise: 'Hear your … wife fussing!' This was late 1921.

In a letter from early 1922, Evatt wrote from his legal chambers, and it becomes clear Mary Alice had had some sort of health crisis. He referred to it only obliquely and his tone was detached; it seemed recounting their private history like the facts of a case enabled him to speak about his worries and fears. He reminded her of a holiday they had taken in Manly the previous December, when they had 'delighted in the surf'. He then added:

> Our chief purpose was to help you in your illness, hoping that an operation would not be required. We were bitterly disappointed in that and I shall never, never forget the anxiety of it all when they took you away from me … in the end you came back home darling and had more illness ... But you won through it all and I could not help thinking of it all as I was there last night.

What this illness was is never specified, but it was obviously serious, and it gives us some insight into their shared history. In a letter to Mary Alice two decades later, Evatt recalled this health crisis, summoning up the memory; his hope that she would get better, that they could 'shake off' their fears, the 'sudden clear cut decision' of her doctor, and 'then the hours of suffering and anxiety that followed'. He never said explicitly what happened; they both knew, of course, and so could write in ciphers that we cannot decode and perhaps have no business trying to decode. What we know is that they survived the crisis, and the course of their mutual affection ran much as Evatt hoped and predicted it would: 'Love and Joy, Anxiety and Sorrow, Hope and Fear – through it all we have got to love each other and value each other more'.

In June 1922, Mary Alice wrote again from the mountains. 'You must be busy, dear one, and I so lazy! I do hope that all goes well. I am with you in spirit at least.' With her there was a Dr Porter, whom she liked: 'He reminds me of you in lots of ways. Being keen on his work, interested and correct about life, decent and not swanky'. This was most likely Hubert Porter, who had attended Fort Street before studying medicine; he played rugby league for Balmain where Evatt was a board member. Porter was the superintendent at Sydney Hospital, and presumably friendship made him available to spend time with her during her recovery. She asked Evatt to send more books, 'a life, political if possible or a good solid novel and something exciting for Ella'. (Ella was employed as a maid and general domestic help.) Mary Alice wrote cheerfully about her convalescence: 'I have never felt better in my life … I hope and trust that a long healthy life will be ours after this. It will be worth the pain and anxiety and separation, dear one, won't it?' From this she moved directly to their future together, and to talking about children. 'Also I have other hopes that you know. Why be ambiguous? A large healthy beautiful intelligent family we desire, and that is worth some trouble to produce. They will all be so proud of you Bert. Just imagine having you for their father!'

She did not have that large family, but they adopted two children, Peter and Rosalind; one of them was infertile, a fact that was clearly significant to them both, but that they wished to keep private. There are some revealing clues, though they are no more than that. The first is that they adopted Peter at some point between July and September 1922; he was a baby, born in January of that year. To move to adoption so soon, only about eighteen months into the marriage, indicates that they knew it was the only way they could have children. The second clue is in Tennant's papers: when she was researching her biography of Evatt, her husband wrote to her that it would be 'rather absurd not to say straight out that Peter and Rosalind were adopted', despite a promise she had made to Mary Alice. He doubted a forthcoming ABC documentary would be so discreet. So it was something of a secret, yet Peter and Rosalind were by this point aged in their thirties and forties. Perhaps they had never been told and Mary Alice was in a quandary, having left it so late and fearing that her secret was about to come out. Perhaps it was a long habit of silence, because at the time adoption was considered slightly shameful and infertility something to be pitied.

Another indication of this secrecy is that Evatt's close friend Hartley Grattan knew they could not have children, but had never been told the details. He speculated in his notebook that one of Evatt's 'frustrations' was 'his failure (inability? or was it Mary Alice's?) to have children ...' The question marks are revealing. The two couples knew each other well, yet Grattan was unsure if the problem was infertility and did not know which of them was infertile. It was characteristic of men of that period to avoid intimate discussions, though it is revealing that Grattan was so much in the dark.

Here we are on the edge of the sort of intrusion that the journalist and writer Janet Malcolm condemned; in her book on Sylvia Plath and Ted Hughes, she described the biographer as a burglar, peeping through keyholes, rifling through drawers and turning over the intimate belongings of their subject. Reading personal letters, she wrote, involves 'the feeling of transgression that comes from reading letters not meant for one's eyes'. She suggested that part of the seductive attraction of biography, for both the writer and the reader, is exactly this licence to be prurient; the reader and author are in 'a kind of collusion ... in an excitingly forbidden undertaking'.

Even with these reservations, it is worth considering the significance of what had happened. A medical crisis had occurred, in December 1921, a year after their marriage. She was ill but it was not life-threatening, because the doctors had time to ponder whether or not she needed an operation; after the operation, she came home but was still ill, and was then convalescing in the Blue Mountains till at least July, or later. By September 1922, they had adopted Peter. Had it become evident early in their marriage that she was infertile, or that some other gynaecological problem required an operation? It was clear that the operation, the anxiety and their separation were related to children.

I had thought that was as far as I could go, trying to interpret cryptic letters and circumstantial evidence. Perhaps it was in any case going too far; being left with some ambiguity at least left Mary Alice

a veil of privacy. But on my last research trip to Adelaide, the librarian in charge of Evatt's papers produced a package of exercise books.
One was a slim black book, with a torn label reading: 'The operation'.
Written in faint pencil, it began on 16 March 1922 with Mary Alice
imagining herself looking down on her body, musing, 'Are you really
going to be cut open tomorrow?' She reflected on how much she owed
to her mother, and to Bert: 'He has helped me and taught me to be a
woman. I was a child when my dear love came to me …' She did not
say what the operation was, only that she was frightened. She wrote a
will, addressed to Evatt; it was not about the distribution of her wealth
but about how she hoped he would remember her. 'Please keep my
little verses and writings and read them sometimes …' She wanted him
to help 'all babies', and to contribute to 'education – our country – our
world'. She told him of her faith in him, and that she would watch
over him: 'Such a work in the world you will do and I will help you –
even if I am dead I will help you'.

The next entry was over two weeks later. Mary Alice was now
recuperating from the operation and had been told she could go home
shortly. She described the intense pain of the two weeks since the
operation, when she 'blew up' till she thought she would 'burst'. It was
clearly a serious infection, and Mary Alice confided in the diary that
she owed her survival to one of the nurses, who pulled her through.
'Even Dr Barrington says so.' On 4 April, the day of the last entry, she
was preparing to go home; she had walked out to the verandah that
morning but was still weak. Her parents had visited and were 'both
very excited', but Bert had 'overslept' that morning, so she 'just saw
him for a moment before he rushed off to court'.

She mentioned Dr Barrington three times in these short entries,
and this was the final clue. I can find only one Barrington in Sydney
in the early 1920s and he was a significant figure. Fourness Barrington was president of the New South Wales branch of the British
Medical Association, and a public advocate of better maternity care
to reduce 'the unduly high death rate in childbed'. He was a leading

gynaecological surgeon at the Royal Prince Alfred Hospital. So Mary Alice's operation was clearly gynaecological. It is unlikely to have been an ectopic pregnancy, which would have been too much of an emergency for doctors to take months weighing up whether an operation was necessary; she was ill for some three months before the operation in mid-March. It could have been an incomplete miscarriage or other condition that required surgery. Perhaps the surgery itself resulted in infertility, perhaps a hysterectomy; or perhaps it was the infection following the surgery that resulted in her infertility. Her long convalescence in the Blue Mountains is consistent with major infection; and while gynaecological surgery was not uncommon in the 1920s, infection following it was also quite common and could be life-threatening in the absence of antibiotics. Mary Alice may have been lucky to survive.

Along with worry about Mary Alice's condition, Evatt's mother's health was deteriorating; by June 1922, she and Clive had both moved into the Evatts' rented house, now at Milton Avenue, Mosman. Jeanie was only fifty-nine but suffering from cerebral thrombosis. In early June, Evatt wrote to Mary Alice from his Wentworth Court chambers: 'Mother does not seem to be better, she had an attack of sickness yesterday as well as the day before and it is very puzzling to know what to do or what can be done'. Evatt had been sleeping 'outside', on the verandah, and could hear the lions roaring at night at the nearby Taronga Park Zoo. He wrote that he had woken up and seen 'a leopard-like figure springing around the tree, a few yards away': 'It gave me a shock and this plus the cold drove me into the sitting room sofa until morning'. This 'fearful creature' turned out to be their cat.

Two weeks later, he wrote again:

Immediately we rang off yesterday I got news that mother was unwell. When I got home I found that she had taken a turn and had to be carried to bed. In fact my aunt thought that mother was dying ... From what I can gather I do not think it was a stroke but a faint owing to her weakness ... I stayed with mother a good part of the evening and played her some music on the ukulele which she seemed to like. She was very drowsy and slept fairly well. This morning she was a little better still. You can imagine how upsetting and depressing it all is.

At around this time, Mary Alice commented that it seemed as if Jeanie was 'breaking up', and suggested they get a bigger house to care for her and have Ella to look after her. 'She would be perfectly happy there and we would know we were doing the best we could do ... After all her hard life and the bringing up of you boys I feel that we should have her with us now. But I could not manage it by myself.' Jeanie caught pneumonia and died in early September, outliving her own mother by only four years. After a Church of England service, her body was taken for burial in East Maitland, alongside the husband who had died two decades earlier. The headstone also records the deaths of Ray and Frank in the war.

Mary Alice's letters include regular praise, pride and encouragement for Evatt. 'I've just been telling Ella about your book. You do know how proud of it I am Bert.' When they had children, she said, she hoped they would 'grow up just half as good and wise and fascinating as you' and she would be satisfied. She had seen him mentioned in the press, and said her heart 'just turned over with pride', though she suggested he provide the newspaper with a better photograph. 'I'll be glad to be home. I feel really homesick and I wonder if I could stand a long while away from Mosman ... Oh I do miss you dearest.' At some time between July and September 1922, her letters suddenly started to mention Peter, adopted as an infant; Rosalind was adopted as a baby ten years later. Mary Alice wrote from the Ritz Hotel in Leura: 'Today is lovely – quite cool and balmy and we have been under the pines all the morning ... I have found it quite easy to manage Peter since Ella came and I am beginning to feel quite rested'. There is nothing else in their correspondence, nor in Evatt's papers, that mentions the adoptions, or what prompted their decision to adopt.

These letters between husband and wife, often sentimental with their declarations of love, reveal their genuine affection; as Mary Alice recovered, there were also oblique references to reviving their sexual relationship. He wrote: 'I missed you last night and dreamed of you so very sweetly ... I love you so much and am looking forward to the time when we will be "married" again and settled down in that dear old home we're going to get'. She wrote back: 'I only feel half myself this week. But I am having a very restful time and I'll be twice the wife I was next week'. In another letter from the Ritz, she wrote: 'Today is the perfection of all days in the mountains. We are warm, yet cool ... Were you here I could dance as doth your frisky colt – also etc.'

The last of this series of letters dates to late 1922; Mary Alice's convalescence was complete. Both of them wrote about their aspiration for a 'home' together, which Evatt described in one letter as 'where you and I are to live and love – wherever that may be – our "monument more lasting than bronze" – because everlasting'. In 1923, *Sands Sydney Directory* for the first time listed 'Mrs H.V. Evatt' at Milton Avenue, making it clear that she was at last 'at home'. From the following year, they were listed at Nuuanu, a large Federation-style house they had bought on Methuen Avenue in Mosman, still within hearing distance of the lions at the zoo.

Law

A courtroom is a sort of theatre. The judges sit elevated, looking down as though themselves on a stage watching those below. Depending on how traditional the courtroom is, they are surrounded and buttressed by the emblems and rituals of power. The wood-panelled canopy over the judges' bench mimicking a proscenium arch, the archaic robes and wigs lifting their majesty out of the realm of the ordinary, the stentorian call of court staff demanding silence – all are part of a performance of the power of the state and the authority of the law.

But this theatre is inverted, for the judges are the audience, and it is the barristers who put on the main show, facing not the spectators behind them but the judges above them. Barristers have to project their voice, using emphasis, inflection and cadence to make themselves persuasive. Facing up to the bench, they either have to project a personality that will carry the judges with them, or dissemble and hide a personality that might intrude on their case. They have to ad-lib, thinking on their feet, responding to questions from the bench; they have to perform under the pressure of examination. Some barristers of course are not good performers, with dull voices and muddled minds, but they are like poor actors who will not thrive.

A courtroom is also more than a theatre; it is a place for sifting and testing evidence and argument, and hopefully it is a place for dispensing justice. But regardless of the quality of argument or evidence available, it has to be presented. A good, even ingenious argument that is poorly presented, poorly performed, may still be persuasive, while even the most convincing and skilful presentation may not, and should not, save a weak, implausible case. Judges are expected to be able to distinguish performance from argument, but cases heard before juries can be much more sensitive to the theatrical talents of the barrister.

On this stage the young Evatt was regarded as a star. This is curious in terms of performance because he was rarely considered an impressive speaker, either in the law or later in politics. His voice was often dull and his delivery flat, but as a barrister he may have made up for it with acuity of mind. Certainly his delivery was not impressive when reading a political speech, though there are some later recordings of off-the-cuff speeches that are compelling and convincing, and perhaps this was more the mode of address he used in court. He was recognised as sharply intelligent, capable of large and ingenious arguments, and some transcripts of his encounters in court show his skill in responding to questioning, in carrying an intellectual position.

One example was in 1925, when, as a barrister now of seven years' standing, he appeared before the High Court to argue against the deportation of two radical leaders of the Seamen's Union, Tom Walsh and Jacob Johnson. A tribunal had ordered they be deported for seditious activities, and the case dragged on for months as Andy Watt and his young junior, Evatt, challenged the legality of the order and the tribunal's jurisdiction. Their arguments were abstruse, centring on the extent to which the constitution allowed delegated judicial authority, and whether the authority of the crown was divisible. Although junior to Watt, Evatt carried the main load. What is most important for our purposes is the sheer confidence and brio with which the young Evatt handled himself in front of a court that included Isaac Isaacs and Henry Bournes Higgins, who had been involved in the writing of the Australian constitution, and alongside them Chief Justice Adrian Knox and Evatt's former law lecturer, George Rich.

The transcript shows just how intellectually nimble Evatt was. He would make a point, Isaacs or Higgins would demand to know 'why', and he always seemed to have an answer. They peppered him with sharp questions, but he was up to the task, clearly across his matter, and showing no sign of intimidation. Even on the bald page, the transcript of exchanges, probing questions and immediate confident answers comes across as an impressive intellectual performance. Over several days, Evatt was on his feet arguing with the same assurance, with quick answers and complete confidence in his brief. It is impossible from a transcript to tell how such experienced judges might have assessed him, though Watt and Evatt won the case. It is revealing of how Evatt's star was rising in labour circles that he was congratulated, by the Carrington Coal and Coke Shipping Union, on his 'great personal effort in obtaining such a magnificent victory in the late deportation case'. It was, declared the union secretary, 'a victory for the Labour Movement' and 'for all freedom loving Australian citizens'.

Evatt's legal practice took off quickly. In August 1919, at the age of twenty-five, he appeared before the High Court as a junior on behalf of the Labor premier of Queensland, T.J. Ryan, in a libel claim. During the second conscription campaign in 1917, the *Argus* had alleged Ryan was involved in something close to a conspiracy to stir up dissent, and he claimed for the large sum of £10,000 in damages. This was not Evatt's first experience of the High Court, but it was a high-profile case and its strong Labor connections indicated his allegiances as a barrister. Throughout the early 1920s, he would be involved primarily in civil cases dealing with matters such as negligence, commercial disputes, libel and slander, contested wills, workers' compensation and defending unions against charges such as conspiring to pervert the course of justice.

Perhaps the earliest encounter between Evatt and Menzies was in 1920, when both appeared in the well-known Engineers' case before the High Court. They were the same age, and recognised as the coming young barristers of their respective home towns, Sydney and Melbourne. Over the next forty years there developed an intense rivalry between the two, with their increasingly bitter struggle on the public stage culminating in the major confrontations of the 1950s. But before the Engineers' case, they may only have been vaguely aware of each other. Menzies had been engaged to represent a union, the Amalgamated Society of Engineers, in a dispute with the West Australian government, and the case brought him instant fame, because it became a landmark decision in the interpretation of the constitutional powers of the Commonwealth.

Menzies later wrote that when he began his arguments in Melbourne, he had suspected he might be able to provoke a reconsideration of the court's earlier rulings on the division of constitutional powers. The judges agreed to that and adjourned the case to Sydney, inviting other states to be represented; Evatt was then involved as a junior support for the barrister representing New South Wales. In an ironic reversal of their later positions, Menzies represented a union and argued for the expansion of Commonwealth powers, while Evatt was amongst those opposing that expansion. The judgement, delivered at the end of August, was quickly seen as a major constitutional reinterpretation. Where the Commonwealth had a power, such as in industrial relations, that overlapped with those of the states it was now decreed to exercise it 'extensively', that is to the fullest extent before the authority of the states began. Menzies wrote that this was 'revolutionary', while the legal scholar Geoffrey Sawer wrote it greatly expanded 'the potential scope of Commonwealth power'. But while the case was historically significant, Evatt's role was minor, and for us it is only meaningful as the first known encounter with his lifelong opponent, Menzies.

Running through Evatt's legal work in the 1920s were two consistent themes: defending *Smith's Weekly*, a populist and often vituperative newspaper in Sydney, against libel claims, and acting for unions and labour causes. In October 1920, he made the first of many appearances with Watt on behalf of *Smith's Weekly*. They regularly defended its owners – Sir Joynton Smith, Claude McKay and Clyde Packer – against equally regular writs for libel. The paper had been sued by a Sydney landlord Emanuel Myerson for describing him as 'Monarch of the Slums', a 'rack-renter' and a 'modern Shylock'. It was characteristic of *Smith's Weekly* that it was so effortlessly anti-Semitic. Four years later, the battle was still going on. A jury, in a retrial, had found in favour of Myerson, but awarded him derisory damages, and his lawyers returned to court to claim an award for costs. Watt and Evatt won the argument when the judge dismissed the application.

During 1921, Watt and Evatt were engaged to assist a royal commission inquiring into allegations that unionists had been discriminated against for taking part in the 1917 railway strike – the strike that had so interested Mary Alice as a schoolgirl. They represented a number of railway workers, including Ben Chifley, then an engine driver and unionist, who claimed to have been discriminated against by being reinstated to lower positions after the strike. Evatt spoke at length about a 'black list' compiled by the railways department; one striker was described as a 'rebellious agitator', another as a 'professional loafer' and a third as a 'Russian agitator'. By the time they had finished, Watt had spent thirty hours addressing the enquiry, while Evatt had taken up another twenty-two hours. Evatt then did his radical profile no harm by writing a series of articles for the *Labor Daily* during 1924 about the royal commission and the discrimination against the railway workers; these were then consolidated into a pamphlet entitled 'The 1917 Strike and the Aftermath'.

Another indication of his rise to prominence was that at the end of 1923, Evatt was appointed by the University of Sydney as lecturer in legal interpretation for the following year. In the same period, he somehow found time to write a thesis for a doctorate of laws that was awarded in 1924; his topic was the constitutional aspects of the royal prerogative, or the reserve powers of the crown, and it was published in 1936 as *The King and His Dominion Governors*. That he could write a thesis while building a busy practice – and, as we will see, also beginning to engage in Labor politics – indicates the prodigious energy he brought to work. He had begun his habit of working many hours past midnight, standing at a writing desk, and surviving on very little sleep.

By the end of 1925, Evatt's legal practice was firmly established. He had appeared before the High Court seventeen times, and in most of the other courts in New South Wales. The *Sydney Morning Herald* itemised 155 reports of his legal work to the end of 1925, the great bulk of it being civil and commercial law, but with a total of twenty-one appearances for unions in either the civil or industrial court system. He had established a reputation as a champion of the labour movement in the courts, and was seen as a prominent new legal figure. Some of this was by design – the republication of his articles on the 1917 strike had deliberately elevated his prominence – while his confidence before the High Court suggested his innate sense of self as well as his legal skills. His relentless success through school and university, winning all the prizes, had reinforced the faith his mother placed in his talents. As a young man making his mark in Sydney's legal and labour circles, Evatt's obvious skill at working with legal rationality made him into a figure of note, just the kind of figure Jeanie had expected him to become.

His rapid rise in the law is important, and it is worth considering how much it shaped his sense of self. I am thinking not so much of how all this success may have turned his head – he never experienced much in the way of self-doubt – but of the kind of person into which he was developing. Being a barrister is a relatively solo occupation, dependent only on one's wits, requiring little cooperation with others; and the law was a sphere in which he excelled, the medium through which he expressed his talent and found recognition. It was not just that he was an exceptional lawyer; he came to invest his identity in being that exceptional lawyer. His capacity to argue a case, to promptly identify key issues and to convince others he was right became his self-definition. Law meant determining 'the facts', and as Mary Alice recalled, he was always asking, 'What are the facts?' As I noted in the introduction, Evatt had a relatively simple notion of epistemology, believing that facts, once established, provided a stable ground from which, after a process of rational enquiry, it was possible for him to determine the truth. He was clearly exceptionally capable in constructing legal arguments, but later critics, such as Hasluck, noted that he chose those facts that suited him – and in any case, winning a legal argument is not necessarily the same as arriving at a truth, let alone wisdom or insight.

The law was where he was most at home and where he could feel most purely and utterly dependent just on himself; and the law was for him what the sociologist Pierre Bourdieu called a 'habitus', a mode of existence with its norms and its practices. Law is not just a profession, it is a habit of mind and a performance of the self, a mode of being in the world, and it came naturally to Evatt. We all need recognition, and Evatt was certainly no exception. In the law he found this recognition. It was not so much that his achievements went to his head, as that his success as a legal rationalist shaped his identity. At university, writing essays on liberalism and on the law, he had shown a talent for

The key to understanding Doc?

working with the themes of progressive liberalism; but he seems never to have really had much interest in political ideas *per se*. Once he had hitched his star to the labour movement, his political views were obvious enough, but in the sense that he had the views expected of him. He had no real passion for political philosophy or theory, for arguing about politics as contending principles or values.

Law was much more important than politics in his formation, and law was the medium through which his intellectual capacity was exercised. In this sense, he was better at law than at politics. Unlike Menzies, who transposed the skills of a legal advocate to those of a *cf* political debater, but who understood the differences between law and *Menzies* politics, Evatt remained a legal rationalist. He believed in the law too much to be a good politician; because he believed that modes of legal reasoning produced truths that others simply had to concede. It was that, more than his undoubted arrogance, that made him so dogmatic, so convinced he was right even when advisers told him he was wrong. It was he, after all, who had the brilliant legal mind and could thus discern the truth. In the fraught political landscape of the postwar years, this would be a serious weakness – but that was far in the future.

4

Politics and Jack Lang

Evatt may not have been well suited to politics, but he wanted to be in politics. What his motivation was in the 1920s is not clear; he had joined the Mosman Political Labor League in May 1920, and by mid-1922 had made a failed attempt to gain preselection for a federal seat. In 1925, he was elected to the New South Wales parliament. But he never really articulated why he wanted to be in the political realm; it was almost as though it was another sphere in which he wanted to make an impact, to excel. Why he chose Labor is somewhat clearer; he genuinely believed that Labor carried forward the progressive liberalism he had written about at university; he had debated Labor politics with Childe and was not attracted to the much more conservative Nationalist side of politics.

'My political attempt'

Among Evatt's papers is the tattered exercise book recording the minutes of the first two years of the Mosman branch. It shows that Evatt was a distinctly inactive member. Six local men meeting on a Thursday evening in February 1920 established the branch; they appointed a secretary and chairman and applied for endorsement to the state executive of the party. Membership grew in ones and twos, each meeting gravely considering new applications. On 30 April a meeting of nine members, all men, approved Evatt's application and he was 'entered into membership', paying his subscription of one shilling. Although the minutes may not be complete, it seems that Evatt, at most, attended only one meeting before early 1922. The members' enthusiasm seemed to be flagging, with a meeting in October 1921 abandoned for lack of a quorum. The minute book presumably came into Evatt's possession after he took over as secretary in 1922.

Mysteriously, the record seems to have been altered for the single meeting Evatt apparently did attend. The minutes of 14 May 1920 read: 'Messrs Grogan, Forge, Mathers, Rose & Evatt Lynch were present …' The original read: 'Messrs Grogan, Forge, Mathers, Rose & Lynch' – but there was a line break before 'Lynch' that left enough space to allow for the later addition of Evatt's name, which was written in a different hand with different coloured ink. The addition might have been entirely innocent, but looks like a retrospective doctoring of the record to make it appear he had attended, a record that could be produced if needed. Yet it is hard to believe someone with Evatt's experience of the forensics of evidence would use the wrong colour ink; it seems amateurish. In any case, during the two years covered by this minute book, he was not otherwise noted and was clearly not active.

Two years later, in mid-1922, he made a bid for Labor preselection for the federal seat of Cook, then an inner-city electorate including Redfern and Surry Hills. In the midst of the letters he and Mary Alice exchanged about her surgery and convalescence, he wrote that he would like her advice on whether to put himself forward. 'Everyone to whom it has been mentioned has been very favourable and as at present advice I am inclined to give it a go.' He expected support from *Smith's Weekly*, the publication for which he did regular legal work. Mary Alice wrote back to him: 'O Bert, if the selectors knew you as I do they would plump for you with one voice'. Once he did nominate, he reported: 'The world received my political attempt with interest and no active hostility'. But he was disqualified because he did not meet the requirement of three years' continuous party membership, only having been a member for two years. It was characteristic of the pushy young lawyer that he presumably thought such a requirement ought not apply to him. He seemed to take the rebuff quietly; perhaps with his mother ill and Mary Alice convalescing, he had decided against politics for a time, though over the next few years he was secretary and president of the Mosman branch, took on honorary legal work for the party, and in October 1924 was appointed chairman of the party's Fighting Platform Committee, tasked with drawing up Labor's policy statements for the next election.

After his initial indecision over the Cook preselection, Evatt campaigned more intently in late 1924 to represent the working-class state seat of Balmain. At the time, New South Wales Legislative Assembly electorates had multiple members, with Balmain returning five representatives. Identifying so overtly with Labor had some professional consequences. Claude McKay, the editor of *Smith's Weekly*, recalled that 'the big interests detested' Evatt's 'brand of politics' and they

> were quick to make [this] known to his disadvantage
> professionally. Briefs which came readily to the young barrister
> on account of his brilliance ceased abruptly and Bert was cut to
> the quick. He couldn't understand the vengeful attitude of the
> money-bags.

But if conservatives disapproved, so too did some in Labor circles. Historian Ken Buckley notes that 'intellectuals were generally regarded with suspicion in the Labor Party', and that Evatt did not help himself by distributing publicity material emphasising his educational achievements and with an image in his barrister's wig and jabot. A leaflet among his papers addressed to 'the Intelligent Electors in the Balmain Selection Ballot' gave 'sixteen excellent reasons' to vote for 'Dr H.V. Evatt, MA, LLD (Chairman of the Fighting Platform Committee and Honorary Legal Adviser to the Movement)'. There was no photograph on this leaflet, but how Evatt positioned himself revealed his sense of self, and how he chose to project that self. Among the sixteen reasons he listed were that boast we have already seen about being 'by far the most brilliant student' of the state education system; as well as the 'rare spirit of courage and steadfastness' he had shown in establishing rugby league at the university despite opposition; the fact that he was 'the most able junior counsel of the day'; and that he had been 'trusted in important cases' for the labour movement. Moreover, he was 'going to win'. He was already Labor's most able writer, he claimed, and was 'certain to become one of Labor's Leaders in the near future'. The political sphere is no place for shrinking violets, of course, but some found Evatt's assertions of brilliance, courage and leadership potential grating. And there were soon criticisms in the *Labor Daily* that he had 'only just blown into the movement', and was the author of a book endorsing liberalism.

Just before the preselection vote, Mary Alice began a journal, a 'commonplace book', which she kept for a year. On the inside cover, she pasted photographs of herself and Evatt, and wrote that marriage to him had 'seen to it that the life of Mary Alice is <u>not</u> a commonplace life'. Her first entry was: 'Firstly, the menus must be re-written, then the housework freshly plotted out'. She was excited about the prospect of his political career and keen to be involved. She recorded events of the campaign, calculated the votes in previous elections, drafted her own speeches, and assessed Evatt's likely vote. She also considered the question: 'Should we move?' and drew up a list of reasons for 'yes' and 'no' which revealed both their lifestyle and the advantages and disadvantages of leaving the middle-class comfort of Mosman for working-class Balmain. Mary Alice was politically canny, yet her list failed to mention the expectation that a member should live in his electorate.

She counted having no maid as an argument both for and against moving. Some of the other considerations she listed were:

Yes	No
Less travelling	Not such good air
House more accessible	Not so pretty

See more of wife	See more of family
Clive's help	Clive's arguments
Live on tram line	Noisy
Not so weathered	Not so cool

She also wrote down a series of questions, with their answers:

Do you definitely intend to go in for Federal politics later on?
Yes. If we move, how soon must we do so to be on electoral rolls
at election? Now. What are the wages of a member? £600
Are schools good? Yes.

That £600 per annum was about $46,000 in today's values, well below
what a thriving barrister could earn; it was only about three times the
male minimum wage, and may have been so low because parliamentarians were assumed to continue their usual professional occupations.
Mary Alice then drew up a domestic budget, calculating how much
they would pay in rent in Balmain and how much it would cost to
maintain Nuuanu if they rented it out rather than selling. 'If we sold
the house for £4,000 we could invest in Govt. securities at 5% free
of income tax – that would give us £200 for rent.' In the event, they
rented out Nuuanu while living in the electorate.

Evatt did well in the preselection, coming second on the list
of five Labor candidates for the five-member electorate. He readied himself for the state elections on 30 May 1925 and his Labor
critics renewed their attacks on his background. His past as a social
liberal continued to be an awkward problem, and he was resented
as an arriviste who had attached himself to the movement. During
the election itself, one Labor opponent described him as 'fresh from
his mansion in Mosman' and seeking to win over the working-class
people of Balmain. One of his strongest critics, T.J. O'Sullivan, was
a member of the Trades and Labor Council, and proposed 'an investigation' into Evatt's eligibility; by publishing *Liberalism in Australia*,

he said, Evatt had 'confirmed the views expressed in the work as his political philosophy'. Opponents pointed to his criticism of preference for unions in employment, and to his objections to the pledge. Evatt's public reply to these critics was disingenuous. He said he had been nineteen years of age, and an arts student, at the time it was written, as if that perhaps excused anything. He claimed the subject of the essay had been selected by the university, which was hardly true. He shrugged off the attacks as 'frivolous and ridiculous', saying that 'with the possible exception of one or two passages, the essay is entirely Labour in feeling, outlook and sympathy'. But these criticisms of Evatt's middle-class life, his Mosman home and his book on liberalism showed that some in the labour movement considered him as simply out of place, if not an interloper.

By the time of the election in May 1925 they were on the Balmain electoral roll, and *Sands Directory* later recorded them as living in Hay Street, Leichhardt. Mary Alice noted in her journal a visit to inspect building works there; a group of cottages was being built on land that was previously a small dairy farm. She supervised alterations to the standard design to accommodate her husband's exacting tastes. Evatt objected to tiled fireplaces; Mary Alice said 'he always held strong views about design' and felt that a fireplace should be 'an open stone hearth or a brick one', and he disliked linoleum. So she designed a brick fireplace by consulting the *Encyclopaedia Britannica* and selected bare timber floorboards.

Mary Alice clearly relished the work of canvassing and campaigning, recalling that it was 'extraordinarily interesting'. She organised a group of women who went door to door in the electorate and was later involved in developing maternal health services and support for women with young children in the area. She enjoyed meeting the miners at the still active Balmain coalmine; she said she 'learnt a great deal about politics' through all this activity. She noticed, too, that Evatt had to learn how to speak again: 'There's no doubt that a lawyer speaks differently in court than a politician speaks on the hustings'. With

Mary Alice such an active campaigner, Evatt came first of the five members elected, despite having to learn how to speak appropriately and despite his Labor critics. The *Sydney Morning Herald* noted, in an article about new members of parliament, that it was claimed Evatt had 'doubled the previous record vote' for a first attempt at parliament. It was exactly the kind of record Evatt was likely to be proud of and draw to the attention of others.

Labor had been returned to power; this was Premier Jack Lang's first government, turbulent but not as turbulent as his second government in the early 1930s. Although a complete newcomer, Evatt promptly tried to have caucus elect him a minister, wanting the position of attorney-general despite it being earmarked for Edward McTiernan. The latter, only two years older than Evatt, had nevertheless already held that ministry in the Storey government in 1920–1922. Evatt failed, winning eight votes to McTiernan's thirty-four, but marking himself as precocious and unwilling to wait his turn. Lang's biographer Bede Nairn commented that Evatt had 'a lot to learn about politics and Lang', while a colleague of Evatt's said: 'Nobody really put the red carpet out for him … if Bert had been a boilermaker he would have been perhaps better off'.

Mary Alice's commonplace book provides glimpses of their daily life. June 22 in 1925 was 'rainy and wet'; she had gone into the city to dinner with Evatt. He had just finished a case; while it was a victory, his client had been awarded only a quarter of the expected damages. Evatt went to the Balmain League after dinner, she recorded, and other meetings were being arranged for the coming week. Two days later, she caught the Mosman ferry to see a Mrs Robertson who had made her a 'new ensemble dress … a brown georgette embroidered with sage green … a brown velvet hat with a feather and brown suede shoes and red gloves'. 'I felt very elegant', Mary Alice confided. It was a new outfit for the opening of parliament. She met her mother in the city and they went together to sit in the gallery of the parliament to see Evatt sworn in.

'I felt a thrill of pride when I saw Bert's dark head amongst the legislators of my country. He was far and away the handsomest man there and received a markedly good ovation.' After the ceremony they lunched with him at Rainaud's, a restaurant they often frequented.

Kept out of the ministry, Evatt still made some political impact in his first term. Unusually, he was given the honour of speaking first after the governor's speech outlining the government's agenda, perhaps as an indication of the profile he had. Lang's agenda included electoral reform to introduce single-member electorates, reform of workers' compensation, and the introduction of widows' pensions. In a long speech, Evatt said the parliament was 'memorable', as the first to which a woman had been elected – the redoubtable Nationalist Millicent Preston-Stanley. (An interjector immediately pointed out: 'She's not on your side, though!') He argued in favour of restoring seniority to the rail workers discriminated against after the 1917 strike, spoke of the need to abolish the Legislative Council, the upper house of the parliament, and opposed the fees for high schools introduced by the previous government, recalling his own debt to the public school system.

Two weeks later, McTiernan proposed that parliament introduce day sittings, overturning the traditional practice of starting mid-afternoon to allow members to continue their day professions. He proposed sittings from 10 am to 6 pm, arguing late sittings had been designed 'to enable some advocate to do his work in the city and come here at 4 o'clock', and that this reflected the interests of a 'small leisured class' rather than the 'interests of the country'. Evatt started scrapping with McTiernan, objecting that McTiernan's comments were 'offensive'. It was not that Evatt opposed day sittings, and he conceded he was 'bound' by the decisions of his party, but he objected to any disrespect towards lawyers. He then launched into a history lecture about changes over time to the hours of sitting of the House of Commons.

Evatt was vocal in parliament, making long speeches in favour of Labor plans to abolish capital punishment, introduce child endowment and cut the working week to forty-four hours; the last, he argued, was supported by the principles of the League of Nations, as well as the decisions of Justice Higgins in the arbitration court. When an interjector claimed Evatt had not always thought so, and asked, 'What about your book on liberalism?', Evatt replied, 'If the hon. member knew anything about liberalism he would know that the fight for liberalism in this country has not been put up by Nationalism or the National Party, but, as I pointed out in the book he refers to, by the Labour party'. That was an explicit indication of his view that progressive liberalism was alive, and that Labor now carried it forward. He spoke in support of Lang's attempts to abolish the upper house, and he chaired a select committee appointed to enquire into allegations, made by the *Labor Daily*, of bribery of parliamentarians. Curiously, he made no comment about the introduction of widows' pensions, despite the fact his mother, now dead, had been a widow for the last two decades of her life.

In July 1925, Mary Alice recorded going into the city to Evatt's chambers, where she answered letters for him. 'Bert and I lunched at the Vegetarian Restaurant and Bert found that he was penniless. However the Vegi cashed a cheque for us without a murmur ...' In November, during the federal election campaign, they had a weekend in the mountains, speaking at a meeting at Katoomba, and then at a 'huge meeting' in Lithgow Park on the Sunday afternoon. 'Bert and I both spoke in support of Mr Chifley. Bert had a great reception. Tea at Mrs Summers place and then ... [the] 6.30 train to Sydney.' A week later, they were in Dubbo and then Orange, speaking at meetings and arguing Labor's case and for Chifley's candidature. Chifley narrowly lost, and was not to enter the federal parliament until his next attempt in 1928.

Mary Alice's commonplace book illustrates how involved she was in Evatt's political career, often speaking alongside him in campaigns. She also held together the domestic realm of their comfortable middle-class life. They had ample money to pay for help, and she organised all this, as well as managing their substantial funds. A few pages of her diary recorded what was evidently a typical morning 'Rise 6.45 – place white clothes in boiler. Start 7.15. Dress Peter 7.30. Straighten library, open house. Breakfast 8 ... Laundress to come at 8 ... 10.30 – Letters and books HVE arrange. 11.10 Tea ...' The cleaner would be there from 8.30 to 5.30; one week she would do the windows and the next week the silver. Mary Alice prepared the food, cared for Peter and stacked the dishes, while others cleaned the house, did the washing and ironing and gardening. There was clearly no expectation that her husband would have any part in all this; he was out at branch meetings, attending parliament and running a legal practice. She did not complain.

For six months in the middle of 1926, Evatt and Mary Alice were in England, leaving the four-year-old Peter behind with friends. Another libel case involving *Smith's Weekly* was being heard before the Privy Council, then the highest court of appeal open to Australians. They left in early March on the *Otranto*, described as a 'palatial steamer' on its maiden voyage, with accommodation for almost 600 first-class and over 1200 second-class passengers. Its decor was luxurious, with spacious dining rooms, a large lounge with marble columns, a smoking room that was 'thoroughly English in character' with cedar panelling and touches of gilt, and a writing room with Chinese figures. The ship also had an electric lift and air conditioning to all the cabins.

During six weeks sailing from Sydney to Southampton they stopped at Colombo, the Suez Canal, Naples and Toulon. Mary Alice began a diary but did not continue it long. She wrote of the 'glorious lot of flowers' given her at the wharf, along with 'fifty pounds from Father'. On the way, when the ship docked in Fremantle, they met John Curtin, editor of the *Westralian Worker*, who had the previous year failed to be elected to the federal seat of Fremantle. In 1924, Curtin had been an Australian delegate to the International Labour Organization (ILO), and Mary Alice recalled that Evatt and he talked about migration policies. When asked later, she gave the impression that Evatt and Curtin always admired each other and got on well, but she was glossing over the fact that their relationship was strained in the early 1940s.

On board the ship the Evatts met the journalist H.J. Cantwell and his wife, Ida, leftists who were moving to England for work. Ida Cantwell liked Evatt and thought he was good company, though in later years she read Tennant's biography and found it far too sentimental; she thought Tennant had listened too much to Mary Alice's biased reminiscences and failed to capture Evatt's contrary side: 'People who knew him well knew he had faults'. On that long six-week voyage she got to know him well, and the friendship between the four of them lasted for decades.

By comparison with the recently married barrister on his honeymoon cruise five years earlier, Evatt was now a much more substantial figure. He could declare himself to his shipboard companions as 'Dr H.V. Evatt, MLA', a member of parliament with a doctorate of laws. On the *Otranto* he became the chairman of the Sports and Entertainment Committee. They were soon busy organising concerts, fancy dress balls and competitions of deck tennis and quoits. Evatt was delighted to discover that the Australian cricket team was aboard, travelling to England for the Ashes. As Ida Cantwell recalled, he 'adored' cricket and got to meet them all: 'I can't imagine Bert being near any cricketers and not knowing them'. The team captain, Herbie Collins, was promptly appointed to the committee Evatt chaired, as was the team manager. Collins was a passionate gambler and a bookmaker, and onboard he organised a daily sweep wagering on the distance travelled.

The Australian cricketers were notably leisurely on this voyage; passengers who had hoped to watch them training in the nets on the ship's deck soon got more used to them sitting in deckchairs, or taking part in the quoits and deck tennis games. H.J. Cantwell sent several articles, titled 'With the Test Team at Sea', back to Curtin's *Westralian Worker*: 'Though they are not doing much training, they are having an overdose of fun'. There were 'days of blazing heat … nights of tropic mugginess' as they steamed through the Indian Ocean to Colombo. A few weeks later, from the Red Sea, Cantwell wrote that, perhaps under Herbie Collins' influence, 'every event becomes a betting event'. At Suez, the beginning of the canal, some had booked to travel overland to Cairo, where they would rejoin the ship for the three-day run to Naples. The cricketers were going, as did Evatt and Mary Alice; Evatt's papers include a photograph of the two of them posing on camels in front of the Pyramids. In this atmosphere of jolly japes, competitive games and fancy dress balls, they arrived in London in late April.

Evatt lost his appeal before the Privy Council, but they enjoyed their time in England. While in London, the Evatts witnessed the 1926 General Strike, which had been triggered by a dispute in the coalmines, and quickly escalated to a shutdown of public transport, the press and much of industry. In a show of solidarity, the Evatts and Cantwells walked rather than take the buses that were being driven by strike-breaking university students. Stanley Baldwin's Conservative government brought in troops and swore in special police, and nine days later, the Trades Union Congress backed down without any concessions being won. It was a complete collapse. Evatt wrote brief notes about the 'unconditional surrender', and the 'astonishment and dismay' of the labour movement. He wondered why it had all collapsed, whether there was some 'betrayal' involved and whether the union movement had been 'ready' to organise a general strike; he queried whether the strike and its aftermath showed that the government was a 'definite part [of] class struggle?' Both he and Mary Alice were first inspired and then dismayed by the quixotic events of May 1926.

Evatt also attended, as a delegate, the World Migration conference in London in June, organised by the International Federation of

Trade Unions and the Labour and Socialist International. Knowing he would be in London for the Privy Council, the federal ALP had asked him to attend, along with W.H. Kitson, a union leader and member of Western Australia's Legislative Council. It was Evatt's first taste of the emerging world of international organisations, and his position on its issues was distinctly nationalist and labourist, rather than internationalist. The conference, dominated by European representatives concerned about growing unemployment, was keen to facilitate labour migration, including migration to Australia. But the conference's proposals for complete freedom of migration clashed with the White Australia policy, and Evatt's defence of restrictive immigration was explicit, orthodox and entirely in line with both Labor and Nationalist positions.

In the report he later wrote he told of 'a very keen struggle' by many delegates to adopt 'a resolution critical of the policy of White Australia'. The conference accepted that 'newer countries' such as Australia could restrict immigration to defend workers' living standards, but expected that 'exclusion' could only be justified on these sorts of 'economic grounds', meaning that race could not be a basis for exclusion. Kitson and Evatt were supported by delegates from the other dominions in defeating the proposals. Evatt wrote that in future European labour organisations would 'recognize the justice and necessity of the accepted principle of Australian legislation'.

Reports from London quoted Evatt telling the conference that the Australian labour movement was 'bitterly opposed' to southern European migration, especially Italian. In any case, he belligerently said, 'Australia is not affiliated to your international bodies, and therefore your resolutions do not bind us.' He had been even more forthright with *The Times*, insisting that Australia 'could and should be developed as a white man's country', claiming that 'coloured labour would lower and ultimately destroy the standard of living' and that 'assimilating Asiatic races without the deterioration of the races concerned' was a practical impossibility. These were conventional views in

Australia at the time, and not only in Labor circles, though they were delivered with a new outspokenness and confidence, and his repudiation of international organisations was ironic in the light of his later enthusiasm for the United Nations.

Evatt's other experience on this trip was as an observer at the International Labour Organization conference in Geneva under the auspices of the League of Nations. He noted criticisms made of Australia's failure to ratify ILO conventions. The justification always given was that the Commonwealth did not have the constitutional power, but Evatt disagreed: 'There is nothing to prevent the Commonwealth Government from ratifying and then legislating under the power of reference by the several States'. This was a revealing inconsistency. He supported labour conventions and felt Australia should be bound by them, but in the case of migration restrictions, Evatt's attitude was a jarring insistence on the sovereign right of nations to be bigoted.

Given Evatt's later reputation as an internationalist, and his work in establishing the United Nations, these small excursions in 1926 are interesting. They show that in the inter-war years Evatt had not yet developed an internationalist outlook, and nothing in his papers suggests otherwise. While other Australians such as the feminist Jessie Street and politician John Latham were intensely involved in internationalist movements, through the League of Nations and in Street's case also through transnational women's and labour networks, Evatt was disconnected from these developments. His approach to issues of labour migration was simply political and nationalist, while his response to the ratification of ILO conventions was legalistic.

Arriving back in Sydney in early September, Evatt warned that another European war was likely, given the 'enmity' between France and Germany; if anything, he sounded like an isolationist. This impression is reinforced by his continued arguments in favour of the White Australia policy. In the New South Wales parliament he expressed ideas much like those he had espoused in London; during a parliamentary debate on factory legislation intended to improve hours and conditions, he suggested that Chinese workers in Australia undercut conditions because they worked long hours without overtime payments. 'It is a very well known principle of British Justice that our own white workers, our own British subjects, should be protected by our laws whilst this competition exists.' That was the conventional underpinning of Labor's insistence on a White Australia, mixing overt racism with a concern that wages and conditions would be undermined.

ie willingness of migrants to work for less?

Jack Lang's 'reign of terror'

By the time Evatt returned from England, Jack Lang's populist and autocratic dominance over his party had started to draw criticism. Before long Evatt was identified as one of Lang's critics. In September, Lang's leadership was challenged and the caucus was evenly divided, with Evatt voting against the premier. The *Barrier Miner* wrote that with barely half his colleagues supporting him it seemed 'only a matter of time before Mr Lang's reign ends'. By early 1927, as the centenary historian of the ALP Ross McMullin wrote, there was 'utter chaos' in New South Wales. 'In March the executive split into two groups, which each purported to control the party.' On one side stood Lang, while the federal Labor party backed a rival group led by Tom Mutch. Sitting in a meeting of the group led by Mutch, Evatt wrote to Mary Alice on parliamentary letterhead. He was frustrated, saying that Mutch seemed 'more and more impossible – nervy, irritable, utterly incapable of leadership'.

Lang headed off another revolt in May 1927 by audaciously dissolving his government and being reappointed as premier by the governor on the understanding he would call an election. Instead, he appointed his supporters to a new cabinet, and prorogued parliament, delaying an election for five months. Following these events, Evatt released a long press statement, describing Lang's rule as a 'reign of terror', and supporting the federal group. Lang's action in dissolving his ministry was 'the most retrograde step in the history of the struggle for dominion self-government'. He claimed his own 'machinery of loyal Labor supporters was ready to spring into action'; the Balmain State Electorate Council supported him, congratulating him 'on his fearless attitude in denouncing the undemocratic dictatorship exercised by Mr Lang'.

On 4 June 1927, Evatt described Lang as 'the biggest crook in the Labour movement'. The next day, he issued another long statement, published in the Sydney newspaper *Truth*, the original of which is among his papers. Lang, he said, was 'wearing the imperial purple of majesty' and claiming for himself all credit for Labor's achievements. Evatt itemised the record: it was McTiernan and himself who had 'worked untiringly' to resolve deadlocks with the upper house, and it was their colleagues John Baddeley and Joseph Cahill who deserved credit for the 44-hour week and workers' compensation legislation. Nor had it been Lang's idea to introduce a widows' pension, he said, though this was unfair – it had been in the governor's speech opening the parliament. Furthermore, Evatt complained, Lang had done nothing about unemployment insurance, and had neglected school education because he hated Mutch, the relevant minister; he had even allowed child endowment to be discounted against the basic wage, which the Nationalist leader Tom Bavin 'openly regards as his greatest victory'.

This litany of faults continued: Lang defied 'the majority over and over in true Lenin and Mussolini fashion'. Lang's methods were 'threats of personal violence and systematic vilification, together constituting a reign of terror quite suitable to countries like Russia, but entirely alien to the ideal of Australia'. Evatt finished with some fine denunciations:

> I say of Mr Lang that he is a menace not merely to good
> government, but to the workers themselves. ... The vanity of
> this man, never small, has grown to colossal and grotesque

proportions. He believes and acts as if he were not merely
the whole Labor party, but the State itself. Other dictators in
Australia have been few and far between ... The Lang bubble will
burst. The Labor Party has had fits of hero worship in the past
with similar results ... The only way to fight Mr Lang is by telling
the truth about him. He has traded on the comradeship and
decency of all the members of the party. He has systematically
violated all its rules ...

This was strong stuff; 'heated indictment' was the subheading. And
being Evatt, he could not resist some self-justification. 'No one in the
Labor Party has worked harder than I have. I gave up a great deal
of my professional work solely to serve my fellow Australians. I was
elected by the greatest vote ever recorded in New South Wales by a
new candidate.'

Evatt's comparison of Lang with Lenin and Mussolini is worth
pausing over, not because Lang was that repressive, but because Evatt
recognised the authoritarian element common to Russia and Italy.
Mussolini would not consolidate a fully fascist regime until a year later,
in 1928, when he established one-party rule, but Evatt could recognise
an authoritarian. Unlike some on the right, including members of the
New South Wales parliament, he never made embarrassing statements
about Mussolini's strong hand being necessary in a decaying democracy, nor praised his skill in running railways. Nor, like some on the
left, was he enamoured of Stalin or the Soviet form of authoritarianism. He was sufficiently a liberal to see the common elements of what
would later, after the full flourishing of fascism, be called totalitarianism. In the 1950s, in the struggle over the banning of the Communist
party, he tried to draw the same parallel between the authoritarianism
of left and right.

Evatt was not alone in his criticisms of Lang, though he was
prominent. But the premier was not finished; during August, when
the party was holding preselection ballots, he took his revenge by

ensuring his opponents, including Evatt and Mutch, lost Labor endorsement. When they announced they would stand as Independent Labor candidates, they were expelled from the party. With his own network of local support, Evatt now presented himself for the October 1927 election as 'Senior Labor Member, Locally Selected Labor Candidate'. The 'senior' referred to the fact that he had been elected first of the five members in the 1925 election.

One of Lang's policies had been to revert to single-member, hence smaller electorates, and Evatt and Mary Alice had, by 1928, moved to Grove Street, Balmain. They were renting, but compared with tightly packed working-class Leichhardt, their new surroundings were more salubrious. The houses standing today in Grove Street are two-storey Victorian terraces with cast-iron lacework balconies overlooking Birchgrove Park. The park occupies a peninsula jutting out into the harbour, and is where the Balmain Cricket Club played; Evatt soon became and remained a staunch committeeman of the club. The house the Evatts rented was more recent, but on the same scale, an Edwardian two-storey red brick house beside the Victorian terraces.

Evatt's 1927 election leaflet shows him looking sternly out of a photograph in his barrister's wig. It asserted he had 'twice secured an absolute majority of League and Union members entitled to vote in the Balmain selection ballot', which was not strictly true; on the second occasion he was endorsed by one half of a split party. Nor was it accurate that he was 'locally selected'; a local coalminer had been selected as the official candidate by Lang's supporters. Evatt had been expelled, and with great brio was committing the cardinal sin of Labor politics, running against an endorsed candidate. Evatt claimed to be 'a vigorous and courageous young Australian', whose school and university career were of 'great brilliance', and who would 'fight for the educational advancement of the children of Balmain'. In another leaflet, he wrote that he would fight for 'the Ideals and Principles of the Australian Labor Party without Communism or Corruption'.

Labor lost to Tom Bavin's Nationalists in the October election, but Evatt – along with Tom Mutch – was returned as an independent. He and Mutch were now divorced from the party in the parliament, and contributed rarely to parliamentary debates. Evatt now had little to do in parliament, with Labor out of office and him out of Labor. Most of this three-year term was taken up with his legal work. By Evatt's usually frenetic standards, this was a relatively quiet period; no trips overseas, no books published and no political campaigns to fling himself into. By the end of 1927, Mutch, followed by Evatt, had the lowest attendance in all votes in the parliament since the election. Though he made a point to avoid voting against the ALP, the public record in *Hansard* and the newspapers shows that he rarely spoke in 1928, and was scarcely even present in 1929 and 1930.

During this lull in his political career, his legal work prospered. Bavin's government returned to afternoon and evening sittings, specifically to allow those with professional practices to attend to their business. In the years 1928, 1929 and 1930, Evatt's practice grew substantially, with over 170 court appearances reported in the newspapers. Prior to 1924, before going into parliament, he had been averaging some twenty-three cases a year, mostly as a junior to Watt. From 1927 till the end of 1930, he was averaging forty-seven cases a year. He was appointed King's Counsel in November 1929, eleven years after being first admitted to the bar.

While he continued with civil law work, mainly commercial, and argued cases in the High Court before the judges he was shortly to join, what is noticeable in the late 1920s is Evatt's increasing prominence in industrial law. He was taking many more cases before the Industrial Commission and the Workers Compensation Commission of New South Wales and the Commonwealth Court of Conciliation and Arbitration. He was invariably on the side of a union in award cases, or a worker in compensation cases. Barristers are in part led by their clients but they also build reputations in specific areas of law, and come to be considered, especially in employment litigation, as being in sympathy with employers or workers. Evatt was, by 1930, highly prominent as a lawyer working for unions and individual workers, but also with a growing reputation for constitutional law. By the time he was appointed to the High Court, Sawer wrote, he was considered a 'leading constitutional silk'.

A story told by Irvine Douglas, a journalist for the *Sun* in Sydney, shows the extent to which Evatt's was a name to conjure with at the time. As the Depression began to bite, Douglas had been involved in his union's struggle against any lowering of award conditions. He was sacked and went to see Evatt, whom he knew well, though he later came to distrust him profoundly. Evatt was away, and Douglas returned to his office. When a colleague, who he knew was close to the editor, asked what he would do next, Douglas bluffed, saying: 'I'm on velvet, I've just been round to see Dr Evatt … I'm a certainty for £10,000 for victimisation, can't lose'. Two hours later, Irvine said, the editor 'sent for me and put his hand on my shoulder and said the whole thing was a most unfortunate misunderstanding'. Just invoking Evatt's name was enough.

Throughout these years, Evatt also continued to devote time to the Balmain District Cricket Club, just opposite the Evatt house. In 1926 he became one of the trustees, was vice-president from 1927, and then from 1929 until 1951 was the club's patron. The club history notes that during 'the off season' of 1930, their patron was appointed to the High Court, but his enthusiasm for the sport was undiminished, including his extraordinary capacity to remember cricket statistics. Whenever possible he linked up with 'his two staunch medico friends', the doctors 'Fuzz' Porter, who had attended Mary Alice in the Blue Mountains in 1922, and Sam Gentile. They would meet in front of the old wooden dressing rooms, and from there they heckled and offered 'advice to any player on either side who happened to incur their displeasure'. Evatt's passion for cricket may have been politically advantageous in the mid-1920s when he was the local member, but his involvement and commitment were genuine, and persisted well after he had moved away from both politics and the suburb of Balmain.

By the end of the 1920s, Evatt and Mary Alice had shared a decade together and among the things linking them were their common interests in books and politics. In November 1928, he gave her as a birthday present George Bernard Shaw's new book, *The Intelligent Woman's Guide to Socialism and Capitalism* inscribed 'from her loving husband'. At the beginning of August 1929, he wrote to her on New South Wales parliamentary letterhead. She was in the mountains again, now at 'Kelmscott', a small holiday cottage they had just built in the Blue Mountains, on the Mall in Leura. (Mary Alice had designed it herself, naming it after William Morris's house and publishing press.) Evatt wrote: 'You are the most sweet and precious thing and I do love you and miss you so much'. He told her that Peter, now aged seven, had just arrived safely home in Sydney on the train, accompanied by Nini, Mary Alice's sister. Evatt described Peter as looking 'like the owner of the train' when he alighted and rushed towards him, eager to tell him about the engines. Since 1925, it had been a political necessity to live in Balmain, but in August 1929 they moved to Beecroft, in the northern suburbs and well outside the electorate he still represented. The move signalled Evatt's increasing detachment from politics. He did not recontest the November 1930 election, when Lang was returned to power. Instead, he devoted himself fully to the law.

Evatt's first foray into politics had been unsuccessful. In his first term, he was not accorded the place and the ministry he expected and found it hard to wait his turn. He had opposed Lang, and doubtless that was courageous, but it hardly made him unusual in the bruising politics of the New South Wales ALP. In his second term, as an independent from 1927, he was on the outer edge of a party that was itself in opposition, an increasingly absent representative and an increasingly busy barrister. By the late 1920s, he was retreating from politics, going back to the certitudes of the law. It might have seemed that he had failed in politics.

5

The judge

By the end of December 1930, with his appointment to the High Court, Evatt had left behind both Labor politics and his practice as a barrister. At the age of thirty-six, Evatt was, and remains, the youngest person ever appointed to the High Court, a record he often mentioned. When he started on the bench, one of his liberal heroes, Justice Henry Bournes Higgins, had recently died, while another, Chief Justice Isaac Isaacs, was known to be about to retire to become governor-general. By taking up a role as a judge, Evatt appeared to have left politics behind forever. As the Great Depression deepened in the early 1930s, he was increasingly removed, but as fascism grew internationally – itself a partial response to the devastation of the Depression – he grew restless. After a decade on the High Court, he would throw himself back into the political realm.

The High Court

Evatt was appointed at the same time as Edward McTiernan, whose claim to be Lang's attorney-general he had precociously challenged in 1925. McTiernan was also quite young, only two years older. But Evatt's commission was dated a day earlier than McTiernan's, apparently, according to the press 'to give Dr Evatt seniority'. Evatt always insisted to McTiernan – quite seriously, it seems – that he was more senior and took precedence.

The appointment of these two young men was greeted with

indignation in conservative and legal circles. The objection was not to their youth, though, but their political colour. As the legal scholar Geoffrey Sawer wrote, the conservatism of the Bar meant that the non-Labor parties did not have to make deliberately political appointments to the High Court. They only had to choose between a small group with appropriate eminence, and those chosen were, as a matter of course, 'supporters of non-Labor parties or apolitical men with middle-of-the-road or conservative temperaments, certainly not likely to be enthusiastic supporters of ALP policies'. Labor had had only one previous opportunity to make appointments, in 1913, when Attorney-General Hughes appointed three judges. As Sawer wrote, he 'did not even try to appoint a Labor man', but chose 'a mediocrity' (Charles Powers), 'a state-righter' (Frank Gavan Duffy), and finally the progressive A.B. Piddington, who was 'terrified into immediate resignation by the screams of rage ... from the reactionary Melbourne and Sydney bars'. Hughes then chose George Rich as Piddington's replacement – one of Evatt's former law lecturers, 'non-political, and constitutionally colourless'.

By 1930, it was less the norm for High Court judges to have had parliamentary experience. The inaugural group of five – Samuel Griffith, Edmund Barton, Richard O'Connor, Higgins and Isaacs – had all come directly from politics, and most had been actively involved in writing the constitution they presided over. Of them, Higgins was the closest to Labor sympathies, and he and Isaacs came from the progressive liberal tradition. Of Hughes' 1913 appointments, only Powers had been a politician – he was a Queensland conservative minister before being Commonwealth crown solicitor. The next three appointments, Adrian Knox, Hayden Starke and Owen Dixon were made by Nationalist governments and had no political experience, though they had their own politics. Starke was a particularly cranky conservative, described by Arthur Calwell as 'an old barbarian if ever there was one'. This was the context for denouncing Evatt and McTiernan as overtly political choices. They had explicit Labor affiliations, with McTiernan

coming direct from the federal parliament, while Evatt had just finished his second term in the New South Wales parliament. And it was
clear that the Labor caucus had been in a hurry to get its own onto the
bench and alter the political balance of the court, despite the objections of the Labor prime minister Jim Scullin and his attorney-general
Frank Brennan, who were in England and had demanded delay.

Evatt kept a file of all the letters of congratulation he received
when his appointment was announced. One was from Menzies, then
in the Victorian parliament. He congratulated Evatt, but with a few
barbs; while commending Evatt's 'very great ability and the industry that has fortified it', he wrote that McTiernan's 'lack of qualifications' for the High Court had led to 'great indignation here at what is
thought to be a "packing" of the Bench'. Appointing judges on 'political grounds', he wrote, was 'a menace to the character and power of the
judiciary'. Menzies evidently had his own future prospects of getting
onto the High Court in mind:

> It is rather hard for anybody, like myself, who has striven hard to
> achieve a standing in the profession which might in a few years'
> time have warranted promotion, to be told that in future political
> standing, and not legal standing, will be the deciding factor.

In a distinctly backhanded compliment, Menzies was offering congratulations and then withdrawing them. The implication – despite
his protestations that he recognised Evatt's merits – was that he was
a political appointment. It was another sign of the rivalry that would
play out between the two of them.

The Victorian bar made an explicit statement along the same lines.
High Court vacancies should only be filled by 'men of the highest legal
attainments and independence of character, irrespective of their political views', but these principles were under threat if appointments were
'to be discussed and regarded as political rewards, or opportunities
for political service, to be dispensed by political parties'. The *Sydney*

Morning Herald was just as disapproving. 'To put it bluntly, these are political appointments, and politics should have nothing whatever to do with judicial office.' An editorial queried whether Evatt had outgrown his early 'impetuousness' and wrote that he had been selected for his politics, 'because he is supposed to hold certain views … these appointments to the Bench leave a nasty taste in the mouth'. There were plenty of others with 'at least, equal qualifications', but they were not members of the Labor party. 'Are politics to be the credential for promotion from Bar to Bench? … Are politics to outweigh essential worth?' The *Argus* in Melbourne could be even more conservative than the *Herald* in Sydney and was just as disapproving. Its editorial 'Politics on the Bench' condemned the hasty fashion in which the Labor caucus had pushed through the decision, and questioned the merits of Evatt and McTiernan; they did not have the 'mellowed experience' required. But rather than experience, the overriding criticism was of political partiality; Evatt and McTiernan had 'the reek of party conflict'.

There was a distinctly muted swearing-in ceremony for the two new judges when the High Court assembled in Melbourne in early January 1931. Many of the court's staff were still enjoying their summer holidays, including Chief Justice Isaacs, who was at Mount Macedon and did not attend; he was in any case about to move to the position of governor-general. The oaths were administered instead by Frank Gavan Duffy. No. 1 Court in Melbourne was crowded, but not with interested onlookers; the corridors were full of stevedores and waterside workers waiting for their case to resume after the ceremony. There 'was not a large attendance' of the bar, and the traditional formal welcome from the profession was not extended, which is interesting, given several members of the bar were present for the waterfront case, including Menzies, who was appearing for the shipping companies.

Both Evatt and McTiernan were described as 'palpably nervous'. The other judges entered in their full wigs and gowns and took their seats. Evatt presented his commission to Duffy, who handed it to the registrar to read, while Evatt 'fixed his eyes on a spot on the ceiling'.

There was some confusion about who was to read the oaths of allegiance to the king and the service of justice; Duffy indicated it was the new appointments. McTiernan was about to read his when he found he had been given the wrong paper; he 'nearly forgot to kiss the Bible'. After the ceremonials, the two new judges took their seats, one at each end of the bench, while Dixon, no longer the most junior judge, shuffled up a place.

Evatt's old headmaster was more enthusiastic than the legal profession had been, saying he was thrilled and deeply moved, and finding words inadequate to express his joy: 'in accepting this position you are making a great sacrifice from a pecuniary point of view', he added, 'but I feel that you have been activated by the loftiest conception of public service'. Kilgour was referring to press comments that prominent barristers could earn much more than a judge, and he was attributing to Evatt the high ideals he had taught at Fort Street. He had been watching over Evatt with fatherly concern. 'I need not tell you, my dear Bert, how deeply interested I have been in your career, though unobtrusively, and how I have glowed with pride that for some years you were under my immediate care.'

Another voice from Evatt's past was that of Henry Boote, the veteran editor of the *Australian Worker*, the influential newspaper of the Australian Workers' Union (AWU); Boote was to be crucial a decade later in assisting Evatt into a parliamentary seat. When he heard the news, he wrote: 'I suddenly had a vision of you as a young student calling upon me at the *Worker* office to ask my opinion of an essay on the capitalist system which you had written at the University. It was a very fine essay ... What a career you have had!' He hoped Evatt's appointment was 'a preliminary' to the chief justiceship, a notion that cannot have displeased Evatt.

There was in fact press speculation that Evatt was in line for the position of chief justice but, if this was the plan of some in the Labor government, it was set back by the controversy about political appointments. The Labor caucus was said to favour Evatt, but when Scullin returned from England, livid that caucus had made the appointments in his absence, 'the moderates in the party' were expected to prevail; that meant the job would not go to Evatt. When, a few weeks later, Duffy was announced as the new chief justice, the *Sydney Morning Herald* commented: 'By its decision today, the Cabinet has overridden the militant section of the caucus'. The *Herald* was pleased, saying: 'The selection of Mr Justice Duffy will be welcomed throughout the Commonwealth'. It would, in any case, have been extraordinary to appoint someone so young to the position, over the heads of the existing judges. There is no sign among his papers that Evatt entertained any hope of it, but he must surely have been aware of the speculation.

Politics and the High Court are invariably intermeshed, in a delicate balance between judicial autonomy and political consequences. The court has often had a part in resolving political disputes, and as the arbiter of the constitution is inevitably involved in determining relations between the Commonwealth and the states. In early 1931, the court considered the constitutionality of Lang's attempts to abolish the New South Wales Legislative Council, ruling that a referendum would be required before he could proceed. In that case, McTiernan was in the minority, while Evatt recused himself because he had earlier provided legal advice, and had appeared in the Supreme Court on the issue.

As Evatt took his place on the High Court bench, the Great Depression was becoming entrenched; unemployment would eventually rise to record highs in 1932, with no provision for unemployment benefits. The suffering of its own supporters left Labor floundering to find solutions, and some of the political repercussions of the crisis that unfolded in the party would eventually be played out in the High Court. It is worth stopping and looking back at the events of the preceding years to understand the origins of this political crisis. Scullin's Labor government had been voted in less than a week before the Wall Street Crash, in October 1929. During its first year in office, economic activity slowed, thousands of workers lost their jobs, and commodity prices fell dramatically. Tax revenue fell as a result, leading to the real risk of Australia defaulting on its foreign debt.

Opinion was divided within the Labor party about how to deal with the economic crisis: Scullin and his treasurer Ted Theodore were groping towards an expansionary response, increasing government spending to stimulate the economy, while others, including Joe Lyons, argued for an 'orthodox' policy, making cuts to public spending to balance the budget. Jack Lang, elected New South Wales premier for a second term in October 1930, argued that Australia should default on its British debts until more favourable terms could be negotiated, and a significant part of Scullin's caucus agreed with him. The factions grew increasingly hostile, and no compromise could be found. During the second half of 1930, Theodore had been out of action, under investigation for alleged corruption during his time as Queensland premier; Lyons stood in as treasurer, and his orthodox views on debt repayment largely coincided with those of the Nationalist conservatives. Shortly after Theodore was reinstated in January 1931, Lyons resigned from cabinet and had effectively taken a small group of supporters out of the party. Menzies was among the conservatives courting Lyons and offering him leadership of a reconstituted conservative party, which came to fruition in May when Lyons joined the newly formed United Australia Party (UAP) as their leader.

Lang and his supporters in the New South Wales branch had already been expelled from the federal party in March, but he retained control in New South Wales. Styling themselves 'Lang Labor' they held the balance of power in the federal parliament, under the leadership of Jack Beasley. When, in May 1931, Scullin and the state premiers negotiated the Premiers' Plan, federal Labor had accepted the bitter pill of orthodox economics; making cuts to public spending, pensions and wages and continuing debt repayments. Lang refused to comply with the Premiers' Plan and proposed to default on debt repayments. In response, Scullin's government passed the *Financial Agreements Enforcement Act* to compel Lang to comply; the Act gave the Commonwealth power to seize state revenues to ensure they did not default. Lang challenged that legislation in the High Court.

By the time it came before the court, Lang's supporters in the federal parliament had, in November, voted to bring down the Scullin government, making Lyons prime minister of a UAP government, and earning Beasley the epithet 'Stabber Jack'. The moves and counter-moves were complex, but the gist was that Labor had disintegrated under the agonising pressure of how to deal with mass unemployment. The party had again split, with a populist left wing going with Lang and a conservative right wing going with Lyons.

The cases before the High Court were like an echo in the judicial realm of all this political turmoil. Lang's counsel argued the *Financial Agreements Enforcement Act* was invalid, and in early April 1932, Evatt was in a minority with Chief Justice Duffy in agreeing. The majority view meant the Commonwealth could proceed with seizing state revenues. But Lang was not finished, applying for leave to appeal to the Privy Council, and for an order requiring banks to return the funds seized. Two weeks later, the High Court considered these issues, and the *Sydney Morning Herald* described the scene: 'The full Bench of the High Court; the strong Bar engaged; the piles of legal volumes to which Bench and Bar constantly turned; and the crowded state of the comparatively small court, all reflected the profound importance of the issues'. The correspondent commented on 'the comparative youthfulness' of Evatt and McTiernan. Evatt asked frequent questions, but it was Duffy who carried 'the main burden of interrogation' directed at the 'imposing legal array' at the bar. A few days later, the court rejected the application to appeal to the Privy Council, with only Evatt dissenting, while on the bank case, a majority, with Evatt and Duffy dissenting, rejected the application to restrain the banks from complying with the Commonwealth.

The High Court had rejected each of Lang's manoeuvres. In each case, Evatt had in effect sided with Lang, but the substance of his arguments hinged on constitutional powers, and on the divided sovereignty between the federal and state governments. While the Enforcement Act purported to compel New South Wales to carry out its obligations, Evatt, with Duffy, thought that was not within the Commonwealth's constitutional powers. Evatt's judgement, described as '35 closely typed sheets' was a complex argument that the subjection of the states to the High Court was accompanied by a perfectly 'equal and undiscriminating' subjection of the Commonwealth to the same jurisdiction. Although the states were not sovereign bodies, he argued, neither was the Commonwealth; both were subject to the court. The Commonwealth was trespassing on the court's role; its legislation attempted to pre-empt 'the exercise by the High Court' of its 'special and exclusive authority' over the federal relationship. It was, ultimately, an argument for the constitutional supremacy of the court, rather than an argument for Lang.

On making State do so

Evatt was then alone as a minority of one when it came to the right of appeal to the Privy Council. He made a somewhat tendentious argument that the decision upholding the validity of the Act was made by a majority of four to two, but one of the minority was the chief justice. If it had been three to three, then the chief justice's side would have prevailed, and 'in a sense' an important constitutional decision had 'depended on the decision of a single Justice'. Given the importance of the issue at stake, he argued the majority was too thin to refuse a right of appeal. Removed as he was from the suffering of the Depression and from the political conflict it engendered, Evatt was nevertheless making small, and in these cases, dissenting interventions into the political realm.

Later in the same year, the High Court heard a case that anticipated later controversies about the legality of the Communist party. Evatt's younger brother, Clive, was now also a barrister, and he represented Francis Devanny, publisher of the *Workers' Weekly*, who had been jailed for publishing an appeal for funds for the Communist party, which was deemed an unlawful organisation under the *Crimes Act*. Devanny appealed against his sentence, on the grounds that the funds were for an anti-war committee representing numerous working-class organisations. At one point Evatt noted the evidence on which he had been convicted was distorted and deceptive. He was not alone in thinking this; Starke also commented that 'every little allegation' had been thrown into the evidence. The court upheld the appeal by a majority of five to one, on the grounds that it had not been proved the funds were for the Communist party, only that they were for a conference of delegates from sixty-four organisations, 'which might or might not include the Communist Party'. The substance of the case was not about whether or not the Communist party should be illegal, though Evatt did speculate that it was doubtful the party was an 'unlawful association' as defined by the *Crimes Act*.

One case in late 1934 that clearly established Evatt's reputation as a leftist judge was that of Egon Kisch. He had been brought to speak at a congress organised by the Melbourne branch of the Movement Against War and Fascism. Kisch was born in Prague into a family of Sephardic Jews, but from the 1920s worked as a journalist and writer in Germany; he was a key figure in a publishing empire run by Willi Münzenberg as a branch of the Comintern, the Soviet Union's international body. Kisch was urbane, learned, subtle and politically committed to the struggle against fascism. He was certainly a member of the Communist party in Germany, but did not mind denying it to what he saw as bourgeois authorities. He signed an affidavit for the High Court declaring that he was not a member of any communist organisation, and instead said cheekily that he was 'a member of the International Society of Proletarian Authors'.

The Lyons government, with Menzies as attorney-general, was determined to prevent his arrival and declared him a prohibited immigrant. The Commonwealth government had advice from the British secret services that Kisch was banned from entering Britain but could not openly admit this, nor obtain clear information, let alone public support, from Britain. They were left making shadowy statements they could not prove, and did not want challenged, because they could not reveal he was proscribed in Britain; meanwhile Kisch was convinced that the Lyons government was acting on Nazi instructions. When Kisch's ship docked in Melbourne and he was denied entry, he jumped to the wharf, breaking a leg, and was then taken back on board. By the time the ship arrived in Sydney, he was a political celebrity, and a series of court cases tested the government's power to prevent him speaking. Albert Piddington appeared before Evatt, applying for Kisch's release, which Evatt granted on the grounds that Kisch was not proven to be a prohibited immigrant. His argument was strictly legal and procedural, but he cannot have missed the obvious political implications. Menzies said shortly after that he was 'somewhat mystified' by Evatt's decision.

A group of sympathisers had gathered on the wharf in Sydney and 'considerable excitement occurred' when Evatt's decision came through for Kisch's release; but Kisch was promptly arrested again. Menzies stated that the government was 'determined … to uphold its authority'. Kisch then failed a dictation test, the notorious pretext under which the Immigration Act implemented the White Australia policy by testing prospective migrants in any European language that immigration officials chose. Despite Kisch reputedly speaking eleven languages, the Scottish Gaelic on which he was tested was not among them. He was convicted as an illegal immigrant and appealed to the High Court. Piddington again represented Kisch, while Watt represented the Commonwealth. Piddington enjoyed himself demonstrating that the immigration officer who administered the test in Gaelic was himself unskilled in that language. His attempt to translate 'Lead us not into temptation but deliver us from evil' had come out as 'As well as we could benefit and if we let her scatter free to the bad'.

The full High Court engaged in grave and learned discussions about philology and dialects, about living and extinct languages, and whether Gaelic was internationally recognised. Eventually they decided Scottish Gaelic was not a European language as defined by the Act, with only Starke dissenting. When a Scottish clergyman then rose up in indignation, objecting in the press to this insult to his Gaelic culture, he added some uncomplimentary thoughts about Kisch. Piddington promptly started proceedings for defamation, but Evatt eventually dismissed that case. It all had more than a touch of absurdity about it, and was excellent publicity for Kisch's visit; in between arrests, he was making frequent speeches.

Kisch was then, for the third time, charged and convicted of being a prohibited immigrant because the minister of the interior had declared him an 'undesirable'. Piddington represented him again before Evatt alone. By early February 1935, almost two months after the whole affair had begun, Evatt had made an interim order that meant the prosecution had to justify Kisch's conviction. Piddington requested an early hearing, because his client was 'anxious to get away'. Evatt replied sardonically that the prosecution also seemed anxious that Kisch should go away, and 'perhaps he would go away with the consent of the prosecution'.

Evatt's comment about the prosecution wanting this troublesome anti-fascist to go away suggested how the affair had turned into farce. Kisch had spoken frequently on the development of fascism in Europe, and the Lyons government's attempts to keep him out had failed. Yet now they were trying to keep him in Australia, and he was trying to leave after a successful tour. Kisch's supporters had skilfully used what they saw as a bourgeois legal system to try to thwart a bourgeois government, and while Evatt was more earnest about the law than that, he must have enjoyed the opportunity to take part, especially as Menzies was then attorney-general.

***

While on the High Court, Evatt began, slowly, to develop an interest in the League of Nations and in internationalism. His focus was primarily on the legal implications that international agreements had for national sovereignty. During the First World War, Australia had seized New Guinea from Germany, and after the war the League of

Nations had recognised an Australian 'mandate' over New Guinea. In August 1933, Evatt read a paper on mandates and sovereignty at an International Law Society conference. The Covenant of the League granting mandates over former colonies, he noted, did not extinguish their sovereignty; powers such as Australia were required to attend to the 'well-being and development' of mandatory peoples and support their 'tutelage'. But if a mandate was exercised only 'on behalf of' the League what did that mean in terms of sovereignty and the law? Did sovereignty in New Guinea now reside with the League, or was it divided and shared? Australia, he argued, had 'legal authority' over New Guinea, but not 'general sovereignty', and international law placed significant restrictions on a mandatory power's 'freedom of action'. It was all a bit inconclusive, but in toying with the problems of sovereignty and mandates, Evatt was starting to engage with one corner of the developing system of internationalism. His interest was not in colonialism and the ways it had shaded into mandates; he was concerned not with justice for subject peoples, but in the legal and philosophical problem of how power and sovereignty were legally constituted.

Evatt's engagement with these questions brought him into contact with others considering the legal implications of international agreements. At the same conference, Kenneth Bailey, dean of law at Melbourne University, spoke about International Labour Organization conventions. He thought they had 'no significance' unless legislation in the 'contracting countries was brought into line with them', and was untroubled by the fact that Australia had ratified only five of the thirty-two conventions adopted by the ILO. Both Evatt and Bailey raised the argument that the Commonwealth could use its constitutional power over external affairs to implement the content of international conventions. That was an early indication of a line of argument that has since substantially increased the powers of the Commonwealth, using the external affairs power to override the states.

In July 1935, Evatt gave a speech at the university branch of the

League of Nations Union in which he discussed Australia's international status. For him, the political fact that Australia had representation at the League signified national independence, 'as an entity separate from Great Britain'. By exercising a mandate over New Guinea, Australia had taken on 'duties for which Australia alone might be held accountable by another member of the League'. In effect, he was saying that engagement in the internationalist system demonstrated Australia's sovereign independence; that was more significant to him than any assessment of the hopes or failures of the League. He was also beginning to argue that Australia should do more to implement ILO conventions, and that it was 'unsatisfactory that Australia should lag in fulfilling its international obligations'. A few months later, he returned to the same theme. In a speech headlined 'Protest by Judge', he argued that one valuable result of the Treaty of Versailles had been the establishment of the ILO, by which nations 'agreed to associate to improve the conditions of labour and to secure some approach to social justice'. Yet Australia's record was 'very unsatisfactory', having ratified too few conventions; in workers' compensation law for example, Australia lagged behind 'the minimum requirements agreed to at Geneva'.

Although rhetorical and somewhat vague, these were nevertheless relatively political interventions for a High Court judge, and they showed he was lifting his gaze, though he could not yet be called an 'internationalist'. In the mid-1930s, he was starting to stake out some positions that would be important when he was foreign minister, and especially at the San Francisco conference founding the United Nations. A decade later he was adamant about Australia's sovereign independence from Britain, enthusiastic about the rule of law being extended through international conventions and interested in the responsibilities of those who ruled over colonies and mandates.

Evatt expanded his intellectual networks in the 1930s, writing to leftist intellectuals in England such as Harold Laski, Stafford Cripps and John Strachey, and maintaining contact with Hartley Grattan in

America. He sent Laski and Cripps copies of judgements, articles and pamphlets and they invited him to visit; they shared impressions of the state of the labour movement and of the impending war. Laski wrote from the London School of Economics and Political Science thanking Evatt for a judgement he had sent: 'It does one's heart good to see that there are still men on the Bench to whom the elementary principles of freedom are still important'. Cripps wrote in late 1936 agreeing with Evatt that he could not understand British Labour's attitude to Spain. They had been unwilling to assist the Popular Front government against the revolt of the military that led to the outbreak of the Spanish Civil War in July. Cripps thought the general political outlook was bleak. He opposed talk about Labour joining a national government in preparation for the coming war; the idea of a bipartisan cabinet including both Conservatives and Labour had been suggested and would be implemented under Churchill in May 1940, with Cripps in fact a member. But as of late 1936, Cripps was opposed and wrote: 'All one can do is go on fighting the situation'. These sorts of correspondents connected Evatt with British political arguments, and contributed to his growing awareness of the rise of fascism and the impending world war.

At home in Australia, Evatt was also in contact with E.H. Burgmann, editor of the *Morpeth Review*, based at St John's College, the Anglican theological school at Morpeth. The *Morpeth Review* was well regarded, and covered social issues with a progressive edge. In 1934, Burgmann was appointed Anglican bishop of Goulburn, and would remain a friend of Evatt's for the next two decades. He proposed Evatt write an article on constitutional law and asked if he could suggest someone to write on 'liberty and the law'. Burgmann wrote that liberty was 'losing ground rapidly', and 'things political and economic are moving relentlessly towards a major crisis'. He suggested they try to do something about the ALP's parlous state:

> No-one within or without the Movement seems to be doing any
> constructive thought for Labour ... Could we not get a group
> or several groups of younger men thinking out a policy and a
> programme. ... Unless something like this can be done brainless
> programmes will carry us onward to the modern version of hell
> towards which we now seem to be moving.

Burgmann seemed to think such a program could be presented ready-
made to Labor once developed. His despair captured the malaise of
progressive thinking in the depths of the Depression. Perhaps that
malaise may have set Evatt thinking about the biography he would
write of the earlier New South Wales Labor premier William Holman;
as we will see, it was as much an analysis of the labour movement as a
study of a life. It was a way for Evatt to think through the history, and
the prospects, for Labor. And perhaps Burgmann's suggestion was also
the initiative for meetings in the late 1930s held in the Evatts' home,
at which, Mary Alice would later recall, they discussed the problems of
the world with Burgmann and young Christian Socialists.

Family

In early 1931, Mary Alice was having Nuuanu renovated before they
moved back in from their temporary stay at Beecroft. Writing from
Kelmscott in the Blue Mountains, she told Evatt, who was in Tasmania with the court, that she was considering buying new furniture.

> I rather fancy a dining table and (light) chairs and sideboard and
> cutlery cabinet ... It is made of walnut with inlaid pattern and
> the chairs are handsome and also very comfortable ... The price is
> £190. What do you think about this matter?

In further letters, she described what she had achieved with the renovations:

> The library is charming with the new bay window and brown woodwork and soft brown-fawn walls, the morning room is like a sunburst, all blue and gold and decorated in the most modern fashion … the bathroom is like a page from the *Ladies' Home Journal.*

The New York–based *Ladies' Home Journal* was the guide to sophistication and modernism in interior design. Shortly after, she wrote that the house looked 'very modern and charming', saying: 'I am very pleased with the library, I am trying to make it exactly the way you would like it. You will have the interesting experience of observing an interpretation of your own taste by Mary Alice Evatt'. That morning, she said, she had been to negotiate with the bank manager, who remembered Evatt from St John's church in Milsons Point: 'You were the best choir boy! How often do you excel, oh my love!' Was she possibly teasing him for his endless striving to excel, or was she feeding morsels to his ego?

Compared with the hesitant and apologetic tone of her letters a decade earlier, when she had promised that once she recovered she would be twice the wife she had been, this Mary Alice sounds much more confident. She was organising removalists and decorators, dealing with the bank manager, and choosing expensive, fashionable furniture. It was the kind of affluent, comfortable life she was used to, and it fitted the wife of a High Court judge better than that of the representative of working-class Balmain (though she did not hesitate to offer her views on the political situation that came to a head with the Premiers' Plan between February and May 1931 – she thought the plan was worth a try).

The modernism Mary Alice and Evatt aspired to meshed with their growing interest in modern art. In the 1930s, Australian newspapers and magazines competed to provide advice on the tasteful achievement of modernism in the home. Blocks of colour in natural tones, simplicity in furniture and 'new' materials such as chrome, glass and stone were all part of 'keeping pace with the times'. The *Australian Women's Weekly* advised how to avoid 'the ornate and the stuffy', striving for 'a simple, fresh, harmonious ensemble', and dispensing with 'the useless accumulations of time'. Modernism in the home was about practicality, space-saving solutions, simplicity and being 'in tune with changing conditions'. As the *Sydney Morning Herald* declared in 1935: 'We are more aware of the science of living, and want our homes to function smoothly, satisfying all requirements of modern conditions'.

By September 1932, Evatt and Mary Alice had adopted another baby, Rosalind. There is nothing in their papers to tell us why they waited a decade to adopt again. Mary Alice wrote to him from Kelmscott, describing herself sitting by the fire, listening to an opera (*The Tales of Hoffmann*) and thinking of him. 'Outside it is raining steadily', she said, 'and has been ever since you left'. Peter played with the dog, reading loudly, while Rosalind interrupted 'with cries of glee'.

From 1936, Peter was boarding at Geelong Grammar, aged fourteen. It was a curious choice, a prestigious private school that was the antithesis of the state education system Evatt was proud to have come from; perhaps with their regular movement for the court between Sydney and Melbourne, boarding seemed to offer stability. Perhaps also they were thinking ahead to going overseas during Evatt's sabbatical leave in 1938. Evatt wrote to Peter offering too much advice and always urging him to work hard. In March 1936, following a meeting with Peter's teachers, Evatt wrote that Peter must try:

(1) To be most punctual. Remember that punctuality is said to be 'the courtesy of princes' ...

(2) To obey the rules always ... The school rules ... are the result of many years' experience – like the law itself ...

(3) Be careful of your books, money, etc. This is a habit too.

Write down the things you have to do and tick off the list as you do the job. Work hard and play hard.

'All these things are necessary not only for themselves', Evatt cautioned, 'but because in adult life it is vital to have already acquired these habits'.

Another letter from about the same period had a similar tone. Evatt started by congratulating Peter on a football win – 'Nothing gives me or Mother greater happiness than to hear that your school work, including sport, is going on well ...' – but he wanted to see more effort:

> We received your monthly report and it continues to show signs of improvement: but not <u>quite</u> satisfactory. Your written work needs greater care. Be careful of spelling ... Try hard to keep up your improvement and reach a higher level. Of course we are pleased indeed but don't slacken off.

Evatt had learned this kind of admonition from his mother, and was passing it on; though his hectoring tone was modified with some genuine congratulation and love.

Over the following years, Evatt kept up this counselling fatherly tone. His letters maintained a relationship with Peter, and Evatt evidently embraced having the responsibility to shape his character. A frequent theme was enjoining Peter to work hard. In 1940, with Peter in his last year at school, he urged him to take his sporting successes modestly, to keep consistently at German and his studies in general, and to watch his health and digestion:

> We want you to succeed as much in life, happiness, as you did last Saturday [at cricket]. Watch my warnings and believe how fond we are of you and anxious for your success in all things.
> Yrs Ever,
> DAD

Shortly after, when Peter was about to come home for the term vacation, his father said that he would organise some German coaching during the break. He went on to tell Peter to 'spend any leisure time you get reading in the library … Remember too that you can get anywhere by industry plus concentration … In German learn 50 words and gender or conjugation per day'. His letters to Peter contain encouragement and affection, but the most persistent theme was always the need to work hard. He was never to drive Rosalind as much, which might have reflected conventional ideas about gender, though she was also ten years younger.

Les Haylen was a journalist with the *Women's Weekly* and went to interview Evatt in 1940, when he was about to leave the High Court. He recalled his impressions of the Evatt home at Mosman, and how he was struck by the contrast between an affluent lifestyle and Evatt's radical reputation.

> He lived out in Mosman with a little dog called Bradman and
> a cat called Molecule, and roses and palm trees and all the
> background of suburbia. And, you know, a little dry wine in the
> kitchen. And I thought, oh this isn't the fundamental socialist, but
> how wrong I was. He was in every way. But he was able to live the
> two.

There is no doubt that during the 1930s the Evatt family was eminently middle class. Mary Alice had brought some resources of her own to the marriage and had continuing income from a share portfolio, while Evatt had been a successful barrister, and was now on a High Court judge's salary of £3000 per annum, about $260,000 today. Statements from their insurance brokers in 1933 indicate that the two houses they owned – Nuuanu at Mosman and Kelmscott at Leura – were insured for £3500. The contents of those houses, and of the apartment they rented in East St Kilda in Melbourne, were insured for a little over £3000. They also owned two cars valued at £400.

Leaving aside Mary Alice's share portfolio, these assets of about £7000 would today be worth about $660,000. This was middle-class professional wealth, though hardly fabulous riches. They were certainly able to employ staff: at Mosman they had a 'permanent nurse, maid, and gardener and/or handyman', and a casual laundress, and at Leura a 'gardener and/or handyman and a casual domestic'.

When Mary Alice's father died in 1929, half his considerable wealth stayed with her mother, with the remainder invested in annuities for his two children and a share portfolio held in a trust. Nine years later, just after they returned from overseas at Christmas 1938, her mother died, and Mary Alice inherited her house at Turramurra on Sydney's north shore, and the residue of her estate after other distributions. Alice Sheffer's estate was valued at £47,000 after estate duties had been paid, the equivalent of almost $4 million today. The papers in Evatt's files show the combined total of Mary Alice's parents' wealth was about $14 million in today's terms. The intention had evidently been to split the wealth equally between Mary Alice and her brother, but there was a dispute about the equity of that division. Letters between lawyers and Evatt show them trying to determine the value of annuities, share parcels and other assets, and arguing over the disparity. In March 1939, Mary Alice signed a deed accepting payment from her brother as finalisation of the dispute; in today's terms it was another $725,000. These figures make it clear that Mary Alice was wealthy by 1939; she had inherited at least $5 million from her parents.

She now had a large share portfolio, the houses at Mosman, Turramurra and Leura were in her name, and by September 1940 she had invested in a block of flats in Sydney, as well as a nearby house in Mosman. This casts a different light on Evatt's own decisions, first to go to the High Court in 1930, and then to step back into politics in 1940. In 1930, some who knew him commented that he was giving up a lucrative practice at the bar for the relatively smaller salary of a judge. In the second instance, in 1940, it was Evatt himself who emphasised the sacrifices, including financial sacrifices, that he was making by moving back into politics; it was disingenuous, but helped shore up his Labor credentials. It was true that his own income dropped on each occasion, but behind that truth was another; that Mary Alice's wealth had expanded dramatically.

Evatt had no need to be acquisitive about money, though he was always acquisitive for recognition. During the Depression, he was at an august remove from the everyday sufferings of ordinary people, but he contributed some of his wealth to charities and especially in Balmain, though he sought no publicity. In March 1930, the Balmain Rozelle Relief Fund wrote to him asking for another donation 'to help relieve the dreadful distress now again prevalent in the district'. They were organising a boxing tournament as a fundraiser. 'So sir if you with your ready generosity will help the fund along my committee will be very grateful.' In 1931, a Sydney newspaper carried the story that since 1927 he had been contributing to the Balmain Distress Relief committee, and by 1931 was donating £40 a month (approximately $42,000 a year). In addition, he gave regularly to a program for 'unemployed youths and girls of the district'.

Although they had moved back to Mosman, Evatt remained loyal to the Balmain Cricket Club. He was the club's patron, and became a silent benefactor; during the Depression, he sent two young cricketers to Bert Oldfield's sports store with instructions he would pay for the equipment and clothing they needed. He later established a trust for young Balmain players unable to afford the club's fees or buy their own equipment, but insisted the arrangement remain secret. We could say he could easily afford to be generous, and it may have eased the discomfort of being a middle-class radical; but nevertheless his generosity with money was genuine. And he continued to go to Balmain club matches to heckle with his friends.

6

The moderns

Evatt and Mary Alice wanted to be modern. Her taste in decor and furnishings illustrate that, and her interest in painting drew them into contemporary art circles. Evatt soon found that modern art also had a political edge and their growing engagement in that world in the 1930s allowed him a form of political activism that was acceptable enough for a judge. It also gave him another field in which to contest with Menzies, who was emerging as a champion of conventional taste; Evatt would be the champion of the moderns by the late 1930s.

The meanings of modernism

With the High Court regularly sitting in Melbourne, the Evatts retained an apartment in East St Kilda, and in 1933 they prepared to move there for several months. Ida Cantwell recalled the entourage – children, the maid and the nurse, friends, and Evatt's tipstaff, a man named Burgess – setting out by train from Sydney:

> It was like something going across Russia, like Dr Zhivago or something … [Bert] was so fussy about things and got very brusque with his retainers … I would never speak to anybody in my whole life like Bert would speak to Burgess or some of these people. You know he really was a contradiction.

They needed to furnish the Melbourne apartment, and on that visit Evatt walked into a shop in Little Collins Street that sold modern, handmade furniture, along with fabrics, sculpture and other artworks. It was to be his and Mary Alice's entree to the Heide group of modern art enthusiasts.

The shop was run by Cynthia Reed, the sister of John Reed, a key figure in the modern art movement in Melbourne; they were children of a wealthy Tasmanian grazing family. John was married to Sunday, who was born a Baillieu. Her uncle was W.L. Baillieu, a major player in the mercantile and industrial life of the city. Sunday was at that time having an intense affair with Sam Atyeo, the talented enfant terrible of the Melbourne art world, a keen modernist who had recently been thrown out of Melbourne's National Gallery Art School for displaying a painting satirising the director of the school, Bernard Hall, who had refused to even hang it. It depicted Hall in caricature. As the art historian Richard Haese noted, 'Not only was it an affront to Gallery School teaching – more importantly, it was a personal insult'.

One of Atyeo's paintings was in the front window of Cynthia Reed's premises and the painter himself was minding the shop when, as he recalled later, 'in walks this old guy'. Though Evatt was only thirty-nine, Atyeo thought the way he dressed made him look forty years older. He described Evatt as wearing a 'butterfly collar, cravat, lavender waistcoat, black tails, striped pants, button-up boots and black Derby hat'. Evatt looked at the younger man and said, pointing to one of the paintings, 'Did you do that?' and added, 'That's a good kick in the arse for the old guard'. Evatt was enthusiastic and said that Mary Alice had just started painting and was also 'a modern'. They went to lunch and Atyeo told Evatt he should do something about how he dressed. They then went shopping for 'a soft hat, grey pants, and open-neck shirt and brown suede shoes'. Atyeo claimed: 'I converted Evatt to modernism – jazz and painting'.

This was the beginning of a strange relationship between the two men. 'Sam was a real playboy as far as the Evatts were concerned',

Ida Cantwell observed – something of a rebel – while 'Bert was a great mixture of a puritan and a larrikin'. Atyeo was often described as Evatt's 'court jester'; he would swear profusely, and joke about Evatt's foibles where others could not. He was a bracing shock for Evatt, who was rather proper while at the same time wishing to be unconventional. The highly talented young artist introduced Evatt to another world, connecting him with the emerging radical art scene in Melbourne. The Heide group were 'so foreign to the kind of people that Bert and Mary Alice had ever known', Cantwell said, that it was 'not only a revelation, but a revolution in their lives'. Amused, she related how they had given him a nickname. 'All this crowd calling him "Judgie" … I mean this prim, rather puritanical man and suddenly he's in with this crowd. He loved it; he just loved it.'

In his new set of clothes Evatt found himself enjoying the company of bohemians and radicals, people who had sexual affairs with each other and who discussed the politics of modernism. It was a world of cultural radicals, far removed from the crusty, conventional person he was becoming as a judge. John Reed recalled their conversations at Heide as 'a sort of free for all when we got together … all of us … excited by the feeling of important things about to happen, by the certainty that the future lay where we were looking'. They would make use of Evatt's profile to advance their cause, and he was more than happy to lend his support to campaigns against the art establishment. Art, and the contest between established taste and modernist experiment, become another sphere in which Menzies and Evatt clashed.

In Melbourne, Mary Alice studied painting at George Bell and Arnold Shore's School of Creative Art, and there met Maie Casey, another aspiring artist, who was married to the young conservative politician Richard Casey. Mary Alice also studied at the equivalent in Sydney, the Arts School run by Grace Crowley and Rah Fizelle. The two schools had been established in 1932 on explicitly modern principles that contested the conventions and authority of the established gallery schools. Mary Alice wrote later of how the Crowley-Fizelle school had influenced her own work and that of other painters; they aimed for a 'balanced dynamic symmetry and harmonious arrangement of colour' and were committed to 'never make terms with custom or prejudice'. Mary Alice was interested in modernism and abstractionism, and it was she who most inspired Evatt's interest in modern art.

The artist Frank Hinder met the Evatts in Sydney and remembered Evatt saying 'he would have preferred the arts to law'. He also remembered 'spaghetti parties' at the Crowley-Fizelle studio, at which Evatt 'enjoyed making remarks which he knew would stir up heated arguments whilst he lounged back and enjoyed the fuss'. Evatt told Hinder that he 'saw' the days of the week in colour; an unusual trait that is characteristic of synaesthesia. Hinder recalled that Evatt's favourite colour was vermilion red, which they came to call 'Jevattred' or 'Judge Evatt Red'.

That vermilion is the dominant colour of a striking 1935 portrait of Evatt by the young modernist Arnold Shore. Sometime during 1935, Shore had been startled when Evatt bustled into his Melbourne studio unannounced. He wanted his portrait painted. One of Nettie Palmer's correspondents, 'Pat', later found a postcard of the portrait and on the back of it relayed the story as told her by Shore, who claimed that Evatt had just walked into his studio, put his coat down and said, 'Paint me. How would this attitude do?' 'Alright', the artist had said, 'your chin is rather fat.' At which, according to Shore, the model gave his head a jerk upwards 'to reduce the said chin'. Palmer's correspondent described Evatt as 'our future Prime Minister'. While the postcard was undated, this presumably referred to the flurry of excitement when Evatt stood down from the High Court in late 1940.

Shore was paid £50 for the painting, which would be about $4600 today. He portrayed Evatt lounging back with his hands in the pockets of his grey waistcoated suit, draped in a vermilion and pink academic gown. He looks out at the viewer with a calm, guarded but rather intense stare. In late 1935, Shore proposed he enter it in the Archibald

MODERN SOCIALIST ART
"It's the spitting image of him, Bert."

Evatt said over and over that the point of modernism was not
photographic realism, but capturing something essential. Here,
in 1953, the point has been turned against him to suggest his
descriptions of Menzies lack all touch with reality. Arthur Calwell,
his deputy as Labor leader, is either being sycophantic, or leading
him on to even greater detachment from reality.

Ted Scorfield, *Bulletin*, 25 March 1953

Prize for portraits: 'if only for the sake of teasing them by having to
look at it'. What he meant was that its style would hopefully disturb
the establishment. The portrait may not have been as disturbing as
Shore hoped, for it was among the finalists that year, but the sentiment
was another signal of Evatt's alignment with the moderns.

Hartley Grattan found it curious that although Evatt's taste in literature, and especially poetry, was conventional, he was an enthusiast
for modernism in art; his taste in painting was 'almost as adventurous

as his taste in literature was conservative'. Grattan wondered whether it was because art had an immediate visual impact, without 'the host of obstacles that he would have encountered in the novel, or post-Victorian poetry'. There is something in this, but it may also be that the modernist novel demanded the sort of introspection that Evatt would rather avoid.

The cultural historian Peter Gay subtitled his book on modernism: *The Lure of Heresy*. One aspect of modernism in art, poetry, architecture and writing was obviously its 'insubordination against ruling authority', by subverting convention and shocking bourgeois taste. But rebellion was only one aspect of modernism. Gay suggested a second attribute was its 'commitment to principled self-scrutiny', to exploring subjective and unconscious worlds. As Gay put it, 'The artist's response to his inner and outer world came to matter more than his fidelity to the model'. Modernism intended to be disturbingly introspective and deliberately uncertain about truths.

It may be that for Evatt this introspection was too challenging. Evatt said many times in speeches championing the moderns that 'photographic' reproduction was no longer the aim, and that modern art sought to remove the extraneous in order to capture the essence of the artist's vision. Conventional taste in art was the enemy of innovation and progress and even of liberty. So while he understood the rebellious aspect of modernism, it was, as Grattan noted, in art but not in literature. An artist might claim their painting was doing something similar to a novel's stream of consciousness, but a painting could still be simply viewed for what Grattan called its 'immediate visual impact'. In contrast, modernist writing required immersion in its inner world.

Evatt wanted to be unconventional but he did not want to be introspective. For him, modernism was attractive as a political stance, and a form of politics that was allowed a judge; he could explain well why unconventionality in art was important. That the Nazis had denounced 'degenerate' modernist art in 1937 meant that supporting the moderns had an explicitly political edge; that Menzies was arrayed on the opposite side, endorsing 'good taste' in art, added an extra dimension. But Evatt was much less interested in the disturbing uncertainties of modernist approaches to subjectivity, or in Virginia Woolf's unsettling question: 'Who am I?'

'I must express my protest'

Nettie Palmer later described Evatt's position on the High Court as one of 'Olympian calm', but the court was clearly not a happy workplace, and there were tensions below the surface. Latham had been appointed chief justice in October 1935, having recently stepped down from federal politics and bequeathed his safe conservative seat of Kooyong to Menzies. He had been the leader of the Nationalists in 1931 when Lyons was persuaded to defect from Labor and lead the new United Australia Party. That meant edging Latham aside, which he allowed with good grace, taking on the role of deputy leader. His subsequent appointment as chief justice was in part compensation – yet the newspapers and the bar did not condemn the appointment as political, as they had with Evatt and McTiernan. But the difficulty of controlling a fractious court may have had Latham wondering if he had won a prize or a penance.

The correspondence between the judges bristles with ego, rivalry and umbrage. Latham tried to calm them all and plaintively asked them to try to get along, but without success. Evatt regularly complained to Latham that the chief justice was not treating him with sufficient respect. He wanted more of Latham's recognition, and like some of the other judges, he was prickly about his dignity. Early in 1937, Evatt complained that Latham had not consulted him about changes in the court registry. 'I must express my protest at this action.' In an earlier exchange between Evatt and Latham, Evatt wrote a note that he needed to get away from the court early for 'an important

Mitchell library meeting'. Latham asked the other judges but they were not as flexible as Evatt had wanted, and Evatt then complained to Latham that it was 'one judge alone', meaning Hayden Starke, 'who prevents the court from being merely courteous to each member ... it is a continual source of irritation'.

Starke was especially cantankerous. He alleged Dixon controlled the court, and all the other judges were servile; he called them 'parrots'. Evatt's associate, John Brennan, who was with him through most of the 1930s, recalled that 'Starke was difficult with everybody ... he was at odds with the entire group'. It was hard to get the judges together to discuss cases, and when they did meet it was tense. According to Brennan, whenever Evatt said something in one of these rare conferences, Starke's reply was to produce a cigar and blow a cloud of smoke. The effect of this on Evatt was 'absolutely devastating', Brennan said. 'It made him sick in every fibre of his being and he'd have to leave the room.' From late 1938, Brennan was replaced as Evatt's associate by his brother Keith, who recalled: 'Evatt despised Rich and did very little to disguise his sentiments. He despised Starke and that was mutual ... They certainly didn't speak to each other in the court precinct'. Evatt had respect for Dixon as an intellectual equal, but was 'highly critical' of Latham, Starke, Rich and McTiernan. 'He thought that McTiernan let the side down', and was not up to the position; he 'shouldn't have been there'. Brennan recalled that Evatt contemptuously called McTiernan 'Eggshell Eddie'.

Menzies was attorney-general through the second half of the 1930s, and that meant he had some influence over the judges' conditions. In 1936, Evatt complained to Latham about renovations to the court in Melbourne that meant his rooms had been moved; there was too little natural light and 'the artificial light is a great strain upon my eyes'. He had asked to return to his old rooms, but Menzies, as attorney-general, had refused, which Evatt thought was 'most paltry'. Could Latham put in a word, Evatt asked, adding: 'I feel inclined to make some public protest but it would only cause scandal'. This sort of vexation and rivalry with Menzies could be repeated in court. John Brennan recalled that when Menzies appeared before Evatt as a judge, Menzies, with his 'lordly manner' and his substantial bulk, deliberately made getting out of his chair to speak 'quite an operation'. Evatt would watch, and if Menzies started to speak 'before being completely upright', Evatt would cut him off, saying 'From your feet, Mr Attorney, if you please'. Brennan thought such scenes were 'lovely', and reflected that Evatt 'had an intense dislike of Menzies'.

Starke appears to have been the biggest problem for Latham. He was cantankerous, prickly and uncooperative. Latham wrote to him in 1937, about a case in which the judges had not been able to find a compromise, and pleaded with him to simply argue his dissent. But it seemed Starke wanted to make a public protest, and was adamant: 'Compromise in matters of right and justice are out of the question as far as I am concerned. I am quite convinced that Evatt has given no attention to the facts and is merely a parrot. Dixon may be right but let an independent majority say so'. It was Dixon who Starke resented most. He wrote to Latham that the court was 'becoming more and more dependent' upon Dixon's opinions, and thought that Dixon 'played up to it'. He resented Dixon's intellectual dominance of the court, and considered the others too easily led. Of one case, Starke wrote to Latham that they had been about to agree, and 'then Dixon suddenly alters his mind … [in] a most confused judgment and the parrots at once agree'.

Dixon had a better relationship with Latham, and wrote to him about how his arguments were received by the other judges: 'I feel frightened of the use of any logical ideas or conceptions of my own because I am only too painfully aware that my methods of thought are hopelessly opposed to those which so far have been authoritatively adopted'. It seemed most of the judges felt on the outer. Starke often took umbrage, Evatt was prickly about his honour and about whether he was sufficiently recognised, and even the relatively mild Dixon felt his mode of reasoning was held in contempt. That was the situation when Evatt left for a sabbatical in early 1938. Latham may well have felt a sigh of relief that at least one of his vexatious colleagues was out of the way.

Europe and America

During Evatt's sabbatical he and Mary Alice were overseas from April to the end of the year, staying in England, France and the United States. They left behind both of the children; Peter, aged sixteen, was at boarding school, while Rosalind, aged six, was left with friends. They took a 'world cruise' on the *Franconia*, stopping briefly in Los Angeles and visiting the Hollywood studios, then through the Panama Canal to cross the Atlantic to London. Mary Alice wrote to Peter that she had been in the London galleries and told him enthusiastically that she had seen the works of Modigliani, Van Gogh and Picasso; Evatt had gone every day to the Ashes cricket. Bill O'Reilly, who was in the Australian team, had known Evatt since 1930 and later told of 'a vivid memory of him spending hours with us at the Oval'. England had a massive lead, and Evatt tried hard to keep the team's 'peckers up', O'Reilly said. 'I couldn't help thinking he was expecting us to lie down and cry.'

When they then went on to Paris, they saw Sam Atyeo again; he had moved there in 1936, breaking off the affair with Sunday Reed. Mary Alice studied at a studio in Montparnasse. 'I worked hard from nine till five every day and enjoyed it thoroughly … it would be hard to imagine a happier atmosphere despite the threats of war outside', she later said. It was the French modern school that most inspired her, while she thought contemporary art in England was dull: 'Such is the inevitable tendency of official art …' They had seen exhibitions of Braque and Klee, and Mary Alice was quoted in a *Women's Weekly* article saying that Evatt had been 'lucky enough to see much of Picasso's new work'.

In August, Evatt wrote excitedly to the Australian writer Vance Palmer from Paris in August. While Mary Alice worked in Montparnasse, he wrote, he spent his days 'haunting' the galleries. 'I find my preference for the Moderns and the Primitives entirely confirmed.' From Manet, Van Gogh, Cézanne, Gauguin and Toulouse-Lautrec to Modigliani and Picasso, he found they had 'in substance returned to painting the clear beauty of the Primitives'. By comparison, Rembrandt and Rubens were 'quite impossible'. But his 'particular wonder and delight' had been discovering ancient Egyptian art in the Louvre: 'Here too the irrelevant has been rejected and the grandeur and styling of the large statues are almost overpowering'. Being in London and Paris also impressed on Evatt the urgency of the rise of fascism; he was struck that 'in London one is so close to the struggle'.

After returning to Australia, Evatt wrote again to Palmer, describing Neville Chamberlain's appeasement of Hitler at Munich as the 'black treachery' of a gang who were 'really sympathetic to Fascism' because they feared socialism more. Atyeo recalled that on this visit to Paris they met Jewish refugees fleeing from the Nazis, and observed:

> Bert became startlingly convinced of the inevitability of war
> and of the true nature of the German, Italian and Japanese
> Governments ... He said Australia was completely unarmed and
> lulled into blissful apathy ... Before leaving I am sure he had
> made an important decision.

Several years later, Atyeo wrote that he recalled Evatt telling him at the end of this visit that he would run for parliament on his return, but 'not to tell a soul, not even Mary Alice'. It is debatable whether it is true that Evatt had decided to step back into politics this early – Atyeo was not a terribly reliable witness – but it is clear that Evatt was much more focused on fascism and the imminent war than he had been previously.

In early September, they sailed for America, and would be based in New York until the end of 1938. There were more galleries to see, including some of the great private collections; Mary Alice told the *Women's Weekly* they had seen the collection of Chester Dale, an investment banker whose wife did all the buying. They had collected Cézanne, Matisse, Renoir and Degas and had 'a whole room devoted to Modigliani', whose portraits combined 'beauty of design ... and a sculptural solidity from which everything that is unimportant has been mercilessly eliminated'. Her theme, the elimination of what was unnecessary to leave something essentially expressive, was also Evatt's in his enthusiasm for the moderns.

From New York, Evatt wrote to Latham, back at the court. This time, there was no indignant tone with his superior. He had met Latham's son in London and assured Latham: 'He is doing well and is highly thought of'. Evatt was developing substantial contacts among American legal academics and had been invited to lecture at the universities of Harvard, Columbia, Chicago and California on constitutional law, labour regulation and administrative law. Many of these lectures were then published in American law journals. Interestingly, he gave no lectures in England; perhaps the Americans were more curious about legal trends in Australia, or perhaps his networks were more developed in America, where a growing friendship with Felix Frankfurter, dean of law at Harvard, opened doors.

He also wrote to Mary Alice's sister, Nini, telling her of his trip to Harvard and his success there. He had taken the bus through New York state and seen the damage from a recent hurricane:

At Harvard I lectured several times to the professors and students and got on very well I think. At any rate I liked the dons very well and I think they preferred my direct method of discussion to that of Lord Wright, the English judge who came just before me to Harvard. Wright is very fond of circumlocution and 'beating around the bush'. They loaded me with books (law books) and letters as I left.

After Harvard, he and Mary Alice travelled to Washington. They met with the Supreme Court judges, and Evatt was delighted to meet President Franklin Roosevelt, to whom Frankfurter had introduced him:

> I met the President who wired me to visit him at the White House. His conversation was most interesting. He is very interested in the future of Australia as far as Japanese aggression is concerned. He seems to me to favour active US intervention in the Pacific. I was with him for nearly 40 minutes while his anteroom was crowded with admirals, politicians and officials. It was most exciting.

Evatt's developing awareness of the threat of fascism and the likelihood of war was reflected in this conversation, as much as his pleasure at being taken seriously by Roosevelt. Mary Alice told her mother Evatt's 'long yarn' with Roosevelt was the highlight of their trip.

Shortly after, from New York, Evatt wrote to Frankfurter, thanking him for his help and saying that Harvard and Washington had been stimulating and inspiring:

> I saw the President and was at once conquered by his directness and his soundness on the things that matter most. I have reason to believe that his opinions on all the matters we discussed so frankly are not different to your own and mine, but that certain practical considerations, military preparedness and local politics for example, have necessarily restrained him.

What this meant was that American isolationism was still constraining Roosevelt from greater preparation for the coming war.

He and Mary Alice were excited by New York. He wrote to Nini: 'New York has really got hold of us and I think we have at last got hold of its rhythms. It is a marvellous city'. They had been to the baseball, the football and the theatre, but they had not, he said, been listening to the radio on the night that the 'End of the World' stunt was put over the air. This was Orson Welles' broadcast of *The War of the Worlds* on 30 October 1938, which gave the impression that a Martian invasion was taking place. He wrote that Mary Alice was having the last of her painting lessons and he had delivered a lecture at Columbia University. Next they were going to Chicago, then the Grand Canyon and San Francisco; from there the boat would take them across the Pacific to Sydney, a journey of about twenty days. He then went into long, detailed arrangements for Peter to be sent to meet them when they stopped in New Zealand. He instructed Nini to ensure Peter had pocket money, and that 'some responsible officer on the boat to Auckland takes care of Peter (eg seat at table, suitable cabin mates, not running silly risks on the deck)'.

A short article in the *Sydney Morning Herald* conveyed back to Sydney an impression of the 'considerable interest' Evatt's university lectures had aroused. He had lectured on constitutional problems and the differences in wage regulation in Australia and the United States; at Columbia he had 'praised the work of the late Mr Justice Higgins on compulsory arbitration' but noted that the level of Higgins' wage in the Harvester judgement had not been maintained. He wrote to Grattan from aboard ship on the way home, pleased that his lectures had been well received. In a relatively intimate letter, he thanked Grattan for his own recent letter and said: 'I hope you will always remember us, and write regularly'. But they did not write regularly. They had first met in 1937, when Grattan was in Australia; whenever Evatt was in New York, as on this trip, they would meet and talk, but they never became habitual correspondents.

After arriving back in Sydney at the end of 1938, Evatt gave a press interview in which he said nothing about the developing international crisis, but much about constitutional reform. He argued it was time that Australia adopted the Statute of Westminster, under which the British parliament had explicitly renounced any legislative rights over its former colonies, now called dominions. He also argued that, like America, Australia should have specific civil liberties inserted in the constitution, namely freedom of speech, assembly, the press and public meetings and the right to trial by jury. He told the journalists he had met Roosevelt, and was clearly enthusiastic about a stronger relationship with America. Trade was obviously important, but: 'Even more important are moral and spiritual ties. The day may come when active friendship with the United States may help to save our integrity as a nation'.

Quite presumptuously, Evatt also intervened with Roosevelt to propose Frankfurter for a recently created vacancy on the Supreme Court. Roosevelt and Frankfurter were close personal friends and corresponded affectionately. Frankfurter offered advice and encouragement, sent him cheeses, and urged him to rest; he was also a well-recognised conduit for others to send their views to Roosevelt. But Frankfurter was scrupulous about not imposing on the friendship. He would have been mortified to think his appointment to the Supreme Court was a result of friendship rather than his own merits, and that Roosevelt might be compromised politically.

Evatt was brasher than that. He admired Frankfurter's liberalism and his eminence, and he admired Roosevelt. After meeting the Supreme Court judges in Washington, he wrote to Frankfurter that he worried the liberal progressive forces on the bench were wavering. 'The next appointment requires a man who is not only a liberal but something of a leader or heir apparent. ... That I could not discuss with the President but if it interested him, my opinion could be written.' Later, Evatt wrote again from Chicago, where he was giving another lecture. He said he had sent a confidential memorandum to the president analysing the situation in the court, arguing the progressive group would disintegrate 'unless unified by an appointee who would combine with the quality of leadership the essential quality of professional public endorsement'. He concluded by saying: 'I mentioned a name that corresponds with your own'.

Evatt had indeed written to Roosevelt on 11 November, saying that he felt it his duty to offer some observations before leaving the country, after three months studying 'Social, Political, Economic and Legal tendencies' in America. He attached a one-page note marked 'Confidential: For the President alone', in which he argued that the Supreme Court was at a 'critical' stage, because the ascendency of liberal, progressive judges was fragile. What was needed, he wrote, was someone whose leadership could restore unity among the loose group of progressives then on the court:

> The appointee must have a social outlook which is in accordance with the general aims and ideals of the Supreme Executive of the Nation ... After a pretty thorough discussion with very many of the Bar and the law teachers, and with some knowledge of the affairs of the Court itself, I would say that Felix Frankfurter possesses all the qualifications; that I know of no one else who does; and that his leadership is vitally necessary.

This was meddling on a grand scale, though it is fair to note that Roosevelt was also receiving letters recommending Frankfurter from law schools, newspaper editors and the general public.

The US attorney-general provided a draft response for Roosevelt with a covering note dryly saying it was 'not an easy letter to answer'. In his reply, Roosevelt thanked Evatt for his 'keen observations', which showed 'a disinterestedness not easily attained by those who are so close to events here'. The US president made no comment on Evatt's unsolicited advice about the Supreme Court, and Evatt seemed not to notice. Less than a month later, Frankfurter was duly nominated for the Supreme Court vacancy. Congratulations poured in, and among Frankfurter's large files of correspondence is a letter from Evatt. It was genuine in its congratulations, but also claimed some of the credit. On his Nuuanu letterhead, Evatt wrote:

Dear 'Mr Justice' Frankfurter,
This is just a very hurried note to tell you of my delight in your
appointment. Ben Cohen may now tell you of my letter to F.D.R
from whom by the way I received a most charming and cordial
letter of thanks yesterday.

The champion of the moderns

After returning at the end of 1938, Evatt was fired up not only about
the developing international crisis but also more firmly committed to
modernism in art. The context was a campaign against the Australian Academy of Art, recently established in Canberra in June 1937.
Menzies was actively involved and hoped to secure a royal charter.
He made his conservative views plain, when opening an exhibition
in Melbourne in April 1937, where he spelt out his vision: 'Great art
speaks a language which every intelligent person can understand. The
people who call themselves modernists talk a different language'. He
went on to talk about the proposal for a national academy of art, in
which he said he had been 'the prime mover'. Every great society has
its art academy, he said. 'They have set certain standards of art and
have served a great purpose in raising the standards of public taste by
directing attention to good work.'

To the modernists, that kind of talk meant the prospect that the
academy would certify good taste and great art, sponsoring some and
excluding others from patronage. They feared it would influence what
was exhibited and bought by galleries, stifling experiment and innovation by imposing conventional standards; it was all seen as what
Richard Haese called the height of 'Edwardian pomposity'. Some,
too, readily saw the academy as simply conservative. But Menzies was
also proposing to commit Commonwealth funds to supporting the
arts, along with the building of a gallery and a national collection;
some involved in the academy, such as artist and publisher Sydney Ure

Smith, saw it as an opportunity for national support for the arts, and assumed it could encompass greater diversity, but the Heide group – and Evatt – were not so optimistic.

The Reeds and their friends saw Menzies as an advocate for a conservative artistic tradition, placing high value on the work of painters such as Tom Roberts, Arthur Streeton and Hans Heysen. The conservative dimension to the Academy was not only its defence of what it saw as good taste; some conservatives were aggressive in their distaste for what they saw as the decadence of modernism. In October 1939, the media baron Keith Murdoch brought to Australia an exhibition of contemporary French and British art and displayed it in the Melbourne Town Hall. The Evatts purchased two paintings, paying £1000 for a 1918 painting by Amedeo Modigliani, *Portrait of Morgan Russell*, and £95 for a work by Maurice de Vlaminck. The ability to spend so much on their growing passion for modern art (about $90,000 in today's values) was a sign of their wealth. They were also collecting the work of Australian moderns, including Sidney Nolan and Russell Drysdale. But Murdoch's exhibition was directly attacked by conservatives such as J.S. MacDonald, the director of the National Gallery of Victoria, where Murdoch happened to be chair of the trustees. MacDonald said he would buy none of the exhibition paintings; he refused 'to pollute our gallery with this filth'. In a similar vein, Menzies was later quoted as saying to the secretary of Sydney's Contemporary Art Society: 'I never liked French art, it was always decadent and the fall of France proved it'.

Dispute about the new academy flared immediately after it was announced, and even some artists Menzies favoured – such as Streeton and Max Meldrum – refused invitations to join. The most concerted opposition came from Melbourne, and was one impetus to the formation of the Contemporary Art Society there in July 1938. George Bell was elected president and John Reed was a vice-president. Leading an attack on the whole idea, Bell argued that the academy would encourage 'the strict preservation of mediocrity', and that its control over patronage and funds would mean 'the acquisition of absolute power' in the sole interest of academy members.

In June 1939, Evatt forcefully aligned himself with the new Contemporary Art Society, launching its inaugural exhibition in Melbourne. He denounced the proposed academy for its 'unwarranted assumption of pontifical authority', claiming it would lead to 'an official imprimatur on every canvas, good, indifferent or bad'. The text of the speech itself is in Evatt's papers, the typed draft scrawled over as he attempted to clarify his thoughts. The Contemporary Art Society, he said, stood against reactionary and retrogressive ideas in art and opposed:

> painting, sculpture and drawing which have no aim but that
> of photographic representation. … it is opposed to the group
> called the Academy of Art which, in its opinion, fosters a spirit
> of exclusiveness and of commercial monopoly very damaging to
> individual artists and well calculated to obstruct the spread of
> modern culture in Australia.

The academy was setting itself up as a 'single authoritative voice', but Evatt argued against authority, because 'all history' teaches us that in the arts 'the principle of authority prevents progress, encourages ossification, discourages genius … the principle of authority is the very antithesis of what is necessary to the healthy development of Art in Australia'. What was needed instead was 'a spirit of agnosticism'.

He went on to claim that Australia lagged in its appreciation of modern art, whereas:

> in France, in England, in the United States … many thousands
> have concluded that the best contemporary work of the moment,
> whether in paint, sculpture or drawing, relates itself to the
> greatest periods in creative art, to the overpowering sculptures of
> ancient Egypt, to the glorious colouring and design of the French,

Italian and Flemish primitives, to the romantic genius of
El Greco and to the superb draftsmanship of Holbein.

He went on to talk of other favourites: Toulouse-Lautrec, Degas
and Matisse, Van Gogh, Gauguin, Modigliani and Henri Rousseau.
Towering over them all was 'that great genius Pablo Picasso'. He was
developing an argument for pluralism, as well as for resistance to
authority, and this linked modernism in art with liberty in politics:

There are a thousand ways in which contemporary thought
and life can be interpreted in painting, sculpture and drawing.
Every single one of them is right ... we must reject the dogmatic
assumption that any particular method of expression is wrong ...
Improvement in art standards has been achieved only through
struggle and sacrifice, often against the conservative groups,
surrounded, as they too often are, by admiring claques of Yes-Men.

Finally, he linked all this to the cultural and political prospects for
Australia, for in art, as well as in some 'more important things', he
said, 'the majority of Australians preferred youth to age, design to flab-
biness, colour to drabness, power to prettiness, and above all, liberty
to authority'.

Two months later, Frank Hinder in Sydney organised an exhibition of contemporary art and sculpture – including works by artists
such as Rah Fizelle, Grace Crowley and Ralph Balson. Evatt made
another speech opening the exhibition. The *Sydney Morning Herald*
noted that many of the women attending were 'hatless', a signal of
their modernism and unconventionality. The *Herald's* reviewer was
unimpressed by the exhibition, describing the works as 'coldly cerebral'
with 'harsh juxtapositions of colour'. Evatt's speech, however, had the
tone of a manifesto; the movement known as modern art had already
'swept the world', he said. Modernism rejected 'camera accuracy', and
it was meaningless to criticise it for apparent 'distortion':

The artist turns his back on realistic illusion and centres on dynamic and formal elements. He asserts and admits that it is of little use merely to imitate things, he therefore seeks to express them through their significant elements … a non-conformance to external objects enables him to select from the object, even to break it up, and to reconstruct it into greater significance and coherence … it is useless to argue whether this movement is justified … The works of Matisse and Modigliani sometimes realize 200 times as much as the works of such artists as Orpen. That is why the galleries of Australia which lack specimens of these masters cannot compare with those in France, Britain and the United States.

Modernism for Evatt meant more than a new form of representation, it also meant an attack on the establishment. In one sense, he was saying that innovation required freedom, and in another he was effectively claiming the market had already decided – modernism had 'swept the world' – and Australia was behind the times. Whereas European modernism had sometimes meant a rejection of progressivism and liberalism, in an Australian context Evatt saw it largely as an assault on the old regime, as representing liberty against authority, creativity against regulation. It was the spirit of a Christmas card sent to the Evatts by John and Sunday Reed in 1939: 'Greetings in the modern manner. Long live Picasso'.

In February 1939, Nettie Palmer noted briefly in her pocket diary that the Evatts had been for dinner. Later, preparing her notes for publication, she wrote about Evatt's enthusiasm for 'the moderns and primitives' and for the 'grandeur of Egyptian art'. Evatt had told them about meeting Roosevelt and Frankfurter. He had brought a volume of the *Harvard Law Review*, with his article on labour relations and Henry Bournes Higgins, Nettie's uncle. With her novelist's eye, Nettie Palmer left us with a vivid portrait of the judge at her dinner table, apparently enjoying life to the full at the age of forty-four:

The man leaves you with a sense of the fullness of life. It's partly physical … but partly his management of energy and time. Ever since – at that fabulously early age, under forty it must have been – he accepted an appointment to the High Court Bench, he has taken for granted that, in this Olympian calm, he can do what he wants. His leisure when it comes is complete – at the close of the day, in vacation. But lately he has been filling it effectively with the writing of significant books, like 'Rum Rebellion'.

7

The historian as judge

Between 1936 and 1940, Evatt published three substantial books and a smaller study. In the same period, he published a series of articles in American law journals. Such an output while working as a High Court judge is testimony not only to his huge energy but also to a growing restlessness. He researched and wrote at night, often standing up and often working close to dawn, while by day he had the considerable demands of the bench. During the day, his nearly illegible handwriting was read out loud by his associate to a typist to produce the first draft. The books demonstrate his interests in the borderland where law and politics blur into each other, and they show his mind at work.

The first book, *The King and His Dominion Governors* (1936), was a rambling but insightful study of the reserve powers of the representatives of the crown in the dominions. The second, *Injustice within the law* (1937), was much briefer, describing the injustice suffered by six rural labourers transported from England for swearing an oath of solidarity. Then came two major works of Australian history: *Rum Rebellion* (1938) and *Australian Labour Leader* (1940).

Injustice within the law, later republished as *The Tolpuddle Martyrs* is a short book, more an extended pamphlet; it was briskly written and bristled with indignation. In late 1834, a handful of agricultural labourers at Tolpuddle in Dorsetshire had formed a trade union. At their inaugural meeting, members were sworn in by kissing a Bible, presented with a life-size sketch of a skeleton, and bound to secrecy. The growth of unionism alarmed the Whig government, and the six labourers were made an example of to intimidate the rest of the growing movement. Forming a union had only recently become legal, but administering a secret oath of association was illegal under old legislation designed to suppress conspiracy in the armed forces; the Tolpuddle labourers were prosecuted under that older law for administering an oath. They were sentenced to seven years' transportation to New South Wales; two years later, following fierce protest, they were pardoned and returned home.

For Evatt, the significance of the case lay in its lesson that the law could be used, quite legally, for repressive purposes; hence his title. The case was all quite legal, yet it was 'the very coronation of injustice'. That showed, he wrote, that 'oppression and cruelty do not always fail', and it appeared to be a revelation for him to imagine that the law could be used for political repression. He drew a somewhat melodramatic conclusion:

> Unless trade unionists throughout the world are prepared
> to sacrifice their personal interests, their safety, or even their
> lives for the amelioration of the lot of the poor, their elaborate
> organisation may perish overnight either in a holocaust of terror
> and force or in the slower process of legal repression.

That may have been an exaggerated sentiment to draw from the case of the Tolpuddle unionists in 1834, but in 1937 it clearly had its context in the rise of European fascism.

The crown and the colonies

The year before, Evatt had published *The King and His Dominion Governors*. It is a large, dry and somewhat disorganised book that grew out of the thesis for which he was awarded a doctor of laws in 1924. Its publication marked him out as an intellectual, in the abstract area of the history of constitutional law. When he saw the book, Kilgour wrote, touchingly, that Evatt's achievements were 'a source of great pride to me and I rejoice that we have been associated ... in the bonds of friendship, may I say affection ... your eminent ability and attainments are widely recognised and I feel sure that this latest work of yours will go a long way to strengthen that recognition'.

In the book, Evatt's central theme was the sheer ambiguity of the reserve powers of governors representing the British crown, and his central argument was that they ought to be clarified. The book was exhaustive; he surveyed a series of constitutional disputes in Britain, and in the settler colonies that were now called the dominions, including Canada, Australia, Ireland and South Africa. In these disputes the reserve powers of the monarch in Britain, or of a governor in a dominion had political consequences for parliamentary democracy. Under what circumstances could a governor refuse advice from the government? Could he or she dismiss a government with majority support in the lower house of parliament? (This was not an abstract question for Evatt: Jack Lang had been dismissed by the New South Wales governor in 1932.) Were governors in the dominions in a different position to the crown in Britain? What were the differences, in federal systems such as those of Australia and Canada, between the powers of state or provincial governors and of national governors-general?

As virtually none of the answers were codified in constitutions, they were the subject of argument among constitutional writers; expectations of what reserve powers existed were governed by conventions and precedents. Evatt was not opposed to the crown having reserve powers, but he disliked their ambiguity: 'It is often impossible to tell whether the conventions are being obeyed, because no one can say with sufficient certainty what the conventions are'. This lack of constitutional clarity, he argued, contributed to an 'element of legalized anarchy'. He was definitely not one of those who said the ambiguity of Britain's unwritten constitution was a source of strength and flexibility; instead his analysis had a distinctly political edge.

Ambiguity, he argued, might have been satisfactory when Whigs and Tories alternated in controlling 'the political apparatus of the State'; they could tacitly assume that certain 'rules of the game' would be obeyed. In those circumstances, he wrote, vagueness and uncertainty did little harm, and 'good form' allowed politicians to live with the 'lack of definition'. But as the vote was extended more widely and as the labour movement entered politics all that had changed. Especially in the dominions, he argued, the parties representing labour were entitled to something more precise than 'a vague gesture towards … constitutional and political morality. They cannot see the "rules" written down in any authoritative way, and they come to suspect the rules the more if they are brought into operation against their desires'. Hence, his argument for codification was principally that the labour movement, with which he obviously aligned himself, was entitled to have these conventions articulated. They were entitled to know the 'rules of the game'.

The book strikes an interesting balance between law and politics. Constitutional law was Evatt's favourite subject, and is the most overtly political branch of the law, as it deals with the legal rules governing government. Evatt was examining the liminal zone where political struggles took a legal form. He seemed to oscillate between wanting rules of constitutional practice written down, and wanting them to be subject to judicial decision-making. Or perhaps it was both – because, if codified, they would inevitably come, in Australia's case, before the High Court for interpretation. They would come before Mr Justice Evatt.

Evatt's analysis of the legal issues is often lucid, explaining the technicalities while keeping sight of the political and historical context, but it sometimes has a slightly dislocated tone, especially when discussing events in which he had been a participant. An example was Jack Lang's attempt in 1926 to abolish the New South Wales Legislative Council; at the time Evatt had been a member of the parliament and provided legal advice. The Labor party's opposition to upper houses was based on the experience that they were a brake on democratic government, especially when, as in New South Wales and Queensland, they were still appointed with nominees rather than being elected. Lang had tried to follow the approach successfully taken by Ted Theodore's ALP government in Queensland in 1920. In that case, a governor had complied with Theodore's advice as premier, allowing additional Labor supporters to be appointed who then voted the council out of existence. But Lang's attempt in New South Wales failed. The governor agreed to additional nominations, but some of them defected and decided against abolishing their new jobs; when Lang attempted to add still more members, the governor refused. Evatt's question, looking back, was whether flooding the upper house in order to abolish it was constitutional – and whether a governor was required to comply with a government wanting to do so.

Evatt adopted a similarly dispassionate tone to describe the dismissal of Jack Lang in 1932 by the governor of New South Wales, Sir Phillip Game. Again one would not suspect how much Evatt's own career had been enmeshed with Lang's. We have seen in chapter 5 that Lang's government was in conflict with the Commonwealth over debt repayment and the Commonwealth's *Financial Agreements Enforcement Act* was designed to force Lang's hand. The premier had unsuccessfully challenged this in the High Court, with both Evatt and McTiernan on the bench. Lang pushed on, and eventually Game dismissed him on the grounds that he was acting illegally, despite retaining a majority in the lower house of the parliament. As Game wrote to the premier: 'You derive your authority from His Majesty through me, and … I cannot possibly allow the Crown to be placed in the position of breaking the law of the land'.

Given the precedent this created for the 1975 dismissal of the Whitlam government, it is interesting to see how Evatt handles it. He thought it was an event 'of great constitutional importance, but needs careful and detached analysis'. That Lang then lost the subsequent election did not, according to Evatt, mean Game's decision was correct. To arguments that Lang's intransigence was 'unjust' and illegal,

Evatt replied, 'This kind of reasoning is a good example of the intrusion of mere political arguments into what are, or should be, questions of legal or quasi-legal character'. But that qualification – 'quasi-legal' – shows how hard it was to separate politics from the law.

Evatt answered his own question about whether Game was 'constitutionally correct in his action' by arguing that it was impossible to say. Game had justified 'the power of dismissal' on the argument that Lang was breaking the law, but only 'a competent legal tribunal' could 'determine the question of legality'. Whether Lang was acting illegally had never been tested in court, and the whole episode illustrated 'the confusion and anarchy resulting from the absence of binding and settled rules for the exercise of the reserve power'. While *The King and His Dominion Governors* is relatively dry, it showed Evatt working his way along the fraught border of law and politics. It was a border of interest to him, a place where the ambiguities of the polity were only partly clarified by constitutional law, and where the judicial power he now exercised bled into the political power struggles he had witnessed both as a member of parliament, and from the court to which Lang's government appealed.

The case of History v. Bligh

By 1937, Evatt was already launching into his next major project. He had been invited to give a series of lectures at the University of Queensland, and seized upon the story of the overthrow of Governor William Bligh. The lectures were reworked and published the next year in book form, with the title *Rum Rebellion*. The book told a sympathetic story of Bligh who, having survived the 1789 mutiny against him as captain of the *Bounty*, had been appointed governor of New South Wales in 1806. He was soon in conflict with the putative leader of the free settlers, the tempestuous John Macarthur. Macarthur was close to the New South Wales Corps, the military force that largely controlled the colony. In January 1808, the commander of the corps, Lieutenant Colonel George Johnston, with Macarthur's active encouragement, led a rebellion to successfully depose Bligh, holding him under arrest until he was replaced.

Evatt took up Bligh's cause with relish. Tennant told the story of how he came to pick the rebellion as his subject. She appears to have heard the tale from W.H. Ifould, the principal librarian of the Mitchell Library where Evatt was a trustee:

> Evatt surged into the library announcing that his time was short, he had to deliver the Macrossan Memorial Lectures ... and he was looking for a topic ... The Librarian suggested that he might consider whether Bligh had been unfairly treated by historians ... Evatt became enthusiastic as he listened. 'I'm *for* him!' he exclaimed.

While Tennant made it clear she thought Evatt identified too much with Bligh's case, she curiously left out a sentence in her draft that came immediately after the lines quoted above: 'He threw himself into Bligh's defence as he might earlier have done as an advocate in court'. That was exactly right; Evatt wrote the book as though he had been retained to represent Bligh, giving an astoundingly partisan account of why Bligh was right and Macarthur was wrong. An advocate is paid to ignore shades of grey, but historians should not, and parts of Evatt's account were comically biased.

Evatt portrayed Bligh as the victim of forces led by Macarthur who felt the governor threatened their interests. Although Bligh had full executive power as the 'head jailer' of the penal settlement, the corps controlled trade, including the rum trade, and Macarthur represented his own pastoral interests as well as those of the military, of which he had recently been a prominent member. Evatt saw this as a conflict between economic and social interests, with Bligh representing 'the agriculturalists and poor settlers', and Macarthur representing 'the rising trading or capitalist group'. He wrote this as a simple polarity, and clearly aligned himself alongside Bligh with the forces of good, even if, ironically, Bligh's was necessarily a 'legal dictatorship'.

Later historians have noticed the partisanship with which Evatt wrote. M.H. Ellis published his sympathetic biography of Macarthur in 1955, ignoring Evatt's book completely. For Ellis, Bligh was 'the uncompromising sea monster in Government House'; he was a tyrant but an ineffective one, while Macarthur represented liberty. A few years later, Ellis revealed what he really thought of Evatt's history, in a *Quadrant* article attacking Evatt's 'grossly inaccurate' account. Others have similarly seen that 'Evatt was blind to Bligh's faults', and commented that his 'unambiguous contest between good and evil … doubtless appeals to enthusiasts for conspiracy theories'.

Evatt certainly took a polarised view of the rebellion, reducing its complexity to a struggle between two men, one of whom must be found innocent and one guilty. He appointed himself character witness for Bligh, and some of Bligh's characteristics evidently resonated with his own. He had read Bligh's log book of the voyage on the *Bounty* with 'a deep sense of respect and admiration, even of affection, for the man'. Bligh showed care for the orphan children of Sydney, which appealed to Evatt. Bligh was self-made, brusque, tenacious and self-sufficient; these were all qualities Evatt might have seen in himself.

But the story held another unique point of appeal for Evatt, beyond politics or personality. In *Rum Rebellion*, he made an astute point about the polity of early colonial Sydney: the only public sphere available was the law. There was no parliament, no press, nor any political associations, not even a theatre – only the governor, the military and a court largely composed of military officers. Consequently the courts were the 'true forum of the little colony' and 'bitter skirmishes between the opposing interests almost necessarily assumed the form of legal contests, because they could not be fought elsewhere'. He made this point about the court being the only public realm several times, as though he felt he needed to justify his approach. The historical sources were chiefly legal records, and that fact made it possible for Evatt to write a book of history by analysing a series of legal cases. Bligh, Macarthur and their agents sued each other, took out injunctions, claimed and counterclaimed. Three years after the overthrow of Bligh, the climacteric was a court martial in London at which Johnston, leader of the rebellion, was found guilty of mutiny.

Drawing on the legal records, Evatt retried each of these cases and delivered judgement. So his chapter titles included the 'Case of the Promissory Note', the 'Affair of Dr Balmain', the 'Case of Sedition', the 'Case of the Imported Stills', and the 'Court Martial of Johnston'. This concentration of politics in court documents – in depositions of evidence, in the arguments of lawyers, and in the decisions of judges – was ideal for Evatt, because he could explicitly claim special skills in weighing up evidence. He relished the chance to retry each case, sifting the evidence, and invariably he found Macarthur guilty.

In a sarcastic comment about the difference between legal and historical modes of thought, he wrote 'I suppose it would be intolerable if the judgments of history had to be pronounced by trained lawyers rather than by persons unskilled in the actual science of legal investigation'. The subtext was that it would not be in the least intolerable if lawyers judged history; historians, he thought, were not trained in the 'art and science' of the law and consequently were at 'a considerable handicap in reaching sound conclusions'. He contrasted this naivety with 'the trained legal mind', saying that:

> The handling of documents for the purpose of ascertaining the facts, of drawing only permissible inferences from facts, is part and parcel of the everyday work of the practising lawyer. Rules and canons of evidence are brought into play for the purpose of avoiding error and ascertaining truth.

Evatt was convinced he could read the truth from the records of the court martial, because the contending accounts there had been tested under cross-examination and because he was master of the 'science of legal investigation'.

His confidence in the capacity of legal reasoning to avoid error and determine truth shines through the book. As he put it in his analysis of Johnston's court martial: given a 'competent and honest' tribunal which takes care to test witnesses and documents for their accuracy and credibility, 'the result will almost inevitably be the detection of falsehood and the triumph of truth'. Unlike the highly political trials in Sydney, he argued, the court martial met these criteria; it sifted evidence to determine the facts and then found Johnston guilty. It was the triumph of truth.

The principles of what most legal philosophers call the rationalist tradition were prominent in Evatt's approach. It is the major tradition within Anglo-American law, especially with regard to evidence; legal rationalists believe that the true facts of past events can be established through rational inquiry, and determining the facts is the basis of justice through the application of substantive law. One writer described truth, reason and justice as the 'holy trinity' of this rationalist tradition, in which true facts are determined, reason is applied to them and justice is the outcome. Evatt was fundamentally convinced of this rationalist mode of determining justice.

In a later interview, Mary Alice told of how Evatt always insisted on being presented with 'the facts'. 'The first thing was the facts ... He worked out a logical approach to the situation ... not one influenced by prejudice.' She made a similar point in another interview. 'He felt that in legal decisions your judgments must be made on the facts and the law, not on your other opinions ... he didn't allow himself to be influenced by anything that he didn't think he should be influenced by ....' When the interviewer pointed out that can be difficult, she agreed: 'It's difficult, but if you are trained in logic, you see, he was a very good philosopher. He won the University Medal for philosophy and he thought all lawyers should study logic and philosophy'.

Evatt's attachment to legal reasoning, particularly to deductive logic, was applied to his reading of Bligh. His legal approach was most evident in his language; while relentlessly serious, it bordered on the comic. He slipped between the language of a lawyer and that of a judge; on some occasions he was counsel for Bligh, and increasingly as the book went on he was the judge. In his examination of a case of sedition that Bligh brought against Macarthur, Evatt wrote about the legal nature of sedition and then pronounced: 'Upon this footing I proceed to an opinion as to each of the three counts of the indictment.' He concluded: 'I am of opinion that Macarthur was guilty of the common law misdemeanour of publishing seditious words', and 'on two counts he was guilty'. The judge was writing history, and the historian was sitting as a judge.

It is no accident that his last chapter was not titled 'Conclusion', but 'Judgment'. He was thinking not merely as a lawyer, but as a judge. Judges do not make arguments as lawyers do, they 'find' and 'pronounce' the truth. 'Sooner or later', he wrote, 'history will pronounce final judgment upon William Bligh. It will be in his favour'. But Evatt had already pronounced final judgement. As one reviewer wrote, presumably with intentional irony: 'Mr Justice Evatt of the High Court of Australia rehears the case of History versus Bligh – and gives verdict in Bligh's favour'.

In writing 'history', Evatt was delivering a judgement, with all its hallmarks of finality. That made his mode of analysis rather different from that of most historical writing, which considers what evidence has been preserved, and why, as much as how it can be read. Historians, unlike lawyers, take into account contradictory motives for human behaviour and rarely assume that one view is absolute. For example, the way historian Alan Atkinson described the same events in *The Europeans in Australia* is more open and complex, treating Bligh and Macarthur as puzzles rather than plaintiffs. But Evatt was not constrained by such doubts.

Rum Rebellion is a good read and an illuminating, if wonderfully biased, description of the events of 1808. But it is also a completely unselfconscious illustration of the centrality of legal rationality in Evatt's intellectual and emotional constitution. His insight – that the court was the only public sphere of the colony – was profound, yet he seems not to have realised its full significance. If the court was the only political arena, then what happened there was both a legal and a political process; but that in turn meant it could not be wholly understood through the application of the legal reasoning he employed. He was transparently appearing for Bligh, and was anything but rational and impartial in his judgements, but could not see it. The irony of his approach accounts for the book's somewhat absurdist tone, and is quite revealing. 'Facts' in politics are rarely absolute, yet Evatt insisted on applying legal reason. He was intrigued by the intermeshing of law and politics, but always hoped that legal rationality would triumph over political power. In politics, that would prove to be a liability.

Evatt's attempts to rehabilitate Bligh's reputation did not end with the publication of his book. He thought Bligh had been unfairly treated by history, and also by Hollywood. The established narrative of Bligh's tyranny had recently been represented in the 1935 film *Mutiny on the Bounty* starring Charles Laughton and Clark Gable. In one of Evatt's rare instances of intentional humour, he wrote: 'Bligh's fate has been to suffer condemnation from Hollywood, the sentences of which have universal jurisdiction'. After *Rum Rebellion* was published, Evatt hoped to interest Hollywood in another film based on his book; it would surely have been a courtroom drama par excellence. His associate Keith Brennan sent the book to Twentieth Century Fox, who replied: 'It is not the type of story this company is interested in.' Paramount Pictures thought it was 'indeed interesting', but clearly not interesting enough. They mentioned that the director of the *Mutiny* film, Frank Lloyd, had recently announced he would produce a picture 'dealing with the further adventures of Captain Bligh'. On Evatt's behalf, Roger Tillam of Film Studio in Sydney wrote to Lloyd touting *Rum Rebellion*'s importance as an account which redressed the 'errors of historical fact' in his film. Nothing came of the attempt but, working through intermediaries, Evatt was apparently flirting with the prospect of himself breaking into Hollywood, where his judgements could have 'universal jurisdiction'.

A Labor tragedian

Evatt's biography of William Holman, published in 1940, was a remarkable book and written in a more conventional historian's style than the Bligh book. At a time when few were writing Australian history, Evatt produced a well-researched and quite radical book that is still absorbing. *Australian Labour Leader*'s narrative structure was clearly that of a tragedy. As biography, it was very much a public portrait, offering little insight into Holman's inner life; his motivations and emotions are largely obscured. The most striking example is that we learn, suddenly, on page 218, that Holman had a daughter to whom he wrote letters, but it is the first and almost the last time she appears in the story. Holman's full character does not emerge, though this may have been due in part to the conventions of biography at that time. It was not so much a biographical portrait of Holman as a narrative of New South Wales politics, focused on the early Labor party.

Evatt appears to have started on the project well before the Bligh book. Holman had only recently died, in 1934, and his widow, Ada wrote to Evatt in January 1936 that she was thankful he was 'undertaking Will's life' and would gladly do her part. She promised to get on with sorting his papers, as she had 'an immense amount of material'. Mary Alice recalled that eventually 'a whole trunkful of papers' arrived, and that she spent six months putting them in order. The trunk included Holman's correspondence about Labor politics between the 1890s and 1920s, including letters from Billy Hughes, as well as letters to his wife and daughter, though these family letters rarely found their way into the biography. If Evatt was expected to return these papers he neglected to; he was well known for his habit of borrowing books and never returning them. The result is that a significant cache of papers relating to the early history of the New South Wales Labor party sits among his own papers at Flinders University.

When Evatt and Mary Alice left for England on his High Court sabbatical in 1938, he was working on the draft aboard ship. A manuscript was with Victor Gollancz in London by August, and Harold Laski assured him he would support publication, saying, 'I am sure we ought to publish your book'. Evatt wrote to Grattan that he was 'awaiting news' about the book, and that Laski had pronounced it 'superb'. Finally, in December, as the Evatts were returning via America, Gollancz wrote rejecting the book: 'One of the tragedies of a publisher's life is that time after time a book comes in which he knows people ought to read, but which he knows also that they won't read'. Gollancz thought people in Britain wanted books on world politics, and were expecting war by the spring. He did not say so, but the book was too parochial. Eventually it was published in Sydney in 1940.

The facts of Holman's trajectory are compelling. He was the son of an actor and theatre manager, and the family had migrated from London in 1888. Holman was self-taught through his reading of Thomas Carlyle, John Stuart Mill, Thomas Babington Macaulay and Karl Marx. He was considered a fine, if acerbic, debater and orator. Alongside Billy Hughes, he was a crucial player in the establishment of Political Labor Leagues in New South Wales in the 1890s, and in the early history of the Labor party. The two of them had led the fight for adoption of the pledge as a means of enforcing solidarity and unity. Holman entered the New South Wales parliament in 1898 and was significant in the period when Labor held the balance of power, explicitly giving its support to progressive liberals in return for policy concessions. Evatt wrote there was no truth to the story that Holman and Hughes tossed a coin to decide which of them would move to the Commonwealth parliament after federation, but it was true 'there was hardly enough room for both of them in the same party and the same Parliament'.

Left The young Herbert Vere Evatt, aged 6 in 1900, the year before his father died. His father was keenly involved in the East Maitland cricket team and had given Bert the bat; it was almost the only memory Evatt recounted about his father. *Flinders University Library no. 1819*

Below The widowed Jeanie Evatt and her six sons, about 1904 in Sydney. From the right are George, with Frank standing in front of him, Clive on Jeanie's lap, Ray sitting on the floor and John sitting behind him. Bert, aged about 10, is standing on the left, looking very earnest, but then they all look serious. Both Ray and Frank volunteered for the First World War and both were killed in France. *Flinders University Library no. 2046*

Above Two young lovers, in images before they married in 1920. The photograph of Mary Alice Sheffer is undated, while that of Evatt is on being admitted to the Bar at the age of 24 in 1918. *Flinders University Library nos 736 and 2014*

Right Evatt, in 1926, as the talented young barrister entering politics and about to confront the implacable force of Jack Lang; his first foray into politics was unsuccessful. *Flinders University Library no. 1239*

Mary Alice and Evatt returning by steamer from England and Europe in 1926. They look very comfortable with each other. *Flinders University Library no. 896*

Mary Alice, undated but during the 1930s, in a forceful and confident image. By this stage, she was very involved in the modern art movement. *Flinders University Library no. 3050*

In August 1940, Evatt announced he would step down from the High Court to re-enter politics for the Labor party; he presented it as his duty to serve in the crisis of the war. He was widely regarded as a celebrity candidate, important enough to warrant a newsreel story about his candidacy. *Still from Movietone newsreel no. 130065; reproduced by permission of Rightsmith*

Above The celebrity candidate and family; in September 1940, this homely image of Evatt, Peter, Rosalind and Mary Alice appeared in the *Australian Women's Weekly*, along with a very sympathetic article. Les Haylen, the chief sub-editor of the *Weekly* had arranged it all, to help boost the profile of the sensational Labor recruit. *Flinders University Library no. 046*

Right In early 1942, as minister for external affairs, Evatt travelled to America and England; he demanded more attention to the war against Japan in the Pacific, more war supplies and a greater voice in war strategy. His media appearances were in part about appealing to the English people over the heads of their own government. *Flinders University Library no. 040*

A formal portrait of Evatt as a minister in the 1940s. By this stage, he was one of the most dominant figures in the Labor government, and was also subject to frequent criticism from his opponents. *Flinders University Library no. 1817*

An unusual image of Evatt, because it captures him in repose, though he still has something to read (undated, but 1940s). *Flinders University Library no. 681*

Right This formal portrait of Evatt and Mary Alice appears to have been taken at the San Francisco conference to write the charter of the United Nations in 1945. Evatt had a significant impact on the framing of the charter, though he made few friends with his forceful advocacy. *Flinders University Library no. 1816*

Below Evatt campaigned hard to be the President of the UN General Assembly, and was elected in late 1948 on his second attempt. Sam Atyeo joked that he was now 'president of the world'. This image is of him presiding shortly after winning the prize; he perhaps looks momentarily content, but his relentless ambition was in fact never satisfied. *Flinders University Library no. 1659*

Above Following the defection of Vladimir Petrov from the Soviet embassy in early 1954, a Royal Commission investigated allegations of espionage and subversion in Australia; it was high drama in the context of Cold War alarms. When some of Evatt's staff were named, he rushed to defend them, and also defend himself as Labor leader. Here he is arriving at the commission in August 1954, and about to ensnare himself in the fraught politics of the Petrov affair. *Still from Cinesound no. 28740; reproduced by permission of Rightsmith*

Left There were not many moments of calm for Evatt in the 1950s, when his leadership was embattled and the party was splitting. Here he is aged in his late fifties, looking reposed but still tense and guarded. *Flinders University Library no 683*

The only way the Labor party could think to bring Evatt's troubled leadership to an end was to offload him onto the New South Wales Supreme Court. After he was sworn in as Chief Justice in early 1960, his mental decline was soon very evident to most, though apparently not to Mary Alice, who insisted he was just tired. *Flinders University Library no. 055*

Evatt and Mary Alice at home following his stroke in early 1962. She continued to hope he could write his memoirs, but Paul Hasluck wrote that when he visited, he met a shell of the dynamic, tumultuous figure he had known and worked with in the 1940s. *Flinders University Library no. 903*

By 1913, Holman was New South Wales premier and Hughes was federal attorney-general, but conflict was building between them; Holman opposed Hughes' failed attempts to expand Commonwealth powers. Holman was also in conflict with his own party; he was criticised for not moving fast enough to implement socialist policies and to abolish the upper house. When Hughes, as Labor prime minister, announced in 1916 his intention to introduce military conscription, Holman sided with him, and in the acrimony of the split that followed, both left the Labor party. A year later, they were leaders of the new Nationalist party formed with the conservatives.

Evatt sent the manuscript to Vance Palmer for comments. Palmer wrote that he enjoyed the political history, but could not see how Evatt's interpretations were supported by the facts. Evatt replied that author and historian Brian Fitzpatrick had said something similar, that 'it looked like two different people combined to write the book'. Evatt said this was a result of the procedure he had deliberately adopted, calling on 'two different capacities'. His intention had been to separate his conclusions and opinions from the 'narrative of the facts', making a clear epistemological distinction between fact and interpretation. 'I have undoubtedly allowed personal knowledge and sympathy to find a place in my judgment,' he said, 'and to that extent it is open to dissent or qualification'.

Palmer thought Evatt was a little easy on Holman:

> I can't believe that a man who had any original core in his character would have shown the fluidity Holman did when he came into power; a fluidity that was obviously changing his disposition even before the conscription referendum. There didn't seem to be any principle of his early life that he held to in his later years.

That may have been a fair criticism, implying that Evatt had failed to find the core of Holman. But neither Palmer nor Fitzpatrick shared Evatt's sympathy for Holman (and Hughes), so they were unlikely to concur with his interpretation. The book has a narrative that is more complex and interesting than a conventional story of 'traitors' to the movement. He had rendered Holman as a tragic figure who had lost everything.

In his introduction, Evatt argued that the examples of Hughes and Holman posed bigger questions about 'social democratic organizations'; this was a nod to Vere Gordon Childe's analysis in *How Labour Governs*. Childe had, in part, argued that representatives of the workers would be tempted to defect when they acceded to power; Evatt saw the solution in loyalty to the party, and kept returning to that theme. He insisted that Hughes and Holman had 'rendered an enormous service' to the labour movement by fighting for the pledge and – in contrast with the views he had expressed in *Liberalism in Australia* – he now affirmed numerous times that the pledge, as a mechanism for ensuring loyalty to the movement, was paramount. But he wrote that the defections of Holman and Hughes were not really a question of 'black treachery'; damaging divisions were caused 'as much by lack of loyalty to the chosen leader as by the leader's failure to appreciate that his primary duty is to the working classes'.

But that only made the fate suffered by Holman and Hughes all the more dismal, because they had broken with the party they helped shape. Tragedy ran as an explicit narrative device through the book. Leaders who defected were denounced by former comrades, regarded with suspicion by new conservative colleagues, and felt at home with neither. His summary was that while the Labor party made 'a great tactical mistake in condemning Holman and Hughes to perpetual exile', they subsequently experienced the 'special mortification' of being regarded by Nationalists as Labor leaders in disguise. Evatt's account of Holman's story was, ultimately, about loss: 'Finally comes the annihilating realization that he should never have abandoned a cause which he first espoused. In that is the element of great tragedy'.

In his account of the conscription split, Evatt touched on two points, both of which are particularly interesting in light of the even

more divisive split he faced as ALP leader in the mid-1950s. The first
was conspiracy and the other sectarianism. The demand for conscription came not only from Australian conservatives, but also from the
British government, which was sending estimates of the number of
troops required that could never have been met by voluntary recruitment alone. Evatt argued Hughes was deliberately misled by British
and Australian military officials about the real pattern of recruitment
and future demands; they had, he said, 'deliberately or negligently' fixed
the monthly quota so high that it was impossible to achieve without
conscription. He referred to the official history for support, where
Ernest Scott wrote that the quotas turned out to be overestimates,
and 'the authorities in London were partly impelled by the desire to
furnish a motive for the adoption of conscription by Australia'.

This was, and still is, widely agreed by historians of the period,
but Evatt drew a novel conclusion that demonstrated his capacity to
detect conspiracies. 'The implications of this last criticism are very
devastating … Was it believed by persons concerned that [their] support of conscription would necessarily destroy the Labour Party?' The
implication that conservatives pushed Hughes towards a conscription
policy in the hope it would destroy the party sounds like an anticipa-
tion of the ways Menzies' ongoing pressure on the anti-communist
issue in the 1950s opened up divisions in the party. But it is an interpretation only Evatt has found in the history of the conscription split.

Evatt moved from this claim to discussing sectarian influences in
the conscription plebiscites. Catholics were just over one-fifth of the
total population, yet religion, Ireland, empire loyalty and Labor solidarity were powerful emotional ingredients in the split in 1916. Britain's fierce repression of the quixotic Easter Rising in Dublin in April
1916 had made some Catholics more anti-British and hence anti-war.
Daniel Mannix, who would soon be appointed Catholic archbishop of
Melbourne, became involved in a public brawl with Hughes. Mannix's
opposition to conscription blended criticism of the war with support
for Irish independence, while some of Hughes' wilder rhetoric railed

against Catholics opposing conscription because they were Fenians and disloyal to the empire. Mannix's biographer, Brenda Niall, commented that the two 'created one another as public figures'. Without Mannix, Hughes as a Labor leader could never have 'captured the King and Empire vote', while Mannix's defiance of the prime minister 'won the hearts of many Australian Catholics'.

Evatt's discussion of all this was significant because later, in the split in the 1950s, fervent anti-communist Catholics clashed with anti-Catholic sectarians, as well as with Catholic ALP figures who thought the anti-communists had overreached. Even before the dust had settled, the Catholic activist B.A. Santamaria and others were claiming Evatt had deliberately set out to repeat Hughes' tactics, provoking sectarian sentiment to save his leadership and drive the Catholic right out of the party. But Evatt's discussion of sectarianism in the plebiscites was not a story of a successful tactical move. He did write that Hughes' mobilisation of sectarianism helped his cause, attracting 'tens of thousands of non-Catholic voters'. But he was not endorsing those tactics, and he knew that Hughes had lost.

Evatt tended to see sectarianism as irrational. He wrote that the conflict within the party between the Catholics and a 'rationalist, socialist, anti-clerical' tendency – with which he clearly identified – was weakened as a result of the 1916 split, largely through defections to the conservatives. Those defections in turn meant that in the popular mind, the party was more closely identified with Catholicism, and he wrote that that damaged Labor in elections, because it deterred those who wanted to vote Labor but were anti-Catholic. But this was hardly a story of the successful mobilisation of sectarianism, because he well knew that Hughes had failed in both plebiscites. His general view of Hughes and Holman was that their rupture with the party they loved was both unnecessary and tragic; they had clung to some political power but had lost everything that mattered.

It is worth reflecting on Evatt's own position at this time. By late 1939, he was already thinking about leaving the High Court and re-entering Labor politics. Seen in this context, the biography could be read as Evatt thinking through his own politics and formulating his views about Labor. It could also be thought of as an application for Labor preselection. Parts of it would have pleased Labor stalwarts, who might otherwise worry about the credentials of an intellectual and a High Court judge. It is also worth remembering that Curtin, the ALP leader, had been fiercely involved in the anti-conscription struggle. This is not to say that Evatt's sentiments were inauthentic, but they were mixed, swinging between orthodoxy on issues of party loyalty, and heterodoxy in his overt sympathy for Holman and Hughes.

As with the Bligh book, the final chapter of the Holman biography is not a conclusion but a 'judgement' – an eloquent summing-up of his major narrative themes of loyalty and tragedy. He even reproduced a cartoon from the *Bulletin*, by the political cartoonist David Low, depicting Holman as the sort of Shakespearean actor his own father had been. Evatt's caption read: 'Even Low could not resist the temptation to depict Holman as tragedian'. He repeated that the split need never have happened, and that there were faults on both sides, and summoned an image of actors caught up in inexorable forces. By breaking with his party, he wrote, Holman 'gave up almost everything worth having'; it was 'tragic' that Holman then 'found himself leading a coalition which included Labour's political enemies'.

While *How Labour Governs* can be detected in the background throughout the book, it was only in the final pages that Evatt explicitly addressed what he called Childe's 'profound pessimism' about Labor. We have seen that Childe had argued three themes, that Labor representatives would be tempted to forget their roots, that the party machine led to an emphasis on means over ends, and that Labor faced the challenge of straddling both middle-class and working-class interests. Evatt chose to focus only on the first of these arguments, quoting one of Childe's best-known statements: 'The Labour Party, starting with a band of inspired socialists, degenerated into a vast machine for capturing political power, but did not know how to use that power when obtained, except for the benefit of individuals'. Evatt refuted this by focusing on the final phrase; Holman had not enriched himself. Evatt rejected pessimism, largely ignoring the other dimensions of Childe's critique, and instead allowed himself a final populist flourish: Labor's idealism must 'be renewed and re-invigorated by constant and continuous contact with the people, the true rank and file'. Avowing the supremacy of the movement made it clear to readers where his own loyalties lay.

Discontents

The body of work Evatt produced in the second half of the 1930s is a prodigious effort for someone also occupied with the work of a High Court judge. While much of the book on the reserve powers of the crown had been done for his thesis in the mid-1920s, the two books on Bligh and Holman were based on intensive research conducted in a relatively short period starting in 1936. In the Bligh book, he had the freedom to retry the case of 'history versus Bligh', a legal problem that was much more interesting than many of the cases he was dealing with on the court; and his final 'judgement' did not depend on consultation with fractious colleagues. In the Holman book, he could rehearse and reconsider the debates he had had with Childe about Labor in power, at the same time declaring his own loyalty to the cause.

Tennant thought these books were about a 'disguised or open dictatorship by the rich' in Australian history. That was exaggerated and romantic, but it is notable that they were all about class relations: the labour movement was entitled to know the rules of the constitutional game; Bligh and Macarthur represented opposing class interests; and the Holman biography affirmed that only organised labour could represent workers against organised capital. There was less sign of the progressive liberalism he endorsed in 1918, though it did still appear in some of his legal articles, especially in his praise for Higgins and wage arbitration. The judge was perhaps becoming more radical, or it may be that his principles were fluid and that, as Palmer had said of Holman, there was no 'original core' to his politics. Evatt had absorbed the views about class current in the ALP's form of socialism, and there is little evidence he had much interest in Marx. The copy of *Capital* in his library (a 1909 edition) was largely unread except for a heavily underlined section on colonialism, and his 1926 edition of Engels' *Condition of the Working Class in England* was unread. Instead, his thinking about class was, as Grattan put it, about opposition to entrenched privilege: he had 'simply decided privilege was wrong'. Grattan frequently referred to Evatt's conviction that Labor was the heir to progressive liberalism: 'Evatt's laborism was a continuation of left-liberalism in a new dress'.

Yet his own class and political position was increasingly compli-cated. He was an arbiter of state power, bewigged and robed, perched in the highest court in the land, and a wealthy property owner enjoy-ing a middle-class lifestyle, tended to by domestic staff. But by night he wrote histories that dwelt on class relations and pondered the prob-lems of Labor politics. Evatt was increasingly uneasy with his position; championing modernism in art was a kind of harmless proxy for rad-icalism, but was not enough. Researching and writing his books may have been a way of dealing with this growing restlessness.

Increasingly aware of the rise of fascism and the coming war, he fretted his legal work was not of enough consequence. His restlessness is suggested by the intellectual games he played. Mary Alice recalled his interest in old English, which he had studied at university; she said: 'Anglo-Saxon, you see, has given us about half our words today', and Evatt would try to write a judgement using only words of old English derivation; at other times, he would try the exercise using only words of Latin derivation. It was, she said, 'interesting to do … just for intellectual exercise'. By October 1939, he was toying with the idea of leaving such games behind, and returning to politics, convinced that his talents were needed.

Mary Alice later recalled discussions at Nuuanu about whether Evatt should leave the High Court. Burgmann, by then a bishop, was 'very fond' of Evatt, according to Mary Alice, and would often come over and discuss the 'problems of the day'. He would bring with him young men from the Christian Socialists, including a young Allan Dalziel, who was to be Evatt's private secretary when he returned to politics. Evatt had come to the conclusion that Menzies' UAP government was incapable of planning for the coming war; Mary Alice recalled he would say: 'I can't bear not to be doing something directly towards winning the war and keeping Australia safe'. It was Burgmann, she thought, who most influenced his decision to re-enter politics. But Grattan thought it was Mary Alice who pushed Evatt forward. His assessment was that, unlike Evatt, who did not understand or have a feel for politics, Mary Alice 'liked' politics, as he several times heard her 'explicitly declare'. But she never presented herself in this way in later interviews; she spoke only of her regret that he had left the court and left behind the opportunity to write more books. He was planning a biography of Billy Hughes, about which Hughes was enthusiastic.

The Olympian calm Nettie Palmer thought she saw in Evatt in February 1939 did not last, and may in any case have been a misinterpretation. By October, he was talking openly about stepping back into politics. After a dinner with the Evatts and other friends, Palmer jotted briefly in her pocket diary that they had had a very good evening: 'Talk both witty and real. Evatt caustic about Government. May leave the Bench for politics'.

8

The celebrity candidate

The development of the war in Europe was a critical factor in Evatt's decision to return to politics. He genuinely thought the nation needed his help in a time of crisis. In September 1939, Menzies had committed Australia to the war, after Hitler invaded Poland, and Britain and France both declared war. The period until mid-1940 is often called the 'phoney war', when nations were readying for the full-scale conflict to come. Hitler and Stalin had signed a non-aggression pact in August 1939, astonishing the world with the vision of Bolshevism and Nazism in collaboration. Communist parties around the world, including in Australia, dutifully supported their incongruous alliance with fascism, but everyone knew the pact was a delaying tactic.

With Russia neutralised, Hitler could turn west and, in May 1940, launched the Blitzkrieg invasion of western Europe. The same month, the Menzies government banned the Australian Communist party, as a subversive organisation which was, after all, supporting an ostensible ally of the Nazis. After buckling under the German assault in France, the remaining British and French troops were evacuated across the Channel from Dunkirk, and a few weeks later, in mid-June, the Germans occupied Paris. In London, Chamberlain's conservative government collapsed and Churchill took his place, establishing a bipartisan coalition War Cabinet with the Labour party. The proposal for an equivalent bipartisan alliance was usually called a 'national government' in Australia; it was an idea Evatt was to champion, but the ALP was to reject. Against this background, the labour journalist Henry Boote noted in June that Evatt was 'more than ever hell bent on re-entering politics'.

From early July, the Luftwaffe attempted to destroy its British equivalent in the Battle of Britain; establishing air supremacy was to pave the way for a Nazi invasion, and it would not become clear until October that the Germans had failed. It was in August 1940, shortly after the first air raid on London, that Evatt announced he was stepping back into politics. He was widely considered to be a celebrity candidate, making a sacrifice for the war effort. It was the beginning of a twenty-year period in which many people projected onto Evatt their hopes, or their fears, their devotion or their animosity. He was to be one of the most prominent and polarising figures of Australian politics throughout the forties and fifties.

'It's no use scolding me'

One indication of Evatt's restlessness on the High Court during 1939 was the rumour that he was being considered for the post of Australian minister to Washington; in effect this was to be the first appointment of an ambassador, though not with that title. Evatt himself had some part in spreading the rumour. Ben Cohen, a senior policy figure in Washington often described as a member of Roosevelt's 'brains trust', had received a letter from Evatt raising the possibility. Cohen wrote to Roosevelt in July that Evatt had said he might be 'invited to become the Australian Minister to the United States for a year or year and a half without his having to resign from the High Court'. Cohen thought 'it would be a fine thing' to have him, as he was so sympathetic to Roosevelt's policies. But it was highly improbable; Menzies, who had become UAP prime minister in April after Lyons' death, was never likely to trust Evatt as Australia's representative in Washington.

Later in the year, journalist Frank McIlwraith wrote from London, where he was the English correspondent for *Smith's Weekly*. He had heard the same rumour, and suggested that if it was true, Evatt should send some publicity material: 'so that I can place a story in the British press'. But he thought it would be a mistake 'if Australia should lose its outstanding jurist'. 'I know you like America and the Americans', he told Evatt, 'but I still think Australia has first claim on you'. He went on to describe the deteriorating situation in Europe, during the period of the 'phoney war', and the confusion in political circles. The British communists were disconcerted that Stalin was 'in close cahoots' with Hitler. The Labour party had joined, at Churchill's invitation, a bipartisan government to fight fascism, but were now wondering if they might end up being drawn into a fight against Russia. The war was becoming a 'mass of contradictions', McIlwraith commented.

On the High Court, Evatt and Latham had another falling-out in June 1939, when Evatt objected to what he saw as lack of consultation about a letter to the chief justice of the Indian Federal Court. Latham had circulated a draft, and all the judges had approved it except Evatt, who sent a telegram saying he was opposed. Latham then wrote to the other judges, quoting Evatt's telegram. Evatt objected and asked for the original to be returned, saying: 'I cannot imagine how it came to be circulated. It was obviously a private message to you'. Latham replied, 'I was not told, and it did not occur to my mind, that there was anything confidential' about Evatt's telegram. He apologised, but he could not resist a final shot: 'I have answered your interrogation and I think we might regard the matter as closed'.

Things soon got worse. A few weeks later, Latham wrote asking Evatt to hurry up with his judgements on cases currently before the court: 'Everybody else was ready last week'. Evatt resented Latham's letter, writing: 'I object to its tone as expressing a desire to ride rough-shod over any suggestion I may make'. He complained that consultation between the judges about their decisions was 'very unsatisfactory', and he blamed Latham for communicating with the judges 'as much or as little as you choose'. Latham, he wrote, had allowed the relations on the bench to deteriorate: 'I think you have exacerbated feelings of unpleasantness, suspicion and even hostility among the Judges … If you persist in this mode of conduct to me, you leave me no alternative except to appeal to authority outside the Court'. While the sentiments were petty, below the surface was Evatt's consistent suspicion that powerful men were not according him respect and recognition.

Latham replied, defending himself: 'You make a complete mistake in thinking that I ride roughshod over your views'. How was he to organise the judges to consult together when they refused to even meet; as Latham wrote: 'You told me yourself ... you would not attend conferences with a certain justice' – by which he meant Starke. Other judges had similar views. 'What can be done in these circumstances – which I found existing when I came to the Court?' Latham said he had tried to 'improve the personal relations' on the bench but without success. 'We ought to be able to enjoy our work and live happily together. Will you not help me to bring this about?' But Evatt was clearly not inclined to respond to this plaintive call, and Latham's own relationship with Starke was if anything more fraught. In May 1940, Starke wrote the chief justice a letter declaring that he resented what he interpreted as a 'dirty insinuation' from Latham about his behaviour and the 'silly schoolmaster attitude' he thought Latham adopted; he signed off: 'I think an apology is overdue ... pray keep your criticisms of me to yourself unless I ask for them'.

Another spat between Evatt and Latham arose in October. The chief justice had written asking for Evatt's decisions on several cases as soon as possible; Evatt had replied by telegram giving his decisions and proposing that Latham compel all the judges to confer. Not surprisingly, Latham took exception to decisions being relayed by telegram, to be 'read by clerks in the post office and others'. He was also frustrated by Evatt's proposal about conferences. They had discussed it before, and he still hoped for something better than the situation he had inherited, but the judges kept refusing to cooperate. Evatt wrote back, conceding that telegrams were not the best method of communication, but said: 'It's no use scolding me about the others' opinions'. He blamed Latham for the poor state of relations on the court; it was not just something Latham had 'inherited', and was now 'a good deal worse than when Duffy was forced off the bench by a combination which included one member of the present bench'.

That allegation that Duffy had been forced out in 1935 annoyed Latham, who was Duffy's replacement as chief justice. Latham drafted a long reply that can still be found among his papers, but it was marked 'not sent'. He repeated that he had tried to encourage consultation, 'but four judges (including yourself)' refused to consult with Starke. He also rejected Evatt's 'gratuitous reference' to Duffy being forced out, with its 'apparent suggestion of some sort of conspiracy'. He finished with another of his plaintive appeals: 'I want our work in the court to be done in an efficient, dignified, and pleasant manner, and I wish I could get your help to this end'. That was the draft, but Latham apparently decided to be more curt. On the same day he sent a note reading: 'Dear Evatt, I acknowledge receipt of your letter of Thursday last – much of it is meaningless to me. Yours sincerely, John Latham'. It was against this background of cantankerous relations on the High Court that Evatt dreamt of re-entering politics.

'Breaking into politics again'

Evatt had mentioned the idea of federal politics at dinner with the Palmers in October 1939, as noted in the previous chapter. At about the same time, he asked Percy Spender to meet him in his High Court chambers in Sydney. They had been at school together at Fort Street, and Spender was a UAP member of the federal parliament and would shortly be appointed treasurer under Menzies. Evatt, Spender later wrote, was 'surveying the lie of the land', and spoke about the need for an all-party government, as in Britain. This idea of a 'national government' was becoming a favourite theme of Evatt's. He now floated the idea to Spender that if Labor would agree to participate, would he, Evatt, 'be acceptable to the UAP as its leader, and thus bring about national unity'. Spender thought the idea 'brave', and 'not practicable', noting that 'only a man of Evatt's insatiable aspirations and vanity could have thought it feasible'. Menzies would not retire in Evatt's favour, of course, and – as Spender said in his memoir, published more than thirty years later – Evatt was unpopular with many. There is no other evidence that Evatt considered entering politics on the conservative side, but it is not inherently implausible; Evatt's politics were not particularly ideological and he was certainly casting about for a way to enter politics.

By early 1940, he had broached the topic with Henry Boote. They saw each other regularly at Mitchell Library board meetings, where Evatt was now the president. Boote, who had considerable standing in the party in Sydney, advised Evatt and acted as a go-between with the Labor organisation. In March, Boote recorded for the first time in his diary their conversations on the topic, but it had evidently come up earlier. After a phone conversation, he wrote that Evatt was still contemplating leaving the bench and breaking into politics again: 'Would rather be in the hurly-burly of the House of Reps than in the austere atmosphere of the High Court'. A few days later, Boote discussed the idea with George Buckland, a member of the ALP federal executive. They agreed Evatt would have to be 'invited' to stand rather than compete for preselection, and they would have to waive the requirement of three years' membership; he was not a member of the party. 'Buckland will make some discrete enquiries', Boote wrote. It seems no one objected that Evatt had been expelled from the party in 1927, and had then competed and won against an endorsed Labor candidate; doubtless they thought that was when the New South Wales party was split and things were quite irregular. But the consequences of the split under Lang were still in the background at the federal level. There were moves afoot to try to bring Jack Beasley's 'Lang Labor' group in Canberra back into the fold, or at least to neutralise them. But if Lang's forces broke away and ran separate candidates in New South Wales, Evatt did not want to be in the middle of a factional fight.

He made an attempt through different channels to seek preselection for the seat of Cook, for which he had made his failed tilt in 1922, but key party figures had already promised it as part of deals done to repair the Lang split. Reg Downing was at this time a key figure in the union movement and was shortly to enter the New South Wales upper house; later he was to be prominent as a Labor attorney-general. He recalled that when they told Evatt the seat of Cook was already committed he was 'pretty upset'. Downing later recalled that when he talked about it with other party figures, he had said they should tell Evatt to 'go to bloody Balmain and have Beasley on'. Beasley held the seat and was 'the toughest Lang man there is'; Evatt should be encouraged to get rid of him. With the electorate of Cook out of reach, and Balmain likely to be a contentious fight, Evatt also made an attempt for the seat of Macquarie, where Chifley was sounded out about moving aside. But Chifley had represented the electorate from 1928 to 1931, and was readying himself for another preselection campaign. He flatly refused to step aside to accommodate Evatt, and would be returned to the federal parliament in 1941.

Through April and May 1940, Evatt and Boote regularly discussed Labor politics in general and Evatt's prospects in particular. Buckland suggested the Barton electorate in Sydney's inner southeast. Although held by the UAP it was considered winnable; it had normally been a Labor seat. In early May, Buckland told Boote that New South Wales ALP leader William McKell was 'in constant touch with Evatt on the matter of his re-entry into politics'. Evatt was working the phones and the negotiations were becoming an open secret. Boote noted in his diary that Evatt had said judges 'were not supposed to appear in politics' and he did not want any publicity. Evatt apparently believed he was 'proceeding very circumspectly', Boote said, 'but such things will out'. News of Evatt's aspirations was indeed leaking.

In March, Evatt published an article in the Sydney *Sun*, arguing that democracy was in danger and urging the need for constitutional safeguards for civil liberties. *The Times*, a short-lived Sydney weekly, responded with sharp criticism, and Chief Justice Latham collected the articles; he was clearly watching a political controversy play out in public. *The Times* described Evatt's intervention as 'mischievous and disruptive', and speculated about 'Mr Justice Evatt's appetite of ambition'. Was he planning 'a couple of brilliant moves' that would land a prime ministership? 'Tired of the High Court! Why not this grand tilt at fortune?' The controversy rumbled on for another week, with a further editorial arguing Evatt had compromised his position on the bench: 'It would appear almost obvious that Mr Justice Evatt has decided on a course incompatible with that of a High Court judge'.

Boote noted rumours that were flying about Labor circles early in April, that Evatt would step down and 'lead an attack on those in control of the ALP and infuse a more militant spirit' into the party. 'Evatt himself has never said anything like that to me', wrote Boote, though he had certainly heard Evatt strongly criticise the party leaders. In early May, Menzies made an elaborate show of deploring the 'unfortunate and embarrassing position' in which Evatt was placed by the rumours. He was replying to a question in parliament from his acolyte Harold Holt, who relayed the rumours and asked 'whether it was not an established tradition for the Judiciary to refrain from political activity'. Menzies replied he knew only what he read in the papers; disingenuously, he said he 'regretted' Evatt was in such an awkward situation.

Claude McKay, editor of *Smith's Weekly*, recalled that he was asked to see Evatt in his chambers. Evatt told him he was thinking of entering federal politics, and felt he was 'too young to be where he was'. McKay said: 'I was frankly dismayed and did my best to dissuade him, stressing security, and honoured position and mentioning that there was precedent for promotion to the Chief Justice'. But Evatt had an answer to each objection and McKay recalled: 'Finally I was forced to say, "It's useless to argue with you; I can see you have made up your mind to step down"'. Others actively encouraged him. Albert Piddington wrote a short note in August: 'I hope you'll stand

and fervently renew my wife's hope expressed to Mrs Evatt a year ago that you will lead the Labor Party'. He enclosed a draft article arguing for a bipartisan national government and asked, 'Can I do anything to help?' The journalist Charles Buttrose remembered that when he first heard the open secret in the Canberra press gallery he was 'very, very pleased'. Evatt had a reputation, while all Labor had, he said, was 'sons of toil' getting into parliament. 'To find a great scholar like Evatt turning up, and at the same time a man with pronounced leftist sympathies, we thought it was wonderful.' The judges were also talking about the open secret. During August, Dixon wrote to Latham, saying that Evatt had given no hint of his intentions to resign and seek nomination: 'I assume that the project is abandoned'. He had a copy of Evatt's biography of Holman but did not have 'the inclination or time to read it'.

Evatt had experienced some brief hesitations; Boote noted after a lunch at Rainaud's that Evatt had said he had 'temporarily abandoned' his bid to re-enter politics, because of the ongoing split between Lang Labor and the federal party. 'He wouldn't take part in a faction fight.' There was another hiccup a few weeks later, when Evatt rang to tell Boote that others seeking preselection in Barton were refusing to withdraw to allow him a clear run. 'He seemed worried about it, as Executive were to endorse candidates on Monday.' That was on a Saturday, but all was cleared away over the weekend and on 26 August, the federal executive formally invited Evatt to accept endorsement for the seat of Barton. Boote wrote that Evatt's public reply was that he 'would carefully consider the invitation', but he then left the party in doubt for several days before formally accepting. He wrote to Vance Palmer the day after the invitation: 'As to politics, they have formally asked me to stand, but I am rather disinclined as I think I could never stand up to the racket of it all'. After all the effort he had put in, this seems disingenuous, but perhaps the offer made him consider the sacrifice he was making – not so much financially, but in giving up the law and the opportunity to write.

While Evatt was still ostensibly deliberating, the *Herald* warned him in an editorial that the Labor party's offer 'confronts his Honor with a difficult and delicate decision'. Unlike Latham, who had just been sent to Tokyo as a minister (in effect an ambassador), Evatt should not expect to be granted a leave of absence from the High Court. He would be a candidate for a party, and that was different; the line between politics and the law 'should continue to be sharply and irrevocably drawn', the *Herald* asserted. The suggestion of leave, rather than retirement, had been made by the ALP president, but there is no evidence in Evatt's papers, nor in the detailed discussions recorded in Boote's diary, that he expected such an arrangement. He was going for broke.

'It is my duty'

Evatt's announcement that he would contest the seat of Barton was made at a press conference at his Mosman home. 'Some of my friends tell me that I am crazy', he said. He talked about the financial losses he was incurring: a salary of £3000 a year, and an assured pension within five years of half that amount. But he positioned himself as nobler than that: 'All I can say about that is … that it is my duty to accept the special call which has been made on my service'. He explained the reasons for his decision:

> But for the emergency which today faces us all alike, I would not
> think for a moment of leaving the Bench where I have served
> for a period of nearly ten years. Yet the emergency is as grave as
> possible. By day and by night, our kinsmen overseas have to face
> unspeakable terrors.

He observed that in England there were precedents for judges taking up political office, and that Latham had recently 'assumed a high diplomatic post' in Tokyo. But even if there were no precedent, he said, it would be 'better to create one at a time when our govern-mental system, including the judiciary itself, is imperilled. In time of war or emergency, following the beaten track may be dangerous, even fatal'. He promised to do his 'very utmost to serve' and noted that the challenges were not only 'the perils and disasters of war', but equally 'restoring and improving the social and economic standards' of Aus-tralians. Knowing the tenacious efforts Evatt had put into his return to politics, knowing his will to power, this of course sounds unctuous, but it was also an understandable way of presenting the decision in the best political light: as an exemplary sacrifice in the interest of the nation. It would have been foolish to say he had been angling for just this opportunity.

From this point dates Evatt's first appearance in a newsreel. Mov-ietone and Cinesound newsreels, hugely popular and shown before the main film in cinemas, were important in presenting Australian leaders to the citizens. A few might meet their local member in person at meetings, and many heard their disembodied voices over the radio, but newsreels were the only way for politicians to visibly present them-selves to a mass audience. Before television, newsreels were a critically important medium not only for reporting the news, but also for citi-zens to see and hear those who made the news, assessing their bearing, discerning their character and putting a face to the name.

Evatt's first appearance on film is short and quite formal. The newsreel opens with a shot of the ornate front of a large building, identified by a simple wooden plaque on a post in the grass as 'High Court of Australia'. Evatt and Mary Alice walk towards the camera, he dressed in a dark suit with waistcoat, hat and overcoat over his arm, she in a smart dress and jacket, with a frilled blouse, rakish hat and gloves. He is holding her elbow as they walk past the camera with eyes resolutely on the future. The camera cuts to a desk in a study, probably the library at Mosman that Mary Alice had designed to modern taste; the desk is strewn with papers and bookshelves are crammed behind it. Evatt enters slowly from right of screen and sits down. He looks a little awkward. At the age of forty-six, he still looks young, with a strong jaw and discerning eyes. Up to this point all has been silent. In a close-up, he takes off his glasses and looks directly and intently into the camera; from that moment, he never takes his eyes off the viewer. He recites a prepared statement without notes. 'After ten years on the supreme judicial bench of the Commonwealth, it is not easy to say goodbye. But the present emergency is so great, everyone must do his duty as he sees it before him.' As the picture quickly fades, he is still resolutely looking into the camera. It lasts only forty seconds, but was enough to establish for a mass audience that a judge was doing his duty and this was newsworthy.

Once announced, Evatt's candidature was considered sensational. Evatt was a celebrity candidate, and some Labor figures were confident his stature and credentials would make the party more attractive to the middle class. Boote wrote that his decision had excited the papers and his name was all over them. 'All references highly eulogistic', he said. Evatt's biography of Holman was being favourably reviewed and Boote said it had appeared at a propitious time for him. 'I know no luckier man.' Clyde Cameron, already a powerful figure in the labour movement, and later to be a critical figure in the 1950s, recalled that Evatt 'brought a degree of respectability to the Labor party. The fact that the Labor Party could attract a High Court judge to its political ranks was seen by floating voters as something in favour of the Labor Party. Don't think there's any doubt about that.' Calwell later argued Evatt's entrance into politics 'won us at least six seats'. Claude McKay thought similarly, recalling that when Evatt announced his move there was consternation in the non-Labor camp: 'For Evatt manifestly would influence the middle-class vote Labor's way. And so it proved to be'.

The day Evatt's candidature was announced, the newspapers carried enthusiastic comments from a range of political figures, including some conservatives. Many spoke of patriotism and of sacrifice. Evatt's decision was described as a 'splendid national gesture', which was 'courageous and public-spirited'. The same theme of sacrifice was central to Evatt's farewell from the High Court, crowded with barristers and solicitors who 'had to find a foothold in the jury box and witnesses' enclosure'. Sitting alone on the bench, Evatt was pale; he 'spoke with emotion, and almost broke down'. A representative of the Bar Association said Evatt was doing his duty in the service of 'Australia and the Empire'. In his reply, Evatt said he was 'deeply touched'. He quoted Isaac Isaacs on the retirement of Henry Bournes Higgins; Higgins had always, Isaacs said, 'searched for the right with a lamp that was lit by the flame of humanity'. That choice to associate himself with Higgins and Isaacs reflected the liberal inheritance he was bringing into the labour movement.

Evatt presented himself in much the same way in a letter to the electors of Barton during the election campaign. It mingled a breath-taking estimation of what he had to offer with explicit references to his sacrifice:

> I now make a personal appeal for your assistance. I believe that you require my services to assist Australia and the Empire in obtaining victory in war and also social security in peace …
> I have tried to give a lead not only to the people of Barton, but to the people of Australia. I have voluntarily surrendered a life of affluence, security, power and comparative leisure in order to face afresh the troubles and anxieties of parliamentary life. I have had in mind the far greater sacrifices of the illustrious men of the A.I.F. I believe you will approve of what I have done.

Before we judge this as more of Evatt's self-aggrandisement, it is worth considering two points. First, Evatt was unknown in Barton and did not live in the area, so it made sense to position himself as making a sacrifice in seeking election. Second, his own sense of self had been inflated by the support he was receiving. Letters of congratulation were pouring in and must have reinforced Evatt's own estimation that he had made a great sacrifice in the interests of the nation. While Labor colleagues often saw the thrusting, bustling Evatt as overly ambitious, many of his supporters saw only the noble side to his actions.

Nettie Palmer wrote with 'general congratulations and perhaps personal thanks'. Even the chronically grumpy Starke wrote to congratulate him: 'How much I admire the big decision you took last week, and how I rejoice that the whole country seems to have considered it the right one'. Evatt's artist friends the Hinders revealed their own priorities by asking he tackle 'a few tasks which need attention'. They asked him to 'kick out the National Gallery Trustees' and 'build a gallery for contemporary art, with theatre attached'. Many strangers wrote offering congratulations; a publisher claiming to speak for the 'middle, non-Labour classes' told Evatt: 'We expect you will give us leadership and inspiration'. The secretary of the Collingwood Football Club wrote to assure him of the club's 'deep admiration and profound respect ... which is now greater than ever by reason of your patriotic and courageous action'. The secretary of the Balmain Leagues Club also wrote with congratulations 'upon your most unselfish and public spirited action'; he offered the use of a car for the campaign.

Some hoped he could heal Labor's wounds. Jim Ormonde, then a journalist and Labor party member, was to be an influential player in the split with the anti-communists in the 1950s. He wrote introducing himself as someone aligned with Beasley, but who hoped Evatt could heal the rift in the party:

> On the day you were farewelled by the members of the Bar, I was
> close enough to the proceedings to realise the great respect you
> commanded from your brother lawyers. I was proud of the fact
> that you were retiring from your position of honour, to take your
> place at the helm of Labor, in the parlous times ahead ... The
> Labor movement needs you, not only as a leader, but as a healer.

Running through these letters, which Evatt kept and filed, were several themes that boosted his estimation of himself. The most obvious was that of sacrifice, while a second was that he was exceptional, and his country sorely needed his talents; a third was the more obviously political expectation that he should provide leadership for the party. None of it would have dampened Evatt's own self-regard, and suggestions that he might take over the helm would only have fuelled his dissatisfaction with Curtin's leadership.

Two letters came from different directions, both dated the day he announced his candidacy. One was from the distant past, from a soldier who had been close to Frank in the war. Congratulating Evatt on 'the splendid step you have taken', he wrote: 'I know Frank would approve what you have decided'. Another was about the future. Les Haylen wrote on the letterhead of the *Australian Women's Weekly*, where he was chief subeditor and leader writer. He offered his services 'in a voluntary capacity ... in publicity and as press liaison man'. He was free in the evenings and gave his phone numbers. In addition, he asked to 'do a domestic story on Mrs Evatt' for the *Weekly*. Evatt took up Haylen's offer and it was the beginning of a long association, in which Haylen always supported Evatt, whom he joined in the parliament in 1943.

The *Women's Weekly* article appeared two weeks later, with a family photo of the Evatts and their children. The big living room at Mosman was described as 'filled with brightness and color'. Peter and Mary Alice were answering the 'almost non-stop phone calls' while Rosalind, aged eight, 'bounced backwards and forwards from the radio to the breakfast table', where Dr Evatt quietly got on with his breakfast. Evatt told the reporter he had 'felt like a kid' when he made his decision. It was Peter, he claimed, who convinced him to stand, in a phone call from school. He spoke about taking risks and being adventurous, and that reminded him of his mother:

> Looking back I realise that my mother was an adventurous, courageous woman ... We were not a wealthy family, but if mother ever had fears for us we never knew them. She was most ambitious for us all, urging us on to grasp every opportunity for more education ... When I won three scholarships I knew she was proud of me, but she also gave me the feeling that I might have won four.

Perhaps poor Peter groaned in the background, but we can see how this talk of opportunity and ambition, and the friendly family portrait of a celebrity candidate, would appeal to middle-class aspirations.

Menzies, meanwhile, was unenthusiastic; he said the precedent of a judge stepping into politics was 'most regrettable', and that Evatt should not be portrayed as a 'sort of non-party candidate', insisting: 'He will be a pledged member of the Australian Labour Party as I believe he was before that party put him on the bench'. Evatt replied that Menzies was 'acting with scant generosity' and failing the 'dictates of Australian sportsmanship'. The *Truth* in Sydney was a little snide, saying that Menzies, 'with his grand manner', had created 'an impression of superiority which he really does not possess'. Evatt was his equal, *Truth* wrote, and 'fear of Dr Evatt has made him churlish'.

'The will to power'

From the end of August 1940, Evatt was set for the election campaign. He had barely been endorsed as a candidate before he was running into trouble with Labor sensibilities and power structures. Boote thought his first speeches disappointing – 'poor matter and dull delivery. Will have to do better to make his mark in politics'. He had focused too much on criticising Menzies, and hardly mentioned Labor's program. At a later public meeting where Curtin spoke well, Boote thought Evatt was still disappointing, though the crowd was determined to be pleased and there was 'more enthusiasm than discrimination'.

Having offered himself as a volunteer, Haylen began working for Evatt immediately, and later recalled the campaign:

> We drank gallons of coffee at the Mocador Café in Elizabeth
> Street and brought strange and sinister men to see him, holy
> men and Union leaders, his old schoolmaster and his old school
> mates, tycoons who were fearful that we were losing the war and
> their profits, and just plain adventurers who wondered how wide
> the bandwagon was going to be and if there was a place on it for
> them ... a massive campaign was launched, and carried on till the
> very last day before the elections. The result was sensational. Evatt
> had a big majority.

After the 21 September election, a *Sydney Morning Herald* editorial conceded Evatt's success 'was regarded as inevitable from the outset', though his majority was even more 'striking' than expected. He had won with an absolute majority of almost fifty-six per cent of the vote, taking the seat from the UAP.

For a week it was unclear whether Curtin had been re-elected in his seat of Fremantle. Finlay Crisp, who was working in the federal public service at the time, wrote in his biography of Chifley that Evatt was 'most ebullient and vocal' in putting himself forward. He later wrote to Tennant that during that week Evatt was 'trying to round up votes' for the Labor leadership, even though he had 'not yet spent a day' in parliament. Evatt began issuing press statements advocating terms under which Labor should join a bipartisan national government; Menzies repeatedly offered the prospect, but it was anathema to Labor, and especially to Curtin. A Labor federal conference had in May explicitly voted against joining a national government, and Curtin feared it would lead the party into complicity with conservative policies and would split the labour movement. Billy Hughes responded to Evatt's overtures by saying he was 'blowing soap bubbles in the sun

… the bigger they are the louder they pop'. And Boote was outraged: 'Has Evatt so soon forgotten that Labor is strongly opposed to joining a Capitalist ministry?' In the days after the election, Boote had discussions with angry labour movement people who thought Evatt was undermining Curtin. At Trades Hall, one 'shook his head over Evatt', saying: 'He's mad for place and power!' Buckland was 'disgusted', complaining, 'He thinks only of his own interests'. Boote wrote of a friendly enough argument with Evatt in his office in which he tried to dissuade Evatt from public arguments for a national government, and noted afterward: 'I could see that he is eager to be a minister, and that this eagerness governed his line of reasoning'.

Once it became clear the election had resulted in a deadlock, with neither party having a majority, the situation changed. Labor now argued they had as much right as the conservatives to form a government. Evatt took that view as well, but still raised hackles with his habit, as one critic put it to Boote, of 'pushing his own barrow too flagrantly'. Buttrose also commented on his impatience: 'As soon as he came to Canberra, of course, he came as though he [had] bought the place'. Once it was clear Curtin's seat was safe, Evatt set his sights on winning the deputy leadership. Boote was asked in mid-October by party figures – 'the boys' as he put it – to tell Evatt not to thrust himself forward so much; it was too early to push for the deputy position, and he 'would be wise to restrain his ambition a little'. When Boote tried to get Evatt on the phone, Mary Alice answered; she was clearly better at soothing the hostilities Evatt raised, assuring Boote that her husband 'only wanted to serve the movement'. A few days later, Evatt took the advice and withdrew his nomination for the deputy leadership.

Menzies' UAP, in coalition with the Country party, was still able to govern, so long as it maintained the support of two conservative independents who held the balance of power. Menzies continued to offer the prospect of a national government, but in October, Curtin again rejected the idea; Labor instead proposed forming an Advisory War Council (AWC), as a joint-party meeting without executive power. On 23 October, the caucus elected Curtin, deputy leader Frank Forde and Norman Makin as Labor's representatives; Beasley represented the Lang Labor group. Evatt had put himself forward, but was passed over. He was ill and missed the meeting, but Crisp would later comment that his precocious bid for the deputy leadership had 'cost him a place on the Advisory War Council', along with 'his indiscriminate preaching' of a national government. The newspapers noted the rebuff, and attributed it to the hostility Evatt's assertiveness was creating.

Evatt now wrote to Peter, at Geelong Grammar, on the letterhead of the House of Representatives. He said he had been ill with influenza. 'At one time it was touch and go with pneumonia ... Mother has been simply marvellous to me – as she always is and I simply don't know what would have happened without her.' He wrote 'in politics, things did not go so well'. He thought Labor had 'foolishly' agreed to the AWC, because it had 'no powers, only a right to give advice'. In the caucus vote, he wrote, he had narrowly missed out being elected, and given his absence, and the fact that he was something of an unknown, for 'few of the men had even seen me more than once', he thought he had actually done well to even come close:

> All the same I was profoundly disappointed and somewhat
> shocked as I might have done something to make the body
> successful ... one must expect setbacks especially as there's so much
> jealousy and pettiness. The thing that's good to remember is that
> I got a splendid vote at a time when being absent was a severe
> handicap ...

As always, he finished by reminding Peter to study hard: 'Go all out for matric, learning vocab and grammar regularly every day and also mastering English grammar which is easy and very interesting – if you set your mind to it'.

He might have written positively to Peter about missing out on the AWC, but he wrote a bitter, peevish letter to Curtin. After thanking Curtin for a telegram concerning his health, he launched into recriminations. He evidently thought Curtin was not according him the respect he was due as the star candidate of the recent election. 'I have good reason to complain that your friendly attitude towards myself was not continued after the day of polling. Many friends of mine have felt this very keenly.' He went back to an earlier grievance; before the proposal for an Advisory War Council had emerged, there had been talk of a conference with the UAP to explore forms of political co-operation. He accused Curtin of having 'hesitated and vacillated' about this proposal; once it was agreed to, Evatt was elected as one of the three Labor negotiators, but felt Curtin had then let him down: 'I was entitled to the frankest and fullest consultation by you. I did not get it. There is no evidence that you did better by ignoring me'.

Evatt's antagonism is palpable in this handwritten letter; he had no respect for Curtin as a leader, who he described to friends as 'nettish', or timid. In spite of all this bad treatment, he now wrote, he had put himself forward for election to the Advisory War Council, and had again been let down:

> Yesterday morning Forde solemnly and deliberately assured me
> – by phone – that I could depend upon you and him for support.
> If I stood, my election would be a certainty! On this, I decided to
> stand. The assurance was not honoured and while on my sick bed,
> unable to encourage my friends or face my enemies ...

The letter broke off here and is incomplete; as I turned the page in the archive there was nothing further. Evatt was clearly working up to a plangent aria of complaints: he was not appreciated, he was being ignored, and on his sickbed he had been abandoned. I do not even know if the letter was sent; if it was, Curtin would surely have shown it to Chifley and Scullin, who were the supports he most relied on. The three of them must have wondered how to deal with this turbulent spirit. Even if it was never sent, as a reflection of his state of mind it blares out his frustration, and his aggression towards Curtin; he had stepped down from the High Court and now his ambitions were being thwarted.

Evatt told Boote at this time that he had been 'seriously ill, pneumonia being narrowly averted', that he was 'disappointed and disgusted' with the Labor party, and they were going to Leura for a few days' rest. Labor, Evatt complained, was afraid to press for power, and Curtin was 'woefully timid'. He said the party had no 'will to power', a phrase he used several times when speaking to Boote. Throughout November, Evatt complained about Curtin's fear of taking responsibility; if Labor would not take up Menzies' offer of a national government, then Labor should seize power by cultivating the two independents to support a vote of no confidence. Boote wrote in early December that Evatt thought Curtin 'hopeless as a leader at a time like the present, when militant action by the Party to defeat the Government and assume power was necessary'. Everyone knew Evatt was avid to bring Labor to power, and his contempt for Curtin was barely disguised.

Evatt's advocacy of a bolder line drew him some supporters, and he emerged quickly as a leader of the 'militants'. Meanwhile Curtin and the party leadership urged restraint. They did not trust Jack Beasley's group of four, who would be needed to form a government; negotiations to bring them back into the party were not concluded until February 1941. A decade before, 'Stabber Jack' had brought down the Scullin government, and Scullin remained a mentor to Curtin. Curtin and his supporters were also uncertain of the votes of the two independents who kept the UAP in power, and would be required to keep a Labor minority government in power. And they worried they would face a hostile Senate. They did not want to come to power just yet, preferring to wait for better circumstances. Labor was often referred to in this period as a 'benevolent' opposition, keeping Menzies in power.

Meanwhile, Evatt was 'like a bee-in-a-bottle after office', as Crisp put it in a letter to Tennant. Curtin tried to rein Evatt in; Chifley, always protective of his leader, resented the pressure Evatt was putting on him. 'Chifley rarely spoke ill of people he crossed swords with,' Crisp wrote. 'But he was fierce about Doc's making difficulties for Curtin on the National Government issue'. In December, Evatt was the only Labor figure of any prominence to campaign in an unsuccessful by-election for the seat of Swan in the west. The press commented that Labor appeared to treat the by-election with 'indifference', because to win another vote in the parliament would force them into government, a prospect that seemed to hold little interest for them. Part of Curtin's reluctance was that he knew the Swan candidate had ties with the Communist party. Evatt was not the only one to complain to Boote, who noted that the 'old brigade' in the Labor caucus were 'afraid of office under existing conditions', and preferred collaboration with Menzies. 'What a situation!' But Boote also saw how Evatt was 'passionately desirous of office', writing in January 1941 that this coloured all he said.

During this period, the war in Europe was moving into an increasingly global phase, though the Pacific war did not begin until the end of 1941. With the Nazis in control of western Europe, and Britain isolated, a new front had opened in north Africa in June 1940. In September of that year, Italian troops had massed in Libya, intending to move east into Egypt and take control of the Suez canal; in early 1941, Australian troops were among those who successfully held up the advance at the Libyan port of Tobruk, which was then besieged by German troops. The Australians were under siege in Tobruk for seven months. In April and May, Australians were part of a disastrous attempt to occupy Greece to block a German invasion. Then in June, Hitler broke the pact of convenience with Stalin and launched Operation Barbarossa, the invasion of the Soviet Union and the largest military operation in history. It was to be a truly titanic struggle, ending in German defeat by mid-1943. Meanwhile, Japan had completed its occupation of Indochina by July 1941, and continued moving south. Churchill was working hard to bring the United States into the war; in

August he and Roosevelt signed the Atlantic charter, which began to outline a postwar order of national self-determination, freedom from want and a new international security system. It showed that America, while still isolationist, was not entirely aloof, even before the attack on Pearl Harbor in December.

Throughout 1941, Evatt was complaining in private about Curtin's timidity, and in public made statements advocating either the formation of a national government or toppling Menzies. When the membership of the Advisory War Council was expanded in March, Evatt was elected, but he remained frustrated that its role was only advisory; power remained with the UAP. When Menzies, in London in April, again called for a national government like that in Britain, Evatt argued that the way to do this was to give the AWC executive power. The *Argus* applauded his 'realism of outlook', but Boote had a fierce argument with Evatt in a phone conversation late that night:

> He denied that his statement in the press was in advocacy
> of a National Government. What he wanted was a Labor
> Government, but Curtin and others would not displace Menzies.
> Failing a Labor Government, he (Evatt) was in favor of giving
> the War Council executive powers … He disputed my assertion
> that if the Labor Party joined the Menzies Cabinet it would
> precipitate the biggest split in Labor's history.

In late May, Menzies had returned from London, arriving by flying boat at a landing pontoon at Rose Bay in Sydney. Evatt went to meet him, representing federal Labor. On his arrival, Menzies famously, and tactlessly, lamented the need to return to 'play politics' once again; it suggested his heart was really in England, and local politics was beneath him, though he may only have meant he was weary of his own precarious political position. Mary Alice recalled Evatt's view at this time; he felt the war was not being waged energetically, and objected to talk of playing at politics. 'He didn't feel it was playing at all', she said. 'He felt it was a serious matter of life and death for the country and the people.'

The day before Menzies' return, Evatt drafted a two-page letter to his old rival. It was an attempt to deal directly with Menzies, behind the backs of Labor's leaders. In it, Evatt rehearsed what he saw as a desperate lack of war preparation and tried to explore a closer form of cooperation. He wanted 'closer association between the parties <u>for war purposes only</u>' and said there were alternatives between the present adversarial system and a complete division of executive posts between the two parties. The Advisory War Council, for example, could be given real power, as had been done in New Zealand. This was to a large extent going over the same territory, advocating a national government or at least some form of executive power for the council. But Evatt now seemed to hint to Menzies he was prepared to act alone. Could he have meant that he would join the government? This seems possible, for Evatt went on:

> I am worried to distraction about the disillusionment and the defeatism which are evident in so many places. I am prepared to co-operate with you to the very limit of my power providing you on your part will go 'flat-out' to achieve the objective I suggest ... My own purpose is to serve this country in the most suitable capacity for the period of this war and then to give up political life as a career. At present I am prevented from performing this service which the people wish me to give.

This was rather delusional, and certainly grandiose; he appeared to think that only he could perform this service.

But he went on to say that there were others 'in the same position', which seemed to hint that he might bring some Labor members with him and cross the floor to support Menzies' government. That may be reading too much into his words, and we can only speculate what Menzies made of Evatt's letter; I could find no reply in either

Evatt's or Menzies' papers. Did Menzies feel a glimmer of hope that Evatt could break off some ALP members to join his government? Did he imagine he could use Evatt's intemperance to split the Labor party? Did he recoil at the prospect of having Evatt in his government? He had enough trouble with his own party and few of them would have welcomed an alliance with disgruntled members of the Labor party. Quite probably Menzies dismissed it all as wild freelance activity, knowing the proposal was not Labor policy, and that Evatt had few followers. Crisp wrote that Curtin knew about this letter and 'squashed this move also'; it accounted for Curtin's 'preoccupation' at the time.

In his memoirs, Menzies mentioned nothing of this letter, and was somewhat circumspect. He wrote that before leaving for Britain in January 1941, he had again proposed a national government to Curtin, and repeated the offer from London. He returned to Australia in May, impressed by the all-party government in Britain operating under Churchill's leadership. In August he proposed that he go back to London to represent Australia in the British War Cabinet, but wanted approval from Labor. 'Curtin was prepared to have a favourable look at this,' Menzies said, but others, including Evatt 'who was a seething mass of frustrated ambitions, took the sinister view that the object of the exercise was to hamper the Opposition during my absence'. At first it appeared Labor would accept Menzies' proposal, but there was a marked shift of view in a caucus meeting. With growing awareness of the Japanese threat, some argued Menzies' place was in Australia. Evatt, along with others in the caucus, argued against releasing Menzies. Evatt was increasingly seen not only as criticising Curtin but also as potentially challenging his leadership, but that only rallied more support behind the leader.

In any case, Menzies' days were numbered; in August 1941, enough of his own cabinet colleagues made it clear they opposed him for him to decide to resign the leadership and he was replaced by the Country party leader, Arthur Fadden, as prime minister. Curtin still insisted that a challenge to the government had to wait till the budget; he was unsure of the reliability of the two independents, Alex Wilson and Arthur Coles. Both had been elected as independents, but were closer to the conservatives. Coles, of the family that built the supermarket chain, had joined the UAP and had then resigned in indignation at how the party had treated Menzies. Evatt was assiduously cultivating Wilson, visiting his Mildura electorate and planning for his support; in September, he wrote to Wilson that matters were heading for a 'showdown', and he suggested that his recent tour of Wilson's electorate had convinced him that 'your people want to see the coalition replaced by a Labor government'. Finally, on 3 October 1941, Wilson and Coles voted with Labor to defeat the government, and a few days later, with the Germans concentrating all their force on a drive towards Moscow, Curtin's minority government was appointed. Evatt was attorney-general and minister for external affairs.

His energetic manoeuvring, his consuming ambition to be in government, had come off. It had hardly been the most edifying episode in Evatt's career, and it had lost him friends along the way, colleagues who forever afterwards saw him as ambitious before all else. But he had not taken the momentous step to re-enter politics in order to wait. Alan Reid recalled Evatt telling him during this period about his family's military service; the deaths of his brothers in the First World War may have been on his mind. A seasoned journalist, Reid thought Evatt's ambition sprang not from wanting power, but because 'he believed he could be of service to Australia in its hour of need'. Reid found Evatt interesting, but was often sceptical about him; on this occasion, though, he was sure of Evatt's patriotism. Others were not, then or later, to make such delicate distinctions about Evatt's will to power.

9

The minister

From October 1941 to December 1949, Evatt was both the minister for external affairs and the attorney-general in governments under Curtin and then Chifley. Although his legal self was eminently suited to the position of attorney-general, during his long tenure Evatt was not a notably active law reformer; he was a legislator. He was responsible for extending voting rights to members of the military below the age of twenty-one (1943), significant changes to company tax and income tax (1941, 1942 and 1943), minor divorce law reform (1945), significant social security, housing and education laws that reflected work in other ministries (mostly in 1945), and legislation ratifying the United Nations and its organisations and dealing with postwar reconstruction (1944 and 1945).

This is not an insignificant, nor complete list, but it indicates the focus on implementing government policies, prosecuting the war and preparing for the peace, and extending Commonwealth responsibility in tax and social policies. Perhaps the most important legislation was the *Banking Act 1945*, which brought the private banks under the control of the Commonwealth Bank and in effect forbade state governments from conducting business with private banks; the later provision was held to be unconstitutional by the High Court in mid-1947. Being thwarted in regulating the private banks was partly what provoked Chifley's failed attempt to nationalise the banking system between 1947 and 1949.

Several major constitutional changes were attempted during the war. In October 1942, the Statute of Westminster was finally adopted, despite conservative protests; the metaphor they often invoked was 'cutting the painter', severing the rope that joined the Australian dinghy to the great British ship of state. Passed by the British parliament in 1931, the statute had effectively declared the political independence and autonomy of the dominions, as the self-governing colonies were now called, but Australian conservatives had resisted its adoption throughout the 1930s. Sawer described Evatt's efforts as 'conciliatory and patient'. His lengthy speech in parliament in favour of the statute was couched in emphatic but moderate terms; careful to steer clear of party division, he quoted Latham's arguments for ratification back in 1931. Canada and South Africa had adopted the statute, he pointed out, and it was in any case necessary to remove anomalies that meant some aspects of domestic law were still subject to the king's approval.

Evatt picked his way carefully through the legal and constitutional complexities; the tone of the speech is captured by one phrase: 'I have explained the origin of the Statute of Westminster … I shall now explain to the House the technical legal position'. He deflected anxieties that the effect might be to 'weaken the Imperial tie', arguing that the real link between Britain and Australia was 'the unity of the Crown throughout the Empire, our common allegiance to the King and the indissoluble tie of tradition and friendship which binds the two people'. Curtin's was still a minority government, so it was necessary to persuade some on the conservative side to accept Australia's status as a dominion in a commonwealth, rather than a colony in an empire. Passing the Statute of Westminster was a success, but Evatt's next project – an attempt to expand the Commonwealth's powers by referendum – was to lead to almost total failure.

'A kind of brute fact of nature'

Rather than being a reforming attorney-general, during the war Evatt inevitably placed much greater priority on his role as foreign minister. In this, he was extraordinarily energetic and quite successful. The Labor narrative is that he was the first foreign minister to strike out in an independent direction, the first to articulate an independent foreign policy, and that his tenure was marked by an ambitious liberal internationalism. There is a good deal in this, though it is worth repeating that he was relatively new to internationalism; his enthusiasm grew out of his advocacy of Australian national interests in negotiating with Britain and America about prosecuting the war.

In his first years as foreign minister, Evatt threw himself into arguments for greater attention to Australia's defence, prompted by Japan's alarming advance through South-East Asia. By the middle of 1941, Japanese forces had occupied the French colonies in Indochina, and in early December, attacked the US fleet at Pearl Harbor, bringing America into the war. During January 1942, the British colonies in Malaya and northern Borneo were overrun, and the US forces under General Douglas MacArthur retreated from the Philippines. The colonial regimes in South-East Asia were collapsing, and in late January, Japanese forces began to occupy the north coast of Papua New Guinea. In February came the first Japanese air raid on Darwin. By 15 February, the British fortress at Singapore had fallen, with thousands of Australian troops captured; three weeks later the Dutch colonists in Indonesia surrendered.

Fear of a Japanese invasion galvanised the Curtin government; one indication of the popular mood was Boote's diary entry in early January: 'All Australia taking the Pacific situation very seriously. A lot of people really scared, fearing a Japanese invasion'. Subsequent historians have doubted that an invasion was ever intended, and seen these anxieties as exaggerated, but they certainly framed Evatt's first overseas trip to Washington and London. He left Sydney by flying boat in mid-March 1942. This first 'mission' to America and Britain was significant for two reasons: it was during this trip that Evatt learnt of an important agreement between Britain and the United States, and he also changed the way the Americans saw Australia. Before the attack on Pearl Harbor, isolationist sentiment had restrained Roosevelt from direct military commitment; America prided itself on being 'the arsenal of democracy', supplying Britain with raw materials and food, ships and planes, but had remained outside the war. The Americans were now actively in the war, but at the end of 1941, Churchill and Roosevelt had agreed that the war in Europe would have priority over the Pacific – the 'beat Hitler first' strategy. The Australian government was not informed, although Earle Page was the minister in London and ought to have been able to report the news. Evatt only clarified this policy agreement during his 1942 mission. The lower priority given to the war against Japan only increased the urgency with which he argued Australia's interests.

Americans had also, until that point, assumed Australian interests coincided with British interests, and that Australia could be understood by reference to Britain. Grattan described this as 'seeing Australia very dimly through the British curtain which traditionally had hung around her'. Richard Casey, Australia's first representative in Washington, was unlikely to undermine this American assumption. A former UAP politician, he had been appointed in January 1940 as the minister, in effect ambassador; his full title was 'Envoy Extraordinary and Minister Plenipotentiary to the Australian Legation'. This was the job Evatt had angled for and, along with Latham being sent to Tokyo, it represented the Menzies government's initiative to have overseas representations beyond the traditional position in England. According to his biographer, Casey saw himself as an 'Anglo-Australian', with a dual identity founded in both countries. A perfect illustration was that just as Evatt arrived in Washington, Casey was considering an offer from Churchill to be the British minister for the Middle East; while Casey had the decency to check with Curtin before accepting, his move into a British government position illustrated how strongly he identified himself as simultaneously Australian and British.

Compared with someone like Casey, Evatt was a single-minded nationalist. As Grattan wrote: 'One of Evatt's contributions was to establish in the American mind the idea that there was an Australian nation. In Evatt they had before them an Australian nationalist of forceful, authoritarian personality'. Grattan emphasised Evatt's sheer physical presence and forceful, demanding advocacy. The Americans were facing someone who was patently not a diplomat, and who did not sound like an Englishman. Instead, Grattan wrote, in Evatt they were confronted with 'a kind of brute fact of nature':

> The Americans had on their hands an Ayers Rock Australian nationalist, standing brutally there and meaning what? It meant, in the present context that the British curtain around Australia had been rent – permanently … suddenly it was understood that Australia would have to be dealt with direct and *qua* Australia as an autonomous nation.

Grattan frequently commented that Evatt's approach was that of 'an advocate, a lawyer'. 'He had a "case" to make and he set about to make it in the only way he knew – the way of an advocate defending a client before a court. In this case the court was the government of the United States.'

Evatt's reputation preceded him and he was expected to be difficult. Concerned cables flew between Canberra, Washington and London. Sir Ronald Cross, the British high commissioner in Canberra, wrote to London in January 1942, describing Evatt and Beasley as wielding a 'strong influence' as 'the Government left wing'. Cross thought Evatt was 'exceedingly ambitious'; he 'probably desires to supplant Curtin' and he displayed 'anti-Whitehall prejudice'. Evatt, Cross wrote, would not 'hesitate to use highly intensified national feeling to gain his own ends regardless of what the effect might be on Empire unity'. Echoing this advice, Churchill – calling himself 'former naval person', as he did with Roosevelt – wrote to the president. Evatt and Beasley had prospered in Australian politics by showing 'hostility to Great Britain'; Churchill thought the failure of British sea power to protect Australia from Japan had only brought this sentiment to a head. He asked about Roosevelt's impressions of Evatt.

This was not only about Evatt's nationalism and 'anti-Whitehall prejudice'. At the end of 1941, worried about a potential Japanese invasion, Curtin had said publicly: 'Australia looks to America, free of any pangs as to our traditional links or kinship with the United Kingdom', and the British had been offended. Conflict between Curtin and Churchill had escalated during February over the return of Australian troops from the Middle East. Curtin was desperate to bring them back, but while they were at sea Churchill insisted on diverting them to Burma. Curtin tried to persuade Roosevelt, and wrote trenchant cables to Churchill insisting the troops were needed for Australia's defence.

Evatt wrote urgently to Felix Frankfurter, now on the bench of the US Supreme Court, to enlist his support. 'The whole incident' of diverting the troops to Burma was alarming, he said. 'Our home defence is most unsatisfactory … I only wish I could speak to you in person.' Evatt also gave his argument a distinctly political edge. Roosevelt should realise that a progressive government, whether in America or Australia, would be 'obstructed by its opponents in war as well as in peace'. They could not have their war aims determined by Churchill, 'so unsympathetic and hostile' to the labour movement. This letter, which Frankfurter passed on to Roosevelt, ended desperately: 'I left the Bench here to help in the winning of the war. I have no other object in life'.

Evatt's group left Sydney in early March 1942. This was his first flight across the Pacific, in a Catalina flying boat loaned by General MacArthur. These journeys were genuinely perilous; they involved flying without radio contact, hopping between Pacific islands in four or five stages, hoping the fuel would not run out, and being undefended against Japanese air attack. With rudimentary seating, the flights could be extremely cold, and in unpressurised cabins they required oxygen masks at any significant altitude. Mary Alice remembered that he hated air travel at first because it gave him 'a terrific headache': 'I think now it's because at that time the planes were not pressurised … later on they were and he never did get a headache then', she said. Evatt's intense fear of flying dated to this first Pacific trip.

Curtin insisted Mary Alice travel with Evatt, astutely recognising that she would calm his anxieties and soften his temper. She recalled that it was 'quite unprecedented' to have a woman on an American Navy plane, and Curtin had to appeal directly to Washington, from where the reply came 'send her over'. She was instructed about what to do if they were shot down or for other reasons had to land in the water; flying boats were cumbersome and slow, but 'in one sense much safer' because they could float. She was shown how to inflate the life raft, and where to find the emergency rations and 'a fishing line and a knife concealed in part of the raft'.

They flew from Sydney to Fiji, breathing in fumes from the additional tins of petrol stowed in the cabin, then to Canton Island (in the Kiribati group), where they landed in the lagoon. Because they had to maintain radio silence, no one knew they were coming; the Japanese had recently bombed the island, and they circled until they were confident they would not be shot down. From there, they flew to Hawaii, and had to dodge a balloon barrage intended to hinder attackers; businessman W.S. Robinson, who was in Evatt's party, recalled going to see the damage to the fleet at Pearl Harbor; his first reaction when he had heard the news of the Japanese attack had been 'great joy', he wrote, because 'it meant the salvation of Britain'. The final leg was in another flying boat to San Francisco. Mary Alice said that halfway across they were told they were reaching the point of no return, but were flying into a headwind with the prospect of running out of fuel. They climbed to higher altitude, where the winds favoured them better: 'So we proceeded on and we arrived with just enough fuel'. Evatt later wrote to Rosalind about this flight, keeping his anxiety from his ten-year-old daughter: 'I slept quite soundly, waking up to peep out of my window and find that I was higher up in the sky than the clouds were and not feeling a bit nervous, but as free and safe as a bird'.

Two advisers were travelling with Evatt and Mary Alice: A.V. Smith, a public servant from the Department of Supply, and Robinson. The latter was a major industrialist who, in partnership with W.L. Baillieu, had been a key figure in developing the Broken Hill mines and building an empire of metal industries. Robinson had advised Australian governments since the First World War and was with Hughes at the Versailles conference. Knowing another war was coming, he had in 1936 joined with the head of the mining giant BHP, Essington Lewis, to pioneer Australian aircraft manufacturing. In May 1940, as the German blitzkrieg overran France, Menzies had appointed Essington Lewis as director-general of munitions supply, with near-dictatorial powers to organise war production.

Like Lewis, Robinson was a distinct type of the patriotic capitalist, who seemed to know everyone in high places in America and Britain. They understood total war meant more than military and diplomatic strategy; it meant the economic mobilisation of production, competition for resources, innovation in industry and above all the politics of command. Japan had occupied South-East Asia not just for territory, but for rice, rubber and petroleum; Rommel had attempted to cross Egypt to seize the Suez Canal because it would sever a vital artery of the British empire. Captains of industry were not all that different from those military chiefs who, at their best, could think in terms of geopolitics as much as military tactics. Later in 1943, Robinson said something about Evatt that applied equally to himself. Evatt, he said, understood the conduct of war was not merely for military chiefs; 'There are vital questions of political and diplomatic policy involved as each phase of the war develops'. Robinson's extensive government and business contacts in Britain and America were invaluable, and by the end of the first trip in 1942, he and Evatt were referring to themselves as 'the Oldtimers'.

Shortly after Evatt's party arrived in Washington, Frankfurter wrote to Roosevelt about how to handle him: 'You know how sensitive poor relations are – and the Australians feel like poor relations. What is needed is to satisfy them psychologically'. He recommended that if Evatt had 'recognized and regularized participation' in decisions, it would prevent 'irritations kept alive and intermittently renewed'; but he added a rider, saying Roosevelt might 'recall Balfour's remark that equality of status does not mean equality of function'. It was all quite patronising, and suggested the clear limits to be placed on Evatt's influence. By the time Roosevelt received this letter, he had already acted, establishing a Pacific War Council, which he chaired, with representatives from Australia, New Zealand, China, Canada and the Netherlands.

Grattan recalled that as soon as they met again in New York, Evatt said to him: 'I have come to bang on closed doors. That's what I have to do, isn't it Hartley?' Evatt had what Grattan called a 'fixed idea' that Australia's future would be determined in Washington, and Grattan thought he was right: 'Therefore he had to get through those closed doors'. At Evatt's first press conference in Washington, he was blunt: 'We want the right to consult the US and the United Kingdom governments on an equal footing'. A few days later, he insisted in a speech that 'effective machinery for consultation' was required: 'It is not a matter of satisfying national pride, for the fate of every Allied nation is involved'. Evatt's forthright speaking impressed American journalists; one described him as 'the most invigorating visitor to the US since Mr Churchill'. But he was soon seen as more amenable. After his first meeting with Lord Halifax, the British ambassador in Washington, Halifax reported: 'Having expected to dislike him, I found myself largely and rather pleasantly disappointed'. He thought Evatt was starting to see the larger picture, especially the need to 'maintain Russia' in the struggle with Germany.

The British ambassador was not alone in expressing such sentiments. In the same letter to Roosevelt in which he described Evatt as like a 'poor relation', Frankfurter went on to tell a story:

Evatt is most eager to play ball and has a fair perspective of the total situation. He said a poignantly moving thing the other night at a private dinner given him by the Council on Foreign Relations in New York, at which I presided. After stating the special situation of Australia, he said, very quietly, 'Please, gentlemen, don't misunderstand me. If I have to choose between my country going under and England going under, I should want my country to go under. For England is the bastion of us all.' And that is really his deep conviction, as I know from intimate talks with him on the basis of old friendship.

Halifax passed the same story to Churchill, and commented that the audience was 'much impressed'. But it is doubtful an Australian audience would have been as impressed by Evatt's choice of Britain's survival over Australia's.

Evatt's relative success in having his voice heard reflects Grattan's comment about his forceful advocacy, often belligerent but impossible to ignore. He was making some progress. He was the centre of attention, and Roosevelt took pains to charm him; Ida Cantwell recalled that Evatt and Mary Alice had, since the 1930s, been 'mad on Roosevelt' and were 'full of admiration' for him. At the first meetings of the Pacific War Council, Evatt had modest success in extracting promises of more bombers to be sent to Australia; he had meetings with Roosevelt's most trusted adviser, Harry Hopkins, and drew attention to Australia's interests in the Pacific. Frankfurter told Roosevelt that Evatt was appeased: 'You certainly have taken the Austrylian into port', he wrote, the deliberate misspelling a wry reference to Evatt's drawling accent. He continued: 'Doc Evatt went off to Canada like a kitten that had wallowed in cream. I am urging him to go to London soon'.

The British evidently also decided Evatt must be charmed. He did not use the term, but Billy Hughes had advised Churchill to 'duchess' Evatt; he wrote that Evatt 'should be favourably impressed', as he was 'inclined to regard Britain with hostile eye'. But he could be brought round:

> If properly handled, given full recognition and himself and wife, taken up by Churchill, made much of, invited to all War Cabinets, given opportunity to spread himself and to announce important help, planes, ships, etc. to Australia he may be won right over. If that can be done it will have far-reaching effect on Government.

Hughes had passed this message through the high commissioner, who also wrote to suggest 'an exceptionally distinguished welcome' would be appropriate, and it would be good if Churchill could 'see a good deal of Evatt', who was 'inclined to disparage him'.

In April, Mary Alice and Evatt made a brief trip to Canada, which he described in a joint letter to Peter and Rosalind. Peter was now in the army in Australia, while Rosalind was staying with family friends. The Quebec hotel they had stayed in overlooked the St Lawrence river, and Evatt described the 'sheets of ice floating down the river in the night and being forced back by the tide in the morning'. It was exciting and dramatic, he said; now they were back staying at the Australian legation in Washington, and he described the squirrels wandering around the gardens. Next they were about to fly to England:

> We miss you both very much and we want you both to help us by looking after yourselves very carefully by being good children and you, Peter, by continuing to pay strict attention to your military duties and seeing Rosalind whenever there is a reasonable chance of doing so.

Rosalind remembered his vivid letters and how they made her feel she was with them; this one seems pitched more to her as a ten-year-old than to the twenty-year-old Peter.

Two weeks later, Evatt was back in Canada on his way to England, but Mary Alice had stayed behind in New York, ill with tonsillitis. Without her, and with only Robinson for company, he was anxious about the impending flight across the Atlantic, as he confessed to Mary Alice in a letter just beforehand:

> I've been so upset at the changes in arrangements that I hardly know whether I'm waking or dreaming: I'm putting a phone call in to you now for a last kiss over the phone ... the one important factor [is] safety and I am sure they are working on that alone. Last night we were instructed in the use of oxygen masks, and fitted out in complete uniforms for cold weather flying – a step-in one-piece suit (lined with sheepskin I think): very heavy but very comforting in the cold weather no doubt.

They flew in a British bomber. Evatt later cabled to Curtin: 'The trip across the Atlantic was bitterly cold and we were under oxygen for 90 per cent of the time'. Robinson remembered the sixteen-hour flight as 'pretty awful – no heating, no seats (not even bucket ones), a five-inch plank to sit on ... flying suits, a cumbersome parachute ... an oxygen mask which has to be lifted off the face every five minutes to prevent its freezing to the skin'. When they arrived near London, Robinson said, they 'struggled out of the bowels of the plane looking like nothing on earth'. Evatt was most anxious to be photographed, he added, 'but I declined'. Despite the ordeal, Evatt was described the next day in the press as 'looking well and rested after his trip'. Stanley Melbourne Bruce, the Australian high commissioner in London, met them at the airport and they were later going to 'dine and sleep' at Chequers, the prime minister's country retreat.

'Every hour may count'

Evatt and Robinson were in England for all of May. At his first meeting of the War Cabinet, Evatt argued that Australia's defences were still inadequate, but that 'if early reinforcements could be sent (particularly aircraft), the Japanese might be deterred from making an attack'; if there was an attack, however, Australia would have to 'divert much larger forces from other theatres'. That was a reminder that Australian troops were being used in North Africa, and that, in the absence of aircraft, they might have to be brought home. He insisted at a press conference that the 'beat Hitler first' strategy was absurd. 'Unless we fight all enemies, all in and all the time, we will defeat none … No decent person could permit the ravishment of Australia and New Zealand by Japan.' As in Washington, his blunt style impressed journalists. One wrote that his press conference was an 'exhilarating' experience: 'He was informative and succinct, and gave hard matter-of-fact replies … [it was] the most aggressive exposition ever heard at the Ministry of Information'. We can imagine how this first encounter with what Grattan described as Evatt's 'forceful, authoritarian personality' was received in London.

Evatt pressed hard for aircraft and additional supplies. He gave radio speeches, in effect going over Churchill's head to rouse popular sentiment. He spoke of the threat of a Japanese invasion of Australia, explaining: 'Even temporary occupation would be little short of death. That is how you felt in 1940. That is how we feel today'. Curtin had likened the fall of Singapore to Dunkirk and the Battle of Britain in 1940, and Evatt frequently drew the parallel with what he called the Battle of Australia in 1942. He also reiterated the ties of kinship, saying Australians owed 'the same allegiance to the King as you do, blood of your blood, flesh of your flesh'. The *Evening Standard* commented that he 'made his case in simple and moderate terms', and that Australia, 'by every plea of sentiment, interests and strategy, has a claim on the maximum assistance we are able to send'.

"Australia is back in the Empire ..."

The British had expected Evatt to be difficult, both due to reports from Canberra that he was anti-British, and due to umbrage caused by Curtin's recent turn to American support. Here he is depicted being welcomed back into the fold, in a telling image that comments on how the British saw themselves as a mother in their relationship with Australia. The caption reads 'Come now, Doctor; give mummy a big kiss and say you're sorry.'

John Frith, *Bulletin*, 27 May 1942

Churchill invited him on a train trip to northern England, where they toured munitions factories. It may have been during this train trip that Churchill spent time calculating how much brandy he had consumed in his life and then comparing this prodigious volume with the volume of the train carriage; it was an exercise which, while it somewhat discomforted the prudish side of Evatt, helped deflect him from nagging Churchill about aircraft. They both spoke at a public meeting in Leeds, and the warm applause for Evatt's speech was said to have impressed Churchill. According to a later report in Australia, it was 'immediately after that public demonstration that Mr Churchill gave his decision on the Spitfires'. The Spitfire fighter planes were to be Evatt's big success.

On 20 May, Evatt was preparing to leave for America, and wrote urgently to Churchill that he was 'desperately anxious to obtain finality' about military supplies; he appealed for Churchill's intervention 'to secure Australia against invasion'. He had a long list of requirements for guns and aircraft, including fighters, bombers and reconnaissance planes. Providing supplies would 'probably enable the majority of our forces serving overseas to continue to serve the Empire', he said, and would be 'a suitable recognition of what Australia has done to help the common cause'. The military bureaucrats were presenting obstacles, and he told Churchill: 'Only you can bring the situation to a head at once – every hour may count'. At the War Cabinet the next day, the military chiefs still argued that their focus should remain on defeating Germany, and that a Japanese invasion of Australia was unlikely. A few weeks earlier, a Japanese fleet had been defeated in the battle of the Coral Sea; it was the first setback to Japan's apparently relentless advance, and seemed to confirm their views. The strategic priorities of the war in Russia and North Africa were debated again, but Evatt kept insisting fighter aircraft were necessary for Australia's defence. Eventually, Churchill ruled that they would dispatch three squadrons of Spitfire fighters to Australia.

Robinson recollected the same story a little differently. He wrote that it was in the garden after lunch at 10 Downing Street – not at the War Cabinet – that Churchill, after hearing 'Evatt's eloquent appeal', finally agreed to send the Spitfires. Lord Portal, chief of the air staff, was 'obviously taken aback', saying, 'But Mr Prime Minister, fulfilment of your order will hurt—', to which Churchill replied, 'Portal, one does not begin to give until it hurts'. Portal was then at the cabinet meeting and proposed supplying American fighters instead; he may have been fighting a rearguard battle, and was overruled by Churchill. Especially in the context of anti-British resentment in Australia, the Spitfire squadrons would, as the cabinet minutes noted, have potent 'symbolic effect'. As Robinson put it, they were 'a great bunch of feathers in the cap of Dr Evatt'. But they were kept secret and it was not until March 1943 that their presence in Australia was revealed.

Evatt drafted a long cable to Curtin, outlining 'the work of our mission'. He said the 'grand strategy' to concentrate on Hitler before dealing with the Japanese had 'come as a great surprise to myself and, I have no doubt to you'; Australia's representatives in Britain had not reported it. He wrote that Churchill and the British military still argued that a full-scale invasion of Australia was highly improbable. Apart from protesting about lack of consultation, Evatt said he had mostly concentrated on ensuring MacArthur, as commander in the south-west Pacific, had the forces and equipment he needed. He now had a keener appreciation of the competing demands for supplies in different theatres of war, especially the titanic struggle in Russia. He told Curtin about the three Spitfire squadrons and suggested that, although they had to remain secret, Curtin make a general statement of appreciation. The mission, he thought, had been successful in raising Churchill's awareness of Australia's interests, and in making 'the British public and press more alive to our dangers and difficulties'.

While in London, Evatt had published a long article in *The Times*, discussing the changing relationship between Britain and the self-governing dominions. His argument combined an assertion of national independence with an appeal to what he called the 'tie of brotherhood and kinship' and the 'call of race'. The dominions had been full members of the League of Nations, which demonstrated their independence, and that had been confirmed in 1926 by the Balfour Declaration, which stipulated that this equality extended 'not only to domestic but to foreign affairs'. He was not inclined to remember the gloss that Balfour had added – and Frankfurter had shrewdly noted – that equality of status was not the same as equality of function. Instead, Evatt insisted that the dominions should 'be heard on all matters concerning the control and conduct of the war'.

Getting ready to leave London for America, he wrote to Mary Alice. He had stayed longer than expected because 'Curtin and Churchill between them wanted so much done here'. He was confident he had succeeded, saying: 'Churchill has become very friendly indeed and I certainly have not abated a single jot of our case for help in our danger'. He and 'Robby' were flying the next day in Churchill's plane, which was, he joked, like the New South Wales upper house – 'the best that money can buy'. Robinson recalled this flight across the Atlantic to Newfoundland, sleeping in what Churchill called 'the bridal suite', two bunks in the tail of the plane. With the turbulence, Robinson was pitched out of the top bunk. The anxious Evatt had not only put on his Mae West life jacket but also inflated it, and got wedged in the door trying to get into the toilet. 'It took the steward and I to release him' his travel companion wrote. After arriving in Washington, Robinson sent a dry note to Brendan Bracken, who was a friend and also Churchill's minister for information. He had overheard Evatt confess that when he arrived in Britain, he was critical of Churchill. 'I know now that I was wrong. Not only is he a Great man, he is the Only Man – the Only Leader in Britain and the Empire. It will be a pleasure to tell Roosevelt so.' Robinson added a postscript: 'He came, saw and Churchill conquered'.

Evatt and his group flew back across the Pacific to Australia by seaplane in late June. They had been away over three months, and he calculated they had flown for 300 hours. On arrival at the Rose Bay seaplane base in Sydney Harbour, Evatt announced his 'vital war mission' had resulted in dramatic improvements in supplies and forces for the Pacific theatre. 'I am certain that in the not-far-distant future nothing will be able to withstand [the] might and power of the United

Nations', he said. The 'United Nations' did not yet have the connotations of a world organisation. It was instead a declaration of unity among those opposing the Axis alliance, a formal agreement signed on 1 January 1942 in Washington by twenty-six nations, including America, Britain, the Soviet Union, China and Australia. The text built explicitly on the earlier Atlantic charter, with signatories pledging not to make an independent peace, and committing to the 'common struggle against savage and brutal forces seeking to subjugate the world'.

Cables back and forth between the British reported that Evatt had returned mollified, and that reports of his mission had alleviated Australian anxieties. Lord Gowrie, the governor-general, wrote to Churchill that Evatt had 'appreciated the personal attention you showed him'; he thought that the foreign minister now had 'a wider outlook on the war as a whole', adding: 'He is a curious creature and could easily be a thorn in one's side if taken the wrong way'. A little earlier, Frankfurter had written to Roosevelt along the same lines: 'The trip of Evatt has been very educative, for the general cause. It made him, largely, a United Nationser instead of merely an Austrylian!' He meant that Evatt had shifted from parochial nationalism to appreciating the larger strategy of the war against fascism. He had advocated for an Australian voice with some success, but in doing so had broadened his own view, learning more about the strategic problems posed by this most global of wars.

'Has Australia's voice been heard?'

Evatt's trip had been widely reported in Australia, though some resented his prominence and assertiveness. Boote recorded one Labor figure telling him many in caucus were disgusted at the publicity Evatt got in the 'capitalist press' and accused him of 'pulling wires to get it'. On the return of Evatt's group, the newsreels reported on his success. In one titled 'Dr Evatt Tells How Victory Can Be Won', he is sitting at a desk, with modernist images of kangaroos on the wall behind him. Only one hand is in view and that is clenched on the desk; he is dressed in a three-piece suit and speaking firmly and deliberately. He tells the viewer in his harsh drawl that MacArthur is a hero, but 'the most valorous man in the world can do nothing unless he's given full and adequate equipment'. Australians and their allies had to work together to get him that equipment, so he could 'achieve a glorious victory against the forces of Japan'. Mary Alice also received attention as the 'behind-the-scenes helper with her husband's important mission', as the *Australian Women's Weekly* put it. 'Mr Curtin told me to take care of my husband and the other members of the delegation', she said. 'That was my job and I did my best to do it well.' Mary Alice also had her opinions, though. Isolationist sentiment in America seemed to have disappeared, she said: 'One feels the Americans are really all-in in the war effort'. She spoke about meeting the Roosevelts and taking part in a women's forum in New York.

It was not until early September that Evatt made a formal statement in parliament about the results of his mission. He outlined the establishment of the Pacific War Council, offering it as proof that the Pacific war was now taken more seriously. He spoke about the struggle being waged in Russia, and reported that Molotov, whom he had met in London, 'showed the liveliest and most friendly interest in this country'. Evatt argued: 'It is essential to the future of the Pacific that Australia should always remain on the closest terms of friendship with Russia'. He spoke of his 'fierce concentration' on the question of supplies while in America and Britain, and finished with a rhetorical flourish: 'Has Australia's voice been heard in the Supreme Councils of the war? ... Yes, to a greatly increased extent'. That was a pointer not only to the purpose of the mission, but to the emotional and psychological resonance it had for Evatt. He had made himself heard.

During late 1942, Evatt was responsible for several events that would have consequences for civil liberties in Australia. While he was overseas, members of the tiny Australia First Movement had been interned, accused of fascist and pro-Japanese sympathies. The movement, led by the publisher P.R. Stephenson, was certainly pro-fascist and clearly anti-Semitic, but its members were never actually tried and found guilty of any offence. After his return, Evatt had some of them released, but three, including Stephenson, remained interned. Some, and especially Stephenson, saw Evatt's preparedness to hold people without trial as a blot on his record. Then in September 1942, Evatt introduced national security regulations clarifying the government's powers; the intention was, as he put it, to prevent 'irreparable injury to the nation' from actions which 'were likely to impede prosecution of the war'. In a context of the war, the regulations increased the powers of the state to suppress opposition, though he insisted they would not interfere with an individual's liberty 'unless there was good ground for belief that he was a menace'. In December, the ban on the Communist party was lifted. It had been imposed by the Menzies government in May 1940, almost a year after the pact between Stalin and Hitler made Russia ostensibly an enemy nation. Since Hitler's invasion of Russia, Australian communists had been released from the tortured position of justifying the pact, and were vigorously committed to the war against fascism. Evatt argued that the Communist party had 'been active in support of the war effort and of war production'. Although he said the decision implied 'no sympathy' for the Communist party, during the Cold War anti-communists would include it as evidence of Evatt's supposed indulgence and unreliability.

From late 1942, he was closely involved in the Curtin government's campaign to expand the Commonwealth's powers over employment, production and social welfare. Evatt's justification, set out in a national broadcast, was that increased powers were necessary to implement the promises of postwar reconstruction, to 'build up a peace economy based upon economic security and social justice'; he was also proposing these increased powers would be balanced by constitutional guarantees of freedoms of speech and religion. The first attempt to expand the Commonwealth's powers was through the constitutional mechanism of 'referral', by which the states would agree to legislate to transfer specific powers to the Commonwealth. But the states would not comply; at a constitutional convention in November, they agreed only to a transfer of a small number of powers, and only for the duration of the war, and even then some states did not go ahead with the required legislation. The other option was for the government to try for a constitutional referendum, but they cautiously decided to wait and not to include it in the August 1943 federal election.

It was not until the end of 1942, seven months after Churchill agreed to send three Spitfire squadrons that they arrived in Darwin. Even then, their presence was kept secret, as Curtin later explained, 'to exploit the element of surprise to the maximum extent'. In early March 1943, they shot down a number of Japanese Zero fighters near Darwin, and the secret was out. Now 'Evatt's Spitfires', as some newspapers called them, were exploited to the maximum extent for war publicity. The Spitfires were said to be 'invincible', having won the Battle of Britain, and sending them was evidence of Churchill's special interest in Australia. They were portrayed as Evatt's great success, and he spoke of them in Churchillian terms:

> Last year I thought that, in the final battle for Australia, as in the Battle of Britain, Spitfire aircraft … would help to make the difference between victory and defeat, and I think so still. By the grace of God, the people of Australia have not as yet been exposed to the horrors of invasion … We shall see what we shall see – our land gradually emerging from the shadow of death and disaster into the sunlight of victory and peace and rehabilitation.

The Spitfires then featured in a five-minute Cinesound newsreel extolling Evatt's success and defiantly challenging the Japanese to try to attack now.

This newsreel provides an insight into how the war was presented to movie theatre audiences, and how central Evatt was to the story.

The breathless narration opened by recalling the Battle of Britain, when Spitfires had 'saved England and the civilised world'. When December 1941 found Australia unprepared, it went on, the government decided that Evatt should go to Washington and London. 'In London, Churchill listened to Australia's voice ... And so, as a direct and spectacular result of Evatt's mission, Spitfires came to Australia ... a continuous stream of trouble for Tokyo.' The newsreel showed Spitfires roaring through the air, to the soundtrack of Wagner's 'Ride of the Valkyries', familiar to modern viewers of *Apocalypse Now*. Britain had remembered Australia in our hour of need, the narrator proclaimed.

Evatt was shown at the Darwin airbase standing before a microphone, surrounded by pilots and aircrew. To see these squadrons, he said, was a dream come true: 'I can't say how I feel about it, gentlemen. We owe their presence in Australia to Mr Churchill and to arrangements he made while I was in Britain'. He sounded diffident, almost humbled. Standing beside him was Arthur Drakeford, the diminutive former union official who was now minister for air. Looking for all the world like a small town mayor receiving beneficence from on high, Drakeford addressed Evatt: 'It is with deep gratification that I receive these aircraft ... as a result of your mission overseas. We thank Mr Churchill, we thank the government of Great Britain, and we thank you, sir, for the results of that mission'. This was rather obsequious – the 'sir' was telling of Evatt's prominence – and it certainly positioned Evatt as the hero of the story. Then followed more Spitfire footage and more Wagnerian music, with the narration building to a crescendo: 'Spitfires over Australia. Thrice welcome addition to our aerial defence ... Up in the north, fresh-faced youngsters expectantly watch the sky: "The Spits are here!" they say. "Now bring out your Zeros"'.

'His virile, disturbing presence among us'

Evatt's second mission to America and Britain in early 1943 had much the same purpose as the first: to continue arguing for more supplies and equipment and to insist on a greater voice in war planning. In January Churchill and Roosevelt had met with their military chiefs to settle strategy for the war at the Casablanca conference. The struggle in Russia dwarfed what was happening in North Africa and the Pacific; the siege of Leningrad was six months into its two-year duration, with famine and cold already taking appalling numbers of civilian casualties. The battle of Stalingrad had just ended with German defeat; it marked a turning point in the war, but that was not yet clear.

Against this background, Evatt was annoyed to be left out of the Casablanca planning, and was still insisting on higher priority for the Pacific war. The high commissioner reported to London that Evatt was 'very disgruntled' that military strategy 'should have been settled without Australia being consulted'. Evatt had criticised Churchill and Roosevelt for a 'lack of respect for democracy'. Curtin cabled Churchill in late February that he was sending Evatt again; when rumours circulated in Canberra that Evatt might never return, Curtin was testy with journalists; the idea was 'an utter fabrication', he said, as were suggestions that there were differences of opinion between the two of them. 'I am getting a little tired of these Press Iagos, who seek to destroy the unity of the Cabinet family.'

Evatt travelled again with Mary Alice and Robinson, as well as John Burton, who worked in external affairs but was attached directly to Evatt's office, and the economist Nugget Coombs, who had just been appointed as director of the new Department of Post-War Reconstruction. Arriving in San Francisco in early April, Evatt said Australia was at the limit of its capacity, and more equipment to fight the war must be made available 'to prosecute the war against Japan'. In Washington two days later, he was described as speaking bluntly in a 'fighting speech'. In New York, his speeches and press interviews attracted wide publicity. 'It is an open secret that Dr Evatt flew to [the] USA to amplify and speed up the flow of war equipment for the South Pacific, but the Australian concern over the postwar situation is not so well known.' Evatt was thinking ahead to American foreign policy after the war and hoped it would include maintaining the peace in the Pacific. He had brought films to show Americans what the fighting in the Pacific was like; they included footage of the naval battle in the Bismarck Sea and fighting on the Kokoda Track in New Guinea. At a viewing for '400 influential Americans', Halifax sat alongside the Russian ambassador, members of Congress and government officials.

Evatt wrote to Churchill from the Australian legation in Washington. He was eager to renew their friendship, 'which greatly helped to save my country from disaster'; he proposed they should have 'more intimate collaboration'. That was a little vague, but was another demand to be given access. In May, General George Marshall wrote to Roosevelt advising against giving in to any more of Evatt's demands for aircraft. 'Frankly he has pounded us with propaganda and personal pressure.' Eventually the solution was to promise the aircraft, but deliver them slowly. Three weeks later, Evatt announced to Churchill he was 'relieved' Roosevelt had approved the planes 'in principle', and he thanked Churchill for his support.

In June, Evatt was alone in New York and preparing to fly across the Atlantic. He wrote to Mary Alice, who was again, as she had the year before, staying behind in America rather than coming to England. Had there been some disagreement? He began by insisting: 'Please <u>never think</u> that I really desired to go on this trip to England alone … I just hated leaving you today – the one thing I yearn for is to be back home with you'. He recalled her constant advice and encouragement, and reminded her of the operation in 1922. He was aged forty-nine, and wrote that he had now been married to her for half his life:

> I'm afraid I have at times led you a merry dance into politics, things outside the beaten track. But through it all – our love has

survived, you have been the perfect wife – the perfect mother too. I'll miss you but almost every waking hour I'll be thinking of you and I'll dream of you too. I'm going off now to catch the plane with Coombs and Robby – they actually seem to enjoy this ordeal. You I suspect do also.

In London, the Australian high commissioner was anticipating another Evatt visit. Stanley Melbourne Bruce increasingly thought that the minister was doing 'incalculable harm', and in early May, he made the first of many acerbic entries about Evatt in his journal. It was hardly surprising the two clashed. Evatt disliked Bruce's patrician ways and thought of him as a 'Nat', the party Bruce led as prime minister when Evatt was in state politics; he suspected Bruce was too enmeshed in British networks and, unfairly, expected disloyalty. Bruce in turn thought Evatt's rudeness was potentially undoing all his own good work; he had been high commissioner in London for a decade and was highly regarded. Perhaps he was teased by doubts that Evatt's coarse colonial ways might remind English colleagues that, after all, he too was just a colonial.

Bruce captured in his diaries the comments of others deploring Evatt's rudeness. He wrote of a conversation in which Bracken praised Robinson as 'a remarkable man', without whom Evatt would be 'helpless and useless' in London – 'a Robinson Crusoe without his man Friday'. He was 'doing no good' in America and the press thought little of him, according to Bracken. A few weeks later, Bruce had a conversation with the British Admiral Somerville, who had recently met Evatt in America. Evatt had 'flared up' and accused Somerville of doubting him; the admiral had said he 'was not prepared to be talked to in that way'. In Washington Evatt had created a bad impression, Somerville said; he always seemed 'to be on the verge of saying something offensive and aggressive'. Bruce sympathised with Somerville over Evatt's 'ill-mannered outbursts'.

Anticipating his arrival, the London *Evening Standard* described him as 'keen-eyed, keen-minded Dr Evatt'. 'We recall his virile, disturbing presence among us a year ago ... He destroyed the complacent view that the then all-conquering Japanese could not invade Australia.' On arrival, Evatt told a press conference that during the previous visit he had not revealed just how weak were Australia's defences, and said again that Australia's position was 'analogous to that of Britain in 1940' and that 'Mr Churchill's allocation of Spitfires had been of inestimable value'.

Two weeks after Bruce lamented Evatt's 'ill-mannered outbursts', the two had a confrontation in London. Evatt had rung Bruce objecting to him meeting Coombs about postwar economic policy; Bruce thought Evatt 'insultingly rude' and when they then met in person, Bruce refused to sit down, saying he was not prepared to allow anyone to speak to him as Evatt had. When Evatt apologised for going too far, Bruce consented to sit and talk. Bruce's detailed record of their exchange is almost comical, with accusations bristling on both sides. Evatt complained Bruce was undermining his authority, and Bruce protested he was loyal to the government, and especially to Curtin, but that if he disagreed he would frankly say so. Evatt said he understood that, and that on his previous visit, he thought Bruce 'had supported him in every way after the first few days'. Bruce bristled at that, demanding to know what he meant by those 'first few days'; Evatt said he felt Bruce had resented his presence. Bruce protested that his 'only desire was to be helpful', but that Evatt must 'restrain his temperament'; he would not tolerate rudeness. Evatt replied that Bruce himself had 'considerable power of being offensive', but possibly was not aware of it.

Bruce then recorded what may have been a flash of insight into the fraught dynamics between them; he wrote that perhaps Evatt 'may have some justification' because any offensiveness on Bruce's part would be 'almost more offensive by being exercised with an infuriating courtesy'. Bruce's lofty and exquisite charm clashed with Evatt's brash and belligerent way with people. We only have Bruce's side of this confrontation, but can almost hear the grinding of teeth on both sides. Part of the dynamic between them was the 'infuriating courtesy' with which Evatt had been put in his place by a grandee of Australian conservatism.

Evatt and Robinson were in London for almost a month and got back to Washington in mid-July. There were no spectacular break-throughs like the Spitfires, and Churchill resisted any suggestion of more access to strategic decision-making. From San Francisco, Evatt sent another joint letter to Peter and Rosalind. He and Mary Alice were about to fly back across the Pacific, and his anxieties were at a peak as he dwelt on the hazards. One of the islands where the plane would land had recently been bombed: it was a 'very long tiring and dangerous trip', he wrote. 'One can never tell the dangers and possible disasters of such voyages.' He turned then to advice about what should happen if there was a 'disaster'. Like any will and testament, it revealed what was important to him:

> If anything bad happens I am sending you this message to tell you both:
>
> 1. That your mother and father love you so very dearly – always – thank you both for making our lives full of interest, happiness and fun.
> 2. That we have done our best to provide for your future but you both must work hard for your country.
> 3. That Peter must always as the elder child do his best to help and guard Rosalind.
>
> We have worked very hard together to serve and help Australia and the future of Australia which consists of the children of Australia like yourselves. It is very, very, very trying and hard to be away from you especially when mother was so ill.

Bless you and keep you safe and happy and busy.
Your loving Dad and Mum

Evatt's anxieties came to nothing and his party safely arrived in early August 1943, just in time for the federal election campaign. Reports had come back from England and America. Later, conservative editors would worry, as already Bruce did, that Evatt's 'virile, disturbing presence' was doing great harm, but in 1943 he was regarded as having succeeded in a necessary struggle to have Australia's interests recognised. An *Argus* editorial praised his 'overseas triumphs'; he was the only Labor minister 'who could impress himself in Washington and London as of equal stature with a Bruce, a Casey or a Menzies'. He would have liked such praise, and welcomed recognition as an equal in such company.

He appeared in more newsreels in the cinemas. One shows he and Mary Alice walking from the seaplane landing on Sydney Harbour, smiling and waving, he in his three-piece suit with his tie askew and she in a jaunty hat. He spoke of his 'delight' to return to Australia. Speaking direct to camera, confident but slow and authoritative, he said he had assured Curtin that large quantities of aircraft and other equipment were coming as a result of his mission, which would allow 'greater offensive action' against Japan. The *Women's Weekly* sketched another word-portrait of Mary Alice, describing her as 'a gifted artist, good-looking, blue-eyed, auburn-haired, with a broad, clever forehead'. She had made radio broadcasts in America where reporters were 'impressed' that she was the first woman trustee of the National Gallery of New South Wales. She spoke of the 'stimulating experience' of meeting 'so many interesting women', including Eleanor Roosevelt and Madame Chiang Kai-shek.

Evatt's prominence in the public realm at this point was remarkable. He was industrious and flourishing, and a leader taken seriously on the world stage. Behind Curtin and Chifley, he was the most prominent member of the government, and working prodigiously hard; he collaborated well enough with Curtin, though Curtin still did not trust him. He was full of physical and intellectual energy and seems to have relished his work; what he was doing was consequential, and exactly why he had resigned from the High Court. Yet he was still restless, and in the election campaign, was again seen to be agitating for cooperation with the conservatives in a national government. Just days after returning to Australia, he praised the cross-party work of the Advisory War Council, saying that it had 'the advantages of a National Government without its disadvantages'. He thought the council should continue, and suggested it would be even more effective if its membership were elected directly by the parliament.

This was not especially provocative, and nor was it an explicit call for a national government; a *Sydney Morning Herald* editorial applauded his 'detachment from party extremism'. But in the inevitable partisanship of an election, Labor figures suspected that Evatt was again arguing for a national government; Curtin was said to be 'mystified', and the Country party pounced on the apparent difference between them. Earle Page, back in Australia from London, said that Evatt, having made all the good arguments in favour of a national government should 'make his inevitable choice'. Arthur Fadden, the Country party leader, declared his pleasure that Evatt was now a 'convert', saying: 'I would welcome Dr Evatt in a National Government, to which our party is pledged'. Fadden was being mischievous. Labor was in power, and less than a fortnight later, would be returned with a resounding majority. While the Country party was reasonably united, the UAP was led by the ageing Billy Hughes, Menzies was still on the sidelines, and the party was disintegrating. There was even less reason than before for Labor to consider an all-party coalition with such a weakened opposition; yet, in this context, Fadden was inviting one of Labor's leaders to defect.

Alan Reid, then a correspondent for the Sydney *Sun*, told a story that appears to date to this incident. Reid asked Curtin for a comment about Evatt; Curtin said it was for Evatt to comment, but Reid said he was ill. Curtin replied, 'I think you'll find he's had a miraculous recovery', and showed him a telegram he had sent, telling Evatt to repudiate the national government proposal publicly or face the consequences, which were left ominously vague. Evatt promptly made a statement that he had been misinterpreted, and denied any thought of a national government. When Reid saw Curtin that night, the prime minister said: 'See. He recovered very fast didn't he?' The day after Evatt issued his denial, it was announced that he would take no further part in the campaign; he was in bed with acute bronchial influenza. Curtin was probably being a little droll when he sent a message that Evatt must 'do nothing to impair his health'.

Evatt had been forced to fall into line, but this episode had a prelude, going back to the previous February, and this may explain why Fadden was so quick to play mischief. Just before leaving for his second overseas mission, Evatt drafted an extraordinary letter to Fadden, though whether he sent it is unclear. He wrote that he had 'always been a keen advocate' of a joint party government, combining those who 'realise the dangers facing Western civilisation'. Labor 'extremists' were opposed, but some 'wiser heads' in the party agreed with him. The postwar world, he argued, would be tumultuous, and would need a government representing all sections of the community. Now he made an audacious proposal to Fadden: 'If we can get unity among the non-Labor elements then it seems that efforts should be directed to making a bridge on which some of the soberminded of the Labor Party may cross. This is not a fantastic dream'. It was, he reminded Fadden, what had happened with Hughes in 1916–17 and Lyons in 1931; in both cases a form of national government was achieved 'by the secession of a number of moderate-minded Labor members'.

What was he up to, and why was it even necessary? His earlier advocacy for a national government had been from opposition, and was a desperate attempt to get into power, but Labor was now firmly in power and he was a senior minister. What purpose was there in exploring what he called 'secession'? The most likely explanation is his ambition for the prime ministership; Labor was in power, but Curtin stood in Evatt's way, as would Chifley later. After all, Hughes and Lyons had not only brought 'soberminded' followers with them, but had each been made leader of a new non-Labor party and hence prime minister. Evatt appears to have been thinking he could do what Hughes and Lyons had done in the previous crises of the great war and the Depression. He may, however, have sensed the risk of what he was doing, for he scrawled across the top of this letter: 'Please Destroy and do not quote', suggesting he realised how explosive was his line of thinking.

Even if he did not send the letter to Fadden, the wily Country party leader would have known he had an opportunity to drive a wedge between Evatt and the Labor party. Evatt was widely known to support a national government, and his desperate ambition was widely recognised, to the extent that there were jokes about it. Hartley Grattan said his favourite was an imagined conversation between Prime Minister Churchill and the king. Churchill said, 'I feel Evatt is after my job', to which the king replied he was relieved: 'I thought it was mine he was after'.

Now, in the August 1943 election when Evatt's suggestions about a national government came up again, ambition was the interpretation many gave. One journalist commented on the 'odd streak' in Evatt which made him do 'puzzling things'; rumours about his 'large ambitions' were circulating, and the journalist suggested that when parliament resumed one should not be 'caught by surprise if Dr Evatt emerges as Prime Minister'. That he even composed the letter to Fadden indicates Evatt's thinking, and it shows that his political allegiances could be inconsistent. But above all, it reflects the consistency of his feverish ambition. Being a prominent minister was evidently not enough.

10

To San Francisco

Labor won a significant election victory on 21 August 1943, widely seen as vindicating their prosecution of the war. After two years of being a minority government, Labor now gained thirteen seats and had a commanding majority. The UAP was in a crisis of disunity, and it would take Menzies well over a year to repair the damage and put a new force together. Before the election, an opinion poll had been commissioned in Evatt's electorate, presumably by his electoral office; it showed that despite his absences and his reluctance to mingle in the tedious work of the electorate, a solid majority of those surveyed were satisfied with his performance. Evatt won in Barton with an increased majority and a swing to him slightly bigger than the swing to Labor across New South Wales. In a safe seat and with a strong government in place, the stage was set for the next, most expansive stage of his career.

The emerging postwar world

Like others, Evatt was thinking ahead to the postwar world, but it is striking how embryonic his thoughts were. He placed an exaggerated faith in the Atlantic charter, despite it being merely a statement of intent made by Churchill and Roosevelt, and then endorsed by other allied nations. He argued in speeches the charter meant nations must accept their international obligations, including obligations to assist developing countries. Australia, he said, regarded the islands to her north as 'crucially important'; the people of South-East Asia and the Pacific must be included in postwar 'economic collaboration', and Australia would have 'a particular interest in closer economic relations with her nearer neighbours'. He was showing some signs of attention to Asia, but this was not so much about Asia's postwar future, let alone decolonisation, as staking a claim to governance in the south-west Pacific.

In October 1943, Evatt made a long ministerial statement to parliament on foreign affairs. Paul Hasluck, who worked in the Department of External Affairs, described the process of writing this speech; a draft was prepared in the department, and Evatt then 'attacked it', converting it into an 'awful mess'. Hasluck was called in, and they worked together until 3 am; 'then the typists and I stayed there till dawn'. This statement, Hasluck said, 'probably has more bits of my own composition in it than any other speech on which I worked as his jackal'. Apart from the chaotic way in which it was written, the statement also shows how limited thinking was about the postwar world in late 1943.

In this ministerial statement, Evatt defended the League of Nations against critics who argued it had failed to prevent the war. The League had enshrined a 'theory of collective security', but he argued some member states had been too irresolute; they had allowed aggression to 'escape with impunity', and that had undermined the standing of the League. The obvious example he gave was Japanese aggression in Manchuria, against which the League had been powerless to act. He expected the League to continue after the war, with some 'clarification and amendment'. But while he spoke about the postwar 'international machinery' for security, it was not clear what that would look like.

In an argument he often made, he stated that Australia could not 'contract out of Europe', for both world wars had begun there. But Australia's 'predominant interest' lay in the Pacific and he expected a leading role in what he called 'an extended Australian zone' of security. He was referring not to South-East Asia, but staking a claim to influence over a crescent of islands – New Caledonia, the New Hebrides (Vanuatu), the Solomon Islands, Papua New Guinea and Timor – which he saw as providing a buffer against any future aggression from the north. At this stage, Evatt assumed the return of the Dutch, Portuguese, British and French regimes to the South-East Asian colonies that had been captured by the Japanese. When he looked north, he tended to see a strong Australian influence in the crescent of immediate islands, and beyond that benign colonial powers holding most of South-East Asia. It was not a vision that would last long in the postwar period, when struggles for decolonisation rapidly reshaped South-East Asia.

The domestic dimension of the postwar order involved Labor's campaign to expand the Commonwealth's constitutional powers for postwar reconstruction and economic and social policy. As discussed in the previous chapter, the attempt in 1942 to persuade the states to transfer certain powers to the Commonwealth had largely failed; the alternative was a referendum to amend the constitution. From early 1944, Evatt led the argument for the reconstruction and democratic rights referendum proposals, which sought expanded Commonwealth powers over employment policy, marketing, company law, production and distribution, national health, family allowances, Aboriginal rights and several other areas. Menzies was adamantly opposed, warning the citizens that Labor wanted to extend the reach of government as a precursor to socialism. Opponents in the states, such as Albert Dunstan, the Country party premier of Victoria, argued these were 'dictatorial powers', which 'paved the way for any aspiring Fascist or dictator'.

During July, Evatt engaged in a strenuous speaking tour in the lead-up to the referendum vote, with speeches across the country. In the Melbourne Town Hall, he spoke to a large public meeting, saying that Australia's development had been retarded by 'provincialism, financial bogies, selfishness, and short-sightedness'; democracy meant not just the right to vote, but 'the right to work and the right to the material needs of life'. After the meeting closed, he sat at the front of the platform and continued a discussion with 'a crowd of about a hundred people, who stayed on till the lights were turned off'.

All this campaigning came to nothing when the referendum was soundly defeated on 19 August. The success of the conservative mobilisation against it provided a major psychological boost to the demoralised non-Labor forces, which Menzies then adroitly brought together to form the Liberal party at the end of the year. A key weakness of the 1944 referendum had been to bundle together extensive powers on a take-it-or-leave-it basis. Two years later, in September 1946, Labor had learnt the lesson and tried again for a constitutional referendum, this time asking three separate questions. One of these proposals passed, extending the Commonwealth's power over social welfare, but proposals for labour relations and control over marketing failed. Apart from the adoption of the Statute of Westminster, the 1946 social services referendum was Evatt's only success in constitutional alteration.

Even after the 1944 referendum ended in rejection, Menzies was wary, suspicious that Evatt intended to use the constitution's external affairs power to achieve the same ends. Under the constitution, the Commonwealth government only has defined powers, with any others remaining with the states. External affairs was clearly a Commonwealth responsibility, and if the Commonwealth government entered into an international agreement within a policy area not strictly within its scope, it might then potentially claim its external affairs power allowed it to implement that international agreement; it might be able to override any state challenge on constitutional grounds. This argument was not tested and accepted until the High Court ruling in the Tasmanian Dams case in 1983, but Evatt, with others, had been suggesting it since the 1930s, when he had proposed that the external affairs power might enable a Commonwealth government to implement international conventions.

Menzies was alert to this in 1944, saying:

Dr Evatt has never made a secret of his view (in fact, Mr Justice Evatt was of the same opinion), that under its external affairs power the Commonwealth Government can make a treaty or agreement with another country, and then give legislative effect to it in the Commonwealth Parliament.

Menzies pointed to recent discussions with New Zealand about jointly pursuing full employment. Employment policy proposals had been among those rejected in the referendum, but what if discussions with New Zealand led to an international agreement and it was then implemented as policy, under the shelter of the external affairs power? The result of the referendum would, Menzies claimed, be 'nullified'. Editorials supported Menzies against Evatt; the latter was attempting to claim that despite the referendum loss, Labor could still go ahead because it had 'residual constitutional powers'. 'No, Dr Evatt, the story is a little too naïve', the *Argus* chided. Perhaps warned off, or perhaps not trusting the political instincts of the High Court in a constitutional challenge, Labor did not attempt to use the external affairs power for significant policy expansion.

He had fought the referendum campaign in his capacity as attorney-general, but as foreign minister Evatt was inevitably involved in more ambitious, international plans. In his statement in October 1943, he had talked about the mutual regional interests of Australia and New Zealand, and when the two nations signed a formal agreement both the British and Americans were concerned. The Australian–New Zealand agreement of January 1944 asserted the two nations had 'full responsibility for policing … a regional zone of defence comprising the South-west and South Pacific areas'. Evatt was a guiding force behind the agreement, which claimed the right to be involved in the planning of the postwar international system, proposed a regional conference on security, and claimed responsibility for the 'welfare of native peoples' in the region. These were rather expansive claims, and the British and Americans were not pleased.

Lord Cranborne, the secretary of state for dominion affairs, told the British cabinet it was 'unfortunate' the two governments had, without prior consultation, made an agreement about 'so many general questions in which we are vitally concerned'. He noted: 'Dr Evatt is no doubt delighted ... and he will be likely to resent anything that he may regard as grandmotherly restraint by the mother country'. Walter Hankinson, the deputy high commissioner in Canberra, chose an equally patronising metaphor when he commented that Australia and New Zealand were 'in terms of nationhood, boys'. He saw the agreement as an attempt by the 'ambitious' Evatt 'to achieve something of historical significance' with his name on it. But he was like a boy misbehaving, which would have been 'impossible if the maternal partner were consulted'.

Without claiming any such maternal prerogative, the US secretary of state, Cordell Hull, was also unimpressed with the new agreement. The Americans objected that the proposed regional security conference would potentially interfere with their plans for devising a new international system; and they resented the claim that Australia and New Zealand would need to agree to any postwar settlements about sovereignty and military bases in the south-west Pacific. Hull wrote to Curtin that he was 'frankly disturbed' at the idea of a regional conference, which would embolden 'other regional groups to make their own exclusive arrangements'. When Curtin was about to arrive in America in April 1944, Hull's department advised Roosevelt to 'tell him very frankly how we feel about Dr Evatt's recent actions'. Some provisions in the Australian–New Zealand agreement were 'aimed, all too obviously, at the United States', especially the claim to have a say about the establishment of military bases on Pacific islands. A month later, Hull wrote again to Roosevelt that Evatt was 'behaving outrageously' and that they had been 'considerably shocked' by his attitude. The issue eventually settled down, when the regional conference was abandoned. But Evatt's latest assertion of independence was a sign of things to come, presaging his clashes with the great powers

over the United Nations charter, drafted at the San Francisco conference the following year.

Evatt's relations with British leaders, especially Cranborne,
continued to rankle into late 1944. Viscount Cranborne, who was
considered a hardline imperialist, was Robert Gascoyne-Cecil, later
the fifth Marquess of Salisbury; a genuine aristocrat, he was exactly
the kind of patrician Evatt instinctively disliked. He and Cranborne
exchanged acid cables. Evatt wrote to Cranborne that the tone of one
of his recent cables reminded him of 'Colonial Office despatches of the
distant past'; he complained about 'failure to consult'. Archly, Cranborne reminded Evatt that Britain had 'world-wide Colonial responsibilities', and individual members of the Commonwealth should not
make unilateral declarations.

In September 1944, Evatt made a long and well considered parliamentary statement on the emerging postwar 'world organisation'; it
was not yet being called the United Nations. His department's work on
'post-hostilities planning' had advanced considerably, and this speech
has a much clearer intellectual framework, presenting the line Evatt
and his advisers would take in San Francisco six months later. Hasluck
had a major hand in writing it and later wrote that he had 'succeeded in
the major task of a speech-writer in thinking my way into the mind of
the speech-maker'. Evatt began with a sentiment he would repeat frequently, saying that, after the failure of the League of Nations, this was
probably the last chance for the democracies to prevent another world
war by establishing the foundations of a new kind of peace. He frequently spoke of the 'lost opportunity' after the First World War, when
'the victorious democracies had the ball at their feet', but 'fumbled' the
challenge. Fascism had grown in the seedbed of depression and unemployment, and the democracies had done too little, too late to confront
the threat. 'It is a miracle that we are given this second opportunity and,
I imagine, the last opportunity for the democracies of the world.'

In his September statement, Evatt developed three main themes.
The first was the design of 'the constitutional machinery' for an

organisation to keep the peace. The failures of the League of Nations showed that the leadership of the new security system 'must have the will to use physical force against a proved aggressor'. Aggression, or threats of it, should be 'countered not by the single State threatened but by the authority of the new organization'. The new structure would include an assembly representing member states (later the General Assembly), an executive of the great powers with a selected number of smaller states (later the Security Council), a permanent secretariat, and a permanent court of justice to adjudicate disputes. The last was significant to Evatt, because he argued international law must become far more important than in the past:

> The body of international law applicable to international
> controversies should be expanded ... the range of justiciable
> disputes will be widened ... and ... to use the phrase of the late
> Mr Justice Higgins ... will open up in the international field
> many 'new provinces for law and order'.

This was obviously his legal and liberal self speaking. Higgins' famous phrase conjured up a vision of industrial law settling disputes and determining fair wages. For Higgins, the 'new province' meant the reason of the law intervening between the contending powers of labour and capital, but it also meant liberal enlightenment brought to bear on social questions such as determining a just wage. Using Higgins' phrase connected Evatt's thinking back to the progressive liberal foundations of his early education, and once again reflected his conviction that legal reasoning was the royal road to divining truth and resolving, in this case, international disputes.

Evatt's second theme expanded on a common Labor sentiment, best articulated by Chifley in a domestic setting, that the postwar world must be founded on social welfare and 'economic justice'. Evatt argued that postwar stability would depend on 'building a way of life in which the various nations and people can live together in prosperity as well as in security'. His prime example was 'the over-riding objective of full employment and improving living standards'. This was in effect internationalising commitments Labor had to building a new domestic social order through postwar reconstruction. At San Francisco, Evatt would fail to have a full employment objective written into the charter, but succeed in giving greater priority to the United Nations Educational, Scientific and Cultural Organization (UNESCO), attempting to make it a mechanism to achieve global economic and social justice. That idea of international social justice has often been seen as the most quixotic of his, and others', commitments to the United Nations, given attempts through a global organisation to influence social and economic policies inevitably clashed with the interests of nation-states, which were not inclined to surrender their sovereignty. At San Francisco, Evatt himself would refuse to countenance international meddling with Australia's migration policies.

His third theme was the balance between great and small nations in the new organisation. Evatt was not as opposed, as sometimes thought, to the exercise of great power politics, but he argued repeatedly that leadership was not intended to be dominance. The original 'big three' powers – Britain, America and the Soviet Union – obviously possessed an 'overwhelming preponderance of the world's armed strength', and he argued that any security system must have their 'full backing'. It followed, he said, that the three great powers must act with unity in the face of threats to peace. This might be called 'power politics', he said, but was common sense; the need for great power unity had been demonstrated by the failures of the League of Nations. But the question was how to ensure the great powers did not dominate the new organisation; they must recognise the equality of states, allowing fair representation to smaller powers. 'No sovereign State, however small, will wish to think that its destiny has been handed over to another Power, however great.' All states had 'a stake in the preservation of peace', so the 'machinery' must be engineered accordingly.

There is a realism evident here that at first glance seems at odds with the idealistic liberal internationalism often ascribed to Evatt. William Macmahon Ball noted this combination in his introduction to a collection of Evatt's speeches. He described Evatt's approach as 'realism ... inspired by idealism', and sketched the trajectory of Evatt's engagement with international affairs between 1941 to 1945, when he began with Australia's urgent need for military supplies, but then, in the fight to make his nation's faraway voice heard in London and Washington, his concerns became broader and more abstract. From seeking influence as a matter of survival, he turned to trying to define the principles that would underpin a stable postwar international order. But this still had a realist focus on survival because, as Ball put it, the future safety of smaller nations such as Australia would depend on ensuring the power of the great nations was harnessed 'for the defence of international law'.

A few days after Evatt's ministerial statement on the emerging world organisation, Richard Boyer wrote him an interesting letter. It demonstrated the hopes being projected onto Evatt's role at the forth-coming conference in San Francisco. Boyer was a board member of the Australian Broadcasting Commission, and was soon to become the chair. He had listened to Evatt's 'splendid' speech, and wrote: 'Frankly, I envy you your great opportunity ... to influence this final step in civilised government'. Boyer thought that smaller countries would have to be persistent to ensure that 'organised collective action' prevailed over the tendency of powerful states 'to retain their individual position'. He was investing high hopes in Evatt's capacity to 'do this country, as well as the world generally, a service of historic magnitude'; it was an opportunity, he said, 'given to few men and few generations. Your speech has quickened the hope of many of us, and we are very grateful'.

'The Charter is a constitution'

The conference to design what was becoming known as the United Nations Organisation was scheduled for April 1945 in San Francisco. In mid-February, Roosevelt nominated Edward Stettinius, the secretary of state, to lead the American delegation; that set the expectation that foreign ministers would lead the delegations from their respective countries. Evatt was preparing to leave, and had arranged to give a speech at the University of California just before the opening of the conference. But then Curtin announced that instead Francis Forde, the deputy prime minister, would lead the delegation, appointing him over Evatt. So began a dysfunctional arrangement in which Evatt was clearly the intellectual leader and treated Forde brutally, while Forde appeared to take little notice and have little grasp of the details. The British high commissioner wrote to London about this curious arrangement shortly after Curtin announced it. He thought Forde was 'genial and likeable', but 'of by no means outstanding brilliance'. Forde might, if he had the weight, 'provide breadth of view as a counter to Evatt's occasionally narrow Australian outlook', the high commissioner said, but 'how exactly they will run in harness, it is difficult to say'.

With both Evatt and Forde in harness, Curtin was clearly intending to rein Evatt in, and he had done the same with an earlier delegation for a conference in New Zealand, appointing Forde to lead it. Hasluck speculated that Curtin's decision to send Forde to San Francisco was prompted by Frederick Shedden, the secretary of the Department of Defence, who wanted to head off John Burton's planning of the delegation; Burton was employed in the Department of External Affairs but effectively worked as Evatt's private secretary. Curtin's biographer David Day suggested it was because Evatt and Curtin differed over colonial policy, with Curtin supporting the British more strongly than Evatt. Curtin asked Roland Wilson, the head of the Department of Labour and National Service, to accompany

Forde; in an interview with Peter Crockett, Wilson said he was 'in a rather awkward position'. Curtin had put the delegation together to 'keep an eye on Bert, because Curtin didn't trust Bert as far as he could throw him'. Curtin told Wilson 'in no uncertain terms' that his role was to be Forde's 'chief bodyguard', to prevent Evatt 'bullying' him. For whatever reason he did it, Curtin's decision was a setback for Evatt and a cause of resentment. 'The rebuff was public. Some dark days followed', Hasluck wrote.

Evatt and Mary Alice, along with most of the officials, left for America in mid-March, again leaving Rosalind with friends. Les Haylen described their departure as 'like Marco Polo going to China'. There had been 'a great frothing' and 'a riot' at the Mosman house 'and eventually "whoosh" they'd all go out, you know. Everything was done on the grand manner'. But while this sounds exuberant, Hasluck recalled Evatt's 'black mood', resentful about Forde's appointment. When they arrived in America, Evatt gave his speech at the University of California, and they readied to fly to Washington. The entire party was flying together, and Sam Atyeo had now joined them; Hasluck recalled the occasion:

> Evatt, his wife, Atyeo and Burton turned up nearly an hour late. Evatt was in a foul temper. He took a dislike to the waiting aircraft and refused to travel in it. He said there was not enough pressure in the tyres … He almost lost his pilot, too, when he started to cross-examine him on how much flying experience he had.

Atyeo had the task of telling the Americans to provide a substitute aircraft. After they flew on to Dallas, Evatt suddenly decided they would stay the night and travel on by train. On the train to Washington, Forde and his wife sat in 'self-contained dignity' at one end of the carriage, while Evatt, at the other, 'made mocking gestures in his direction'. Hasluck said Evatt 'embarrassed some of us by his derisive comments' about Forde. It is not a flattering image; while Hasluck recognised Evatt's talents and was even somewhat fond of him, he was a critical witness of his behaviour. And he observed how crucially Evatt depended on Mary Alice; only she could influence him and warn him away from a course. Hasluck wrote that she soothed his tantrums, and mothered him against his enemies, encouraging him to do better. The relationship, he thought, was 'much more like that of mother and son than wife and husband'.

At the end of March, the party flew to London for a meeting of the Commonwealth delegations prior to San Francisco. As they left, Frederic Eggleston, an Australian diplomat of many years' experience, wrote from Washington to warn Curtin that the arrangement between Forde and Evatt might lead to trouble. Forde was senior, but Evatt insisted he was head of the delegation and had forbidden his staff to show any papers to Forde's staff. 'Why Evatt should regard the matter in this light, I cannot imagine … all he needs to do is to give formal precedence to Forde and the latter will be satisfied. If both open their mouths, it is obvious to everyone who is the master mind.' But Eggleston doubted Forde had 'the guts' to settle the issue.

Hasluck described the flight from Washington to London in a specially fitted Liberator bomber. 'Most of the way we flew at 20,000 feet in the most lovely ethereal landscape of moonlight on clouds … We had to sniff oxygen and we kept warm by thrusting our feet in great fleece-lined flying boots and swaddling ourselves in rugs.' Evatt was distraught and anxious, worrying that ice was forming on the wings, and convinced that the weight of the ice would make them crash: 'He thought we were losing height already and the engines were labouring'. He sent Burton to warn the captain. Evatt's fear of flying was legendary; in later years, his Labor colleague and adversary Eddie Ward would tease him during flights, inflaming his anxieties by asking whether he had noticed if the plane had been refuelled, and did he think those hills up ahead were too high to climb over. But Hasluck paid tribute to Evatt's courage in continuing to fly when he was prey to such violent fears.

This Commonwealth meeting in London was intended to clarify, if not coordinate, the positions they would take to San Francisco; Australia, New Zealand, Canada, South Africa and India were all represented. When Churchill met them he warned it was still possible Russia might refuse to attend the San Francisco conference. He described the British Commonwealth as 'the third of the Great Powers' and said they could only maintain their influence 'by our superior statecraft and experience and, above all, by ... unity'. But there was a revealing slip in that formulation: he seemed to suggest it was the Commonwealth, rather than Britain, that was a great power. Churchill was implying they must speak with one voice, and it should preferably be Britain's. It was the sort of thing Evatt resented and it would be a major source of tension at San Francisco, when he would insist on his independent voice.

Before this visit to London, Hasluck thought Evatt was not really focused, but now with 'furious concentration' on the papers, he developed an 'amazing' expertise. 'His intellectual powers never impressed me so vividly as they did during this period of rapid learning in London', Hasluck wrote. Evatt identified what he saw as two key flaws in the draft charter which had been composed at the Dumbarton Oaks conference in Washington in October 1944. At Dumbarton Oaks, the 'big three' had become four – with China added to America, Britain and the Soviet Union – and their draft was the basis for the San Francisco conference. Evatt now objected to the veto claimed by the four powers, by which any one of them could halt discussion or action by the Security Council, and he objected to the vagueness in the draft about what would happen after the war with colonies, as well as territories held under trusteeship or mandate. Hasluck thought Evatt seized on these as good issues for a fight, and 'became a crusader on both topics'. He brushed aside the objection that the Soviet Union had made the veto a condition of their participation, and although he had not yet developed clear views about the future of colonial states, he insisted the new organisation should monitor the welfare of dependent peoples. By the end of these London talks, Hasluck said, Evatt had grown into the role he would take at San Francisco, the champion of the smaller nations against the great powers. This had an 'elevating effect' on Evatt, Hasluck explained: 'He knew already that he was in command and was going to play an effective part on the broader stage'. He had mastered his brief.

Evatt explicitly saw the task at San Francisco as one of writing a constitution. One of his objections to the great powers possessing a veto was that it meant the charter could only be amended by the 'unanimous consent' of the great powers, and would make the constitution 'unworkable' and inflexible. He objected to the veto in general, but especially to it being applied to 'constitutional alteration'. At his address at the University of California he said that a permanent system of security could be made 'effective and acceptable' only if its constitutional framework was flexible enough to meet the needs of a changing world. It was a recurring theme. The charter was a constitution and needed to be specific about mechanisms for amendment, as well as about the relative powers of the Security Council and the General Assembly.

In a later speech to parliament moving the adoption of the charter, he said explicitly: 'We should remember that the Charter is a constitution'. It established a legal and political framework, rather than formulating solutions to specific problems. He was drawing parallels to national constitutions, which established the political rules of the exercise of power and which, like the Australian constitution, were subject to legal interpretation by a superior court. He wanted the United Nations charter to be interpreted and governed by the new world court, because 'judicial institutions are indispensable as a check to executive power'. In addition to specific aspects such as the veto and the future of the colonial world, Evatt had clarified that San Francisco was to be an exercise in constitution-making, his favourite area of the law.

In mid-April Evatt was back in Washington, having meetings with the newly installed President Harry S. Truman, British foreign secretary Anthony Eden and Soviet ambassador to the US Andrei Gromyko. Molotov, the Soviet foreign commissar, had arrived and insisted on a bulletproof car. Evatt told journalists that 'we must keep our eyes on the ball', even though there would be 'side issues' at the conference: 'The great thing is to get the charter of the organization framed', he said, 'so that it will be neither too rigid nor too flexible, and so under its terms it will be possible to stamp out aggression ruthlessly'. From Washington, they took the train for San Francisco.

'Persistent fighting under great difficulties'

The conference started on 25 April, with more than 600 delegates representing forty-six nations, a reported 3000 advisers and consultants, and – in the phrase of one journalist – 1000 'crack international newspapermen'. But only part of the world was there. The Axis powers were of course not present; the German surrender that brought the European war to an end came shortly after the conference opened, while Japan's surrender was not until August. The European colonies in Africa and Asia were absent, or rather were represented by their European masters. Only three African states, Liberia, Ethiopia and South Africa, attended, and from Asia only China, India and the Philippines; most of South-East Asia was still under Japanese control, but the European colonial powers assumed they would resume their rule after the war. That presumption greatly complicated debates at San Francisco about colonies and trusteeship.

The Australia delegation stayed at the Sir Francis Drake hotel, with Evatt's entourage on one floor and Forde's on another. Evatt demanded that none of his staff talk with Forde's. Alice Jackson, editor of the *Australian Women's Weekly*, was in San Francisco and sent home a story. While Forde and Evatt were 'working almost ceaselessly', she wrote, 'their wives are working almost as strenuously'. The Evatt suite was 'sandwiched in between the Panamanians and the Greeks'.

Mary Alice was especially busy, Jackson reported, and had hosted a party 'of friends, old and new' to celebrate Evatt's fifty-first birthday; Eden, Atlee, Halifax and Cranborne were all there. Mary Alice was in demand as a speaker at women's clubs, and she also spent time 'visiting different delegates and promoting general friendliness'.

It was to be an extremely energetic two months, as Evatt moved between committees, working late into the night, intervening in everything. Eggleston wrote to Bruce about chaotic and frenzied activity, with everything 'done by Evatt, or under his instructions'. 'As you know', Eggleston wrote, 'Evatt is not very tactful, and, in addition, his manners are none the best, in fact he can be exceedingly rude and he did not restrain himself'. With his intense concentration combined with his brusque manners, Evatt attracted a good deal of attention and almost as much criticism. The Australian journalist Harold Cox, who was in San Francisco to cover the conference, recalled what he called Evatt's 'amazing flair for doing very good work in the very worst possible way', working indefatigably but creating 'ill-feeling from almost every other delegation'. But many of those who were there, including Eggleston and Hasluck, judged that Evatt made a significant difference to producing a less imperfect charter.

Hasluck, a member of Evatt's group, called the divided Australian delegation 'a Calf with Two Heads at the Great World Show'. He made it clear the fault lay with Evatt, while Forde bore Evatt's rudeness with something between patience and oblivion. Cox told a story that illustrated the relationship between the two men perfectly. The American shipbuilder Henry Kaiser was producing ships at the rate of 'one every two or three days' and invited each head of a delegation to launch one. Forde was invited as the head of the Australian delegation, and Evatt objected. Then new invitations arrived announcing a 'Double Launching', with both Forde and Evatt named as 'leader of the Australian delegation'. The two ships were launched simultaneously, meaning journalists had to choose which to attend. Cox went to Forde's launch and they were then taken off to dinner. The next day Evatt was furious, demanding to know 'why everybody went to Mr Forde's launching last night and nobody came to mine'. Hasluck's account was slightly different, but still ludicrous. At midnight, he wrote, 'There gathered at the shipyards two separate groups of Australians, the adherents of Forde and the adherents of Evatt, each at the bows of a Victory ship in adjoining stocks … Afterwards we sat on opposite sides of the hall in a supper room'.

Evatt is Don Quixote on a wooden horse. Throughout the 1940s, he was frequently criticised as the self-appointed champion of those 'in or out of distress'.

Mick Armstrong, *Argus*, 24 September 1945

Evatt had regular disputes with the British delegation about the trusteeship chapter of the charter. After the First World War, the League of Nations had established trusts or mandates over former German colonies; for example, New Guinea was an Australian mandate, while Britain controlled Tanganyika. As noted in chapter 5, Evatt had written about the Australia's New Guinea mandate in the 1930s, both as a puzzle about the nature of sovereignty, and as a measure of Australia's independent status. The Dumbarton Oaks draft assumed a continuation of this system of mandates, and at San Francisco Evatt strongly supported the sentiments of the final wording of the charter, which stated that mandates were held 'as a sacred trust', with an obligation to promote the wellbeing of the inhabitants, including their 'progressive development towards self-government or independence'. But he went further.

Evatt argued explicitly that the 'sacred trust' should apply not only to mandates, but to colonial territories. 'What is good in one case should be good in another', he said, as a general pledge 'covering all non-self-governing territories'. That would mean that imperial powers would be accountable to the United Nations for their 'stewardship', but the British were not intending to allow such interference with their colonial system. In March, before San Francisco, the British cabinet had discussed how to deflect any threat. Lord Cranborne advised that Australia and New Zealand intended to propose that any territory could 'voluntarily be placed under trusteeship', but if 'voluntary' meant a 'dependent people' could take the initiative and request being placed under a mandate, he saw a threat to the fabric of the empire. What if Britain's colonial subjects requested a mandate? The different standards applying to mandates would mean the emerging United Nations system had oversight of Britain's empire, and, Cranborne wrote: 'We shall be continually under pressure from some elements in the United States ... to bring the whole of our Colonial administration under international review'; it would throw 'the whole Colonial Empire open to discussion by this motley assembly'. The cabinet resolved to insist that being placed under trusteeship must never happen at the initiative of the subject people; it could only be at the initiative of what Cranborne liked to call the 'Parent State'.

In San Francisco, Evatt clashed with the British delegation over the text of the trusteeship chapter, protesting when Cranborne blocked his suggestion that trusts could be established 'not only on a voluntary basis, but on a compulsory basis', which clearly implied intervention by the UN. On another occasion, he proposed that colonial powers had the same responsibilities as states with a mandate, and should be required to report to the UN on the condition of their subject peoples. Cranborne scotched the idea: 'We could not possibly agree … It must be for the nations concerned to decide what they will or will not make available'. In the end, the relevant chapter emphasised the rights of dependent peoples, but it was only about trust territories and did not mention colonies. At the conclusion of the conference, when Halifax claimed that the British delegation had taken the lead in writing the chapter, Evatt complained that was 'unfair', not giving Australia 'her full credit for the part taken in the expansion of the Trusteeship and Colonial chapter'. It was a significant slip of the tongue on Evatt's part, because the relevant chapter did not apply to colonies. Halifax was right to claim the credit, for the chapter represented a successful British campaign to ensure the empire was not subject to review by 'this motley assembly'.

The ways that Britain consulted with the other great powers but not with Australia or other dominions continually vexed Evatt. Amendments to the draft charter were being agreed between the great powers, he argued, without consultation with any Commonwealth delegates. One section that concerned him dealt with what constituted 'domestic jurisdiction', about which Britain was negotiating with the other great powers; Evatt feared that changes might mean migration policies could be subject to an order of the Security Council. He insisted the White Australia policy, as well as tariff policies, were off limits; intervention in domestic politics should be restricted

to breaches of the peace, but as Sawer noted, this was 'scarcely consistent with his general policy of strengthening the authority of the
United Nations'.

More generally, what became clear at San Francisco was that the
priority of the British delegation was to maintain unity with the other
great powers. Evatt complained the British had surprised the dominions by consistently voting with the great powers, especially in debates
about the veto. As Halifax and Cranborne put it, the great powers
had decided, 'rightly or wrongly' to consult on every departure from
the Dumbarton Oaks draft; it had been necessary, they said, to 'keep
the Russians in the fold'. Evatt objected to this British commitment
to great power unity, complaining the British 'appeared to think that
the Dominion delegates should be seen but not heard' – precisely as if
Britain were the 'mother' it presumed itself to be, and the dominions
its unruly children, echoing Cranborne and Hankinson's earlier use of
such imagery.

The battles about the veto power were fought out in the committee on structure and procedure. The journalist Alistair Cooke
wrote that the committee room became known as 'Madison Square
Garden', after the venue in New York then used for boxing matches.
Evatt attempted to persuade the great powers to surrender their right
to a veto; having failed in that, he then argued the veto should be
limited to decisions about armed intervention. It should not be possible for a great power to veto attempts at conciliation and peaceful
settlement. Reprising his earlier description of international law as
a 'new province for law and order', he told the committee members:
'In Australian labour disputes it is the understood duty of both parties to conciliate. And it should be the duty of the Security Council
to conciliate, not its right to use or waive that method'. Evatt lost
comprehensively on the veto power; each of the great powers wanted
to retain it and it was pretty much a condition of Soviet participation. He warned that unless the veto was used with restraint, nations
would begin again to settle their quarrels outside the organisation,

'a fate that in the end had doomed the League of Nations'.

One question on which there was not a great deal of disagreement was strengthening the role of the International Court of Justice, and the application of international law in resolving disputes. Sawer considered this an achievement to which Evatt contributed: he succeeded in having 'legal, moral and ethical standards and methods' written into the language of the charter. In addition, Evatt had argued for an expanded role for what became UNESCO; though attempts to include a commitment to full employment in the charter failed, there was a greater emphasis on the potential social and economic intentions of the new organisation.

Finally, the other major debate in which Evatt had some success concerned the relative power and role of the General Assembly; the great powers had effectively proposed the assembly could only debate what they allowed it to, because any member of the Security Council could veto what was discussed. Evatt argued that the assembly should be able to bring international disputes into the open. Smaller countries, through membership of the assembly, should be able to debate issues of international concern. The idea that conflicts should be resolved in an open public realm and not in secret by powerful alliances was in one sense internationalist, but it was equally about Evatt's nationalist demand that smaller nations must have a voice.

Drew Pearson, an American journalist who clearly admired Evatt's role at the conference, published his reports in the *Argus*. On the constitutional role of the assembly, he reported what he described as 'a closed-door debate as hot as anything San Francisco ever witnessed'. Evatt had proposed an amendment allowing the assembly to debate any issue. Pearson, presumably based on what Evatt told him, wrote that Stettinius, the US secretary of state, summoned Evatt to his penthouse and 'begged him to withdraw his amendment', saying: 'If you push it any further the bigger nations may be forced to withdraw from the United Nations entirely'. 'I'll take my chances on that', Evatt had apparently replied. Evatt eventually lost the debate, but the great powers agreed to a compromise. As the conference concluded in late June, Alistair Cooke described the atmosphere: 'At noon the word came from an excited Secretary Stettinius that Moscow had approved the slightly amended Evatt text defining the debating powers of the General Assembly'. Evatt claimed that the powers of the General Assembly were now 'five hundred times broader' than he had first envisaged.

As the conference wrapped up, there was a good deal of discussion in the Australian press about Evatt's standing at San Francisco, some of it simply repeating American reports. The *Argus* ran a statement from the *New York Times* saying that Evatt was 'the greatest fighting man' of the conference. At the final meeting of the conference steering committee, the Peruvian delegate thanked Evatt as 'the great champion of the smaller nations', and the delegates reportedly rose to their feet with applause. However, Roland Wilson, there to protect Forde from Evatt's bullying, suggested that Evatt had himself arranged for this recognition of his role. The fiercest arguments had been over the veto, which Evatt lost, but he was now able to make a joke about it. Though apparently 'overcome with emotion', he thanked the committee, and glanced up at the head table where the big power representatives sat, saying: 'I would like to say a great deal more, but I'm afraid somebody might exercise the veto power against me'. One report noted that 'even the dour-faced Soviet Ambassador Gromyko … joined in the laughter'.

Pearson also described 'the hard-hitting lawyer from a little town in New South Wales' as the champion of the small nations. While Molotov had the early publicity, and Stettinius 'got most of the play in the newsreels', Pearson wrote that it was 'Dr Evatt who did the day-in day-out crusading for real democracy in preventing war'. In the 'uncompromising battle for a liberal post-war United Nations policy', he had lifted Australia from 'silent membership of the family of nations to a place alongside the Big Five'. Evatt had evidently spoken to Pearson about Ray and Frank, for the journalist attributed Evatt's

THE CONCERT OF EUROPE.

In the 'concert of Europe', Evatt is represented as blowing his own trumpet, an early version of a frequent criticism that he was speaking only for himself.

Ted Scorfield, *Bulletin*, 10 October 1945

motivation to the deaths of his brothers in France. 'Ever since, Evatt has made it a life work to try to root out seeds of war.'

As the conference wrapped up in late June, Evatt had a final fight with the British. He mischievously claimed that the British had so slavishly pursued the unity of the great powers – which were now five following the addition of France – that Australia and New Zealand should now speak on behalf of the British empire: 'Britain's voice must hereafter be tempered by the demands of Big Five unity'. A *Sydney Morning Herald* editorial described that as 'an unhappy piece of arrogance', and scolded Evatt for marring 'the worthy part played by the Australian delegation' by deliberately starting another quarrel with Halifax. Certainly the British delegation, writing back to London, thought Evatt had been 'the leader of the opposition among the small powers … hasty and suspicious; constantly pressing for full support for his various purposes'. Evatt's behaviour, they reported, had 'certainly dispelled the illusion that Dominion representation means six votes for the United Kingdom'.

Evatt's role at San Francisco has subsequently been regarded as a high point of his career, when through sheer force of character and hard intellectual work he helped draft a constitution for the new global order. Hasluck thought his contribution had been significant, while Eggleston thought the causes he championed were worthwhile, even if his manner was rude. Eggleston wrote to Bruce from Washington saying just that:

I know all Evatt's weaknesses and have no admiration for the way in which he works but … I believe that he played a very constructive part at the conference and that he pointed out the weak points of the main scheme, conducted a very fine campaign against them and that on the question of the Economic & Social Council and the Trusteeship clause, he was very largely responsible for the draft which appeared. Here is where the main conflict took place with the British delegation.

Eggleston also thought Evatt was right to oppose the veto, the use of which threatened to 'paralyse' the new organisation:

> You must not take it that Evatt's campaign was merely a small power vs. a great power campaign. It was a campaign against the defective principles of the Charter. It certainly brought a number of rather undesirable small powers on his side, such as the Latinos and the Arabs. I suppose that cannot be helped. You must not take this letter as a defence of Evatt. What I want to do is show that we had right on our side and must not be penalised because Evatt got a bad name.

While Evatt's will to dominate and his desperate desire to make his mark contributed to his success in San Francisco, there was something more to it: he was drawing on his strength in legal rationality, because at the conference politics took the form of writing a constitution.

Legal rationality was both the métier in which he was most comfortable and the mechanism by which he hoped to tame great power conflict. If international relations could be a 'new province for law and order', the law would objectively determine the facts and dispense justice. That was the promise Evatt saw in the United Nations. This was a liberal internationalist stance, but he mingled realism with internationalism. 'Realism' meant recognition of the dominance of the great powers, and the assertion of national interests, which could only be protected within a stable international order. When he asserted the claim of smaller powers to take their part in designing the United Nations system, he was motivated by nationalism, even as he helped to shape an international constitution. Rather than interpreting his attachment to the United Nations as only idealistic liberal internationalist aspirations, we should equally note his impassioned, legalistic defence of national interests.

But, of course, it was also about his will to power. Part of how Evatt himself saw the conference is revealed in a letter he wrote shortly afterwards to Felix Frankfurter:

> Frankly, at San Francisco the attitude taken by the great powers on some questions was appalling. It was only due to persistent fighting under great difficulties ... that the Charter was radically improved ... Some of those present tried to treat countries like Australia ... as though they had no right to make their voices heard. However they were disillusioned.

11

'The president of the world'

The five years from early 1945 to the end of the Chifley government in late 1949 were a time of intense activity for Evatt, most of it on the world stage. They represent the zenith of his career. His urgent drive to be recognised and to have his voice heard was being realised, in London, at the San Francisco conference, and at subsequent UN meetings in Paris and New York. He was out of Australia for a total of twenty-seven months during this five-year period, almost half the time. Mary Alice accompanied him on all these trips, while Rosalind stayed in country New South Wales with friends, except when she went with them to Paris at the age of sixteen in 1948.

The dizzying, frantic round included, in 1945, almost five months in San Francisco and later in the year four months in London and America at UN preparatory meetings; in 1946, almost five months in London and Paris, including the Paris peace conference; in 1947, a month in Japan and then later three months in America at UN meetings; and in 1948, six months in Europe – in Geneva and Paris, as president of the UN General Assembly, and in London to argue an appeal before the Privy Council on bank nationalisation. In 1949 he was slightly less busy, but still spent three and a half months in London, again at the Privy Council, and attended UN meetings in New York. All this frenzied work took a toll. Although it was punctuated by several sea voyages during which he could recuperate, by the late 1940s Evatt was clearly exhausted. Eggleston thought he had burnt himself out at San Francisco and was never the same again; others noted his exhaustion in 1948 and 1949, when he was simultaneously

241

appearing before the Privy Council and being president of the UN General Assembly. Hartley Grattan saw him in 1948 and remembered he was 'terribly tired'.

These frequent overseas absences inevitably also led to criticism. In mid-July 1946, the deputy leader of the Country party, 'Black Jack' McEwen, sardonically asked Chifley when Dr Evatt might visit Australia. It was becoming a favourite joke in parliament. Chifley was asked if he intended to call 'Marco Polo' home, and whether there was 'the remotest possibility' Evatt might 'pay a fleeting visit to Australia'. Cartoonists regularly represented him as flying away to more urgent business. John Frith of the *Sydney Morning Herald* pictured him, when he returned to Sydney by ship in January 1949, with a crew member asking: 'Shall we wait, sir, or will you be staying awhile?' Foreign ministers are always ridiculed for their frequent flying, but with Evatt there was something more; the criticism was always that he was more interested in being a major actor on the world stage than a minister in Australia, and that he made up foreign policy on his own. Conservative opponents said that no other government member would comment on foreign affairs 'because they knew Dr Evatt would not permit' it. He was also the attorney-general but his attention was elsewhere; Senator Nick McKenna regularly acted for him in the role, and although he was loyal and dutiful, he remembered that Evatt never thanked him for his diligence.

'No longer merely an echo'

Roosevelt had died just at the beginning of the San Francisco conference and then Curtin died just as it ended in early July. Curtin had been hospitalised in late April, and by the middle of June he was back at the Lodge, but clearly declining; he told visitors that he was satisfied his work was done, even though he would not see the end of the war. But he was not going to resign. The press speculated about the succession, with the likely candidates expected to be Forde and Chifley; the latter had impressed with his leadership and had the backing of the New South Wales members of caucus, while Evatt's popularity, despite the splash he had made at San Francisco, was said to be less 'pronounced' than some time ago. In fact there was speculation that Evatt would be welcome on the new world court established by the UN charter, though he said he had 'no ambitions in that direction'.

Curtin died on 5 July, and when they got the news in San Francisco, the journalist Charles Buttrose recalled:

> We were having a drink in Bert's office in the Sir Francis Drake, and he said, 'You know I'm going home by boat'... I said, 'Have you got any chance of being prime minister?', and he said, 'No ... I've been in touch with Canberra and Chif's got the numbers.' I said, 'Well, if you need the bloody rest, why don't you go on the ship'. So that's what he did.

Once on the seas, Evatt could not change his mind about the leadership; the ship had no radio communication and there was no way to contact the party, but Forde, as acting prime minister, found a way to contact him. Passengers were mystified when a plane began circling the ship, anxious it might be Japanese attack. But instead of attacking, the plane dropped a bag containing a letter from Forde that notified Evatt caucus would meet and elect a new leader in his absence. Under caucus rules, those who could not attend were automatically considered candidates, unless they stipulated otherwise. Alan Reid later said Evatt's nomination was 'regarded as a bit of a joke' as he had no chance. When he arrived in Sydney, Evatt said he had not known his hat was in the ring, and that 'it must have been generally known to my colleagues that I was not a candidate'.

These were still early days for opinion polling, but gallup polls announced after Curtin's death that they had been polling about the Labor leadership for several weeks. Among Labor voters, Curtin was first choice with 58 per cent, followed by Evatt with 20 per cent, and Chifley with 5 per cent. Among non-Labor voters, Evatt had even more support (26 per cent), placed between Curtin (55) and Chifley (11). That suggested significant warmth for Evatt among the citizens, especially in the middle class, and his profile in reports from San Francisco may have boosted this support. One journalist thought that 'swinging electors … looked on Dr Evatt as Number One Labour hope after Mr Curtin'. Yet the real contest was widely assumed to be between Chifley and Forde, because as the *Sydney Morning Herald* pointed out, 'Labour would be abandoning all its precedents if it were to seek a leader from outside the trade-union line'. It turned out that Chifley was much more popular among caucus colleagues than among the citizens; he had a surprisingly low profile, given his role as treasurer and key supporter of Curtin, but his opportunity to demonstrate leadership had come when Curtin was ill and both Forde and Evatt were overseas. In the caucus election, Chifley had 45 votes, with Forde 15, Norman Makin 8 and Evatt only one. In the election for deputy, Forde was re-elected by 68 votes to Evatt's one. It looked like a rebuff, but Evatt had not actually tried for the leadership.

Six weeks later, he and Mary Alice flew out again for London, for a Preparatory Commission of the UN and a Council of Foreign Ministers meeting, then returned via America by sea in early January 1946. A few months later, in mid-April, Evatt and Chifley left by flying boat for a Commonwealth prime ministers' meeting in London, and Evatt then attended another Council of Foreign Ministers meeting. After that was the Paris peace conference, which was to deal with Italy, Hungary, Romania and Bulgaria but left both Germany and Japan still off the agenda. Prior to the peace conference, Evatt was already staking his claim to be heard. The foreign ministers of America, Britain, the Soviet Union and France had met and agreed on drafts of the treaties, and had agreed that each of them, as great powers, would have a right of veto over any changes. Evatt protested such 'prior bargains' were contrary to 'the principle and procedures of justice and democracy'. Commenting on his statement in an internal memo, the Dominions Office in London worried that they were again 'placed in the San Francisco position' which they had been 'anxious to avoid'. Prior arrangement of the treaties might produce more objections and the dominions might consider the conference 'a farce'.

The Paris conference opened in the Luxembourg Palace in late July 1946, attended by twenty-one nations, with most of Asia and Africa remaining under colonial rule. Security was tight, with the French organisers worried there could be attacks on the representatives by the violent Zionist Stern gang, which was agitating for a Jewish homeland, or by fascist agents coming across the border from Spain. Hotels and cafes were searched and cars carrying diplomats were driven at high speed to deter attack. Bodyguards were everywhere, and police with machine guns were placed around the palace itself; according to the Australian press, even Evatt had a bodyguard, who 'embarrassed him with his attentions'.

In the Luxembourg Palace, built in the seventeenth century and now housing the French Senate, meetings were held 'under the high gilded ceiling and richly-painted room of the former Throne Room of Napoleon III'. One commentator noted how the smoke from 'scores of pipes and cigarettes' rose each morning in a 'friendly blue haze against the priceless Gobelin tapestries and sparkling chandeliers'. All delegates wore a small enamel emblem designed by Cartier with the globe in blue and a white dove of peace. The *Women's Weekly*'s Anne Matheson described Molotov, the Soviet foreign minister, as a 'grim battler in session' who nevertheless cut a 'genial figure' at the opera. The *Weekly* always supported Evatt in this period, and described how he 'shared the limelight with Molotov and won great admiration for his battle for the small nations'. Matheson wrote of speaking with young mothers in the Luxembourg gardens who saw in 'this outspoken man from Australia … the hope for a more secure world for their growing children'. Mary Alice's activities were also reported back to Australia: she had visited the Louvre, and held discussions about arranging for art exhibitions to be exchanged between Australia and France. She recalled later that during the conference the works stolen by the Germans during the occupation had been returned to Paris and were on display.

At the beginning of the conference, Evatt caused a 'minor sensation' when he insisted again on the right of smaller nations 'to have a part in the final and definitive making of the peace treaties'. He objected to a proposal that a two-thirds majority would be required for any amendments to the drafts, demanding a simple majority. Molotov insisted on the two-thirds majority, knowing it made it much harder to approve any amendments, and suggested that Evatt's objective was 'to ensure a majority for the Anglo-American bloc'. Over the following days, Moscow Radio also criticised Evatt on the issue, claiming he was playing 'a clumsy game' and was doing the work of the western powers. Evatt lost that debate, but he was not so much doing the work of the western powers as once again throwing himself against the presumption of the great powers that their interests should prevail.

Molotov and Evatt also had 'heated exchanges' about the election of a chair for the conference; the great powers had agreed the chair would rotate between the four of them. When Molotov accused Evatt of trying to open up 'a rift between members of the United Nations', Evatt reportedly shouted back at him, 'That is not so!' The question, he said, was 'simply the right of an international conference to elect its own chairman'. The Soviet delegation then opposed Australia's claim for a place on the eight-member secretariat of the conference. Andrey Vyshinsky was the Soviet deputy foreign affairs minister and had been one of Stalin's most lethal prosecutors during the purges in the 1930s; he described Australia as 'a rather temperamental member', and said it might be better to have 'the representative of a calmer nation'. He suggested Ethiopia, but Australia's candidacy went ahead.

Mary Alice recalled that they actually got on well with the Soviet representatives, and these clashes were in a sense ritualistic. Evatt's view was that smaller nations had as much at stake in the peace, and when he returned to Australia he said, 'We do not want to be handed treaties and told here they are without being able to make recommendations or amendments'. It was a matter of 'ordinary justice'; treaties must be made 'in a just and democratic way'. But his claim that Australia had a right to shape the European peace was not always winning friends. When he accused the Czechoslovakian foreign minister, Jan Masaryk, of having deserted democratic principles, Masaryk replied acidly: 'What do you, with your kangaroo-filled open spaces, know of the problems of a Europe where every time you spit you hit the next man's boots? You know, if I really wanted a holiday from serious problems I think I should like to be Foreign Minister of Australia'.

Reports in the Australian press reinforced Evatt's reputation for assertiveness. One quoted an anonymous 'close observer' who said that Evatt was 'certainly the leading lady at the moment', though he was spoiling the effect with his 'repetitiveness and pugnacity'. 'He is as belligerent as ever', this source said. 'I feel like blushing when Dr Evatt gets up on every possible occasion and speaks boisterously and repetitively.' Such reports drew criticism in Australia. A *Courier-Mail* editorial castigated Evatt for his belligerence 'in his self-chosen role of David slinging stones at the four-headed Goliath of Big Powers'. Menzies commented that a combined voice of the empire was better than 'Australia's (or Dr Evatt's) single voice'. Hughes, who had himself been a notoriously pugnacious presence at the Versailles peace conference after the First World War, now criticised Evatt for 'making a great noise', saying that Australia should speak 'as a member of the British Empire, not as a shouting unit'. Conservatives certainly thought that Evatt was carrying self-assertion too far.

Evatt and Mary Alice arrived back in Australia at the end of August, on a specially chartered Lancastrian; they were accompanied by John Burton, who was described as Evatt's 'external affairs counsellor'. Rosalind met them at Sydney airport; during their absence she had been staying with family friends at Gulgong and attending school there. Answering his critics, Evatt said he was glad that Australia was

MOSTLY FROTH AND BLUBBER.

A savage criticism of Evatt landing back on Australian shores.

Norman Hetherington, *Bulletin*, 2 July 1947

no longer considered a 'rubber stamp' for Whitehall. The most serious obstacle to peace, he said, was 'the abuse by Russia of the power of the veto' in the Security Council, which could 'paralyse' the United Nations, and was already holding up the resolution of the peace treaties, including negotiations with Japan. 'If we do not tie up the loose ends of the Second World War a third world war is inevitable', he claimed.

Only days after his return, Evatt launched into the campaign for the federal election held in late September; he was 'looking as fit as a fiddle and fighting mad', according to one commentator, and would be 'one of Labor's trump cards'. But there are stories that he had wanted to step out of politics at around this point; even though it would have been difficult to do so in the lead-up to an election. Arthur Calwell remembered that in 1946 he wanted to go back to the High Court, but 'Chifley didn't want him to'. Les Haylen had a similar recollection, but was less precise about the timing: 'After early disappointments he had tried to get back to law in Chifley's day. He was dissuaded by Chifley and stayed on'.

Mary Alice too recalled that Evatt 'had not intended to take any part in politics after the war'. She said later she had wished he would leave politics, and that he had said to her, 'Well, once we get the war under control, once we, in fact, succeed in winning the war, I will give up politics and take to writing'. The plan was not necessarily to return to the High Court, but to go back to research and writing; the biography of Hughes beckoned. But then, she said, he decided he should contribute to postwar reconstruction: 'Before I think of retiring, I must see that everything's functioning ... that there is a life worth living for all, not just for a few people'. The postwar reconstruction he was most focused on was international rather than local.

Whatever Evatt's true intentions were, there was no sign of ambivalence in his election campaign. His international profile was a theme in his own election speeches, and his pride in what he had achieved was reflected in his claim that Australia 'had won a high place among the nations'; Australia was heard with respect in world councils, he said, and was 'no longer merely an echo of someone else'. But Menzies attacked on the same point, arguing that Evatt's 'notoriety at Paris had been bought too dearly'; he consulted nobody in the government, Menzies said, and parliament was not briefed on his policies; the man himself was 'the sole repository' of foreign policy. Evatt claimed to have put Australia on the map, but 'what he meant was that he had put himself in the headlines'. But Evatt being in the headlines did no damage to Labor's prospects, and in the election he held his seat with a large majority; although Labor lost some seats, it was returned with a comfortable majority of fourteen. Forde lost his seat and Evatt was elected deputy leader. The social services referendum proposal passed, and Labor now had an electoral mandate, if not the full constitutional powers, to push ahead with postwar reconstruction.

Campaigning for the presidency

During mid-1947, Evatt and Mary Alice sailed to Japan on the *Kanimbla*, a merchant ship converted during the war to carry troops. His aim was to meet with General MacArthur and discuss the Japanese peace treaty, and he reported back to Chifley that he and MacArthur had 'complete over-all understanding'. Nevertheless over the next few years, Evatt insisted on a punitive treaty with Japan, and argued that Emperor Hirohito should be tried as a war criminal, both proposals that the Americans were not intending to countenance. Japanese atrocities during the war had profoundly disturbed Evatt, perhaps even more so than the Holocaust. It may be that he identified Frank and Ray with the young Australian soldiers who suffered at the hands of the Japanese.

Significantly, this trip to Japan was his first and only visit to Asia, apart from brief stopovers during flights to Europe. When he thought regionally, it was about Australian interests in the south-west Pacific, and that was increasingly in relation to America as a Pacific power. Asia was something of a blind spot for him, in terms of an active interest, and some who worked with him at the time recalled they were uncertain about his views on South-East Asian decolonisation. We have seen that in the mid-1940s, Evatt took it for granted that the European powers would regain their colonies after the war, and that his battles over the trusteeship chapter at San Francisco had been about extending United Nations oversight to those colonies.

Yet in August 1945, when the Japanese occupation of South-East Asia collapsed, the whole situation changed rapidly; Ho Chi Minh declared Vietnamese independence from the French, and Sukarno and Mohammad Hatta declared Indonesian independence from the Dutch. The new situation in South-East Asia was one of open conflict between European powers attempting to re-establish control, and movements struggling to establish national independence. (Meanwhile, Britain was more pragmatically preparing itself to release India, Pakistan, Burma and Ceylon, while firmly insisting on retaining control of Malaya.) The debates at San Francisco were soon redundant, replaced by a new era of decolonisation, which itself was increasingly tangled with Cold War global rivalry.

Geoffrey Sawer, who worked with Evatt in the late 1940s, thought he was largely sympathetic to these new anti-colonial movements; late in his period as foreign minister, he made a parliamentary statement arguing that South-East Asian nationalist movements were a bulwark against communism gaining control, which was a line of argument that Chifley often pursued in support of decolonisation movements. But Macmahon Ball, who represented Evatt in Jakarta and then in Tokyo, confessed that he was 'always unclear' about Evatt's position, in particular on Indonesia. Looking back in 1969, Ball thought all he could say with confidence was that Evatt hoped to see 'a great reduction in the influence of the European colonial powers – Holland, France, Britain – and a marked increase in Australian influence'. Evatt seems to have been slow to notice how decolonisation was transforming South-East Asia in the late 1940s, and slow to realise that the rule of the European powers was coming to an end.

The Dutch were determined to regain control in Indonesia. When they launched a military offensive in mid-1947 to crush the republic, Chifley quickly referred the conflict to the UN Security Council, which established a three-nation 'Committee of Good Offices' to negotiate a ceasefire, made up of America, Belgium and Australia. Eighteen months later, when the Dutch launched a second offensive, Chifley proposed that the United Nations should intervene to hold 'an immediate election'. Evatt wanted international mediation by the United Nations, but seemed also to want the Dutch to maintain a presence. He had less of Chifley's instinctive sympathy for independence, and was more concerned with expanding Australia's role in the region, which he thought would depend on cooperation with European colonial powers. Chifley at times overruled Evatt, and it was Chifley's hand that appears more evident in the negotiations that led to Dutch withdrawal and Indonesian independence at the end of 1949.

One aspect that may have influenced Evatt's ambivalent position on Indonesian independence was his campaign to be elected president of the United Nations General Assembly. Hasluck recalled that Evatt had this in mind as early as 1945; by 1947 he was seriously lobbying for the position. Holland had a vote, but Indonesia did not, and Evatt was on occasions cautious not to alienate the Dutch, or other colonial powers. His campaign for the presidency in September 1947 was a close race, but ended in defeat; his opponent, Dr Osvaldo Aranha of Brazil, was running for a second term and had the support of the Latin American bloc.

Evatt was offered a consolation prize: the chair of an ad hoc committee on Palestine. The British held a mandate over Palestine, but it was to expire in May 1948; an earlier UN special committee had, without being unanimous, recommended partition into separate Arab and Jewish states. The committee Evatt chaired was established to consider the alternatives, and he is widely seen as guiding it to supporting partition, which was formally approved by the assembly in November 1947. Felix Frankfurter wrote thanking Evatt for his 'firm and constructive statesmanship' on the Palestine question, telling him: 'The Nations of the world shall arise and call you blessed'.

Evatt saw the establishment of a Jewish state as a question of justice and was firmly in favour of Israel. His stance had little to do with the Holocaust; he saw it instead as a question of national independence, and was clearer about the issue than he was on Indonesia. In early 1948, with the British mandate soon to expire, there was violent conflict in Palestine, and some Arab states were threatening force to prevent partition. The Americans proposed a renewal of the trusteeship, which would have delayed developments, but Evatt remained actively committed to partition. In May, Jewish leader David Ben-Gurion proclaimed the creation of the state of Israel from an air-raid shelter in Tel Aviv, while Egyptian planes bombed the city. The situation was complex, as it remains to this day, but Evatt's enthusiasm was undiminished, and he received the congratulations of Zionist groups in Australia. Evatt and Chifley both favoured recognition of the new state of Israel, while Britain was opposed until the conflict was resolved.

Eventually, in May 1949, Israel was formally admitted to the UN General Assembly, when Evatt was in the chair as president. He later spoke of it as his greatest achievement as president. Frankfurter wrote to him again: 'As one of the midwives of the state of Israel, you must have had a particular satisfaction in welcoming Israel to the family of nations'. At the end of that year, W.S. Robinson sent him a press clipping reporting a rumour Evatt was being considered for a UN position as governor of Jerusalem. Robinson wrote: 'You can't walk out on us for a job like this!' He was doubtless joking, but his good-natured teasing shows how closely Evatt was tied to the foundation of Israel, though he was surely too much of a partisan to govern a divided city shared by both Arabs and Israelis.

Supporting Israel in 1947 and 1948 involved some risk for Evatt, as it put him at odds with both the British and the Americans, both of whom were less willing to push aside Arab Palestinian interests and were concerned about the continuing violence. That in turn meant he risked their support for the next campaign for the presidency, on which he was focused from mid-1948. In July, he arrived by air in London, with Mary Alice and Rosalind about to arrive by ship. He was lobbying hard for the presidency; one report had it that he 'spared no effort to gather votes for his election', though the Americans opposed him, reportedly due to his 'unpredictable attitude'. By this stage, both the British and the Americans thought Evatt was unreliable on Cold War issues and too inclined to support the Soviet Union. In addition, the British and American intelligence services knew that there were significant leaks from Evatt's Department of External Affairs in the late 1940s. They knew this because Soviet signal codes had been broken, but this 'Venona' intelligence, as it was called, was kept secret, in order not to reveal that the codes had been broken. Leaks from Evatt's department were among the reasons for the establishment of ASIO in 1949 by the Chifley government. It did not mean that Evatt was himself corrupted, though he was notoriously sloppy with security; there are numerous stories of him leaving sensitive documents behind in hotels.

In the end, the Americans decided not to oppose Evatt for the presidency and he insisted to the British that they 'had already committed themselves to support' him, a point which the Dominions Office conceded. By the time the assembly met in Paris in September, Evatt expected the support of India and the South American countries, and was certain of British support. The assembly meetings took place in the Palais de Chaillot, an enormous 1930s modernist building across the river from the Eiffel Tower. Evatt was duly elected president in September, taking his seat 'on the great Louis Quatorze chair to preside over the momentous gathering of fifty-eight nations', as the *Women's Weekly* reported. Sam Atyeo joked that Evatt was now 'the president of the world', but the presidency of the UN General Assembly is not quite as august or powerful a role as it sounds. Elected annually by the member states of the assembly, the president is chairperson when the assembly is in session; the position has some capacity to influence events, but is hardly an executive role.

Just after his election, another *Women's Weekly* article reported that the Evatts were staying in 'a small apartment half way between the Australian Embassy and the Palais Chaillot'. Mary Alice and Rosalind, now aged sixteen, attended most sittings of the assembly and watched Evatt presiding. Rosalind was studying the flute with the Paris Opera's chief flautist, and taking French lessons. She later remembered her adolescence as 'terribly exciting', explaining, 'I was able to go overseas … that's not a normal upbringing for a child, yet I would never give it back'.

Mary Alice told the *Weekly* she had not yet had time to visit the galleries, but she was delighted that Evatt had been elected president, because 'he really believes that it is the one organisation which can make peace possible'. The *Weekly* was enthusiastic about Eleanor Roosevelt's work on the Universal Declaration of Human Rights; the assembly formally adopted the declaration in December, with Evatt in the chair. Although he is often associated with it, and although he certainly supported its intent, the declaration was predominantly Eleanor Roosevelt's achievement. Her papers contain a good deal of correspondence relating to the committee she chaired to draft it and, while Australia had a representative on her committee, Evatt himself was not centrally involved.

As president, Evatt could be quite informal, even ostentatiously so. He sometimes walked to work at the Palais de Chaillot, and often insisted on taking the Metro, despite the security guards saying it was too risky. Mary Alice said that he liked the sociability of public transport and considered private cars to be antisocial. He was described arriving for his first session as president of the assembly; other dignitaries arrived in limousines, formally dressed, while Evatt was sitting next to the driver of a modest, late-model Ford, in his baggy lounge suit, his tie off-centre. He muttered a nasal 'see you later' to the driver, let himself out and shambled up to the official entrance – where he was barred by a gendarme whose instructions were to admit 'dignitaries only'. The guard had to be informed that this dishevelled character was the president of the United Nations General Assembly.

Evatt's year as president was marked by the escalation of Cold War tensions in Europe. He clashed further with the British, over Palestine in particular. One of the British delegation to the UN, Francis Cumming-Bruce, told his superiors in London that Evatt was unable to deal with anything properly, due to 'the enormous number of irons that he insists on keeping in the fire at once'. He thought that Evatt was 'manipulating' the assembly 'almost exclusively in the interests of his own personal ends, and desire for publicity'. Over the partition of Palestine, Cumming-Bruce complained in December that Australia pursued 'an extreme appeasement policy with the Jews and failed even to go through the motions of consulting with us'. They had disagreed, too, about how to handle the Berlin blockade, which had begun in mid-1948. Berlin was divided into four zones – one controlled by the Russians and the other three held by America, Britain and France – and the city was isolated within communist East Germany. When the Russians blocked supplies to the western-held zones, the US and Britain responded with an airlift of supplies. The blockade was not lifted until May 1949, when the Russians backed down; the crisis was a clear sign of the escalating Cold War tensions between Russia and the west.

Evatt had earlier, in 1948, commissioned some work in the Department of External Affairs to assess the onset of the Cold War. The analyses revealed a division within the department between two broad groups identified as 'realists' and 'liberal internationalists'. The realists largely agreed with the Anglo-American view that the Soviet Union was aggressive, and argued that Australia should align itself with the US and UK strategy of containment. The liberal internationalists, on the other hand, saw fault on both sides and proposed that the UN should appoint a group of third-party member nations to act as intermediaries between the antagonists. Evatt was predominantly on the liberal internationalist side of this debate, as was Burton, whom Evatt had appointed secretary of the department in April 1947. In a similar vein, as president of the assembly Evatt tried in November 1948 to urge the major powers to find a solution to their Cold War tensions, especially the blockade of Berlin, lest it develop into open war. He was acting in concert with the UN secretary-general, the former Norwegian politician Trygve Lie, but to Evatt's chagrin, the issue was referred to the Security Council, where it was blocked by a Soviet veto.

THE ESCAPIST

Mr. Menzies, criticising Dr. Evatt's championing of UNO, said it was fantastic to bandy words about fine theories and airy schemes when lawless and revolutionary forces were on the march.

As Cold War divisions undermined the aspirations of international cooperation, Evatt's continuing commitment to the UN was often ridiculed by cartoonists; here Frith represents him as 'the escapist', smoking opium and drifting away, his head clouded by illusions.

John Frith, *Sydney Morning Herald*, 17 February 1949

Evatt's opposition to the veto was already well established, and his objections proved to be well founded. By December 1949, the end of his period as foreign minister, the right to veto had been used in the Security Council a total of forty-eight times; all but two of those veto votes were cast by the Soviet Union, which blocked action on debates related to Spain, the Berlin blockade, Greek frontier incidents, Czechoslovakia and Indonesia. In addition, the Soviet Union regularly vetoed applications for membership of the United Nations from individual countries. The internationalists, including Evatt, placed their hopes in world governance, but the realities of Cold War conflict were quickly sidelining the fledgling United Nations. Into the 1950s, as the Cold War tightened, the conservative parties in Australia argued a strongly 'realist' position while Evatt's continuing attachment to the ideals and hopes embodied in the United Nations started to appear anachronistic.

'The quick change artist'

While he was president of the assembly in 1948 and 1949, Evatt was also, as noted previously, involved in a Privy Council appeal in his capacity as attorney-general. This resulted in yet another frantic stream of work. In late 1949, the cartoonist John Frith represented Evatt's multiple roles as president, as foreign minister and as attorney-general as those of a 'quick change artist', the kind of actor who dashes off the stage to then reappear in another costume and another role. The call boy comes into Evatt's dressing room saying, 'You're on for the Prime Minister's act, sir'. It was another reminder of Evatt's ambition, but his multiple parts were also exhausting him.

The Privy Council appeal was about the Labor government's attempt to nationalise Australia's private banks; resentment of the power of the banking system to dictate economic policy was a strong memory, especially for Chifley, that led back to the traumas of the Depression. Legislation had been passed in November 1947, and the banks were mounting a vigorous public campaign in opposition. In February, they mounted a constitutional challenge to the legislation and Evatt appeared in the High Court in Melbourne presenting the government's case. The diminutive Garfield Barwick represented the banks. Evatt had not been in the court since he left it in 1940, and he immediately roused Starke's antipathy by arguing that several judges should recuse themselves because they held shares in private banks; Latham, still chief justice, overruled that. The case ran for weeks, with Evatt creating a record by taking seventeen days for his arguments. In sweltering heat, Evatt famously and idiosyncratically ordered that the windows be closed as he was worried about catching a chill; Latham ordered them opened again.

In August, when the High Court's decision was published, it had gone against Labor, declaring that the nationalisation of private banks was unconstitutional. But both Latham and McTiernan had dissented and some of their arguments were thought to favour Evatt's views. On the basis of those dissenting judgements, Chifley decided on an appeal to the Privy Council in London. By this stage, Evatt was already in London and Kenneth Bailey, former dean of law at Melbourne University and now Commonwealth solicitor-general, was sent across with volumes of papers.

Brendan Bracken wrote from London to his friend Robinson in Australia that he had had dinner with Evatt, and 'tried to persuade him not to appear before the Privy Council'. Bracken suggested an alternative barrister and Evatt agreed, but then they discovered the barrister in question had already been engaged by one of the banks. Bracken thought Evatt had some reservations about the case: 'I gather from our friend that the Government would like to find a face-saving compromise with the banks. [Evatt] is very critical of some of the judges. He says they are very old and very reactionary'.

The first part of the appeal (in which the Privy Council would decide whether it would hear an appeal) was held in late October, just as the UN General Assembly was meeting in Paris. Evatt attended both events simultaneously. The Privy Council was reportedly less formal than an ordinary court; the press in Australia described the five Lords of Appeal without their robes and taking their seats at a table facing the barristers. By the time the Privy Council ruled in early November it would hear an appeal, Evatt had already dashed back to Paris for the assembly, and Bailey apologised for his absence.

When the assembly completed its session in late December, Evatt and Mary Alice hosted an official party in the Palais de Chaillot. 'All the fountains were illuminated', Mary Alice said, and she had arranged for some comedians to give a performance. The interior of the building still showed some war damage and 'looked a bit drear', so she arranged to borrow modernist paintings to cover the walls. Evatt, Mary Alice and Rosalind then had the relaxation of a sea voyage back to Australia.

The Privy Council appeal was then a gruelling marathon from mid-March to early June 1949. Mary Alice and Evatt flew this time. Evatt spent twenty-two days presenting his case, and Barwick, leading the case for the banks, took another nine. It set a new record for the duration of a Privy Council case; two of the judges died before a decision could be reached. Finlay Crisp, Chifley's biographer, thought that Barwick was much wiser and more sensitive in taking up less time, and that Evatt went on far too long. Barwick led the judges towards his conclusions and then congratulated them on being right, while Evatt lectured them, but seemed to sense he was losing ground. He was at the same time juggling flights to New York for meetings of the General Assembly, which was still dealing with the Berlin blockade and the risk of open confrontation between Russia and the west.

Geoffrey Sawer was part of Evatt's legal team in London, working day and night for weeks; he later recalled that at the end of another exhausting night working on their legal arguments, he announced to Evatt he had decided to take a break and go on an Easter pilgrimage to Canterbury cathedral. 'Instead of blowing me up for my base desertion,' he said, 'Evatt proceeded to recite the first thirty lines or so of the Prologue to the Canterbury Tales by Chaucer'. Sawer wrote that the incident illustrated Evatt's 'fundamental humanity' as much as his 'prodigious memory'.

The Privy Council decision was announced in early July. It was a triumph for Barwick and another defeat for the government, bringing Chifley's attempts to control the banking system to an end. And it left

Evatt seriously exhausted; Grattan saw him during this period in New York and noted that he was 'terribly tired' and not really fully engaged by what he had to do. At the age of fifty-five, he appeared to need 'more than just a holiday', Grattan wrote. 'He seemed to need – and want – a completely new occupation; he had had politics.'

Communists and Groupers

By the middle of June 1949, when Evatt and Mary Alice returned to Sydney by air, his time as president of the assembly was over, though he did not know it. He was expected back in New York for the opening of the next session in September, which would elect a new president, but there were already press reports that he might not attend, given a federal election was due by the end of the year. When it was later announced that Norman Makin, now the ambassador to the US, would preside in his place, it was speculated that Chifley had told him to stay. It effectively marked the end of his time on the international stage and by the end of the year Labor was out of government.

The Evatts arrived back just as the coal strike was about to start. Australia ran on coal, fuelling power stations and industry, which made the Miners' Federation a strategically important union. Trouble had been building through June and the miners went out on a nationwide strike at the end of the month. Labor saw it as a direct and aggressive challenge to their government by the Communist party, which controlled the Miners' Federation. Evatt was often out of the country throughout the late 1940s, and had little connection with what was happening within the labour movement. In any case, he did not have the same relationships in the labour movement as someone like Chifley. But the struggle developing between the Communist and Labor parties was to be a defining feature of the late 1940s and early 1950s. It would have significant bearing on Evatt's tortured period in leadership from 1951.

In 1944, the Communist party had over 20,000 members and the allegiance of between 25 and 40 per cent of the union movement, through CPA union leaders being elected, usually openly as communists. The CPA had some substantial strength, in the unions and also culturally, among intellectuals and writers. Their opponents assumed the elections bringing communists to union leadership must be rigged in some way, though Clyde Cameron, already a veteran of the corrupt practices of his own Australian Workers' Union, noted that most of the CPA unions had clean ballots. Just as importantly, the CPA's union strength was strategic; they did not much bother unionising shop assistants or public servants, but they were very strong on the waterfront and the railways, and in the steel industry and the coalmines.

During the mid-1940s, both the ALP mainstream and those associated with Catholic anti-communist circles in Victoria began to organise to defeat the CPA in union elections. B.A. 'Bob' Santamaria, the key figure in Catholic Action in Melbourne, had diagnosed the strength of the CPA and noted the strategic importance of the unions they held. He argued that the ALP was in danger of being taken over because affiliated unions had significant influence through sending delegates to Labor conferences, where they voted on Labor policy and on senior administrative appointments. As Santamaria put it:

> The deep nation-wide penetration of the trade unions by the
> Communist Party has as one of its effects great Communist
> pressure on the structures of the ALP, because the trade unions
> are the dominant factor in the ALP. If the Communists are
> allowed to consolidate their control over the trade unions they
> must inevitably control the ALP ... This is mathematically
> inescapable.

If that happened, he claimed, a Labor government would be at best neutralist in the Cold War, and at worst would support the Soviet Union and China. By this relentless logic, the global Cold War and the fight to control the unions were intimately entwined with a struggle for the soul of the ALP.

Beginning in Melbourne in 1942, and with the moral and financial support of Archbishop Mannix, Santamaria organised Catholic unionists into the Catholic Social Studies Movement with the intention of working against communist union leaders. The 'Movement' was a network of well-organised and secretive anti-communist union activists, and in Melbourne they worked closely with the Trades Hall Council and its secretary, Victor Stout. Paul Ormonde, a strong critic of the Movement, described clandestine meetings of small cells of dedicated members, usually in church halls with the windows blacked out to disguise the fact that anything was happening. Admission was by invitation only, and an indication of the conspiratorial climate was the use of 'split letters' for communicating information; members would be sent one half of a letter, and it was only when they came together that they could piece together the full message – a subterfuge to prevent the complete letter falling into 'enemy' hands.

In parallel, the ALP from 1945 onward itself established 'Industrial Groups', first in New South Wales, with a similar aim of contesting CPA influence in union elections. Santamaria later wrote: 'The basic principle of counter-organisation, which had been pioneered in Victoria – to oppose cadre with cadre, "fraction" with "fraction", cell with cell, and to give effect to the entire enterprise with tight central direction – was being put into operation throughout Australia.' There was significant overlap in membership between the Movement and the Groups, but while the former was explicitly Catholic, the latter was a more diverse mix of anti-communist labour activists, including some former Marxists, such as prominent leaders Laurie Short and Dinny Lovegrove. Over time, the Movement and the Groups became almost indistinguishable, and were known simply as the Groupers. For convenience, I will use the term Groupers, but it is important to recall that they always had a more Catholic flavour and fervour in Victoria, where the church had backed them with little reservation;

in other states, the Catholic hierarchy was more wary, and the Groupers had a more secular orientation. Outside Victoria, anti-communism was more about the right and centre of the labour movement struggling to re-establish the control it had lost to the CPA – a power struggle rather than a moral crusade.

The aggressive stance the CPA took in the late 1940s culminated in the demonstration of strength in the 1949 coal strike, when Labor certainly thought it was being openly challenged. Jack Ferguson, a close confidant of Chifley, recalled the coal strike as 'a revolutionary situation' in which the CPA was testing its strength. Until 1940, Ferguson had been a member of the CPA and had come up through the Railways Union; he and Chifley agreed that this was not an ordinary strike, and he later recalled Chifley saying: 'Ah, well, Johnny, we're into it boots and all'. Beazley later wrote that the coal strike infuriated Chifley. He dispatched troops to work the open-cut mines, horrifying Labor stalwarts. Ferguson persuaded his union, the Railways, to transport the coal, while Evatt quickly prepared legislation to freeze CPA union funds to prevent them supporting the strike. Under the terms of the *National Emergency (Coal Strike) Act*, four union leaders were then jailed.

The Liberals were in furious agreement with Labor's repressive legislation, which Evatt justified in parliament by referring to circumstances of 'economic war'. He argued that: 'The community, through the national parliament, is acting in self-defence against aggression that is completely unjustified in the circumstances of this case'. Evatt's legislation was in line with Chifley's thinking, but it would later be cited against him personally, as would the legislation he had drafted a few years earlier suppressing communist-led union boycotts against the rocket testing range established by the British at Woomera in remote South Australia. In both cases he was subsequently accused of repressive action inconsistent with his reputation as a champion of civil liberties.

The distinction Evatt tried to maintain in 1949 during the coal strike was between illegal action, as determined by the courts, and freedom of expression, which should flourish. His feelings on this question had been made clear the previous year, when banning the CPA was debated in parliament; the Country party wanted a legislative ban, but the Liberals were not yet in favour. Evatt argued that making it 'a criminal offence for people to hold or express views in favour of communism' would undermine democracy; it was in the repressive spirit of the Nazis, and of 'a police state'. When the prominent Liberal politician Percy Spender interjected that communists were 'a criminal conspiracy', Evatt replied, 'It is a criminal conspiracy if it is proved to be. If sedition can be proved, court proceedings may be taken'. 'Propaganda', he said, should not substitute for 'argument and ascertainment of the facts'. This was his legal self speaking and it meshed with his liberal self when he argued that:

> Communism can be suppressed, not by coercive means but in
> open encounter. We can deal with communism by applying
> the famous maxim of … John Milton: 'Let truth and falsehood
> grapple. Whoever knew truth to be put to worse in an open
> encounter?' Let the encounter be free and open.

In 1948 this was a view still shared by Menzies, but the Liberals, urged on by the Country party, were moving towards a policy of banning communism itself, and would take that policy to the December 1949 election.

The actions of the Chifley government in putting down the coal strike were forceful, using the military, freezing union funds and imprisoning some leaders. The intention was to starve the miners back and it worked; the strike collapsed, and in the subsequent union election the CPA lost control of the New South Wales branch of the Miners' Federation. But both Cameron and Beazley thought the consequences were demoralising for the labour movement. Beazley wrote that Chifley's actions were 'the antithesis of his whole approach to unionism', while Cameron said, 'a lot of grass roots Labor people became disenchanted, temporarily at least, with what the Government had done and, in a spirit of cussedness, voted informal or perhaps even went to the point of voting for the Opposition'.

It is doubtful that is enough to explain the loss of the 1949 election to Menzies' revived Liberal party. One historian of the party, Ian Hancock, thought the strike helped the Liberals, because it allowed them to 'link socialism and communism'. In the Cold War period, it was not hard for conservatives to drawn a connection between their existing opposition to what they saw as Labor's socialism and emerging anxieties about communism. But given the Chifley government had acted so forcefully against the strikers, it was a stretch to claim that Labor was 'soft' on communism. The disenchantment of Labor's own supporters may have been important, but in any case the Chifley government was seen as tired and remote; it was still insisting on the rationing of goods such as petrol, and could be painted as a government of the past rather than the future.

In the election in early December, Labor's primary vote nationally fell to 46 per cent, and in the lower house the Liberal–Country party coalition had an advantage of seventy-four members to Labor's forty-seven. In Barton, Evatt had been confronted with an effective Liberal challenger in Nancy Wake. She had genuine glamour, having been a British agent in the French Resistance during the war. The election result gave Evatt 'one of the biggest shocks of his political career', when Wake came within a few thousand votes of upsetting him; during the count it had seemed a lot closer. With Menzies back in power, growing tensions over communist influence within the labour movement, and the developing Cold War eclipsing hopes of international collaboration, Evatt's period of ministerial power was now over. He could not have known that it was over for good. Nor could he have known that this combination of Menzies' resurgence, domestic anti-communism and the international Cold War would destroy him.

12

The Labor leader

In early 1950, Jack Ferguson was fishing in a dinghy off the New South Wales south coast when a motor launch approached carrying a message that Evatt needed to speak to him urgently. Ferguson was one of the most powerful men in the administrative wing of the ALP, and was described as 'Chifley's faithful lieutenant'. He was president of both the New South Wales and federal branches of the party. Still in his fishing clothes, he went to meet Evatt, who announced that he wanted to step down from politics and join the New South Wales Supreme Court. The state Labor government was presenting obstacles and he wanted Ferguson to use his influence. Ferguson told Tennant he refused, saying, 'It was not the proper thing for him to do'.

When I first read this, I thought the date was mistaken; it was in 1960, not in 1950, that there was a flurry of activity to get Evatt out of politics and onto the Supreme Court, and the state government resisted. But Ferguson mentioned both New South Wales premier Jim McGirr and state attorney-general Clarrie Martin as individuals he was supposed to influence – both of whom died in the 1950s – and Ferguson himself had long since retired from politics by 1960 and would have had only residual influence at that time. Evatt's private secretary, Allan Dalziel, also wrote that in 1950 Evatt was 'talking privately of quitting politics'. So it seems that after the 1949 election defeat, Evatt was again toying with the idea of getting out. Hartley Grattan, who had seen him so exhausted in 1949, wrote that 'it would have been far better for him' if he had left politics, and that continuing and then taking on the leadership was 'the great mistake of his life';

he felt it was only Mary Alice urging Evatt on. Mary Alice herself claimed that they had talked about retirement after the election, but that it was 'practically impossible' for her husband not to stay on: 'You can't just give up something because it's getting harder; at any rate it wasn't in his nature to do that. The harder it got the harder he would try to do it'. She did not say if she wanted him to give it away, and she only ever attributed the loftiest motives to her husband.

If Ferguson had brought his power to bear, Evatt's career would have run a very different course, and possibly the trajectory of post-war Australian politics would have been different too. For Evatt was entering the most turbulent period of his turbulent life. The story has been told in detail; there is a huge literature about the unfolding of the Cold War in Australia, about Menzies' failed attempts to ban the Communist party in 1950–1951, about the defection of the Russian spy Vladimir Petrov in 1954, and about the tensions building within the Labor party and leading to the split in 1955. After the split, acrimony and exhaustion debilitated the party. Evatt was leader through almost all this period, and was central to the action. Looking back on the wreckage, many would blame Evatt, and say his flawed decisions in this period indicated instability, paranoia and even madness. Others thought of him as a champion of reason and liberty in a time of irrationality, suffering calumnies and smears for his principles. In the fierce politics of the Cold War, Evatt was an intensely divisive figure. But to assess this tumultuous period of his life, we have to disentangle his actions and motivations from the building tensions splitting the labour movement as Menzies' coalition government relentlessly pressed the issue of communism that divided Labor.

Banning communism

Many on the left saw Stalin's successful incorporation of central and eastern European states into the Soviet empire in the 1940s as defensive – an attempt to create a buffer between Russia and NATO-aligned Europe – but critics on the right saw it as relentless aggression that must be contained. In 1949 the Soviet Union tested its first nuclear bomb, fuelling these existing fears of communist expansion in the west. In the same year, the Communist party came to power in China, and in June the following year, war broke out in Korea, setting Cold War alarm bells ringing. In August Menzies warned that a third world war could be expected within three years.

Evatt, like many others, would often describe Australian anti-communism as a homegrown form of McCarthyism, the virulent anti-communist campaign spearheaded in the United States by Senator Joseph McCarthy. Anti-communist sentiment in the United States often took the form of a frenzied search for traitors, conducted with all the passion of a witch-hunt. But while Australian anti-communism was also vigorous, it had at least three important differences. The first was that it did not have the overt religious character of the US campaign. American historian Richard Hofstadter described anti-communism as an expression of a 'paranoid theme' in American politics, underpinned by a division of the world into good and evil: those who are with us and pure, and those who are against us and evil. In *The Crucible*, first performed early in 1953, the American playwright Arthur Miller explored a similar idea, drawing parallels between the Salem witch trials and McCarthyism; he later wrote about the guilt experienced by those 'holding illicit, suppressed feelings of alienation and hostility towards standard, daylight society as defined by its most orthodox proponents'. Drawing on these ideas in her study of Menzies, Judith Brett described Australian anti-communism as less 'lurid', with less of this religious undercurrent. That communists were atheists was not as central in Australia as the idea that they were alien and beholden to a foreign power; they were 'threats to the social order rather than purveyors of sin'.

A second difference was that Australia had a genuine communist party, significant both culturally and in the union movement, whereas the party in the US was negligible and had no influence in a weak labour movement. It was fanciful, even paranoid, to see the party as a threat in the US, but in Australia there was a legitimate struggle between real forces. Anti-communism in Australia was less about chasing shadows and rooting out evil, and much more about practical political struggles.

Finally, and because of this second difference, anti-communism had direct political implications in Australia. Control of the unions translated into power within the ALP, with consequences for policymaking, appointments of influence and the candidates chosen for preselection. The struggle between communism and anti-communism in the labour movement directly affected the party, and it provided an ideal wedge issue with which the Menzies government could divide its opponents.

At the 1949 election, the House of Representatives had been expanded from seventy-six to 121 members. New members on the conservative side included many ex-servicemen. When the new Labor caucus assembled in February 1950, the Groupers' parliamentary representation was vocal but still relatively small. The most prominent, talented and passionate of the eight Victorian MPs aligned with the Groupers were a former public service union leader, Stan Keon, and a former member of the Victorian parliament, John Mullens. Clyde Cameron, who opposed the Groupers throughout, described the new Victorian group as 'tough and dedicated sons of the Church whose main interest in life was to fight Communism'. A few others, such as Tom Burke, who had represented the seat of Perth since 1943, were similarly aligned, but in a total caucus of eighty-one, including senators, they were a small group that did not yet reflect the changing balance of power in the labour movement. At this stage, the Groupers were stronger in the party organisation and the unions than they were in the parliament.

By 1949, the Groupers were largely in control in Victoria and had used their majority on the state executive to force out secretary

Pat Kennelly. A talented backstage operator often described as a clas-
sic machine politician, Kennelly had been supremely powerful in the
late 1940s. A Catholic himself, he was implacably opposed to the
Groupers; he thought they were becoming an intolerable party within
the party. Now he had lost power in Victoria but not his power base;
he was also the party's federal secretary from 1946 to 1954. In other
states, the Groupers were not yet powerful, but their influence in New
South Wales was growing; since the mid-1940s they had been aligned
with the AWU under its national secretary Tom Dougherty. During
1950 and 1951, the vociferous group in the federal caucus was small
but implacable.

Until well into 1949, there had been some dispute within the
Liberal party hierarchy about the wisdom of banning the Communist
party; it was also something Santamaria was sceptical about. Menzies
had been reluctant, preferring argument and education to proscription, but the Country party enthusiastically endorsed a ban. The pre-
vailing view among the Liberals was that it was not feasible and that
driving the party underground would make control more difficult. But
by late 1949, this had changed, in response to the challenge of the
coal strike and the escalation of global Cold War tensions. During the
December 1949 election campaign, Menzies was quite explicit about
his intentions:

> Communism in Australia is an alien and destructive pest. If elected,
> we shall outlaw it. The Communist Party will be declared subversive
> and unlawful, and dissolved. Subject to appeal, the Attorney-
> General will be empowered to declare other bodies substantially
> Communist … These are far-reaching proposals. But half-measures
> are no good if, in the bitter conflict between the Communists and
> our decent, peaceful people, the people are to win.

In April 1950, the Menzies government tabled its legislation.
The *Communist Party Dissolution Bill* declared the CPA unlawful,

dissolving it and other bodies suspected of being affiliates or fronts, and imposing five-year jail terms on members who attempted to carry on. It defined a communist as someone who supported the 'objectives, policies, teachings, principles or practices' of Marx or Lenin, and stipulated that a person 'declared' a communist would be banned from employment in the public service or a union. Most contentiously, it reversed the usual onus of proof, requiring accused citizens to establish their innocence; it was not the state's responsibility to prove their guilt.

The sweeping breadth of the proposals, their ambiguity, and the reversal of the onus of proof were all grounds for attack, but Labor was in a bind. Menzies could, as he did regularly, say that opposing the bill meant supporting and protecting communists. The proposal was popular; an opinion poll in April found support for a ban at 74 per cent and opposition at only 20 per cent; two months later, approval had risen to 82 per cent. As could have been predicted, Labor was internally divided, and vulnerable to being depicted as soft or unreliable on communism. Initially, Chifley was inclined to oppose the legislation outright, though he knew the tensions in the caucus meant that was difficult. Some sided with Chifley in opposing the bill; others were inclined to let the legislation through, thinking it would be impossible to enforce, while the right-wing Groupers vigorously supported proscription. Chifley was explicit in private about the dangers, saying that the legislation was 'a political measure aimed at splitting the Labour Movement'.

In the parliament, Chifley gave one of his most famous speeches against the bill:

It strikes at the very heart of justice. It opens the door for the liar, the perjurer and the pimp to make charges and to damn men's reputations and to do so in secret without having either to substantiate or prove any charges ... Nothing could be more hateful than witch hunting, which gives to liars, perjurers and

informers opportunities to make statements without being called
upon to substantiate them in a court of law.

Chifley based his arguments on ideas of 'liberty and justice', arguing
that the legislation was akin to 'the machinery of tyranny'. Evatt would
later follow suit, but Jack Ferguson recalled that the deputy leader was
initially reluctant to oppose the bill, and had fought him on it, saying it
was 'ruinous for the labour movement to be too closely identified with
the Communist party'. Once the party resolved to oppose the legislation, Evatt fell into line. Ferguson said later: 'He seemed relieved that
the decision had fallen out and was happy and free to follow it. But he
had fought that decision to the last ditch'. Having taken up the cause,
Evatt's opposition was forceful, but some would remember his wavering as evidence of uncertain principles. The pragmatism he showed
in this case was inconsistent with his arguments when banning the
CPA was debated in 1948; back then he had insisted that existing laws
could deal with illegal actions, and had quoted Milton: 'Let truth and
falsehood grapple'. Now he seemed more concerned with blocking
Menzies' attempts to divide the Labor party.

In June, Labor's federal executive decided that amendments
should be forced in the Senate, where Labor had a majority, to restore
the onus of proof to the prosecution, to provide for trial by jury and
to extend the right of appeal. The Victorian executive openly opposed
the federal decision, proposing that the bill should be voted through
intact. When Kennelly asked for the views of each of the state representatives on the federal executive and collated their responses for
Chifley, the party was clearly divided. The Victorians favoured no
amendments; New South Wales, South Australia and Western Australia all supported the amendments; the Tasmanians were divided;
and the Queensland delegates were ambivalent. Labor used its control
in the Senate to force the amendments, which the government then
rejected. Cameron wrote that Chifley was worried the Groupers might
defy caucus, and decided that 'the safest way to avoid a damaging

division' was to refer the issue back to the federal executive, which had power to instruct the caucus how to act.

At the beginning of October, the federal executive met and again instructed the parliamentary party to insist on the Senate amendments, but opinions on the federal executive were finely balanced and Tom Burke, the Grouper MP from Western Australia, returned to Perth and convinced that state's executive to change its vote and to oppose the Senate amendments. Joe Chamberlain, Western Australia's state secretary, considered resigning but travelled back to Canberra to reopen the issue and vote against his own view. He recalled Chifley was 'greatly disturbed'. Labor's resistance was collapsing and Chifley had been humiliated. Some feared the threat of a double dissolution election over the CPA bill, but the about-face also signalled the growing strength of the Groupers.

The federal executive now instructed the party to pass the bill intact, and Chifley made what Cameron described as 'the bitter announcement that all he had said in previous debates now had to be stood aside'. In caucus, Chifley warned the party to hold together and accept humiliation, saying 'recriminate, and we shall split'. The Liberals were understandably jubilant; Menzies described it as 'surely the most abject surrender in the history of the once great Labour party'. In an assessment prepared during the subsequent referendum campaign, the Liberal secretariat exulted over Labor's 'great retreat'. The Labor senators then dutifully voted for the legislation on 19 October 1950, and the Communist party became illegal the following day. Members of the CPA had been preparing to go underground, setting up a clandestine network that would not unravel if some were arrested. Communists buried their books, or housed them with friends who would not be searched.

A few days later, the CPA and ten of its unions mounted a constitutional challenge in the High Court. Everyone was staggered when it emerged that Evatt had taken the case for the Waterside Workers' Federation, a CPA union. It seemed a reckless act, and Evatt often ignored advice when he felt himself to be right, but there are indications that in this case he sought the opinions of others; it was not a decision he made lightly. Frank Green, the left-leaning clerk of the House, recalled being told by Jim Healy, the leader of the Waterside Workers, that 'a lot of pressure had to be put on Evatt before he agreed to "go into the ring"; he was afraid it would injure him politically with the Catholics'. Evatt also consulted Ferguson, who recalled him asking what the party's attitude would be if he were to take the case. Ferguson said he replied: 'What you are proposing to do is ethically correct, professionally sound and politically very, very foolish'. Ferguson rang Chifley; he later said it was the first time he had ever known Chifley to be at a loss, hesitating and then sighing deeply. 'Ah, well, Johnny', Chifley said, 'We've got to remember what Bert did for the railway union after 1917. And we've got to remember that he has a brilliant mind. That's the trouble with brilliant minds. They make hellish awful mistakes.' Approaching Ferguson at least indicated some caution, though it seems Evatt was careful to avoid asking for Chifley's approval, perhaps to give his leader room to say he had not approved, or to prevent Chifley talking him out of it.

The announcement that Evatt was to appear in the High Court had, in the words of one journalist 'set legal as well as political circles buzzing'; in light of recent political events, the embarrassment to the Labor party could be 'enormous', he wrote. Another wrote that while some in Labor praised Evatt's courage, others were annoyed that 'another critical angle to the Communist issue had arisen'. And Evatt's decision caused uproar in the caucus. Cameron described questions put to Chifley at a party meeting – had he known and had he approved. Chifley said he had not known, but had Evatt asked for his permission, he would have given it gladly. A motion was proposed dissociating caucus from Evatt's action; when the vote was taken on the voices, Chifley declared it lost. Cameron was convinced the majority was against Evatt, but when Burke called for a division, Chifley refused to accept it. Cameron described the scene: 'By this stage the caucus was in a state of bedlam. Members were shouting across the room ... calling the Victorians all sorts of things and they were retaliating.' Burke moved a motion of dissent, whereupon Chifley sucked on his pipe, stood up and walked out, saying, 'There will be no dissent from my ruling. The meeting stands adjourned'. Cameron commented that 'no one else could ever have done that and got away with it'. A few days later there were press reports that another attempt to censure Evatt had been blocked; Labor people were criticising 'his lack of political acumen, his secrecy or his desire for publicity', but the Liberals' attacks on him had been so fierce the caucus reflex was towards solidarity.

The High Court case began in mid-November, with Garfield Barwick appearing for the government. Three judges remained from Evatt's time on the bench – Latham, Dixon and McTiernan – and there would be no grumpy repartee from Starke, as he and Rich had recently retired; the talk was that they had waited until Evatt was no longer attorney-general so he would not decide who replaced them. The court announced its judgement on 9 March 1951, declaring the Act was invalid because the government did not have the constitutional power to legislate to ban a political party in peacetime.

The journalist Harold Cox remembered that when the news came through on a teleprinter there was confusion; the first message was that the Act had been validated, then the mistake was corrected. Cox went to Chifley's office, where he found 'a small wake going on in the corridor'. Chifley saw him and said, 'Harold's a bloody old Tory, but he'll tell me the truth. Is it true that the bill has been sustained?' Cox explained the confusion and confirmed the legislation had been rejected. Chifley said, 'Well, this is wonderful. I must go and ring up bloody old Ivan and congratulate him'. After his appearance in this case, Cox explained, Chifley generally called Evatt 'Ivan the Terrible'.

Menzies was for the moment defeated, but he had popular support on his side. He promptly called a double dissolution election for 28 April, ostensibly because the Senate had rejected the government's banking legislation, though banning the CPA was another prominent issue. Labor gained five seats, but the 1949 loss had been so deep that the new seats only nibbled into the government's majority; and as Menzies had expected, the coalition won control of the Senate. One anecdote highlighting Evatt's idiosyncrasies may date from this election. Haylen wrote about a small town meeting in Tasmania 'in sub-arctic weather' at which Evatt had spoken for an hour. Haylen asked how he endured the cold and was surprised by the response:

> Evatt opened his coat. Inside he was entirely wrapped by the *Hobart Mercury*. On his feet as gaiters he had the Saturday edition of the *Launceston Examiner* … Grinning at his own cunning Evatt said, 'I have never been closer to the capitalist press in my life.'

During the election campaign, Liberal press advertising regularly featured Labor's divisions and associated Evatt in particular with communism: 'Labor is hopelessly divided: on defence; on communism; on secret ballots'. One ad had a cartoon of Chifley, Evatt and Eddie Ward with the caption:

> They walk along the Political way
> The bright pink Socialist three.
> But what they carefully do not say,
> Is how <u>Red</u> they would like to be.
> SOCIALISM IS THE FIRST STEP TO COMMUNISM;
> HELP MENZIES TO DESTROY THE RED MENACE IN
> AUSTRALIA

Another advertisement stated that behind Chifley stood Calwell, Ward and Evatt. Calwell was characterised as 'the Standover man', and Ward was 'irresponsible, hot-headed Eddie', while Evatt was 'the Communist champion'. That was nicely ambiguous; did it mean that

Evatt had championed the communists, or was himself a communist?

After the High Court challenge and as they prepared for the election, the Liberal federal secretariat identified Evatt as a Labor vulnerability. In his history of the party, Ian Hancock wrote that they decided to 'associate Dr Evatt with members of the Communist party … [to] make Evatt himself the issue in the campaign, and … highlight divisions within Labor ranks over the association with communists'. Even though Menzies argued against linking Labor with the Communist party, the Liberal party officials 'had every intention of doing so'. During the campaign, Menzies had promised that though the High Court's decision invalidating his legislation created 'great difficulties in dealing with the alarming Communist conspiracy', the Liberals would 'go on with the fight'. His plan was to propose a constitutional referendum giving the government the power to ban communism. This proposal was popular, with 80 per cent of Australian citizens polled in July saying they would support the referendum.

Leadership

In mid-June 1951, only six weeks after the election, Chifley suffered a fatal heart attack in his room at the Hotel Kurrajong in Canberra; he had refused to dress up and attend the ball being held in nearby Parliament House to celebrate fifty years of the Commonwealth. He had had an earlier heart attack, but when asked why he did not retire said he was worried about the succession. He told Clyde Cameron, 'Bert is my Deputy, but I honestly don't think he could do it'. Others recalled hearing Chifley voice his reservations. Fred Daly, who had been a Labor MP since 1943, wrote that when he suggested to Chifley he should retire, he replied, 'I'll wait for a few months as I want the right man to lead Labor and he may turn up within that time. Evatt's a brilliant man but I don't think he would make a successful leader'. And 'Jo' Gullett, the Liberal government whip who was no fan of Evatt's, later wrote to Kylie Tennant that Chifley was 'under no illusions' about Evatt's capacity to lead the party; he recalled Chifley telling him, 'As long as I am here I can hold the Catholics and the left wing reasonably well together but I cannot see that the Doc or Arthur [Calwell] will be able to do it'.

Clyde Cameron remembered Evatt 'sobbing like a child' when the news that Chifley had just died reached the ball at Parliament House. Ferguson recalled they met in Evatt's office: 'Evatt was crying. Arthur Calwell was deeply grieved but Menzies was as deeply grieved as he'. Evatt's affection for Chifley was genuine; he never openly opposed him, unlike Curtin. Evatt had, Alan Reid thought, 'an almost small boy reverence' for Chifley, which he had never shown with anyone else. Evatt's respect for Chifley was met by the latter's good-humoured indulgence of his deputy's waywardness. Les Haylen suggested that, while Chifley admired Evatt, he did not even attempt to understand him. 'His belief was that Evatt was a special kind of man and you met the situations he created like a land mine in the back yard, when such a situation arose.' Possibly in losing Chifley he had lost another father, or perhaps an older brother; certainly, he had lost a restraining influence.

Despite all the doubts, Evatt was elected unopposed as Labor leader on 20 June 1951, with Calwell as his deputy. The caucus minutes recorded Evatt's short speech of appreciation, in which he reminded the party that he had been 'closely associated' with both Curtin and Chifley, and vowed to 'spare no efforts in trying to follow their illustrious example', cautioning them that they must be 'vigilant and united'. In one sense, he was the obvious choice; at fifty-seven, he had a high public prolife both in his own right and as Chifley's deputy, and was the last of the three large figures of the war years. Others who had made some mark as ministers in the previous Labor govern-ments – such as John Dedman, Jack Beasley and Jack Holloway – were gone; Norman Makin had returned from Washington and was back in parliament, but was never considered leadership material. Although he had Pat Kennelly's support, Calwell was not highly regarded, and being a Catholic who opposed the Groupers was a complication, while Ward was too incendiary.

There were few contenders, though plenty of Labor people shared Chifley's reservations about Evatt. Ferguson later told Tennant: 'The

Dr. Evatt will start early on his campaign for a "No" vote in the anti-Communist referendum.

Evatt and Calwell preparing for the referendum campaign; the musical score is 'No, No, a Thousand Times No', but Labor's opposition to the ban on Communism was less harmonious than that.

John Frith, *Advertiser*, 17 August 1951

Caucus had doubts about Evatt as leader ... He had offended too many of them'. He also cited Evatt's 'political incompatibility' as a cause for concern, which may have been a reference to Evatt's intellectualism and his grounding in radical liberalism rather than traditional Labor values. In this, Evatt was like Gough Whitlam, but a generation earlier; it was one of the reasons for the enmity between Evatt and Calwell, who regarded Evatt as an intellectual out of place in the labour movement, and later despised his own deputy, Whitlam, for the same reason. That Evatt's election was unopposed was as much a reflection of the depleted ranks of the party as recognition of his prominence.

Evatt's leadership was almost always precarious. Over the next nine years, he survived four formal leadership challenges and numerous other votes in caucus that tested his position. He had no real power base, and no feel for the labyrinthine ways in which the party and the union movement worked. Where Curtin, Chifley and to a lesser extent Calwell could read the labour movement, maintain their alliances and ensure support, Evatt had never been able to do so. He was like a cork tossed on rough seas. He had become leader in the build-up to the worst split in Labor's history; it was not a good time to be Labor leader and he was not well suited to the task.

'Justice is the thing'

Evatt was, however, well suited to fight a constitutional referendum. The proposal put to the citizens was threefold: to insert a new clause in the constitution giving the Commonwealth the power to legislate on communism, to validate the *Communist Party Dissolution Act*, and to give parliament the power to alter that act. That was a much more complicated proposition than simply saying yes or no to banning the party, making it easier for Evatt to raise doubts about the government's true agenda. Both he and Menzies launched into nationwide campaigns, with public meetings and rallies, some of them broadcast over national radio. Menzies' meetings were often interrupted by organised interjectors, reported in the press as rowdy and turbulent; some of his radio broadcasts were barely audible over the noise of the protestors, and he was goaded into responses such as 'communist scum', 'organised communist rabble' and 'dirty lot of rats'. He seemed to be thrown off balance by both the strength of this organised opposition and Evatt's success in widening the front to include economic policy. Menzies complained that Evatt was trying to turn the referendum into another election campaign, and Evatt was indeed keen to expand the issues, inviting the people to judge the government on its record in general.

The itineraries among Evatt's papers show the furious pace of his campaign. He started earlier than Menzies, campaigning from early August till voting day on 22 September 1951. Weeks before the official launch of the campaign at the Sydney Town Hall, he spoke at meetings in every state capital, as well as Cairns and Townsville; during the first three weeks of September there were some twenty-two short speeches broadcast on radio. Others, such as his deputy Arthur Calwell, were also scheduled to speak, but Evatt carried the main load of the campaign. During September, he gave speeches in Sydney, Newcastle, Bundaberg, Brisbane, Wagga, Adelaide and Melbourne.

The CPA, too, threw itself into the campaign, spending substantial funds for a party with a small membership, but it remained ready to go into hiding. Eric Aarons, one of the CPA's emerging leaders, was about to sail to China. Should the existing leadership be 'wiped out or incarcerated', he said, his instructions were that his group would form the nucleus of a new 'leadership in exile', a prospect he admitted was fleetingly romantic. Labor was careful to keep its distance from the CPA and in fact had a formal ban on any cooperation. At one point in the campaign, Ernest Platz, secretary of the left-wing Jewish Council to Combat Fascism and Anti-Semitism, was present when a CPA member approached and thanked Evatt for his efforts. Platz recalled Evatt later saying: 'That little reprehensible man. I wouldn't lift a finger for him. It is the principle I fight for. What did you tell me? First in Germany it was the Communist Party the Nazis attacked, then the Socialists, then Labour and the Catholics'.

* * *

Of the fifty-four metropolitan newspapers, only the *Argus* endorsed a 'no' vote. It was widely assumed that Labor's 'no' campaign was losing a rather quixotic battle, but opinion divided sharply within Australian society. As the historian Russel Ward commented, only the conscription plebiscites in 1916 and 1917 were comparable in the intensity of passionate debate roused. 'Voluntary organisations, political parties, even families were often divided against themselves.' And the referendum divided Labor, especially in Victoria. In early July, the federal executive had voted by eight votes to four to oppose the referendum, with the representatives from both Victoria and Western Australia dissenting. On the same day, the Victorian branch voted to support the referendum. During the campaign, the state branches that provided the least cooperation were Tasmania, Queensland and Western Australia; South Australia and New South Wales were largely united and ran extremely active campaigns.

The party in Victoria was itself intensely divided, with disputes breaking out between those for and against the referendum. The prominent Grouper Stan Keon made it clear he was not going to assist the 'no' campaign, and there were suggestions the federal executive would discipline him; Santamaria's paper *News Weekly* campaigned for a 'yes' vote with its usual verve, attacking Evatt and Ferguson in particular. John Burton, no longer at External Affairs and angling for a run at politics, was enlisted by a local branch to speak for the 'no' case, but the meeting was cancelled by the Victorian executive; in an indication of how anti-Catholicism and anti-communism were being inflamed, Burton declared, 'I no more like Australia receiving instructions from Rome than from Moscow'. The stresses of the referendum were exposing the rifts within Labor and these were being widely commented on in the media.

The astute political men who ran the Liberal party organisation were monitoring all this. The federal secretariat's Public Relations Planning Committee had responsibility for campaign strategy, for 'propaganda' and 'selling' their message, as they put it. This committee included shrewd operators such as federal director Don Cleland, public relations officer Edgar Holt, who wrote insightful research papers, and the state secretaries, including the very able John Carrick from New South Wales and John McConnell from Victoria. In July, McConnell commented that there were 'many strong personalities' in the labour movement in Victoria who privately supported a 'yes' vote but 'would not appear publicly on either side'. Three weeks later, he noted Victorian Labor was 'still divided' and that some Labor members had already indicated that they would be 'on holidays' during the referendum campaign. But Carrick, on the other hand, said the New South Wales labour movement was united, and strongly against the referendum; the campaign would be 'very intense'. Evatt, he said, should not be underrated, as he 'could be relied upon to put a strong legalistic case'. Tasmania, Queensland and Western Australia expected an 'easy run', while the South Australian secretary expected a hard battle. These were accurate diagnoses of what was happening.

The committee also discussed the problem of convincing Liberal supporters that the ban on communism was necessary. On 13 August the committee members were joined by Menzies, who insisted they should not try to associate the Labor party with the CPA in the 'yes' campaign. He predicted that much of the 'no' case would be directed at 'liberals with a small l' and that the advocates of the 'no' vote would be feted as champions of free speech and freedom of association. These minutes show how alert the Liberals were to the risk of losing some of their support base, fearing small 'l' liberal supporters would see the issue in the referendum as incompatible with principles of individual liberty.

Evatt used exaggerated language in the campaign, linking Menzies with totalitarianism; he said Menzies was adopting the methods of Nazism and the referendum proposals were 'fascist in spirit and a definite step towards the police state'. The cartoonists pictured Evatt shouting out of the radio about 'a police state' and 'fascism'. Commentators and historians agree, describing Evatt's 'alarming' and 'excitable' language and his 'wild allegations'. I used to agree, too, that Evatt was

HALLUCINATION

The Opposition Leader, Dr. Evatt, in an electioneering speech on Monday night, accused the Menzies Government of following the same road as Hitler, Stalin and Mussolini.

Even before the inflammatory language of the referendum campaign began, Evatt was depicted as hallucinating when he drew parallels between Menzies' legislation to ban the Communist party and the totalitarianism of Stalin, Hitler and Mussolini.

John Frith, *Advertiser*, 18 July 1951

extreme in his language, given Menzies was obviously not intent on a police state. But listening to a scratchy recording of Evatt's last speech of the referendum has made me reconsider, because his voice is genuinely authentic and his arguments quite persuasive.

Evatt made innumerable speeches over his career, in parliament, at the United Nations, launching art exhibitions, during elections and elsewhere. His voice, the voice he had demanded the Americans and British hear, was rough; some of his colleagues thought he deliberately adopted a harsher tone to disguise his class background. The voice was why Felix Frankfurter referred to him, to Roosevelt, as 'the Austrylian'. There were stories about stenographers at the UN taking dictation whose transcripts came back full of mysterious references to 'the human rice' and 'the Australian papal'. His delivery was often flat, and he had few of Menzies' oratorical skills – his pauses, his literary flourishes – and he often lacked Menzies' gravitas. Mary Alice said that when Evatt stepped down from the High Court he had to learn again to find the right voice for politics, and many commented that his speeches read better than they sounded.

The speech that changed my mind was given at Bondi, in front of a sympathetic crowd of 1200 on 20 October, the last night of the campaign. It was broadcast nationally over the fifty-nine radio stations of the Macquarie Broadcasting Network. Evatt was speaking virtually without notes, and repeating what he had been saying throughout the campaign. Listening to it, you can hear he was working the crowd in front of him, as well as appealing directly to a national radio audience. Menzies' opening speeches several weeks earlier had been raucous, the booing and shouting of hecklers prompting his intemperate replies of 'communist scum'; the tactics of his opponents made it clear to radio listeners that the referendum was being passionately disputed. By contrast, Evatt's last speech had an obviously partisan audience to reinforce his message for the listener; they laughed at his jokes, cheered at the mere mention of Chifley's name and applauded loudly when he made an emphatic point.

Both the timbre and the substance of what he said were persuasive, passionate, intimate and authentic. Cameron and Haylen both considered this the best speech of his life. Cameron thought it 'just tipped the scales' to defeat the referendum. Haylen said what came over the radio was 'a man talking with utmost sincerity':

> That night Evatt was the supreme lawyer, the civil libertarian, the man with that strange rapport he could conjure up sometimes that went out beyond his supporters to the people themselves ... He wrote into our minds the sort of country we should continue to live in and the rule of law which we dare not live without. Blasé politician that I am it moved me deeply ... I believe the real, the essential Evatt reached out that night and got the people to believe him and understand him.

Even remembering that Haylen was one of Evatt's staunchest supporters, this is significant. Evatt brought to his case a conviction that he was on the side of liberty and the rule of law. He spoke with his odd mix of legal expertise and political naivety, and a transparent authenticity. In covering the substance of his arguments, I also want to try to convey how he sounded, to capture the performance he gave.

The gist of his argument was that a constitutional change is much harder to reverse than mere legislation, yet Menzies was asking for the constitutional power both to validate the existing CPA Dissolution Act, and to enable parliament to amend any of its provisions, including its vague definition of a 'communist'. That, he argued, meant that future governments could legislate to suppress dissent of either the right or the left. The recording starts mid-sentence with Evatt saying, 'it's a tragic thing to find any government putting these proposals forward ... putting the courts out of the picture ... By making parliament or the politicians the judges of these things the government is introducing totalitarianism'. Throughout the campaign, Menzies had vainly tried to counter that only communists were covered by the proposal, while Evatt consistently raised the doubt that any dissenters might be caught in the net. 'The basic ingredient, after all, for the arbitrary control of men's lives, is the gradual elimination of all forms of opposition.' Here his voice falls into a homely, conversational tone. 'Comfortable, isn't it, at the outset to consent to the removal of these disturbing minorities; they're very noisy, very troublesome, very fractious.' That led to a long description of how Hitler had consolidated his power by suppressing opposition, and how that led to world war and the concentration camps. Evatt was reminding listeners of a familiar, recent history.

Then comes a section that starts loud, rapid and declaratory:

> And I say that in this country we can't take these steps, because under these constitutional powers a reactionary government of the right like the Menzies–Fadden government could eliminate opposition from the left; and equally [*here his voice is slow and thoughtful*] a government of the left…. could gradually eliminate opposition from the right.

Then he was back to his loud, insistent voice, saying that each of these courses 'would destroy democracy'. 'Labor stands for democracy and freedom', he said, 'and we utterly resist these infamous proposals'. There was sustained applause, after which he dropped back to a slow measured voice.

> Now, Mr Chairman, there's a famous speech by Pastor Niemöller … and I think it puts the case that I've been trying to sum up in a few sentences. He says, 'As Hitler attacked the communists, I lamented, but did nothing. Hitler attacked the Jews; I lamented, but did nothing. Hitler attacked the trade unions; again I lamented, but did nothing. Hitler then attacked my church' – that was the Lutheran church – 'Hitler then attacked my church; I acted, but then it was too late.'

This was all said in a grave, quiet voice, but he ended loudly and emphatically: 'You can't allow the first steps towards totalitarianism to be taken'.

This was followed by a long, rather wayward section about how the High Court might interpret what 'communism' meant, and how that might affect the powers of the parliament and might influence policy decisions about public ownership or state intervention. It was hardly convincing, but raising doubts and ambiguities was a key part of his strategy, and that was also why he spent a long while pondering who might be caught up in the net. 'Mr Menzies says that these proposals apply only to communists', he says, and pauses, then adds, 'He doesn't define what he means by communists'. A muffled voice from the crowd calls out, 'Anybody who interjects!' and Evatt took that up. 'Ah, yes, anybody who interjects at his meetings, perhaps.' There is laughter. 'I don't say he seriously thinks that, but that's the way he talks … When he says that this applies to communists – it's not much information, unless he says what he means by it.'

His voice here drops back down to a quiet, conversational tone:

But I go further than that. I'm dealing with the general power, but the particular power is to pass the Act of 1950. I've told you about that Act. There's a definition of communist in that. It means people who advocate the doctrines of Marx and Lenin, and I don't suppose there are many people … who could state what those doctrines are, in the aggregate. Much of what Marx advocated is commonplace in the legislation of Australia. Things like free and compulsory education by the state and matters of that kind.

Here his voice rises again to be loud and insistent:

But the point is this … Mr Menzies wants power to alter that Act of 1950, with respect to anything contained in it …

If parliament's got the power to make laws with respect to matters mentioned in the Act and one of them is a definition of communist, that says plainly to the parliament you can redefine what is the meaning of a communist and therefore it's clear that parliament could give the government of the day, or a minister, or a police officer, the right to define and characterise as a communist persons whom they so chose to include. That would practically include any group in the community.

His voice then slows, expressing genuine puzzlement: 'It's amazing to find in certain circles how ignorant people are of the dangers of it'. Immediately, he moves to a more direct, urgent tone: 'You'd have a system here analogous to the totalitarian countries, once the rot starts. You mustn't allow it to start. You must preserve the democracy of this country. Think of this not as a problem concerning communists alone, but as concerning fundamental principles'.

There is a break in this recording. Evatt says nothing in the recorded parts about the reversal of the onus of proof, but perhaps this was in a missing section, because the recording starts again as he says that some people will not receive justice, but everybody else will. 'That is not justice,' he says, and goes on:

Justice is ... to assign to every person the measure of the law, apply that to all. It's not peculiar to British law, it was enunciated 2000 years ago and more, in ancient days. [*His voice is quiet and calm.*] It's the basis of everything, justice. And the labour movement – if I had to describe in one word what it stood for – it's the principle of justice. [*His voice grows louder again.*] The principle of justice for which Mr Chifley fought all his life, and he thinks this is unjust.

He was playing the crowd well, and by recalling the memory of Chifley he also drew attention away from Labor's divisions.

Evatt then moves into a different register, deploying irony and playing for laughs. The government had recently obtained legal opinions stating that the constitutional changes could only be used against communists. 'Mr Menzies throws the opinion on the table and he says, "That proves I'm right". Well, it's the joke of Phillip Street.' More laughter and applause. He then quotes Julius Stone, a professor of law at the University of Sydney, who had commented that the opinions 'so elaborately procured' were interesting, and important indeed, but they were wrong. When the laughter dies down, Evatt's voice falls into a quiet conversational tone:

> I said justice was the objective. Social justice: that sums up
> the views of Labor, and the labour movement … Labor has
> always stood for the ordinary man and woman, and especially
> the children of Australia … We know that. I'm not saying it
> boastfully, but why do you think we are opposing these proposals?
> It'd be easier for us to say, oh, what does it matter, fold our
> arms, and pass by on the other side. We don't do that, ladies
> and gentlemen, because it's a matter of fundamental principle.
> I've told you by reference to Hitler what happened in Germany,
> what Pastor Niemöller said; it's the same in countries which are
> totalitarian on the left.

His voice continues quietly, with a genuinely puzzled tone:

> But I can't understand, for a moment, why anybody in a
> responsible position in Australia should say that the end justifies
> bad means, and that we should adopt totalitarian methods of the
> right, that is fascist methods, in order to deal with communism,
> which is a totalitarian movement of the left.

Then he returns to irony, describing how the British had viewed Menzies' legislation.

In Britain, they walked around Mr Menzies' precious bill in 1950; they said, 'What a wonderful thing this is. Look at this document that's come from Australia, twenty-seven sections. That's the way to deal with communism. Never mind about the courts of justice – let the government take the place of the courts of justice.' But the reception in England was cool, not to say frigid. [*That gets a laugh.*] And the conservative party wouldn't look at it, the Liberals wouldn't touch it, because in England the Liberal party believes in liberalism, which is the rule of law. Not so Mr Menzies – he's departed from that.

He goes on to address his audience directly, in the hall and over the radio:

President Truman – I am going to tell you, I'm quoting from him – how we are *not* going to fight communism. And I want the people of Australia, and each of you, to follow this. [*His voice is slow and even ponderous, building to a crescendo at the end.*] 'We are *not* going to transform the FBI into a Gestapo-like secret police. We are *not* going to try to turn the United States into a right-wing totalitarian country in order to deal with a left-wing totalitarian threat. In short,' said President Truman, 'we are *not* going to end democracy.' And I ask the people of Australia to take no risk of ending democracy by adopting totalitarian methods, not only in legislation, but incorporating them permanently, *permanently*, into your free constitution.

Then he evokes Chifley's name again, saying that when he asked his leader about the bill shortly before he died, Chifley said, 'I wouldn't have a bar of it'. Chuckling is heard from the audience before he continues, carefully and slowly, 'We know what Mr Chifley meant. We know what he stood for. He stood for justice. Justice is the thing. To the best of my ability, I've stood for it'.

It is striking that Evatt spoke as much about 'justice' as about liberty. He conflated his own abstract notions of justice, democracy and the rule of law together with Labor's commitment to social justice, as though they were much the same thing, and were what Labor stood for. While it made a somewhat incongruous bundle, it *sounded* plausible. It has been suggested that this was fundamentally about a British cultural inflection to his view of justice, and that may have appealed to some listeners; but Evatt's commitment to the law was not that it derived from Britain, but that it derived from reason. Evatt was being perfectly sincere, and it comes through in the voice:

> Now look, I want to finish now. Justice can't be limited … justice must be given to all. You must always fight for justice for all people, you can't have politicians dispensing justice, you must have the courts of law, the principles of British justice. We must always fight for that, that's fundamental.

From this point he is building to his conclusion:

> These are dangerous proposals, infamous proposals. I can't use language too strong to characterise them. I've not stated it to beg the question, I've tried to analyse them throughout this campaign, and act fairly, to try and conduct a campaign to educate the people. And I ask you here in this great audience at Bondi, and each of you in your home listening to me throughout Australia, to save Australia on Saturday as a democratic country for you and your children. And don't forget that the soldiers of Australia fought to preserve this country from totalitarianism, and don't let Mr Menzies introduce it by the methods of a democratic referendum. Therefore, vote 'no' on Saturday.

The broadcast ended with loud cheering and applause. As noted above, both Cameron and Haylen thought this speech may have tipped the balance in the campaign. We cannot know that, though many would have heard it, because we know radio audiences for major policy speeches during election campaigns were large; the scheduling of radio speeches was advertised widely in the press. But what is most interesting about this speech is Evatt's voice. It is relaxed, sometimes conversational, and while it is often emphatic, it is never extreme or wild. He is sure of his subject matter and sure of the crowd. He modulated his voice to fit his different themes, by turns homely, earnest and intimate, declamatory, ironic and even sentimental, but always genuine, always authentic. As an unscripted piece of rhetoric it is highly skilled and entertaining, with all these variations of style provoking real feeling in his audience, persuading them to Evatt's point of view.

Through it he was making a coherent argument about the risks involved, about the importance of democracy and dissent, and implicitly about the priority of the courts over the legislature. Perhaps the most telling line is that in which he asks his listeners to 'think of this not as a problem concerning communists alone, but as concerning fundamental principles'. In this context, his talk of totalitarianism sounds plausible rather than alarmist – he was not so much alleging Menzies was a fascist as warning about of the erosion of the rule of law. Just as at San Francisco he had flourished because they were making a constitution, in the referendum his core commitment to legal rationality was in tune with the demands of politics. Perhaps, unlike many of his speeches, this one sounds better than it reads. And perhaps, as Haylen had said, Evatt had been able to conjure up a rapport with his listeners: 'The real, the essential Evatt reached out that night and got the people to believe him and understand him'.

The referendum vote was held two days later, on 22 September 1951. The Labor campaign was largely Evatt's campaign, and had shifted opinion from a peak of 82 per cent supporting a ban in mid-1950 down to 53 per cent only a week before the referendum, and then 49.4 per cent on the day. It was a narrow victory but a stunning one; it had been assumed the popularity of the measure would see it sweep through. It was seen as the triumph of Evatt's reasoning, and his 'finest hour'.

Nationally, the 'no' vote was 50.5 per cent. One estimate was that 14 per cent of non-Labor voters had voted no, while 11 per cent of Labor voters had voted yes. New South Wales recorded the highest 'no' vote, while in Tasmania, Western Australia and Queensland, a majority supported the ban. It had been expected that most religious denominations would vote along party lines, except for Catholics, who, while they were much more inclined to vote Labor than Liberal, were also more inclined to support the referendum. But something curious happened in Victoria, Menzies' home state, where his standing was high, and where the Catholic Groupers were by far the strongest. In Victoria 51.4 per cent voted against the referendum – a figure slightly higher than Labor's estimated two-party vote in the election held five months earlier. So it seemed that even in Victoria, the leakage of 'small l' liberals rejecting Menzies' referendum outweighed the anti-communist Labor vote supporting a ban.

In the immediate aftermath of the victory the caucus congratulated Evatt by 'acclamation' – surprisingly, without dissent. Evatt responded, saying the campaign had been more important than an election: 'It was an educational campaign and a crusade associated with the name of Mr Chifley.' Even more surprisingly, the Victorian executive wrote congratulating him on 'the splendid victory', which they said resulted 'in large measure' from his personal leadership. A letter to Evatt from the South Australian Trades Hall argued for retribution against those who had not supported the campaign, but Evatt was conciliatory. He wrote back that while some in the labour movement had not given active support, the citizens had shown a 'political maturity which over-came the hysteria and panic'. Labor should display the same maturity, he said, and not start out now on a road to 'heresy hunting'.

But members of the federal executive, particularly Jack Fergu-son, wanted retribution, and in late November they resolved to 'sternly rebuke' those who had refused to participate in the campaign, and to proscribe *News Weekly* for supporting the 'yes' campaign. Banning *News Weekly* put it in the same category as the Communist party's *Tribune* and Jack Lang's *Century*. Archbishop Mannix, who had briefly supported Evatt in his 'no' campaign, then publicly criticised the proscription of *News Weekly*. Though Menzies had failed to expunge the Communist party from the polity, the struggle was not over. Evatt's success led to increased hostility from the Groupers, reinforcing the developing split within the caucus and the party organisation – while at the same time allowing Menzies to position him as 'the Communist champion'.

13

The Petrov affair

The Menzies government was widely seen to be struggling during the period between the referendum in late 1951 and the sensational announcement in April 1954 that a Soviet spy had defected from the embassy in Canberra. The referendum loss affected party morale, but more important were the effects of the 'horror budget' handed down shortly afterwards; it raised taxation and slowed the economy. The Liberal party's public relations officer, Edgar Holt, wrote a gloomy 'Political Appreciation' at the end of 1951, arguing that the decline in the government's popularity largely resulted from attacks by its own supporters, dissatisfied with controls and the economic slump. He wanted the party's 'propaganda' to emphasise 'development, opportunity and a great future'.

Over the next few years, opinion polls brought bleak news for the coalition, and Labor's confidence that they could win back government in 1954 rose. At the end of 1951, W.S. Robinson wrote to Evatt: 'Your future looks brilliantly bright. You appear to have a comfortable grandstand seat from which to watch the mass suicide of your opponents. Don't spoil the effect by attempting to speed up the show'. A year later he wrote another of these cheering letters, saying that he doubted economic conditions would improve enough to save Menzies' government. 'When this Parliament has run its course – if not before – you will be Prime Minister ...' Robinson's confident prediction was wrong and Evatt, along with many in the Labor party, became convinced that the Petrov defection was the cause. But the political divisions developing inside the labour movement were equally part of the story.

Within the labour movement

In this period, caucus meetings were relatively quiet, but deeper in the labour movement the power of the Grouper forces was growing, particularly in New South Wales. In 1949, in response to the CPA's aggressive industrial policies in the coal strike, Evatt had amended the *Conciliation and Arbitration Act* to allow court investigation of alleged corruption in union elections; in 1951, the Menzies government strengthened those provisions, allowing new elections at the request of a union or some of its members. Groupers had won the New South Wales branch of the Miners' Federation in elections following the coal strike and then won control of the Federated Ironworkers' Association in 1951. The ironworkers' union was a rich prize, one of the largest and wealthiest in New South Wales and long controlled by the CPA. Laurie Short, formerly a communist and then a Trotskyist, but now an ALP member and strongly anti-communist, led an Industrial Group in the 1949 union elections. Having lost, he challenged the result in the courts and, after protracted legal battles, was installed as national secretary in 1951. In 1952, a concerted Grouper effort won control of the union nationally.

That significantly shifted the balance of power in the New South Wales branch, when combined with the right-wing AWU. A coalition of Groupers and the AWU successfully moved to depose state president Jack Ferguson, though he remained as federal president. In Queensland, the Groupers were not as strong, but had the AWU, and won control of the Waterside Workers', Ironworkers' and Clerks' unions. Western Australia and Tasmania had not established Groups; and in South Australia, Clyde Cameron ensured the relatively weak group network was disbanded in 1951. But with substantial power in Victoria and New South Wales, and some in Queensland, the Groupers were in the ascendant in the ALP federally by late 1952.

Evatt had only fragile ties to the Labor machine and little standing among the unions, and was trying to court the Groupers on the right. The premier historian of the Labor split, Robert Murray, suggested Evatt had little choice but to try to forge an alliance with the Groupers, even though they had not forgiven him for fighting the Communist party referendum. Evatt made public statements designed to appeal to the right; he explicitly ruled out recognition of the communist government in China and, six months after it had been proscribed, he convinced the federal executive to lift the ban on *News Weekly*. Bob Santamaria wrote in his memoirs that Evatt courted the right rather than allow the party 'to continue to rend itself apart'. Santamaria thought this was Evatt's way of trying to secure his leadership, 'although, as always with this complex man, his motives were obscure'. If Evatt had kept diaries, or written more letters, we might be able to decode his thinking. Was it simply about survival, or was he attempting to hold the party together?

One small clue as to Evatt's thinking was his response to a letter, in mid-1952, from a woman who warned him about the dangers of 'the Catholic influence' in politics and the caucus. The danger of 'Roman Catholicism', she thought, was that it was 'lasting', and only the Soviet Union stood up to Catholic 'fascism'. She wrote that Catholicism was 'thriving on anti-Communism, and slipping in quietly behind', arguing: 'This foreign power should also be thrashed out in Parliament; we non-Catholics are being squeezed out in all walks of life'. She recommended a book (*Freedom and Catholic Power*) which was available for twenty shillings at the CPA's bookshop. Unusually, Evatt wrote back and, because he so rarely wrote letters, his reply is worth quoting at length. He acknowledged these problems were 'difficult':

> Mr Chifley was acutely aware of their importance. What I would like to see in the movement is a spirit of tolerance and mutual forebearance. There must be many differences of opinion in any social democratic movement and the special difficulties of the Labor movement in Australia are apparent enough. I think that it is correct to say that my views on freedom of expression and

freedom of association are well known and that everything I have said publicly in the Referendum I firmly adhere to. My deepest regret is that Mr Chifley's death prevented his witnessing the set-back to totalitarian methods which resulted. The book you mention was brought under my notice during the Referendum campaign and I am obliged to you for referring to it. Yours faithfully,

H.V. Evatt

This reply is undeniably formulaic. Evatt was often accused of being foolish in politics, but it would have been very foolish to unburden himself to a stranger on a sensitive issue. It is nevertheless clear that he was in a conciliatory mood, speaking of 'tolerance and mutual forebearance', accommodating 'differences of opinion' and supporting 'freedom of expression'. He did not explicitly disagree with his correspondent's anti-Catholic views, but nor did he take the bait. Through the 1950s, he received many of these unsolicited letters encouraging him to resist Roman influence, often from people identifying themselves as part of the Protestant cause. He scarcely ever replied and, although he was accused of exploiting sectarianism in the split, there is nothing in his papers to clearly suggest he agreed with such sentiments. To his secular mind, these sorts of passions were irrational and obscure.

Evatt's motives were unclear but Santamaria's were becoming increasingly clear, even though he was not a figure known to the wider public, or even to many in the Labor party. Within the secrecy of closed meetings of the Movement, Santamaria spoke about the opportunity to translate union power into political influence over the Labor party, to ensure the Movement's social and foreign policies were followed. Some of this began to leak into wider circles. At the same time other Catholics were becoming anxious about the power of the Movement; one who would play a role was the Sydney journalist Jim Ormonde, who had written to Evatt in 1940 congratulating him on entering politics and hoping he could heal Labor's divisions. He was emerging as a key figure in a strand of Catholicism associated with the left wing *Catholic Worker* magazine and opposing the Movement. The Catholic hierarchy in Sydney had never been as openly supportive of the Movement as had Mannix in Melbourne, and in Sydney they worried the church was being drawn too much into Labor's tensions; something of a split was opening up among Catholics aligned with Labor.

Ormonde leaked to the ALP leadership the transcript of a speech Santamaria made at a Movement meeting titled 'The Movement of Ideas in Australia'; accounts vary about when this meeting was held in 1953, but according to the historian Bruce Duncan, the transcript was circulating by February 1954. Ormonde's undated cover note to Evatt told him it was his last copy. Evatt wrote across the top that the author was 'Robert Santa Maria', signalling just how obscure Santamaria's name still was, and he proceeded to underline and annotate the text heavily. In his speech, Santamaria had spoken about 'the job lying in front of us, industrially and politically, in the year 1953', and about new challenges the Groupers faced from 'people opposed to us'. They had had successes in the unions – 'our forces started to win in Australia – you remember the wins culminating in the cleansing of the Ironworkers' Federation'. To counter those in the labour movement who were saying that the anti-communist struggle was over, or that the Groups had become too influential, Santamaria said: 'We have got to answer the ... argument that the Groups threaten the structure of the Labor party'. If that was not done, then the Groups would be under attack. He had also said that 'within the Labor Movement we must fight to destroy their use of the Chifley legend'. He meant that Chifley was often invoked as though 'infallible', but he had not been as pro-American as Curtin; Santamaria preferred 'the now forgotten Curtin legend'. This reference to 'the Chifley legend' did not help when people read it; it sounded like disloyalty to an icon. Santamaria was not yet saying that their wins in union elections translated into power within the party, but it was the language in this leaked document that struck readers – the use of 'us', 'we' and 'people opposed to us' – indicative of a new force within Labor with a separate identity and interests. It was quite a leap to conclude from this speech that Santamaria intended to take over the party, but some were well prepared to make that leap.

At about the same time, Evatt was cultivating Santamaria, who responded warily. Santamaria later told Tennant that in February 1954 he had received a letter from Evatt suggesting a meeting and that Mannix had talked him into agreeing. They met in the Hotel Windsor in Melbourne, where Evatt usually stayed, and had a subsequent meeting at Santamaria's office. The account of this meeting in Santamaria's memoirs was detailed; he said they talked about removing Pat Kennelly, and Evatt asked about 'the type of measures' Santamaria would like to see from a Labor government, promising he would legislate for clean union ballots, provide financial aid to Catholic schools and make Grouper Stan Keon a minister. 'It was all rather disgusting', Santamaria wrote. 'I told my wife that I had encountered the impossible – a man without a soul.' While Evatt left no record of these meetings, they clearly happened, sometime between February and April 1954.

By July, Santamaria was speaking more explicitly, still within the privacy of a Movement meeting, about the need to translate the Movement's industrial strength into political influence. He had earlier diagnosed the danger of CPA control of unions leading to political influence over Labor, and now the same logic applied for the Movement; victories in union elections inevitably had political consequences, he said, 'because the trade unions are affiliated with a political party', and union election victories won 'representation in that party'. The Movement then had no alternative, he argued, but to use the political influence it had gained to 'preserve the structure of the Industrial Groups and the policies and legislation which are essential to its fight against Communism'. But then he went further. Given 'the southward march of Chinese Communism', he said:

The decisions which will determine the fate of both Church and
Nation are not confined to the industrial field but will be largely
political decisions in the higher sense of that term – decisions
of foreign policy, of immigration policy, of defence development
and economic policy ... such decisions may not be left to the
unguided action of political parties.

Admittedly, this was written in a specific context: Santamaria was justifying the Movement to church critics who worried it was becoming
too political and that the church was too involved in Labor politics.
The statement was not made publicly; nevertheless, it made a forthright case for the necessity of political action, and had it been leaked it
would have been explosive.

Santamaria always claimed the issue dividing the Labor party was
not sectarianism, not Protestant versus Catholic, or even Rome versus
Moscow – it was a struggle between the ALP and the CPA. Certainly
there were alliances between anti-communists in the union movement, whether Catholic, Protestant or non-religious. But the political
theory he worked with was itself sectarian; he argued that communism
was necessarily evil, godless and materialistic, and this seemed more
important to him than the fact that it was dictatorial. He saw communism as an expansionist ideology on the march and argued that, for
these reasons, the old separation of religion and politics no longer held.
He was proposing a vigorous combination of defence and aggression –
defence of religious belief through aggressive political action. In doing
so, he necessarily brought religious difference and sectarian antagonism into the open, involving them in direct political contest – precisely what he would accuse Evatt of doing in precipitating the split. If
the Catholic Movement had the right to defend 'Church and Nation',
intervening in 'largely political decisions' to ensure policies were not
made 'unguided', then surely other churches had the same right. Santamaria was zealot enough to think there was only one church, but
others would call that sectarianism.

Meanwhile, the Liberal party secretariat were keenly observing the divisions emerging within the labour movement; in September 1953, they discussed the potential advantages of 'the split in Political Labor's ranks, the weakening of the unity between Political Labor and the Industrial movement, and the absence of real and unanimously held beliefs'. They agreed the existing 'line' they had taken – contrasting Menzies with Evatt – was still as strongly in their favour. John McConnell, the Victorian state secretary, suggested that the 'split in Labor might not be apparent at election time', and the Tasmanian secretary, V.L. Ockerby, agreed, saying that the split was not too apparent as yet, but attention should be drawn to it.

By 1953, with the Groupers in the ascendancy, there was growing disquiet among senior Labor powerbrokers that the party itself was being taken over, and that the influence wielded by the Groupers was expanding from their original industrial purpose to more political ends. The party secretary, Pat Kennelly, had always been implacably, even vengefully, opposed to the Groupers. During 1953, Joe Chamberlain was saying privately, 'We have to get the Groups before they get us'; from the end of that year, Chamberlain was a federal vice-president, and during the actual split was acting president. The federal conference in Adelaide in January 1953 was attended by 'two sharply divided, bitterly opposed and well matched factions', those of the Groupers, strongest in Victoria and New South Wales but with support in Queensland, and those aligned with Kennelly. The Groupers attempted to depose Kennelly but he outmanoeuvred them. As 1954 approached, the tide was moving again inside the labour movement. Kennelly and Chamberlain were preparing to act, and AWU national secretary Tom Dougherty was shifting his union away from the Groupers. Evatt, who had been trying to cultivate the right, would be caught up in these manoeuvres.

The Petrov election

The next federal election was due in late May. Menzies was going the full term, and Labor had high hopes they could win. Evatt would finally be prime minister. Much press commentary assumed Labor had a good chance. At a by-election in the New South Wales seat of Gwydir just before Christmas 1953, Evatt had campaigned hard and was ebullient. He and Mary Alice were driven around the electorate by a local man whose baritone voice had won him amateur radio prizes. A journalist accompanied them on one trip and got to see a different side of the Labor leader:

> Dr Evatt suddenly said: 'Bill, let's do "The Old Hundredth"
> – Vaughan Williams' arrangement'. The hymn is Dr Evatt's
> favourite … Then we all joined in for 'A Maiden Fair', 'Oh, What
> a Beautiful Morning', and other songs … When we reached
> the town proper, Dr Evatt once again became the eminent
> constitutional lawyer and leader of Her Majesty's Opposition.

Evatt might have been dwelling on the next line of 'Oh, What a Beautiful Morning': 'Everything's going my way'. But Gwydir was a solid Country party seat, and the anticipated swing to Labor did not occur.

A month earlier, Rosalind had married Peter Carrodus in St John's Anglican Church in Canberra. Bishop Burgmann did the honours, and among the 250 guests present were political leaders, diplomats and friends, though press reports commented that Menzies was not there, and only Arthur Fadden attended from the government side of politics. Evatt had always been very protective of Rosalind, now aged twenty-one; he did not demand that she strive for excellence as he expected his son to, and he thought she should not go to work. She recalled later how he would pick her up early from parties, and would accompany her and her future husband to the cinema, sitting beside them and embarrassing her. He had taken extra precautions before walking her down the aisle, she said, with two spare wedding rings in his pockets belonging to his mother and Mary Alice's mother, 'in case the best man lost ours', and three bottles of emergency medicines, in case she fainted or had a spell; he clinked as they walked down the aisle. For the honeymoon he had filled their car boot with books, because they would need reading material. These images are charming, but they reveal his underlying anxieties.

Evatt's relationship with his son seems to have been both more distant and more fraught. Peter excelled at rowing, and when he won the Australian sculling title in early 1953, Evatt was pleased, saying, 'It makes me realise there are more important things than politics'. Peter told Kylie Tennant a story of one race and, although the details of when and where it took place are unclear, the idea it gives us of their relationship is not. Evatt had said he could not come to see the race as he was 'too busy', but then he did come and was described as being 'like a cat on hot bricks', jumping up and down on the bank with excitement, saying, 'Where's Peter? I can't see him'. Peter won the race but did not know his father had seen him win. According to Peter, Evatt had not come afterwards to congratulate him; when someone said he had been there, Peter said: 'You're nuts. He hasn't been near me'. That Peter was still relating this story in his early thirties suggests that his father withheld approval from him just as Jeanie had withheld her approval from her boys, and it reveals the awkwardness between Evatt and the son on whom he had urged so much hard work and effort at school.

If Evatt sometimes realised there were 'more important things than politics', that kind of balance was about to be swept away. The tense mix of loyalties and enmities building in the labour movement, and the hopes that Labor might win the May 1954 election, were exploded by the defection of Petrov from the Russian embassy in April. Whether or not it was the political stunt Labor saw it as, and whether or not it cost Labor the 1954 election, Evatt was convinced of both. His intervention in the royal commission that followed, alleging conspiracies against himself and his party, is often cited as evidence that his judgement had become unbalanced, and it further inflamed the tensions between the Groupers and the rest in the parliamentary party.

Before the election, set for the end of May, there had been a royal tour, with the young Queen Elizabeth and her consort in Australia for most of February and March; it was only the presence of the royal couple that prevented a 'bitter political fight', according to media reports at the time. Frank Chamberlain commented on the antipathy between Evatt and Menzies, writing that Evatt was 'the political foe … Menzies disliked – no, detests is the word – more than any other'. He later recalled speaking to Menzies and asking if he was 'staying in politics a long time' because he wanted to keep Evatt out. Menzies replied, 'Most definitely. I would leave politics this 1954 but for Dr Evatt. He's a menace to Australia and he must be kept out of office by hook or by crook.' Chamberlain was convinced it was by 'crook'; he regarded the Petrov affair as a trap set for Evatt, who was too much a political innocent to see the danger.

On 13 April, Menzies announced to parliament that Vladimir Petrov had defected and asked for asylum in Australia, and that the government was setting up a royal commission to investigate espionage in Australia. This was the evening Evatt was flying to Sydney to give a speech at Fort Street, when Haylen had chatted with him on the tarmac about his mother. Officially, Petrov was a diplomat, as third secretary in the Soviet embassy; unofficially, he was the representative or 'resident' of one of the key Soviet intelligence agencies, the MVD. He had been cultivated by ASIO for almost a year, and was worried about his fate if he went back to Moscow. The news set off a panic about communist influence and espionage within Australia, in a context of heightened Cold War tensions as the French were being besieged by the Viet Minh in Vietnam. About a week later, Petrov's wife was escorted onto a flight to Moscow by two armed Russian 'couriers'. It was not clear whether she was being prevented from defecting, whether she regarded her husband as a traitor, or whether she believed the Russian story that Petrov had been 'kidnapped'. At Sydney airport, there were wild scenes as a crowd of anti-communist eastern European migrants tried to prevent the plane leaving; then, when the plane stopped to refuel in Darwin, her minders were disarmed, Evdokia Petrov was released, and she too sought asylum.

It was all highly dramatic. The defection of a Russian spy and the implication he had brought with him documents detailing spying and subversion in Australia were political sensations. The Labor politician Gil Duthie wrote in his diary on that day: 'SENSATION – Petrov … seeks asylum in Australia. Offers evidence of spying in Aust. Brings jubilation to the Menzies government. Press filthy in handling of political repercussions. Talking of ALP men being involved, etc.' Immediate media commentary noted the electoral advantages. Chamberlain described the 'dramatic revelations' as 'world-shaking'; the electoral mood had already 'been moving ominously against Labor', he said, and now their hopes were 'fading'. A political columnist writing for the Sydney *Sun-Herald* under the pseudonym 'Onlooker' observed drolly that Menzies had claimed 'demurely' that he would rather the Petrov affair had not come up just before an election. But Onlooker's analysis was that it had 'one of the biggest strokes of luck' for a government previously in doubt about its re-election, and was 'a shocking mischance for Evatt'. 'His great personal victory in the anti-Communist referendum of 1951 will backfire on him now. Labour's Catholic Action wing, which detested the Evatt policy on Communism, will be saying: "we told you so".' Labor's hopes for the election were dwindling, though whether the outcome was due to the Petrov defection is debatable.

At his policy launch, Evatt announced, without any consultation, a Labor proposal to abolish the means test on the aged pension. Ironically, this had been a non-Labor position for at least a generation; the predecessors of the Liberals saw the means test as socially and ethically 'demoralising', because it rewarded those who had not been thrifty and saved for old age, and penalised those who had. In the 1920s and 1930s, they had attempted to introduce a contributory insurance system of social welfare, while Labor had always supported the means-test. Now Evatt suddenly proposed the abolition of the test as Labor policy, without any estimate of what it would cost. Bill Bourke, the Victorian Grouper who had shadow portfolio responsibility for welfare, immediately voiced his dissent in public. The Liberals were able to portray Evatt as reckless; they calculated the costs and trawled through Hansard for Chifley's previous statements that such a measure would be irresponsible. Press advertisements titled 'The High Cost of Evatt' used Chifley's words against his successor.

Menzies derided Evatt's means-test policy, saying Evatt was 'as innocent of financial knowledge as a frog is of feathers'. That was both evocative and not far wrong. Most on Labor's side were ignorant of economics. Chifley had been responsible for all that; he had taught himself, but unfortunately had taught no one else. At one point Menzies said of Evatt: 'I don't know the state of mind of a grown man who can put such drivel before the people. Financially speaking, it is criminal'. Evatt responded that this was just 'a series of insults' unsupported by facts. The two had been battering at each other for decades now, and their animosity and rivalry was widely noted in the press. 'Onlooker' wrote of the election as a 'duel to the death' between Evatt and Menzies, especially bitter 'because they are personally antipathetic'.

The outcome of the election was close, with Labor gaining just over 50 per cent of the vote, and five seats, but that was not enough: they needed to gain ten. How much the Petrov affair had contributed to this outcome has been the subject of much argument. Evatt was convinced the defection cost Labor the election, and that it was all a conspiracy designed to deny Labor the government and him the prime ministership, but there is little clear evidence to confirm this view. Labor's position had been slipping since early 1954, and its internal divisions were not helping. Opinion polls had for a year been showing support was turning towards the government, while the dominant issue in the campaign was Evatt's means-test promise.

Menzies wanted no mention of the Petrov defection during the election; he was concerned it would be seen as making cheap political capital out of the issue. But others, such as Arthur Fadden, told audiences Evatt could not be trusted to implement whatever came out of the royal commission. More generally, the issues of communism and Labor's divisions were prominent in Liberal advertising, with Evatt again targeted as a communist champion. One Liberal advertisement had a cartoon of Evatt walking with a disreputable-looking Russian, with the claim: 'LABOR AND RED POLICIES IDENTICAL ... MENACE TO AUSTRALIAN FREEDOM ...The A.L.P. bosses and the rulers of Communist Russia have the same avowed objective – Socialism'. Another read:

> DON'T GIVE THE REDS A SECOND CHANCE! The communist conspiracy was the greatest challenge to progress and security during the eight years of Federal Labor government ... yet Dr Evatt:

> Removed the ban on the Communist party.
> Defended the reds in the arbitration court.
> Was a bitter opponent of the secret ballot legislation.
> Led the fight against the Communist Party Dissolution Bill.
> Whom can you trust to deal with the Communists? Menzies or Evatt?

Other advertisements spoke of 'Labor's history of appeasement of the Reds' and declared that communism was still a world menace and 'could become a menace in Australia again if Evatt ran true to form'.

As with the referendum campaign, Menzies told his party he wanted a clean fight, while the party secretariat was less scrupulous, keen to associate Evatt with communism. When the Liberals' public relations committee later reviewed the election, they mostly thought that the mean-test promise had been decisive, though the Victorian director thought the 'disunity of Labor' had helped and they had run a 'good PR campaign particularly tying Labor to Communists'. Given the stridency of advertisements associating Evatt with communism, it is probable Petrovs' defection had some impact, though impossible to demonstrate how much. It is not hard to imagine that when citizens heard of the communist menace in general, they thought of the recent and particular sensation of the defection of a Soviet spy.

'Evatt at Spy Probe'

Parliament and hence caucus did not meet until early August. From that point until the split in March 1955, the defeated Labor party was, as Robert Murray put it, perpetually 'on the boil'. Few members of the caucus were ever to forget those months, Murray said. The pressure in the parliamentary party rose with every twist and turn of the Royal Commission on Espionage, particularly over Evatt's precipitous responses. When they met on 3 August for a marathon thirteen-hour meeting, Evatt's leadership was challenged by Tom Burke, the member from Western Australia aligned with the Groupers. Evatt won 68 to 20, and Calwell was re-elected deputy unopposed. It appeared a reasonably convincing win, but almost a quarter of the caucus had voted for Burke, who was relatively junior and had hardly organised, showing that Evatt's support was crumbling. 'Onlooker' said that the 'whispering in the corridors' was that 'the Doc's had it', and commented, 'there is no doubt about the cleavages opening in the Labour Party. Who can re-weld it into a disciplined, effective fighting force in Parliament? Dr Evatt? Few think he is the man for that job. He is respected for his brains and energy, but not trusted enough'. Chamberlain wrote that 'a ruthless struggle for power must come'.

The royal commission had met briefly before the election, and then following the election its hearings provided front page news for

months. Most in the Labor caucus were desperate to avoid more controversy about the royal commission, but in August Evatt was determined
to bring on a bitter debate attacking Menzies and the commission; his
exchanges with Menzies were highly charged. During Evatt's speech,
the government backbenchers were described as hounding him with
derisive laughter, 'like a bullfight crowd at the death scene'. The government had made a substantial payment of £5000 to Petrov after
his defection, ostensibly for his living expenses, and Evatt argued that
this constituted 'improperly influencing the people ... at the general
election'; he meant that they had paid Petrov to defect and he argued
that Menzies had timed the defection for electoral advantage. He was
not yet alleging that the documents Petrov provided were forgeries,
but said 'when the tangled skein of the matter is finally unravelled, the
Petrov–Menzies letters case will rank ... as an equivalent to the notorious Zinovieff letter ... or the burning of the Reichstag'.

Evatt rarely did things by halves but this was playing for high
stakes. The Zinovieff letter in 1924 had been a forgery, purportedly
from the Comintern, instructing the British Communist party to
infiltrate the Labour party, and it contributed to Labour's defeat;
Hitler blamed the burning of the Reichstag in 1933 on communists and used it as a pretext to round them up, while the fire was
almost certainly set by the Nazis. Drawing such parallels raised
the expectation he could prove conspiracy, but over the following
months he would fail to do so. Drawing such parallels, a *Sydney
Morning Herald* editorial sniffed, was 'hysteria', and 'too wild and
fantastic to be worth discussing'. Menzies was equally contemptu-
ous, describing Evatt as 'so hysterical as to indicate a grave state of
panic'. Menzies defended himself against the accusation that the
timing of the defection had been managed, or that it was 'an election stunt'; he had, after all, remained silent on the issue during the
campaign. The inveterate Liberal anti-communist Billy Wentworth,
then member for Mackellar, claimed during the parliamentary
debate that Evatt's foreign policy had always had 'a pro-Communist

thread and bias'; to which Evatt responded, 'You dirty little liar'.

The documents Petrov brought with him when he defected were picked over extensively during the royal commission, and it was this that drew Evatt into intervening as an advocate, as he might once have done in court. 'Document H' was a summary of the political leanings of Australian journalists, written for a Soviet press representative. The author was Fergan O'Sullivan, Evatt's press secretary, though he had written it two years before he took on that role; when his authorship came out, Evatt wrote curtly to O'Sullivan saying he was 'amazed and disgusted' and he was dismissed. Then, in July, the chairman of the royal commission stated that another two of Evatt's staff, Allan Dalziel and assistant private secretary Albert Grundeman, were mentioned in another of Petrov's papers, 'Document J'. This long analysis of the Australian political scene had been composed by the well-known CPA journalist Rupert Lockwood, though he denied having written it. O'Sullivan, Dalziel and Grundeman were all listed among his sources. ASIO had in fact been watching all three, and the director-general had earlier warned Evatt about O'Sullivan's leanings. Whether or not it was true that Evatt's staff in the early 1950s had connections with Soviet intelligence, the public naming of them was very damaging; now Evatt seemed implicated. W.S. Robinson wrote to Evatt from Queensland saying he thought the main objective of the commission appeared to be 'the elimination of one H.V. Evatt'.

There was speculation Evatt might appear at the royal commission to defend Dalziel and Grundeman, and some Labor members attempted to call a caucus meeting to prevent it. Evatt knew he was being damaged by whispers that he was somehow involved in the espionage networks that were being uncovered, and he was understandably suspicious Menzies had not warned him some of his staff were named in the documents. He was also motivated by loyalty to Dalziel and Grundeman and described the public naming of them as 'McCarthyism'. But he seemed unaware that taking up the role of lawyer again to defend his staff, and hence himself, would draw him further into the net; he seemed oblivious, too, that all this also exacerbated pressure within the party. Even if he succeeded before the commission, the *Sydney Morning Herald* wrote, 'a complete split' with the right-wing group could develop. Frank Chamberlain was already writing that Labor was 'split beyond further camouflage'.

For three weeks from mid-August, Evatt appeared before the commission, representing Dalziel and Grundeman, but increasingly appearing to represent himself. Headlines such as 'Evatt at Spy Probe May Split Party' heightened the drama. A Cinesound newsreel shot on his first day showed people milling about the doors of the Darling-hurst courthouse in Sydney, in what the breathless narration described as 'an atmosphere of almost electric tension'. Individuals called to give evidence were identified by the narrator while press photographers jumped in front of them: O'Sullivan, Grundeman and Dalziel, all of whom, of course, looked shifty; being called to give evidence at a 'spy probe' inevitably looks suspicious. Then Evatt walked into frame, looking calm and lawyerly; this was his territory. 'Here is Dr Evatt now', the narrator said: 'There's a flurry among press men, and photographers dash to vantage points for close-ups'. The narrator described appearing at the commission as 'a bold decision which could affect his political future', providing 'another highlight in an enquiry which is likely to remain front-page news for a long time'.

Evatt had sent telegrams at the last minute to inform his colleagues he was going to the royal commission. The *Sydney Morning Herald* wrote that his action would 'consolidate both his supporters and his opponents' in the party. On the first day, when he cross-examined O'Sullivan, the press reported that Evatt 'spoke excitedly, waved papers in the air and thumped the Bar table loudly on two occasions'. At the end of the day's hearing, a crowd of hundreds of people 'cheered and clapped Dr Evatt as he left the court at Darlinghurst'. For three weeks, Evatt was in Sydney, haranguing the judges, alleging a conspiracy to damage his staff, himself and the party. He wanted to examine the documents in forensic detail and was convinced at least part

ROYAL COMMISSION

Dr. Evatt and his clients leaving the Royal Commission

Many, including the commissioners, felt that Evatt was
unable to distinguish between his own interests as party leader
and as a barrister representing his staff.

George Molnar, *Sydney Morning Herald*, 8 September 1954

of 'Document J' was a forgery. All this undermined his position as leader, infuriating the right and generating doubts for the remainder. The press regularly reported the developing crisis in the Labor caucus, predicting a split. Chamberlain wrote that the feeling in Canberra on both sides of politics was that Evatt was 'finished as a political leader' whatever happened in the royal commission. During his absence in Sydney the factions were waiting; Chamberlain wrote: 'Caucus still simmers and predictions of an explosion are still sound'.

A week into his appearance at the Petrov enquiry, the right in caucus challenged Evatt's participation; after his first appearance at the royal commission, Bill Bourke had described him as 'the Communist Party's greatest asset'. The parliamentary executive, the shadow cabinet, had initially proposed to the caucus that 'it be left to the Leader's own judgment as to how long he should remain at the Commission', but the caucus voted thirty-seven to thirty that they wanted a more detailed report. Caucus was clearly not willing to sign a blank cheque, but while opinion was intensely divided, the party nevertheless waited to see what the outcome would be of his appearances at the commission. While the right thought Evatt was once again supporting communists, others on the Labor side assumed the enquiry was politically motivated, but worried Evatt's actions were exacerbating the tensions. Senior Labor figures like Reg Downing later recalled they thought Petrov's defection was engineered. 'We all felt that while Bert was right he fell into the trap set by Menzies for him … he was obviously right but we felt he took the bait too savagely.'

When Evatt alleged that Petrov's 'Document J' naming his staff was a forgery, he was depicted as obsessive and conspiratorial; it was a characterisation he could not escape. Victor Windeyer, senior counsel assisting the commission, was scathing, describing Evatt's 'vagueness and irrationality'. Only if 'some sort of persecution had warped his mind', Windeyer said, could a reader interpret the document as 'brought into existence solely to make it appear that two of Dr Evatt's secretaries gave information to the Russians'.

After three weeks, the commissioners simply withdrew Evatt's leave to appear. Justice Owen, chairing the enquiry, told Evatt, 'You cannot dissociate your function as an advocate from your personal and political interest'. Evatt's claims of a conspiracy were putting them all in an 'embarrassing position', Owen said, and a climax had been reached when Evatt had issued a public statement about the commission. Evatt insisted that statement had been made in his capacity as Labor leader, not as an advocate, but Owen said that just illustrated the conflict between his two capacities. Evatt, he said, had lost 'the impersonal detachment proper to an advocate', and when Evatt protested, saying,

'I submit it is a wrong judgment', Owen was blunt, 'Please resume your seat'. 'Judges Ban Evatt' read the headline in the Adelaide *News*. In effect, they had thrown him out, after three weeks of sustained legal conflict during which Evatt had held the floor, haranguing the judges, alleging conspiracy but being unable to prove it, and becoming more frantic as it became clear he was not winning the argument. Outside the court, Evatt made a press statement that the decision interfered with his rights and duties as opposition leader. A 'huge crowd' had gathered and 'cheered and applauded'. One journalist wrote of how a sobbing woman tried to grab hold of Evatt, saying, 'They treated you worse than Hitler would'. As he strove to get through the crowd, Evatt apparently replied, 'No, no'. Brendan Bracken reported to Robinson that it was all over the front pages in England; he thought Evatt's going into the royal commission had been a great mistake, and said, 'I can't help feeling that he has done himself limitless harm by his appearance in Court as Counsel'.

Evatt returned to Canberra in early September, and spoke at a tense caucus meeting, again dissecting the documents and the evidence given by Rupert Lockwood and Fergan O'Sullivan. Gil Duthie noted he spoke for seventy minutes. He claimed again that the Petrov case was more significant than the Zinovieff letter, and waved a copy of *News Weekly* from January 1953 which had predicted – over a year before the event – that a defection was imminent. After Evatt left the room, there was a chaotic attempt to move a vote of confidence in him, and Duthie recorded in his diary that scuffles broke out, with a 'very heated' exchange between Eddie Ward and another MP, Albert Thompson. Ward flung 'nasty accusations' at Thompson, saying he had supported the Premiers' Plan, his tenacious memory casting back to betrayal in 1931. They had to be separated. People were worried Evatt was becoming unstable, and the party itself was showing the same symptoms.

There are indications and hints in all this about Evatt's state of mind, and also about how his opponents were raising doubts about his state of mind. Windeyer's acid comment about persecution warping the mind was a strong hint, as was the judges' reference to his lack of 'impersonal detachment'. On 10 September, a devastating sketch of Evatt appeared in the Adelaide *News*, under the headline 'Is Dr Evatt Facing Breakdown?' It described disturbing and disturbed behaviour: 'He seizes almost any opportunity to analyse the Petrov affair, shouting his conviction that the documents in the case are concoctions. Parliamentarians, officials, Pressmen, and even House attendants report having been buttonholed'. The report described him as 'fanatically obsessed' that the Petrov affair was a conspiracy against him, and after his 'angry tirade' at a press conference, journalists were saying that they had 'never seen such a display of tension, emotion and nervousness by a political leader'. Fred Daly was a hostile witness, but his judgement seemed accurate when he wrote: 'The Petrov Commission infuriated Evatt and marked the end for him politically. He was fanatical, developed a persecution complex and waged his campaign against those who opposed him ... His judgment and tolerance were non-existent'.

Evatt's files on the Petrov affair are enormous and dishevelled. He kept notes on scraps of paper, worked through the transcripts of the hearings as they were produced, had sections of testimony typed up, drafted evaluations of contradictions, wrote analyses of the Petrov documents and of handwriting studies, compiled a synopsis of the infamous Dreyfus case in France, studied the differences between Petrov and the similar Gouzenko defection in Canada in 1945, compiled chronologies of the events, and more. He also typed up what looks to be the outline of a book, in five parts. It suggests both how he saw the Petrov affair but also how he dramatised it. Part One began with the lead-up to the election, with chapters such as 'The Declining Government', 'The Desperate Necessity for the "Rabbit out of the Hat"' and 'Enter the Lady Defector'. Part Two was titled 'The Truth Enters Slowly', and included chapters called 'Was O'Sullivan Protected?', 'Hard Struggle Towards the Truth' and 'Why was Dr Monticone Rejected?' (Monticone was a handwriting expert.)

NOT KIDDING!

Evatt's handling of the Petrov affair was starting to divide the party.

Ted Scorfield, *Bulletin*, 29 September 1954

Part Three dealt with 'The Documents', with chapters including 'The "Ring In" Page' and 'The Frame-up Exposed'. And so on. If it was to be a book, it was to end with chapters titled 'Security Service and the Police State' and 'Labor is at the Crossroads'.

Leafing through it, it all feels quite obsessive. It certainly involved a great deal of work and energy. He was furiously looking for the piece of evidence that would unlock the case; Allan Dalziel described Evatt absorbed late into the night on his 'latter-day Sherlock Holmes deductions' as he picked over the documents and transcripts. But despite his formidable legal and forensic skills, despite his belief in the law's ability to uncover the truth, he would never find the key, never prove his claim the documents were forgeries, never prove a conspiracy. Nor have most subsequent historians who have spent time in this labyrinth found any definitive answers.

There are few hints of what his home life was like at this time, but it must have been fraught. Rosalind, who lived at home with her parents until November 1953, was asked in an interview about Evatt's 'difficult periods' and said that he would come home 'pretty down'. She said she hated to see him worry, and that he used to get 'very depressed' and he couldn't understand why his Labor colleagues 'didn't go along with his viewpoint'. The question was imprecise, though, and it is not certain she was talking about this period in the 1950s. All Mary Alice said was that the Petrov affair was a 'very, very strange, sad affair':

> It upset my husband very much. He felt quite sure that most of these allegations were untrue, but … unless they were proved to be untrue … in the case of any people who were connected in any way with his own staff, that it might be brought up against him at some other time. And so he set out to defend them.

The way she presented her husband in interviews later in life was always in his favour, and she provided little insight into his thinking beyond asserting that he was always rational and ethical. If she had more to say, we will never know; in 1973, when she was seventy-five years old, Mary Alice participated in oral history interviews conducted for the National Library by Mel Pratt, but they had only just got to the Petrov affair before taking a break of some weeks, during which she died.

In late September 1954, news got out that Evatt had applied to return to the commission; he had further arguments to make, but the judges said nothing had changed. In caucus, after he had given another report on the royal commission, members of the right proposed a motion forbidding him to appear as a counsel, 'nor make any further public statements' about the commission 'without the consent of the Parliamentary Labor Party'. This motion was effectively a gag; the intention was to rein him in. Nine members had their say, including Evatt; as usual, nothing of what was said was recorded in the minutes, except that 'after discussion', the motion was withdrawn. But Gil Duthie gave more detail in his diary:

> Bill Bourke viciously and spitefully attacked Doc Evatt in a way
> that staggered us … Caucus overwhelmingly behind Doc this
> morning and his own statement on why he sought to appear
> in Royal Commission again last Thursday did much to remove
> hostility … Stan Keon was silent … Bourke's attack was shocking
> in view of his own disloyalty over the anti-Communist Bill.

Bourke's 'disloyalty' – when he had three years earlier engineered the backdown over the Communist Party Dissolution bill and had humiliated Chifley – was not forgotten. But there were plenty of others in the caucus who resented Evatt acting without consulting them. At the time Clyde Cameron wrote in his diary that Evatt's attendance at the commission was seen 'as an act of contempt'.

The royal commission was a high-profile public event, and although Evatt's actions divided opinion, there were plenty who supported him. His papers include letters of encouragement from strangers, reminding us that he was acting on a public stage and that ordinary citizens were drawing their own conclusions and projecting them onto him. He also received letters from ALP branches swearing their support, and petitions of encouragement from unionists in tramways workshops, on the wharfs, in post offices and in the no. 1 yard of the New South Wales state brickworks; these supporters saw the royal commission as a deliberate political manoeuvre and commended Evatt's actions. He kept letters from Russian émigrés about the extent of Soviet intelligence and espionage, letters from ordinary people saying they could reveal more about the conspiracy, and some letters from people with outlandish theories. Some clearly would have reinforced his own belief that he was exposing intrigue, and that his obsession was warranted. One wrote that he knew all about O'Sullivan's father, who had been an agent provocateur in Dublin; he offered to put Evatt in touch with 'interesting people'. Another wrote congratulating him on his 'moral courage', saying, 'your action will be remembered as a decisive set-back to the establishment of McCarthyism in this country … your many supporters are staunchly behind you in your present crusade against the forces of intrigue and calumny'.

The novelist Frank Clune also wrote, saying that after Evatt had won this case, 'as win you must', he should 'go tell Caucus to jump in the lake … and give them back their leadership … Go back to the Bar and Ten Thousand Pounds a year, and be captain of your soul …' But Evatt was never again to have the balance necessary to be captain of his soul. The idea may in any case be inappropriate for him; Grattan's diagnosis of unappeased and undisciplined ambition seems more apt. The drives that impelled him – to win the prize, to be proved right, to defeat all the enemies pressing in on him – may never have allowed that kind of balance and composure. He was driven, but seemed unaware what drove him. With the Petrov affair, he had met an impasse; his fundamental identity as a lawyer and judge simply failed him. If he could not find the truth through a process of legal reasoning, how could it be found?

14

'The wrecker'

The events leading up to the split in April 1955 were parallel struggles, one spectacular and public, in the caucus; the other a longer-term arm wrestle in the wider labour movement that largely took place out of sight. Caucus meetings were divided and much of the tumult focused on how Evatt responded to Menzies' pressure on the issue of communism. In 1950 and 1951, it had been about his part in the High Court challenge and then the referendum. Later, during mid to late 1954, it was about how he dealt with what he insisted was the Petrov conspiracy. After the acrimony in caucus between August and October 1954, a split now seemed inevitable. But this drama, vividly reported in the press and frequently the focus of Labor recollections of the period, was only the most visible part of what was happening. Less visible were the shifts, intrigues and tensions developing inside the union movement.

The split

From mid-1954, the federal executive was mobilising to defeat the Groupers. The state ALP conferences in New South Wales and Victoria in June 1954 were stormy, with recriminations over the election loss. The Groupers had substantial control in both branches but it was never absolute, and both conferences heard indications of the fight to come as the counterattack against the Groupers began. At the Melbourne conference, Pat Kennelly launched an attack on what he called an 'outside influence' that he said was using the Industrial Groups to try to dictate the party's policy. The Groups, he said had gone far beyond the purpose of fighting communists in unions. At the Sydney conference, AWU national secretary Tom Dougherty surprised everyone by not re-nominating for the state executive; he told the media he 'forgot' to stand again. It was another straw in the wind, indicating he was shifting the AWU out of the Grouper camp. Dougherty's defection made a significant difference to the balance of power in the party. There were diverse elements, representing different forces and sentiments, in this counterattack against the Groupers. It came in part from the left against the right, and in part from figures such as Jim Ormonde, the journalist who had leaked Santamaria's speech, reflecting the growing disquiet of some Catholics. In many cases the suspicion of outside influence had a sectarian basis, when that influence was seen as the Catholic Church, so often imagined by its opponents as controlled from Rome; though that was not the case for Kennelly, who was Catholic himself and one of the key participants. It was, fundamentally, an attempt to seize back control from what was seen as 'a party within the party'.

The motives for Dougherty's decision to defect are obscure. They were certainly not ideological. He may have feared the Groupers' close alliance with the Queensland secretary, Joe Bukowski, which threatened his position as national secretary. He may have feared the Groupers would press for clean union ballots in the AWU, which would threaten his hold over what was acknowledged to be one of the most corrupt unions in the nation. The Groupers had always demanded policies to ensure clean elections, but they had till now held their noses and exempted the AWU because it was an ally. For whatever reason, by October it was known Dougherty planned to attack Santamaria in the *Australian Worker*, the paper Henry Boote had edited. The journalist Frank Chamberlain saw Dougherty 'in and out of [Evatt's] office a great deal' at the time, and thought he was now arguing that 'unless something was done to stop the activities of the Roman Catholic group in the Labor Party, it would become the Catholic Labor Party'. Cameron also thought it was Dougherty's intervention that spurred Evatt to make a public statement denouncing *News Weekly* and the Movement.

Evatt worked on this statement at his Mosman house, reportedly in collaboration with Ormonde, Haylen, Dalziel and Alan Reid. He released it to the media on the evening of 5 October, and it is widely considered to be the match that triggered the explosion. In it, he said publicly what many in the labour movement, and some in the press, knew. But saying it in public was a direct challenge to the Groupers, and particularly to Santamaria. Evatt blamed the 1954 election loss in part on the 'thinly veiled use' of the Petrov affair by the government, but in greater part on a disloyal minority in Victoria, which used methods he described as similar to 'both Communist and Fascist infiltration of larger groups'. They had attacked Labor policy and leadership; the example he gave was Bill Bourke's rejection of the means-test policy during the election. Their 'disloyal and subversive actions' inside the party, Evatt said, were 'intended to assist the Menzies Government, especially in its attempt to initiate ... the un-British and un-Australian methods of the totalitarian police state'. This minority was largely directed from outside the labour movement, he said, and the Melbourne publication *News Weekly* appeared to 'act as their organ'. He said he would take the issue to Labor's federal executive for 'appropriate action'. Naming *News Weekly* made the accusation explicit, and limiting it to Victoria was sensible, focusing attention on the Catholic Movement, rather than the wider alliance of the Groupers. Evatt described this influence as 'outside' and 'subversive' – powerful and, in the context, provocative language.

Clyde Cameron was an astute, knowledgeable and active participant in the politics of the split. He wrote that the AWU defection was very significant, and that Evatt's public statement was then crucial, spurring on others who opposed the Groupers: 'All this time they had been waiting for somebody like Evatt to pull the trigger'. Gil

Duthie recorded his reaction in his diary; as a Methodist minister, he had little tolerance for the Catholics in caucus. Evatt, he wrote, had finally named the Victorians as 'disruptors and disloyalists'. Duthie was pleased, saying, 'It's about time he took them on for they have got away with too much already ... these disruptionists must be disciplined ... Why don't they form their own Catholic Party and be done with it?' Now that Evatt had 'thrown down the gauntlet', he said, the fight could begin. 'It had to come. Their attitude is anti-Labor and intolerable.' Duthie was not a major figure in the party, though it is worth noting he was one of the Tasmanian representatives on the federal executive that would shortly sit in judgement on the issue. But his response reveals the building tension that had been released, and the sectarian hostility and resentment the Catholic group provoked.

Evatt received a letter the following day from Harry Alderman, a senior legal figure in Adelaide, who had been friends with Evatt since the 1940s. Alderman wrote: 'I was wondering how long before you made such a statement ...' Alderman was of Scottish Catholic heritage and went on to warn about the danger of sectarianism, given the long association between Catholicism and Labor. There should be a place in the party for all views, within the bounds of loyalty, he argued. 'I hope that this does not develop into a mere "R.C. v others" dispute. It gives strength to the anti-R.C.s in the party who also have their proper place there. The Liberals are already circulating the idea that "the Labor Party is going to expel all R.C.s"'. He wrote that Evatt need not trouble to reply, adding: 'Not that I have ever regarded you as a good correspondent'.

Over the next two weeks, there were turbulent meetings in caucus, reflecting the antagonism provoked by Evatt's public statement. Cameron, who had come through the hard political school of the AWU, later wrote: 'The bitterness between personalities was something that I had never seen before in my life'. On 13 October, the right mounted a challenge to Evatt's leadership. In caucus Evatt proposed a motion trying to clamp down on public debate: pending consideration of his allegations by the federal executive, he said, no caucus members should make public statements without consultation with the parliamentary executive. After a long debate involving more than twenty speakers, the motion was carried 54 to 16. Duthie recorded in his diary that the discussion was 'ninety per cent calm', though 'Doc got emotional in defence, showing strain of the battle'. Then came the anticipated challenge to Evatt's leadership. Duthie was scathing that this had been 'prophesied in the Press before the meeting!!!' 'With much stumbling and amateurism', George Cole moved a motion that 'all positions of the Party be declared vacant'; Duthie described him as 'a bitter Catholic activist' who was putting his Catholic allegiances above the party. But a motion that all positions be spilled could only be put on notice, and Kennelly, who was in caucus now as a senator, proposed it be dealt with the following week. Duthie wrote that many of them were 'disgusted' that Evatt's deputy, Calwell, was prepared to stand against him. 'What price loyalty. What price personal ambition … Treachery and disloyalty I hate like sin itself.'

An indication of Evatt's own thinking is a telegram he sent two days later to Percy Clarey, who was in New York. Clarey was a member of the caucus and a former president of the ACTU, and Evatt was hoping to enlist his support from afar. He told Clarey that 'the extreme right wing' was moving to depose him as leader, but he was 'almost certain' that the move would be defeated. There had been 'systematic attacks' on him in caucus which were then leaked to the press, and it was all happening because:

> I strongly attacked right wing especially small Victorian group
> … it seems possible that because [of] very strong support I am
> getting from trade union movement, [the] Victorian executive
> will be disciplined … I have come to the conclusion that we can
> never advance at all while we tolerate a party within a party.

He asked if Clarey could send a public message of support, but said he understood it was hard for him to judge the facts from a distance.

The formal minutes of the violent caucus meeting the following week are delightfully bland. It opened at 9 am on 20 October. Cole's motion was put and six members spoke alternately for and against Evatt. Then Tom Burke moved that the position of leader 'be declared vacant'; Cole's earlier motion had been too sweeping and included all positions. Evatt ruled that was out of order, and Keon moved a motion of dissent, which was lost. The debate continued, with another nine speeches. Then the vote was taken and the motion was lost, 52 to 28. 'Meeting adjourned at 1.10 pm.' The minutes of the whole meeting only take one typed page. But accounts by some who were there are more detailed and revealing. It ended in an open brawl.

Daly wrote about this meeting: 'It was a bitter debate. Feelings ran high and the attacks of Keon, Mullens and Bourke on Evatt were vitriolic and devastating. Insults, interjections and abuse filled the air as emotions and frustrations rose to fever pitch. I doubt if a worse scene has been witnessed in Caucus'. Duthie's diary began:

> TEST OF DOC'S LEADERSHIP … cool heads except John
> Mullens who spoke for 22 minutes using dramatics and verbosity
> to slate the Doc and then dramatically throwing down on the
> table documents charging Doc with disloyalty.

Duthie recorded in his diary only small sections of the debate. One was Keon's interjection, during one speech, that 'Doc Evatt has not always been a Labor candidate', a reference to rumours Evatt had been prepared to stand for the Nationalists in 1925. The reply was that Keon 'should have never been a Labor candidate'.

Cameron recorded dialogue much more extensively. He took notes at the time, then dictated them onto tape, which was typed up into his diaries. He recorded Cole saying directly to Evatt: 'You, Dr Evatt, have failed this Party in your leadership because you've put your personality above the principles of the Party'. By making his public statement denouncing outside influence, Cole told Evatt he had 'started something that is going to destroy the Party and himself'. One of Evatt's supporters, Joe Fitzgerald, said: 'If it wasn't for some of the traitors inside this Party Dr Evatt would have won the election'. He accused John Mullens of being 'a Labor rat' who was stabbing Evatt in the back, 'so your right-wing fascist mate could achieve his ambition of destroying our party'. Mullens then heaped scorn on Evatt:

> Your great weakness, Dr Evatt, is that you are devoid of principle, you are devoid of loyalty, you are devoid of decency and you are devoid of concern for what your selfish, self-centred motives might do to the Party … Step by step, you have taken us all to the brink of the precipice of disaster we face right now.

Accusations of ratting, of treachery, of undermining the leader, and of destroying the party flowed. Stan Keon said dramatically: 'If there is a majority of this Caucus in favour of keeping Dr Evatt as our Leader in today's vote, I shall fasten him upon you with bands of steel!' He said Evatt's own allies were intending to stab him in the back. Eddie Ward demanded he name who he meant; Keon said, 'You're one'. Ward retorted that Keon's anti-communism was 'a campaign of political terrorism', going on to say: 'You and your mates are more in line with Menzies and his mob than with the great ideals of the Labor Party … Your mob take your orders from *News Weekly* and Pope Santamaria, don't you?'

Then Evatt spoke to defend himself:

> I never spared myself in the last campaign. No human being could have done more than I did to win … frankly I can't understand how any person could say I shouldn't appear before the Royal Commission in defence of my own staff! … According to Mr Mullens, if anyone is a Communist he must be

automatically found guilty of treason or the like. This attitude is a thousand times worse than the infamous Zinoviev letter or the Reichstag fire.

Responding to interjections from Keon, he said: 'You're worried, aren't you, because I'm standing up to you?'

When the vote on Evatt's leadership was finally taken, according to Cameron:

> Evatt jumped on the table and tried to count from there. Eddie Ward shouted, 'Take their names' … the whole Caucus degenerated into a riot … [It was] easily the most sensational Caucus meeting I have ever attended … The bitterness was so intense, the hatred so deep.

Duthie and Daly also described Evatt jumping on the table; Duthie noted that he 'had to get on the table to be seen and heard as we were all standing'. Daly wrote: 'The motion was clearly defeated on the voices, but that did not suit Evatt and Ward – they were going for the kill'.

Who it was that said 'take their names' is contested, and a point worthy of trivia buffs. Daly said it was Evatt. Cameron would later insist that it was not Evatt but Ward. Duthie noted only that 'someone' called out, but he added that six of those originally supporting Evatt changed sides as soon as this happened, because taking down names was seen as so vindictive. Daly was one of them, later writing: 'It was Evatt and Ward at their hating best … It was a degrading and disgusting spectacle – twenty-eight members lined up like Japanese war criminals by colleagues with hate, vindictiveness and triumph written all over their faces'.

It was a powerful act in Labor's drama. The hatred of the Groupers for Evatt was palpable, and the hatred of many of the others for the Groupers was equally vicious. After years of baiting each other, the animosities had boiled over and there was no turning back. Accusations and imagery of rats and betrayal, of outside influence and control, of sectarian sentiment and of Japanese prisoners of war all conjured up powerful emotions. Duthie wrote in his diary: 'I went out very sad at heart to think such a cleavage, such behaviour, such bitterness existed'. The press quickly had the full story including the list of those who had voted against Evatt. Duthie found that disturbing: 'I don't agree their names should be published'. Some thought the final vote was a victory for Evatt, but Cameron noted in his diary: 'It was not a vote *for* Evatt ... it was a vote *against* the Groupers'. The antagonism towards them was 'open and very intense'. Duthie's entry for the next day starts: 'No heart for anything ...'

A week later, the federal executive began meeting in the Hotel Kingston in Canberra. Though evenly divided, they were getting ready for intervention into the Victorian branch. Evatt produced a long accusatory document teasing out in more detail what he had said in his public statement in early October. Debate went back and forth between Evatt and the others, with questions from the executive members. Joe Chamberlain recalled that Keon, Bourke and Mullens all attended, 'very bitter in their attitudes'. When interviewed many years later, Chamberlain's recollection of these events was a little oblique, as though he was not a crucial figure in them; he said 'they' rather than 'we', yet along with Kennelly he was actively seeking action against the Groupers: 'So they then decided the thing was so serious, that they couldn't close their eyes to what was happening and hope for the best, that these people had to be fought'. On the following evening, the executive resolved, in the brisk minutes they kept, that the charges against the Victorian branch were 'grave' and that a further investigation should be held in Melbourne.

These investigative sessions started on 10 November in the ACTU boardroom, in Lygon Street, Carlton, and ran through to early December. The federal executive heard evidence from a cluster of anti-Grouper unions; from Victor Stout, the president of the Melbourne

Trades Hall, who had been a Grouper but had turned against them; from a number of Grouper politicians including Frank McManus and Keon; from Evatt; from the Victorian executive; from Victorian premier John Cain; and many more. The minutes, which do not record what was said, have a quasi-judicial tone, as though the powerful executive was investigating for the first time a struggle they had no prior knowledge or opinion of. But their views were still divergent. The to-and-fro included an amendment to censure Evatt for going public, and then a decision that 'permission be granted' for this motion to be withdrawn. Cameron reported that Dinny Lovegrove, the Victorian state secretary who was on the federal executive, was – behind the scenes – being assured that he still had a future if he defected from the Groupers.

The crucial decision was finally taken on the afternoon of 3 December; when Chamberlain moved a motion to intervene, Lovegrove spoke in support. The federal executive decided to intervene in the Victorian branch, calling a special conference of the branch to elect a new state executive. In two decisions intended to ensure that the special conference voted the way it should, the federal executive ruled that unions that had disaffiliated from the Victorian branch would be permitted to be delegates, and the normal requirement that a delegate be a paid-up member of the party would be waived. Under these conditions, when the special conference met in February, it elected a new anti-Grouper state executive that significantly included Kennelly, Stout and Lovegrove.

There were now two Victorian executives, old and new, because the old Grouper executive refused to resign. Normally it would be the next federal conference, scheduled for Hobart, which adjudicated on which should be recognised, but that was too risky. Cameron encouraged Joe Chamberlain to make a ruling beforehand, and just before the conference opened, the federal executive ruled in favour of the 'new' state executive. It was irregular, Cameron conceded, 'but when you are in a war, fighting for survival, you can not afford to be

"HE PLAYED HIS UKELELE AS THE SHIP WENT DOWN."

Before the split in Hobart in March 1955, the predictions were already in, and most held Evatt responsible. In this cartoon, Calwell is trying to warn him, but Evatt is oblivious, playing the ukulele he had had since he and Mary Alice went to Hawaii on their honeymoon in 1921.

Ted Scorfield, *Bulletin*, 26 January 1955

worried about technicalities'. When the Hobart conference opened on 14 March 1955, the old Victorian group attempted to gain entrance and were blocked; but nor could anyone else enter the hall. The following day, conference reconvened to another hall without telling the Groupers where it was; but the Groupers, including the New South Wales delegation and parts of those from Tasmania, Western Australia and Queensland, had now decided to boycott the conference. It was a huge, intense fight and a ruthless operation, played out on the front pages of the press.

With all the boycotters absent, the conference, now firmly in the hands of Kennelly, Chamberlain and Cameron, was barely large enough to function. But it voted to remove 'political recognition' from the Industrial Groups in Victoria, on the argument that recognition had enabled them to 'enter fields other than those intended by their founders'. They were not disbanded, but were being trimmed to the sphere of union matters only. That meant they were finished in Victoria, but it left New South Wales to sort out. The conference also took decisions moving Labor's foreign affairs positions further to the left, which were anathema to the Groupers; it endorsed recognition of China and its admittance to the UN, and opposed the dispatch of Australian troops to Malaya. Robert Murray described the 'grand strategy' as changing the Victorian delegation to Hobart, confirming Jack Schmella, Kennelly's choice as his successor, as federal secretary, and ending the factionalism with a decisive defeat for the Groupers. Then, he said, most felt 'Evatt would have to go'. That was effectively what happened in the split, except that Evatt did not go; he hung on for another five years as leader, increasingly a liability, but doggedly fighting off challenges while the party despaired of how to remove him without granting a victory to those they had defeated.

What followed over the next month in Victoria was bloody. On 7 April, the new state executive met in the ACTU boardroom for what Murray called the 'night of the knife'. Over 100 members were expelled from the party, including members of the federal parliament, the state parliament, the Melbourne city council and many others. A week later, Stout wrote to Evatt on the Victorian central executive letterhead, advising him formally that Keon, Bourke and four others had been excluded from membership for failing to accept the decisions of the Hobart conference and for supporting 'a bogus breakaway Labor Party'. Mullens had previously been expelled. This was the bureaucracy of retribution, and the Grouper members of state parliament retaliated a few days later, using their numbers in the parliament to destroy John Cain's Labor government by voting with the conservatives. These Groupers in the Victorian parliament were then wiped out at the consequent state election at the end of May. Their federal equivalents now sat in Canberra, calling themselves the ALP (Anti-Communist) and vicious disputes broke out between what they increasingly called 'Evatt Labor' and the anti-communists, who were in return called the 'bogus' or the 'corner' Labor party. After years of build-up and intimations, the Labor party had finally split.

'The wrecker'

The image of Evatt as the 'wrecker' of the Labor party is a powerful one. For many, it is the one thing for which Evatt is remembered. As leader, should he bear the blame for the erratic and intemperate judgements that precipitated the catastrophic split of 1955? This question goes to the heart of any attempt to understand the complex and tumultuous events within the labour movement in the 1950s; it also goes to the heart of biography, because it asks whether our subject is an actor with a degree of control, or is acted upon by overpowering events and influences. Evatt had triggered the split, but was he its cause, the guiding hand who should take responsibility?

In the fraught period after the split itself, and before the federal election that they understood would wipe them out, the Groupers in the federal parliament turned their hatred on Evatt. The 'Joshua–Keon

THE WRECKER

Evatt as the 'wrecker' was already a leitmotif even as the split unfolded.
Ted Scorfield depicts him conspiring with the communists – the man
beside him has a hammer and sickle on his shirt – to draw the ship of
the ALP onto the rocks to be broken up for its cargo.

Ted Scorfield, *Bulletin*, 6 April 1955

group', as they were called, opposed Evatt more than they opposed the government. In late April, Bourke alleged Evatt had accepted funds from the Communist party during the 1951 referendum campaign. Evatt, he said, had 'won an assured place in history for himself ... as the man who wrecked the Australian Labor Party and a man who is the best friend the communists in this country have ever known'.

Liberal party election advertising had explicitly targeted Evatt since 1951 as a 'Communist champion', and in 1954 as not to be trusted to deal with the communists. In the December 1955 election, which Menzies had called to capitalise on the split, this focus on Evatt intensified, explicitly naming him as 'the wrecker'. One ad compared Menzies and Evatt, using the line: 'PROVED LEADER OR PROVED WRECKER'. Another advertisement said: 'EVATT HAS WRECKED THE LABOR PARTY. DON'T LET HIM WRECK AUSTRALIA'. A third claimed: 'When Dr Evatt split the Labor Party he re-opened the door for the Reds. REMEMBER! A VOTE FOR LABOR IS A VOTE FOR EVATT'. This focus on Evatt as the wrecker would have appealed to those distraught Labor supporters devastated by the trauma of the split and seeking someone to blame.

Evatt was certainly the catalyst, touching the match to a powder keg. The split might not have happened had someone with cooler judgement, and who could command greater loyalty, been in place as leader; and as leader he had to bear some responsibility. In retrospect, Labor figures tried to assess the degree of that responsibility. Fred Daly thought, like many, that Evatt was a poor leader and contributed to the split: 'Although a great lawyer, Evatt possessed few, if any, of the qualities needed to lead the Labor Party'. He said in a later interview that the split was never inevitable: 'Had Chifley been leading the party ... with his background, his patience and ability and all that, that would have been avoided'. By contrast, Clyde Cameron's detailed reminiscences were mostly about the intrigue and workings of the party machine, and he did not explicitly blame Evatt. Cameron had an insider's knowledge of the workings of the Labor machine, but Evatt was not prominent in his account.

The historian Robert Murray ultimately laid the blame for the split at Evatt's feet. Despite describing in great detail the machinations within the party and the union movement, the build-up of factional tensions and alliances, and the pivotal role played by senior figures, he wrote that:

> The central figure must remain Evatt, the gifted but tragically inappropriate intellectual at a time when Labor needed intellectual distinction at its head. Evatt's failings were enormous: his egocentricity, his naiveté, his lack of feeling for economics … his sheer lack of judgment and his disastrous errors, under pressure, over the means test, the Petrov inquiry and then in touching off the split.

He suggested Evatt was by 1954 'extremely disturbed'; that his obsessions and conspiracy theories may have been part of a 'deeper paranoia' and 'deepening instability'.

Some saw Evatt as the mastermind behind the whole turbulent struggle, because he was the leader and because his public interventions fanned the flames. Alan Reid's *The Bandar Log*, a fictional rendering of the events, depicted Evatt as 'Kaye Seborjar' (i.e., Cesare Borgia), the party boss, hated and feared, skilful and self-deluding, ruthlessly scheming for his own survival and place in history. Reid had him deliberately deciding to stir up sectarianism, calculating that expelling the Catholic right would win him more support from Protestants. Reid said in several interviews that Evatt had told him that for every Catholic vote he lost he would gain two Protestant votes. Reid wrote: 'If Machiavelli were alive today he'd rewrite *The Prince* with Seborjar as his model'. There were others – particularly the Catholic right – who interpreted the split much the same way.

Jack Kane, the main Grouper organiser in New South Wales

similarly wrote that Evatt had turned on the Groupers, determined 'to drive them, by a violent sectarian campaign if necessary, out of the Labor Party'. Santamaria blamed Evatt for triggering a sectarian war, and doing so quite deliberately; he told Tennant that Evatt had studied the use of sectarian tactics when writing about Holman, and 'knew they had worked before'. Later, in his memoirs, Santamaria wrote that Evatt 'set out to guarantee his political survival' by stirring up anti-Catholic feeling in his attack on the Groupers. And yet we have seen that when he had written about Holman and Hughes, Evatt had not endorsed sectarianism. Even if Hughes' sectarian rhetoric against Catholics and 'Fenians' had drawn him some support from the right, he had still lost both the conscription plebiscites and he had split the party. Evatt wrote of the 1916 split as a disaster, and of Holman and Hughes as tragic figures; it was hardly an exemplar of success.

There certainly was sectarian sentiment in the 1950s, and it was aggravated by the split. Evatt received numerous letters that encouraged him to act against an alien Catholic influence. One wrote urging him not to step down from the leadership: 'This would be much regretted by a great many Protestant adherents of the movement. It would be another win for the Roman Catholics'. Another commended him on his 'exposure of the plotting of the Santamaria party, who ... were out, not to overwhelm Communism, but to get the power into their own hands'. A third correspondent commended Evatt's record, listing his achievements: he had 'triumphed over Fascism at the Referendum, debunked the Royal Commission ... rebuked the R.C. Hierarchy, swept away the powerful agent of outside forces'. The letter writer concluded: 'I honor you and pay you my personal thanks'. There are many other such examples in his papers. It is important, however, to recognise that while those tensions existed and had been stirred, Evatt had not so much deliberately deployed them as stumbled into them.

The trouble with the idea that Evatt deliberately triggered a sectarian backlash to preserve his leadership, and engineered the split through conscious action, is that it exaggerates his control over events, control over the party and perhaps control over himself. The issues leading to the split were fundamentally about a power struggle, and went deeper into the labour movement than Evatt himself. He had very little influence, compared with some of the key powerbrokers such as Santamaria, Kennelly, Dougherty, Cameron, Ferguson and Chamberlain. They were people who controlled loyal forces, who knew how the machine worked culturally and procedurally, and who could influence the unions, ALP state branches and the federal executive. Evatt had no real base in the party, and no feel for the machine.

Frequently, interviews with Labor figures pointed out that Evatt did not understand the party, and the party did not understand him. Jack Ferguson shared the widespread reservations in the New South Wales party about Evatt's trustworthiness, and later said Evatt 'never took any notice of what was for the Labor Party'. Evatt was for Evatt, he said. Joe Chamberlain thought that Evatt's legal training meant he found it 'extremely difficult to move easily in the political field, particularly in the hurly burly of Labor politics'. Pat Kennelly was closely aligned with Calwell and they shared an antipathy to Evatt's intellectualism. When asked in a brief interview in 1967 what sort of prime minister Evatt might have been, Kennelly said only that 'those who administered the party at that time' – by which he meant he and Ferguson – 'may have had moments of anxiety to be quite honest'. Daly was more direct, writing that Kennelly had 'no great love' for Dr Evatt. 'He once said he would walk over red-hot coals to do anything for Ben Chifley, but he wouldn't walk over an eight-inch-thick carpet to do anything for Dr Evatt.'

Evatt's position was precarious, and at key moments he looked to be out of his depth, desperately trying to save his leadership by shifting alliances. When the Groupers were in the ascendant he attempted to cultivate their support, but when key powerbrokers such as Kennelly, Chamberlain and Dougherty mobilised to fight against the Groupers he aligned himself with them. His vacillation only reinforced the view that he could not be trusted, but it was also a sign of desperation and weakness, and of not really having a grasp of the political complexities. In this sense, he was still the outsider he had been in Lang's party in the 1920s, an arriviste from a different political tradition, with little understanding of how Labor worked.

But it goes further than this. It was not only that Evatt was out of his depth in the intricacies of Labor politics, he was out of his depth in politics. He had few of the skills needed for political leadership: the ability to work cooperatively, the skill to assess political situations, the open-mindedness to recognise differences of opinion and seek compromise, and above all the ability to persuade others and to engender trust and loyalty. Joe Chamberlain touched on this when he observed that Evatt could not understand the fact that belonging to a political party meant that 'everybody was deemed to be equal, had the right to express themselves'. He was just that kind of man, Chamberlain said. Grattan saw some of this, too, and thought it was why Evatt taking on the leadership was a tragic mistake. 'Bert was a lousy politician,' he wrote, and 'not by nature or cultivation' someone who could work as part of a team; he 'never really understood, let alone liked, politics.' Grattan always returned to the insight that Evatt was essentially a lawyer, an advocate.

This goes back to the shaping of Evatt's identity through the law. A barrister can be successful, as he had been, as a sole actor, making their case without needing to accommodate others; the mode of address is largely partisan, convincing others of the correctness of your case. As a foreign minister, Evatt had to work with others, but was often accused of being the sole repository of foreign policy. Making his case in Washington and London, and later in Paris and New York, he was seen as belligerent and uncooperative, but that was the nature of his address, of his advocacy. When arguing about constitutions in San Francisco and about justice in the referendum campaign, he was deploying the skills of an advocate and had some significant success. But as a leader of a political party, the narrow range of his skills was exposed, and his inability to understand and read the complexities of politics was a liability. In the dangerous and paranoid atmosphere of the Cold War, with a labour movement building to a crisis, these were major flaws in his leadership.

But did this mean his flaws were the problem, or did his failure to grasp the situation just mean he was all the more powerless? While Evatt's October statement was the match that set off the split, the powder keg already existed; the struggle inside the party organisation was between factions in the union movement, between the federal administration and the state branches in Victoria and New South Wales, and within the finely balanced numbers on the federal executive. One way to think about this is to imagine Evatt was not in the picture; could the problems of the labour movement have been resolved, and the pressure released, in a less damaging way? Counterfactual or 'what if' histories involve taking one actor or one key event out of the sequence, to try to guess what would have happened; they can help to reveal the deeper historical forces in play. If we change one actor for another, is the plot still the same? What might have happened if Evatt was not a player? Is it possible to imagine the split being avoided?

Fred Daly said that: 'When Chifley died the only man capable of avoiding the split left the party'. With his caution, his authority and the respect of most of the labour movement, Chifley might have been capable of avoiding a conflict while assisting the party leaders to regain control. He might have been able to prevent others from provoking the split. The enthusiasm of Movement activists in Victoria was waning during 1953 and membership was known to be falling. While Santamaria was moving in a more militantly political direction, that in turn was causing anxiety in the Catholic hierarchy; there were attempts by the church to rein him in. Might this have meant the zealotry and the influence of the Movement faded? Santamaria's influence might have declined over the next few years, while Kennelly and Chamberlain might have worked out how to rebalance the party;

Keon and Mullens might have gone on to be the cabinet ministers they were marked out to be.

The successful efforts in 1955 and 1956 to prevent the split spreading to New South Wales might provide a model for such an 'altered past' in which the pressure was defused; but the pressure was largely in Victoria, and New South Wales was different because there were many there who remembered and were determined to avoid a repetition of the split under Lang. Kennelly and Chamberlain led a concerted effort to regain control and that inevitably would have led to conflict with the Victorian branch. But could the way they coopted Dinny Lovegrove, who was assured that if he supported intervention he would still have a future, suggest that the Victorians might have been contained? Cameron had dismantled the weak Industrial Group network in South Australia, and it might have been possible either to reduce their vigour or contain them to union matters elsewhere.

But it is hard to imagine an alternative trajectory in which the split did not occur. Fundamentally, Evatt had little grasp of what was happening, and little control over events; in the deeper struggle inside the labour movement, it is hard to see his hand at work. Certainly, his actions provoked existing antagonisms, but the hatred in caucus was intense, and more importantly the confrontation building in the wider labour movement was always likely to be bloody. We can never know, which is the way of counterfactual histories; I am not intending to exonerate Evatt, but the powder keg he touched off was already in place and it is difficult to imagine how it could have been made harmless had he not been in the picture. Nevertheless, Evatt was in the picture, and after all this turmoil and all the hatred directed at him, he was even more determined to stay.

15

The wreckage

The split formally occurred during March and April 1955, but it had been coming for many years before and continued for some time after. The Hobart conference had not been the end point, but a spectacular set piece in a drama playing out deep within the labour movement. After the Hobart conference, Evatt was one of the fiercest in wanting to pursue the purge and his language was still quite extreme. On 24 March, he told a Labor rally in Wollongong that a 'Menzies-Fadden-Santamaria-Fascist cell' was trying to push the ALP 'even further to the right than the Liberal Party'. But wiser heads, including Kennelly and the New South Wales Labor premier Joe Cahill – who were both Catholics – were to prevail.

The aftermath

The struggle that occurred in the New South Wales party was in large part about how to avoid another split; many had memories of the divisions under Lang from the late 1920s to the early 1940s and were intent on avoiding a repeat. In that conflict, there were some expulsions, but they did not go as deep as in Victoria. A remnant of the New South Wales Groupers formed the Democratic Labor Party (DLP) in September 1956, but the split had been contained. Evatt's younger brother Clive was one of the casualties of this turmoil, expelled in July 1956. He had been a minister in Labor governments since 1946, and his expulsion was not because he was a Grouper, but because he was a maverick and had voted against party policy; there are suggestions that he expected Evatt, as the federal leader, to intervene to save him and resented his inaction.

In Queensland, the split was local, relatively petty and quite protracted, as a feud developed between the AWU and the ALP government under the pro-Grouper premier, Vince Gair. The AWU in effect controlled the party in Queensland, and Joe Bukowski was both state secretary of the union and state president of the Labor party; over two years of internal strife ended when Bukowski and the state branch expelled Gair and his supporters in April 1957, and then Gair's government collapsed in June. Gair also founded a DLP branch, and from August 1957 the DLP was nationally organised.

Just as important are the ways in which the rumblings of the split continued in local party and union branches. Throughout 1956 and into the following year, the party's federal secretary, Jack Schmella, received numerous letters making charges and countercharges against individuals in branches; so too did Evatt as the leader. ALP or union members found themselves accused of being Groupers and sought help, appealing their innocence and loyalty; resolutions came in from local branches notifying the executive of allegations and expulsions. Much of this correspondence was from New South Wales, where from late 1955 local branches identified themselves as 'Australian Labor Party (Official)', the tag that had also been used during the Lang split. These letters are all about loyalty and treachery, recriminations and old wounds, solidarity and defiance, rebel groups, breakaways and unity; above all else, their language demonstrates the emotional energy, the angst and the sheer distraction of ordinary members in the labour movement. This preoccupation meant the Labor party was debilitated in Victoria, New South Wales and Queensland.

A flurry over Evatt's lapse of party membership in early 1955 was characteristic of him, but also of the internal strife in the party. He had been a member of the Canberra branch in previous years, but had failed to renew his membership. Suddenly those opposing him saw a chance to remove him from the leadership because he was not even a member of the party. The leader of the New South Wales Groupers, Jack Kane, was reportedly confident the plan would work. The Canberra branch, then led by Finlay Crisp, refused to help, and it seems Crisp and John Burton, who was a member of the branch, were in open conflict with one another; Evatt's leadership was, incredibly, collateral damage. But Frank McManus, Kane's equivalent in Victoria, wrote later that the plan to use his lapsed membership to depose Evatt was 'a smoke dream', adding: 'There were too many whose tenure of newly gained power depended on Evatt as a symbol, since they had built him up as the saviour of the Labor Movement'. At the end of March, Evatt urgently applied for membership of the Mosman branch; eventually he was issued with a member's ticket by the Brighton-Le-Sands branch in his electorate of Barton; it was backdated to 18 January.

By contrast with Labor's disarray, the Liberal federal secretariat in this period was professional and politically astute. As they watched the split building in late 1954, the Liberal's public relations committee had read an internal discussion paper about the Industrial Groups and the history of the dispute. They agreed that policy on communism 'on the national and international level' was the great issue dividing Labor, and that in future political campaigns 'this division should constantly be kept before the public mind'; perhaps 'more legislative action' against communists would help, they thought. During these discussions, though, they consistently reminded themselves they should also have a positive message about development, rather than rely only on anti-communism and Labor's strife. In June 1955, they discussed the split: John McConnell, the Victorian secretary, suggested 'a big section of the Catholic vote was lost to Labor for many years'; Howard Sleath, the Queensland secretary, commented that the split was 'of immense advantage', and that Evatt was 'the Liberal's best asset'; while John Carrick, from the New South Wales division, said the swinging Catholic vote should largely come to the Liberals, although there was a danger of a few Protestant votes going to Evatt. Carrick then rehearsed the potential advantages of calling an early election before the end of the year: the Menzies government was currently popular and the budget should be well received, over the coming months the anti-communist Groupers in parliament 'would continue to trouble Evatt', and the release of the final Petrov Commission report 'would help'. That was an accurate diagnosis of the immediate future. Preoccupied with its internal power struggle, the Labor party was no real match for the calm and professional Liberals, as they compiled research, collected intelligence from the states and acutely analysed the weaknesses of their opponents.

The Molotov letter

The Petrov Royal Commission final report was debated in parliament on the evening of 19 October 1955. Evatt was extremely eager to have a long debate, despite attempts in caucus to restrain him. Some of his colleagues felt the Petrov issue was dead, and should not be 'dug up', but he disagreed. Because the report had recommended no prosecutions, there was a sense abroad that Menzies was vulnerable. Certainly, on the left, many thought the royal commission had not delivered what Menzies hoped for, which turned the focus back to the accusation that Petrov's defection had been used for political advantage. The leftist historian Brian Fitzpatrick had written to Evatt the previous week: 'All your friends are looking forward to your impending destruction of the commissioners and their report'. Fitzpatrick thought it was an opportunity similar to the referendum to confound Menzies, but he urged Evatt not to get bogged down in technical analysis of documents. Instead, he should emphasise the fact that no spies had been uncovered, and the inquiry had been costly for no purpose. Fitzpatrick advised Evatt to 'flummox Menzies, by presenting at the outset ... a short series of simple points', and repeat them at the end of his speech 'by way of challenge'. Sending 'blessings on your anxious undertaking', Fitzpatrick said he would be listening on the radio.

Evatt started his speech at 8 pm and went on for two hours. The public and diplomatic galleries were full. He repeated all his previous charges: that the Petrovs had been cultivated over several years, that Menzies had timed the defection for maximum political advantage in the 1954 election, that at least parts of the documents were forgeries designed to damage the Labor party, that the Petrov case was all a 'political fraud' and 'far worse than … the notorious Zinovieff letter'; he had, by this point, dropped the reference to the Reichstag fire. He ended by saying that had he been in a court or commission it 'would probably have taken me twelve days to finish my remarks'.

The speech itself reads reasonably coherently, though it is obvious Evatt could not prove his core claims of conspiracy and forgery. However, as we saw at the beginning of this book, he fatally undermined his position by announcing, early in the speech, that he had written to Molotov, the Soviet foreign minister, to ask whether Petrov's documents were genuine, and that Molotov had denied it. This is where we began, and for many it was where Evatt's career ended. The laughter and incredulity that immediately erupted showed how little credibility Evatt had remaining. Menzies wrote in his memoirs of the 'great gusts of laughter' in the parliament. 'What an absurdity this was', he said. To ask Molotov about the authenticity of the documents was 'too ludicrous for words' and the 'derisive laughter rolled on'. Evatt's speech was punctuated throughout by heckling from the government side and from the now-expelled anti-communist Labor members, particularly John Mullens and Stan Keon, who goaded him about Molotov. It was an unusually unruly debate, with the speaker unable to maintain order above the pandemonium. When Mullens said Evatt was 'suffering from strain and overwork in making such wild claims', a government voice reportedly called out: 'He's nuts'.

Later, Russel Ward revealed in his memoirs that he had had a hand in writing the speech. He and Ron Heiser, 'two unknown young men from the university' as Ward described them, had been invited to Evatt's room in Parliament House the night before to work on it with him; Burton was also there. No mention had been made of a letter to Molotov. On the night of the speech, there was a party at Burton's house to listen to the debate on the radio; Ward wrote that 'drinks flowed freely and expectations soared'. Then Evatt announced he had written to Molotov, and they were stunned into silence. Ward recalled that when Evatt later joined the Burtons' party for supper, he looked 'a bit wild-eyed and more dishevelled than usual'. Ward asked 'why in God's name he had been so mad as to write to Molotov, and so much madder as to announce the fact', and Evatt merely replied, as noted in the introduction, that it was established judicial practice. 'In opening a case one must always ask counsel for the accused for his version of the events', he told Ward. Evatt knew Molotov from all their many earlier encounters, but this was a critical mistake in the climate of Cold War politics, when anti-communism was so intense, and when Evatt was so often targeted as a communist sympathiser.

The immediate media reaction was one of disbelief, followed by speculation that Menzies would call an early election to capitalise on Evatt's blunder. The response of the *Canberra Times* was typical: it commented that Evatt's letter to Molotov was 'handing to the Government on a platter a complete election victory with every prospect of a crushing Labour defeat'. But Menzies waited before announcing the election; he intended to crush Evatt first, in a speech in parliament a week after Evatt's. This speech was described by Menzies' sympathetic biographer, Allan Martin, as 'one of the most brilliant and powerful of his political career', but also one of the 'cruellest'. Menzies wrote in his memoirs: 'I decided that I must dispose of the charges once and for all without any mercy for the man who had made them'. And it is a merciless speech; after decades of rivalry and antagonism between the two of them, Evatt had fatally weakened himself, and Menzies was going in for the kill.

The galleries were again full; people had been queuing for hours to get in. Menzies spoke slowly and deliberately for ninety minutes, alluding frequently to Evatt's 'illogicality', 'the erratic course of his arguments', and his 'bewildering variety of charges'. Evatt, he said, was 'driven on by this extraordinary obsession of his'. He ridiculed the idea he had influenced the timing of the defection and defended the integrity of the judges at the commission and of ASIO. The 'very fury' of Evatt's obsession, Menzies said, had even diverted him from 'his consistent battle on behalf of the Australian Communists to make his now celebrated appeal' to Molotov. Evatt's letter would be childish, he said, 'if it were made by an obscure nonentity', but it became 'atrocious when made by a leader who is an aspirant for the Prime Ministership'.

Over and over, Menzies made pointed references to Evatt's state of mind. Any 'sane and sensible person', he said, could see that Evatt was 'suffering from persecution delusions', and inhabiting 'a world of sheer fantasy'. He was not just swatting away all Evatt's allegations; he was also positioning Evatt as delusional, obsessive and irrational. At one point, Menzies said: 'He is troubled. He made a monumental exhibition of himself last week. I am not adding to the monumental exhibition; I am merely sealing the tombstone on top of it'. The exchanges between Menzies and Evatt were poisonous and demonstrated Menzies' ascendency over his rival; at one point Menzies told him not to 'mutter and mumble', and Evatt protested 'I am not muttering. I am trying to yell'. 'Just take it!' Menzies sneered. To one of Evatt's interjections, Menzies said, 'I understand your feelings perfectly. You are in a very agitated state of mind'. Evatt protested, 'Not a bit', but the headlines in the papers said: 'Evatt Under Delusions'. Menzies finished by saying that the security services, the judiciary and 'decent and patriotic Australians' were being undermined by Evatt 'in his own interests and with the enthusiastic support of every Communist in Australia'. The man on trial in this debate was Evatt himself, he concluded.

A few days later, Menzies announced a federal election, barely halfway through the term of the parliament. Calling an early election was clearly ruthless exploitation of Evatt's folly and the despair it generated in the Labor party. The government also saw the advantage of bringing the House and Senate election cycles back into line, as they had been out of sequence since the 1951 double dissolution. Menzies wrote to his daughter: 'It would be flying in the face of Providence not to seize the opportunity ... to clean up the political position and to write "terminus" to the career of the Right Honourable the leader of the Opposition, whose mental oddities grow upon him'. Menzies was making the most of this chance to entrench the split and perhaps finally see Evatt off the political stage.

Evatt's 'Molotov cocktail' had left a 'nasty taste' in the party's mouth, according to a newspaper back in his birthplace in the Hunter Valley: 'Never has the prestige of Dr Evatt in particular and the whole Labour cause been so low'. The *Canberra Times* editorialised about his 'political stupidity', commenting: 'No one can even guess what surprises Dr Evatt may still have in store for stunned audiences in the coming election'. As the parliament broke up a few days later, Labor members were despondent, 'like unwilling troops moving into a disastrous battle'. Evatt was demanding that Menzies table the original Petrov documents, which he refused to do.

The Labor party attempted to constrain Evatt in the lead-up to the election. His policy speech was to be 'strictly vetted' by the federal executive, to ensure he would not 'spring last minute surprises'. A week later, the executive instructed Evatt not to refer to Petrov in his election speech; he was 'virtually gagged' and told that only if government speakers raised the issue during the election would he have a right of reply. But he was hard to restrain and clearly wanted to distribute his Molotov speech. The day after he made the speech he had ordered 500 copies from the government printer; two weeks later, after the party had attempted to gag him, he ordered a further 5000 copies for distribution. A year later, the invoices had still not been paid.

Although Labor hoped it would not come up again, the royal commission and Evatt's letter to Molotov were raised frequently in the 1955 election. Menzies ridiculed the 'broken Labor Party, its old ideals lost … and its leadership deeply distrusted, even by its own supporters'. Evatt, he said, was 'struggling to emerge from his trafficking with Molotov and the wreckage of his Party', and was adding 'to this election the final touches of bewildering phantasy'. Evatt had 'worked himself into a state of mind in which he found nothing but incompetence, conspiracy or fraud' around him. At an electoral meeting in Bondi, as police moved through the crowd to quell interjectors, Menzies replied smoothly to an accusation that he was smearing Evatt, 'I have no intention to hurt him'. A voice called out, 'Why don't you produce the Petrov letters?' and Menzies replied, 'The letters from Molotov?' This quip was met with laughter from the crowd.

This jeering came not just from the government and its supporters, but also from Grouper-aligned Labor forces. In the closing days before the election, Evatt came to a turbulent meeting of 1500 people in the Richmond Town Hall in Melbourne. This was Stan Keon's electorate, and Keon was being challenged by a young Jim Cairns, who would go on to be deputy prime minister under Whitlam. The audience was divided, with Evatt being both cheered and booed as he spoke. A group of hecklers kept up a 'barrage of interjections', calling out, 'What about Petrov?' and 'Molotov!' Evatt found himself pleading with opponents in his audience to at least preference Labor ahead of the Liberals: 'Vote first for your own candidate, then for your ALP candidate, and put the Liberals last'. Menzies repeatedly made the all too obvious point that Labor was divided, and Liberal newspaper advertisements emphasised this message: 'A Labor Party that cannot govern itself has no claim to govern you'.

Edgar Holt later wrote an assessment of the campaign for the Liberal party. Labor, he said, had been 'quite deliberately' forced to an election when 'its ranks were hopelessly divided, its leadership under deep suspicion'. The Labor party 'had no illusions about the outcome', Holt said; it expected defeat. But Holt warned against complacency claiming that, without the split, the government might have lost. Nevertheless,

Labor was soundly defeated, the only solace being the fact that the anti-communist group was also wiped out. Labor lost ten seats, half of them in Victoria, and its national primary vote dropped from just over 50 to 44.6 per cent. The 1955 election demonstrated starkly the effects of the split in Victoria, where Labor's primary vote dropped from over 50 per cent to only 37.1 per cent and where the ALP (Anti-Communist), not yet called the DLP, gathered almost 16 per cent, delivering much of that vote via preferences to the conservatives.

In the following years, the DLP vote was always highest in Victoria, remaining around 15 per cent into the 1960s; in other states it started lower and declined more quickly. Victoria had been the epicentre of the Movement and of militant anti-communist Catholicism, and this was reflected in the higher support there. Labor was to lose the next five federal elections, and it would require another intervention into the Victorian branch before they could win national government in 1972. In the meantime, the DLP acted as a bridge for middle-class Catholics to cross from Labor to the conservatives, though to some extent that process was already underway before the split. In the aftermath of the 1955 election, Edgar Holt reported that most of the ALP (Anti-Communist) voters in Victoria were Catholics voting against Labor for the first time; but that in Queensland there had already since 1949 been a Catholic drift to the Liberals. Subsequent analysis confirmed this impression; in New South Wales and Queensland, some middle-class Catholics had become detached from their traditional allegiance to Labor by the end of the 1940s, but on class rather than religious grounds. By contrast, in Victoria, middle-class Catholics had largely stayed with Labor until the split, when the fierce storms of anti-communism broke the allegiance of many.

Evatt had barely survived in his own seat of Barton, where the Liberals had mounted a concerted campaign; he was returned by a majority of only 226 votes after preferences and it took ten days to determine the outcome. During that period, there were media suggestions that some in Labor hoped he would lose and solve at least one of their problems, but his narrow victory meant they would have to face the question of his leadership. Menzies had not yet written 'terminus' to his career but, for Evatt's own sake, it would have been a mercy to have lost his seat and exited the stage; that humiliation would have saved him from humiliations still to come.

Evatt the symbol

Evatt was now weakened as a leader, an object of hate and abuse for the Catholic right, and burdened with the reputation of a 'wrecker', psychologically unstable and politically unpredictable. Why did he not walk away? Why could the party not persuade him to walk away? It was another four years before he resigned to join the Supreme Court in Sydney; these were miserable years for Labor, and ought to have been miserable years for Evatt. He survived a small leadership challenge after the 1955 defeat, and a more concerted one from Eddie Ward after the next defeat in 1958. His lack of self-awareness may have protected him from the wreckage around him, but others in the party were well aware of it.

The sheer debility of the Labor party after the split partly accounts for their inability to move Evatt on. They were reactive and had no real strategic capacity, let alone policy development capabilities. They were still dealing with the fallout of the split, and recovering from its traumas. In the state branches, only New South Wales premier Joe Cahill had much power; Joe Chamberlain as federal president was significant too, and Pat Kennelly was still a member of the Senate and hence of the caucus; but his chosen replacement as federal secretary, Jack Schmella, was drinking heavily. The caucus was divided between those still backing Evatt and those who opposed him.

The more he was attacked the more he dug in. Brendan Bracken observed in a letter to W.S. Robinson from London that other politicians who had made Evatt's mistakes 'would have been sunk without trace'. 'Our old friend Bert is really unsinkable', he concluded. Kim Beazley senior, one of those who opposed his leadership, wrote that Evatt seemed indifferent to the hostility directed at him, and that the party 'still had the Irish attitude that the more their leader was attacked, the more they stuck to him'. Frank McManus, who had gone with the DLP in Victoria, thought that after the split Evatt was a symbol, and therefore impregnable, 'defended even by those who detested him'. But McManus did not say precisely what Evatt symbolised after the split.

The letters of some ordinary citizens who wrote to Evatt may provide clues to what he symbolised; they expressed the hopes and sentiments invested in him as a public figure and a leader. Some thought he had saved Labor from Roman Catholicism, some that he stood for the defence of liberty, and some that he stood for sacrifice in the face of calumny. Katharine Susannah Prichard, a writer well on the left, wrote in 1958 commending him after a speech on foreign affairs: 'Although the way has been rough and difficult lately, your courage and noble character are shining through the dark. I believe a majority of people will realise this more and more'. When the press reported he was ill, people would write urging him to look after himself: one wrote that Labor leaders were developing a tragic tradition of untimely deaths, 'due in part to the bitter frustration of giving all in their power, for the common good, and receiving little but vilification in return'.

Perhaps Evatt also now symbolised how Labor had been traumatised by the great split. Of the three fractures in Labor's history, the 1955 split was the most profound. In 1916 and 1931, part of the leadership had peeled off to join the conservatives, in each case providing a prime minister to lead the newly reconstituted conservative party, with Hughes leading the Nationalists and Lyons leading the United Australia Party. But while those events had been bitter, and had depleted Labor's strength, it was only in 1955 that the labour movement itself was so fundamentally divided; 1916 and 1931 were like chips off a block, while 1955 fractured the rock entirely. Some unions had abandoned the ALP for the DLP; it was a separate party commanding a fraction of Labor's previous vote, but it was there to stay – or so it seemed at the time – and delivering its supporters to the conservatives through preferences.

The ALP took a generation to recover, and that was both Evatt's inheritance and legacy as leader. Yet deposing him might have seemed like giving in to the Groupers, suggesting that all the trauma and angst of the split had been suffered in vain. If Evatt was aware of all this, he said nothing; if he wondered again about getting out and returning to writing books or practising law, he left no record; if he was bruised and battered by what Haylen called the 'brutalising experience' of caucus meetings, he did not complain. He still had energy and ability; during the Suez crisis in 1956, he made some powerful speeches attacking Menzies' mishandling of the tension, arguing as always that the United Nations should be brought in to resolve the dispute; Beazley wrote that Evatt was 'superb over Suez'. Throughout the second half of the 1950s, it was one of the few moments when Labor's spirits revived.

In mid-1956, Evatt met the literary figure Barrett Reid for the first time. At this point Evatt might reasonably have been shattered by all that had gone before, yet Reid was struck by his vitality. Reid had come to Melbourne in 1951 to live with John and Sunday Reed at Heide, and recalled Evatt as a 'presence' in the house even before they met, because he often rang for late-night phone conversations. 'I can remember Sunday saying "oh bloody old judgie … rings up and never gets off the phone" … it would be Bert Evatt on the phone wanting to know all the gossip and tossing ideas to John Reed.' They met face to face when Evatt gave a speech at the opening of the new Gallery of Contemporary Art in Melbourne. Reid told Peter Crockett that he found Evatt enormously approachable and extraordinarily energetic, and that he never stopped talking. 'You got the feeling of a man enjoying life … I always felt excited in his company because of the torrent of words and ideas that poured out of him.' Reid left us a sketch of Evatt's physical presence: 'a conventionally-dressed roly-poly figure with a very fine head, quite a handsome head … a thick-set man of medium height, always talking, very vital, always wanted to be the centre of attention'.

To open the gallery, Evatt gave 'a marathon speech', which Reid recalled was off the cuff and, although too long, 'quite fascinating … a very intelligent and very detailed speech'. Afterwards, the crowd departed, but 'Bert was in no mood to go home'; they stayed on into the night, with music, talk and drinking. John Reed then wrote to Mary Alice thanking them both for coming:

> Bert's talk gave people a sense of what they never get at Openings
> – a feeling of listening to someone who really knows what they
> are talking about, who does not mind saying what they think,
> and who are able to do so in a way which embraces rather than
> excludes the audience. It was nice of you both to come down
> from Canberra … all the young people felt it was a very friendly
> gesture.

Embattled in politics, hanging on tenaciously to a traumatised party, Evatt still had time for modern art. He and Mary Alice were still buying paintings and attending exhibitions. In the 1930s, his engagement with the art world had been a form of politics by proxy; he could indulge his growing interest and passion, while also intervening in the public realm and squabbling with Menzies about the virtues of modern versus conventional art. By the 1950s, art must have been more like a refuge for him. He was still sought after as a speaker; people still wanted him to lend his stature to openings and launches. Perhaps most importantly, he was not being perpetually challenged in art circles; he was listened to and valued. Although he was diminished in politics, in the realm of art he was still a champion.

In 1957, he published a short article about Tom Bass's abstract cubist sculpture *Trial of Socrates*, a copper panel placed above the entrance to Wilson Hall at the University of Melbourne. Evatt often visited this sculpture when in Melbourne. He saw in it a story of freedom of expression, writing that Bass had depicted a 'tragic theme' of Socrates' courage in 'choosing death rather than fail to speak out against what he regarded as public abuses'. Evatt went on to write of the Cold War context, the background of 'indirect restrictions on freedom of speech and expression designed to curb or limit political non-conformity and dissent'. This was subtler than his earlier speeches railing against the creation of a police state; this was about the 'gradual silencing' of a McCarthyist climate, about promotion being withheld from dissenters, about the difficulty of publishing 'radical or left-wing statements', and about quiet conformity. His theme was still liberty, though, and he might perhaps have been thinking about his victory in the anti-communist referendum. 'The truth', he said, 'is that liberty of expression … has to be fought for in every generation.'

In April 1957, Evatt's old friend Vere Gordon Childe returned to Australia, having retired from his position as professor of archaeology at the University of London. Some who saw Childe thought he was depressed about the state of politics; he stayed with the Evatts at Mosman, and his biographer suggests that 'Evatt's despair may have influenced his old friend and coloured his impressions'. In October, Childe's body was found at the bottom of a cliff in the Blue Mountains; he had been studying the rock formations and may have slipped, or more likely it may have been suicide. Evatt helped arrange the funeral, but said nothing publicly. Ten days later, he wrote to the editor of *Meanjin*, saying that Childe had mailed to Mary Alice a study of the Blue Mountains area, which reached them after his death. He proposed that he would write something for *Meanjin* about Childe, but we can only speculate what he had in mind, as the article was never written. Evatt was not the kind of man to reveal himself in writing about friendship and loss, and if he had tried to write about the significance of *How Labour Governs* that could have raised awkward issues about Labor and the leadership. Childe had written that Labor leaders

A brilliantly self-explanatory image of the ALP and DLP
fighting it out after the split, with Menzies an effortlessly
triumphant matador.

John Frith, *Herald*, 23 October 1958,
reproduced with the permission of Jeffrey Frith

were tempted to betrayal, and although Evatt had not defected, he had
led the party in a devastating split.

Still he doggedly hung on, arranging to switch from the now precarious seat of Barton to the safer seat of Hunter for the 1958 election. He had a connection with the area – after all, he had been born
there – but had not lived there since childhood. By then Evatt was
sixty-four, still vainly striving for the prize of the prime ministership.
He revealed another of his surprises in the November 1958 election
campaign. Following a policy speech that generally received a good
response, he then announced at the opening of the campaign in Victoria that he would resign as leader if the DLP would allocate their
preferences to Labor instead of to the conservatives. Joe Chamberlain

called this a 'magnificent' and 'magnanimous' gesture, but it was also a curious one. It meant asking people to vote Labor into office with the identity of the prime minister to be advised. The DLP response the next day was that this offer was not enough. They insisted Evatt must go but clearly did not trust him to fulfil his promise, and they also demanded a reversal of the 1955 conference decisions on foreign policy, reinstatement of the Groups, and an end to the 'unity tickets' in which Labor and CPA unionists collaborated in union elections. The episode reminded citizens again of the split and started another public squabble between the DLP and what they called 'Evatt Labor'. A week later the DLP leader in the Senate described Evatt's offer as a 'blatant confidence trick'.

In the election, Labor lost another two seats and its primary vote fell further to 42.8 per cent. The DLP was now gathering votes in Queensland and Western Australia. Afterwards, John Carrick wrote that 'the voters wanted to change the government', but Evatt and the ALP had made too many blunders. The advantage of a good policy speech had been lost by reviving memories of the split, and Evatt had then made statements about what Catholic voters thought that drew Mannix out to contradict him, saying that the Communist party wanted an Evatt victory. The Liberals were wary, though, conscious that they could not rely on the Labor split to keep winning, and began to worry that anti-communism, which had in the past been 'a potent factor' in election victories, might now become 'of less political value'. But as the decade closed Labor was still paralysed by the trauma of the split, and the continuing crises that surrounded its leadership. They were generally reactive, responding to the government rather than setting the agenda, and often that response was dictated by Evatt's own, often unpredictable reactions.

The madness question

Mutterings about Evatt's sanity had started in the mid-1950s, fuelled by his wilful misjudgements and his obsession with the Petrov affair, but also by the animosity he aroused in opponents. We have seen how Menzies brought the issue into the open in his reply to the Petrov Royal Commission speech, when he spoke of Evatt 'suffering from persecution delusions', but Menzies was not alone in that; cartoonists regularly depicted Evatt as driven by his conspiracy theories. His decline into dementia from about 1960 then had people projecting back into the past to try to determine when the infirmity had set in. 'Was Evatt mad?' is a question often asked of a biographer.

The two most explicit subsequent judgements have come from historian Robert Murray and former intelligence analyst Andrew Campbell. Murray first raised the question of Evatt's 'insanity' in *The Split*, writing: 'Cunning concealment of the condition … would also be consistent with paranoid behaviour. The judgement of mental illness is one men seem more likely to make of Evatt in retrospect than in the desperate heat of the mid-fifties, but never with any certainty'. Murray was more explicit, and much more certain, in a later retrospective in 2004. When Evatt denounced the Groupers in October 1954, Murray now wrote, he had 'made an existing problem a dozen times worse'. Other characters in the drama behaved badly, erratically or vengefully, and there were deeper issues of principle, of sectarian sentiment and of 'trade union power struggles', but Murray wrote that these tensions were all 'immensely aggravated' by Evatt's 'psychiatric problems': 'The simple explanation, which Australians of the time found so unpalatable that they usually looked for other explanations, was that Evatt had gone mad and his paranoia flowed down through society'.

Andrew Campbell was even more adamant. In an article appropriately published by one of Santamaria's organisations, he analysed Evatt's 'psychopathology'. Campbell was no admirer of Evatt's, and his article is a useful compendium of all the things people have written over the years about Evatt's flaws and neuroses. He detailed Evatt's lack of empathy for others and his ruthlessness in politics; his mood swings and duality in behaviour; his suspicion and distrust of those around him; and the 'pathological sense of entitlement' that led him to flout the rules. Campbell also commented on Evatt's grief at the loss of his father and his brothers, noting that suppressed grief 'increases the risk of psychiatric disorders in later life'. His conclusion was that Evatt's 'fundamental pathology' was a phenomenon psychoanalysts call 'the compulsion to betray'.

In his appearance at the Royal Commission on Espionage, Campbell said, Evatt displayed 'paranoid psychosis and persecutory mania', and he was also prone to 'narcissistic rages', which Hasluck referred to as 'tantrums' – explosions of temper that left him child-like and helpless. Campbell carefully catalogued Evatt's eccentricities: his fear of flying, again described as 'pathological'; and the way he 'regressed' by retreating to bed with illness, sometimes working in bed with his boots on. Evatt had 'bizarre beliefs', Campbell said, 'including seeing days of the week in colours'; this last has previously been noted as the entirely benign characteristic known as synaesthesia. The only oddity that Campbell seems to have missed is Evatt wrapping news-paper around his torso to keep out the cold, which for some writers has been the clincher. It is an impressive range of symptoms, though Campbell is careless in failing to distinguish between eccentricity and psychosis, and in the end the only diagnosis he offers to tie them all together is 'polymorbidity'. He did, however, heroically and censori-ously, conclude that without the 'soothing understanding' of his wife, Evatt would most likely have been 'institutionalised'.

In sorting through this issue, it is useful to distinguish between Evatt's underlying personality or character, the changes in his behav-iour evident when he was under extreme pressure in the mid-1950s, and the influence of dementia on his conduct in later years. Evatt had a baseline of eccentric behaviour, deep suspicion and exaggerated self-regard, but in the period from 1954 to 1955 these eccentricities

TOO MUCH OF THE ONE THING.

"Dr. Evatt, while in New York, was reported to be suffering from exhaustion."
"What you need is a change. Try to get away from yourself for a while."

During the 1940s, cartoonists often lampooned Evatt's self-regard.
Hetherington has him here surrounded by images of himself and under
a spotlight. The caption reads: 'Too much of the one thing. Dr Evatt,
while in New York, was reported to be suffering from exhaustion'.
His doctor advises: 'What you need is a change. Try to get away from
yourself for a while'. The joke is that he could not get away from
himself, but it also suggests how Evatt was trapped within the self he
had created, captive to the drives that made him such a forceful and
dominant personality.

Norman Hetherington, *Bulletin*, 25 May 1949

and character flaws gave way to obsession, evident in disturbed patterns of mind and behaviour. Then, from 1960, or perhaps somewhat earlier, these problems were compounded by cerebral arteriosclerosis. I will look at each of these three factors in turn in considering the question of Evatt's sanity.

First, even if we forgive him for wearing newspapers and for having his boots on in bed, Evatt was a flawed character. That is hardly unusual in itself, though Evatt's flaws were most obviously his narcissistic and paranoid personality characteristics. Narcissists believe that they are special, craving success and admiration, but lack empathy, often taking advantage of others to achieve their own ends. Evatt fits this description. An inflated, even grandiose sense of self-regard fuelled his ambition and led him to trample on others if they got in the way. But while narcissism provides part of the explanation of Evatt's personality there is one important difference: usually narcissists have a grandiose sense of self-importance 'without commensurate achievements', yet Evatt's achievements were considerable, constantly reinforcing his self-regard, even though they were never enough. In addition, narcissism is not madness, and some of these personality traits could characterise many driven people, including political and corporate leaders.

Narcissism is often accompanied by paranoia, because narcissists experience any disagreement as an assault. Paranoid personality traits include pervasive distrust and suspicion of others: the conviction that others are harming or deceiving one; unjustified doubts about the loyalty and trustworthiness of friends and colleagues, and reluctance to confide in them; perceiving attacks where there are none, and so on. Many people commented on Evatt's suspiciousness and distrust, and often noted that it was reciprocated by the distrust of others. He lived in a world frighteningly devoid of trust, and this was evident well before he was Labor leader, when he had much less cause to worry. John Brennan, his associate in the 1930s, described Evatt as 'an extraordinarily distrustful man' who was 'infinitely suspicious of people's motives'. 'It's a frightening thing to say really', Brennan said.

'I think it was a thing that left him bereft of friends.'

Keith Brennan, Evatt's other associate at the end of the 1930s, also highlighted these qualities when describing Evatt, but insisted that he did not change when he went into politics; he was always the same. He said there were two things to understand about him:

> One is that Bert thought Bert was good ... He was intellectually convinced that he was a man of ... outstanding intellectual stature and much of what he did was based on that premise ... the second thing is that he had great difficulty in understanding ... that other people could in good faith hold an opinion different from his. The truth was so apparent to him that he couldn't understand why people would be thinking differently from him, and this is one of the reasons why he so consistently attributed bad motives to other people.

This seems to me sad rather than mad. Brennan was tying together Evatt's narcissism and his conviction he was outstanding, with his suspicion of the motives of others when they opposed him. While both inflated self-regard and exaggerated distrust are hardly unusual, they can be fatal in a political leader. They were personality traits that were debilitating for Evatt in the intense pressure cooker of the labour movement during the Cold War.

We have explored the extraordinary stresses Evatt faced in the mid-1950s in the preceding chapters. The Cold War was a time of fear, distrust and paranoia, marked by accusations of treachery and fears of subversion. The labour movement was intensely divided and stumbling towards the split, its internal animosities intensified by the extreme pressure of Menzies' adroit prosecution of anti-communism. Evatt, as leader, was at the epicentre of what was happening in the Labor caucus, despite his distance from the unions and the Labor machine. For Evatt, the period between April 1954 and December 1955 was brutal. An intense election campaign led to bitter defeat, followed by a

Well before the debacle of his Molotov letter speech, Evatt was depicted as obsessed with conspiracies and as a failure. This cartoon, titled 'The Fossicker', shows Evatt as a washed-out goldminer working his 'Great Conspiracy Claim'. Unlike many of Scorfield's acerbic images of Evatt, this one is almost sympathetic.

Ted Scorfield, *Bulletin*, 22 June 1955

leadership challenge in August, appearances before the royal commission in August and September, his denunciation of the Groupers in early October and then the intense fight in caucus; he wrote his letter to Molotov in January 1955 and the Labor split occurred in March and April; the final report of the royal commission was delivered in August and he made his foolish speech about Molotov in October, which led into another election defeat in December 1955. The pressure was enormous, and Evatt, poorly equipped for it, handled it badly.

His conviction that he was right, his confidence that legal rationality was the path to truth and he was master of its methods, were frailties rather than strengths in the Petrov affair. His judgement in politics had never been good, which was ironic given how central the idea of judgement was to the self he had constructed through the law. Like others in the party, he knew how damaging the Petrov allegations were to Labor, but he refused to take advice from others and plunged in. He was under regular and often vicious attack – from the Groupers, from the government and from some in the media – and he knew that moves were being made against his precarious leadership. His predisposition to see conspiracies flourished in that climate, and he was publicly exposed as delusional, as obsessed with conspiracy.

The most vivid descriptions of his mental state come from this period. I have previously quoted the newspaper article describing him returning after being rebuffed by the Royal Commission, buttonholing parliament attendants and telling anyone who would listen about the forgeries, shouting allegations about the police state in parliament and scaring journalists with his tirades. The editor of the *Sydney Morning Herald* during the 1950s, John Douglas Pringle, recollected a long conversation in May 1954, shortly after the election loss. 'My impression', he wrote 'was that he had lost control of his personality and was totally in the grip of his obsessive suspicions. It was difficult to have a rational conversation with him, and it does not seem to me unkind to suggest that he was already suffering from some mental imbalance'.

In their later accounts of the period, his Labor colleagues often tried to work out when things started to go wrong. He would eventually be diagnosed with cerebral arteriosclerosis, and they wondered when it might have begun to account for his behaviour. Clyde Cameron thought it dated back at least to 1951:

> Some people say that Evatt's mental deterioration began with the Petrov Inquiry. I think his complaint, which was a sad disease, started to manifest itself even at the time of the Communist Party Dissolution Bill. His decision to write to Molotov … was quite irrational. The reaction of his colleagues was utter disbelief … only a madman would have made the approach in the first place. That was a manifestation of his decay.

Kim Beazley senior put it only a couple of years later: 'I noted strangeness in his behaviour in 1953, and more so in 1954'. He said the Molotov letter, sent in 1955, was 'so wildly improbable, granted the strength of his unaffected intellect, that one must speculate about the onset of the condition'. Fred Daly dated the decline to the Petrov affair, saying that his powers were declining and his judgement was being swayed by 'the obsession that this was a plot'. Evatt was no longer 'the intelligent, reasoning, former High Court judge', he said. This is all necessarily imprecise, but it seems to me that in this intense period in the mid-1950s, Evatt was somewhat unhinged. It is impossible to determine, though, whether this was due to a physiological condition affecting his mind, or just the extreme reaction of a paranoid narcissist put under incredible pressure. It is notable, however, that he calmed down after 1955. It is possible that he was taking medication. Tennant's biography of Evatt was heavily dependent on Mary Alice's recollections, and a stray sentence in her account of his stroke in 1962 mentioned that he had been taking tablets prescribed to relax him, 'later discovered to be powerful depressives'.

His diagnosis finally came in the early 1960s, after the stroke he suffered in 1962. Kenneth Noad, a prominent neurologist, told Peter Crockett that he examined him and diagnosed cerebral arteriosclerosis: roughly, a restriction of the blood supply to the brain. In 1963 or 1964, Douglas Miller, a leading neurosurgeon, would also examine Evatt, and later told Ken Buckley he was 'demented' – both physically uncontrollable and completely out of touch with reality. Miller also told Rae Else-Mitchell, one of Evatt's fellow Supreme Court judges, there was 'a disintegration of the brain cells', but that Mary Alice had insisted 'it must be possible for something to be done'.

There are several, very obscure, scraps of evidence that might signal something earlier. Buckley, Dale and Reynolds speculated about epilepsy; their only evidence was that Evatt sent a cable back to Australia in 1943, to be passed on to Dr Gilbert Phillips, a neurosurgeon. In it he wrote, 'Agree to your diagnosis. Might try combination of Luminal and Dilantin'. Luminal (or phenobarbitone) became available in 1912 and was a major tranquilliser; Dilantin (or phenytoin) was available from 1938, and used to control epileptic seizures. Epilepsy had a good deal of stigma attached to it, though once it could be controlled with drugs it started to be seen not as a psychiatric but a neurological disorder. This is not much on which to base the idea that Evatt had epilepsy, and there are no accounts of him having fits among his various ailments, but it is not impossible.

Two other suggestions that Evatt's deterioration started earlier are very tenuous. When Les Haylen was being interviewed for the National Library's oral history program, he said that 'a medical man' had told him that Evatt had the beginnings of a 'brain lesion' since he was forty. Haylen felt this accounted for what he called Evatt's 'uncontrollable outbursts of violence'. The interviewer, John Thompson, then asked about 'a quite serious breakdown ... just before he went to the High Court'. Haylen replied: 'Yes, that's right ... this specialist in brain surgery was telling me ... at forty-two he could have saved Evatt, but he didn't see him until he was sixty-seven, you see'.

He said that something vital had 'burnt out' and Evatt was 'living on one side of his brain'. Haylen's account is rather garbled, but the suggestion that Evatt, while still a young man, had some kind of episode before he joined the High Court in 1930 is tantalising.

The other fragment comes to us third-hand. Kylie Tennant's husband, L.C. Rodd, wrote that he had spoken with Allan Dalziel, who had been told by one of the Evatt family that Evatt should have received treatment for a 'mental condition he had when he was forty', back in 1934. He wrote that 'Evatt himself was conscious that something was wrong; he was always reading medical books about mental illness'; Dalziel had said that on one occasion when Evatt encountered a friend with a book on the subject he said: 'Here, give me that, it's a subject I'm most interested in'. He took the book and, characteristically, never gave it back. These are only fragments, though. The 'mental condition' Dalziel mentioned, and the 'breakdown' and 'lesion' Haylen referred to could have been epilepsy, or could have simply been burning out from the intense pace at which he worked. It is very unlikely that what became dementia by the early 1960s reached back to the 1930s.

It is possible also that Evatt was suffering, before 1960, from the onset of vascular dementia, the result of small strokes damaging parts of the brain. It is a different ailment from Alzheimer's disease, a form of dementia thought to be linked to organic degeneration of parts of the brain, with relatively consistent symptoms of memory loss and difficulty processing new information. Vascular dementia, related to the blood supply, leads to minor strokes and produces less predictable symptoms, because it depends where the damage occurs. It can lead to rigidity in habits of thought and can affect some higher level cognitive functioning, such as judgement and insight. This form of dementia tends to reinforce and enlarge existing personality traits; it can start quite slowly, but proceeds something like a set of steps, in the sense that there are sudden marked declines to a new level. And as with Alzheimer's, the onset of vascular dementia is both disorienting and frightening, but can be covered up by maintaining familiar habits and practices; a sudden shift to a new field, such as moving from politics to the Supreme Court, can trigger a deterioration, because the scaffolding of the familiar has suddenly been removed. Evatt's decline from 1960 was precipitous, and although there were references to his health in the press in the late 1950s, there were no explicit comments about his mental capacity.

What does this all add up to? Evatt had certainly developed dementia by the early 1960s, and with his family history of 'cerebral events' and high blood pressure it is likely to have been vascular in origin. If so, it may have started to reinforce his existing personality traits – narcissism and paranoia – well before it was diagnosed. But his underlying personality is probably enough to explain his supposedly 'mad' behaviour in the mid-1950s, when he was clearly obsessive and irrational, at least at times. He had an exaggerated self-regard, and showed many of the traits of narcissism, except that he had driven himself to exceptional achievements that justified and reinforced his grandiosity. In the intense period of the Cold War and the Labor split, Evatt's misjudgements and excesses were disastrous – but he was hardly imagining it when he thought people were attacking him ferociously.

16

'Dropping the pilot'

Evatt's embattled leadership continued on throughout the late 1950s, and he was regularly reported ill, variously with pneumonia, flu or high blood pressure and fevers. He had to drop out of his Victorian election campaign commitments in April 1957 due to bronchial influenza, and was sick again during the Queensland elections in July 1957 with a fever after returning from Israel, where he had given speeches recalling his commitment to the foundation of the country. During the 1958 election campaign he had retired to bed with pneumonia; when he returned to speak at a meeting in Launceston, he was 'ashen-faced', his speech cut short by coughing and wheezing. The election result was another defeat; Labor's primary vote was still declining.

In February 1959, the *Sun-Herald* commented that Evatt was 'obviously feeling the strain of leadership', and his serious illness during the campaign had shown the strain was affecting his health. That same month, Eddie Ward challenged and gathered 32 votes to Evatt's 46. It was interpreted not as a sign of the left on the rise, but as a censure by the right, who had voted for Ward while knowing he could not win; the vote was said to indicate 'the loss of support for Evatt rather than the extent of Ward's real strength'. Evatt cancelled meetings in May 1959, retiring to bed with flu; again in August he was ill. By now he was being written off by the journalists. One commented in July that Evatt had 'lost his grip on the party', and that the 'obvious deterioration' in his health meant a change of leadership was likely: 'Many Labor men believe that if he does not resign because of health, he will be told to go'.

But there was one final controversy to close out Evatt's contentious political career: the federal Labor party tried to tempt him to resign by offering him the chief justiceship of New South Wales, from which Kenneth Street was about to retire. In September 1959, there was speculation Evatt would leave politics to take up this position 'within about six months'. He was in fact appointed to the chief justiceship, but only after a long and humiliating delay. As the rumours about the Supreme Court appointment fluttered about in October, he said he had no comment, but journalists were writing that the rumours had substance, that 'soundings had taken place'. But the affair dragged on for four months, and the appointment was not actually announced until February 1960, with the protracted delay caused by divisions in the New South Wales Labor cabinet. The premier, Joe Cahill, had been approached by the federal party and agreed to Evatt's appointment, and Evatt had reportedly been sounded out and also agreed. Then Cahill died suddenly in late October, and his successor, Robert Heffron, inherited the promise. Heffron, unlike Cahill, did not have the requisite support in the New South Wales party to deliver on this commitment. Cahill had held Labor together in New South Wales, but the Groupers who had remained within the party now saw an opportunity for revenge on Evatt.

The New South Wales attorney-general, Reg Downing, was also adamantly opposed; at the time, he was reported as insisting it was his prerogative to make the recommendation. But he said in a later interview that he knew Evatt was in decline, and was being off-loaded onto them by the federal party. 'Evatt was downhill at this stage, he was going down rapidly ... I felt that Evatt was not suitable to be appointed Chief Justice because of his physical and mental declinement ... that is the only reason I opposed him.' Public discussion nevertheless centred on the fighting within the New South Wales party, and Evatt was left hanging and humiliated while these disputes played out in public. Calwell meanwhile assumed the role of heir apparent.

In early December, the appointment was said to be 'expected

within the next fortnight'; and Evatt was regarded as 'certain to accept it'. But by January, there was still no decision, and the New South Wales cabinet remained evenly divided. Evatt was powerless, his fate uncertain and public humiliation absolute. Yet even during his worst days, there was a little light relief, when Menzies and Evatt attended a banquet to farewell Sir William and Lady Slim, who were returning to England after Slim's governor-generalship. Menzies had presented Slim with two silver fighting gamecocks, and Slim joked that he would call one Bert and the other Bob: 'the guests, including Evatt and Menzies themselves, roared with laughter'. The animosity between the two of them, so evident in the debates about the Petrov affair, was now abating, with Menzies triumphant. All that was left to Evatt was the possibility of a dignified retreat.

In Sydney, the Liberal opposition attacked Evatt as unsuitable for the position of chief justice and roundly criticised the state government's handling of what was becoming a fiasco. Robert Askin, the state Liberal leader, said Evatt was a 'damagingly controversial' figure who had 'for years been the centre of a bitter sectarian dispute', and was 'altogether too friendly with the Communists and their sympathisers'. Askin pointed out that Evatt had been too long away from the law, and others also raised doubts about 'his capacity to pick up threads' of a legal system that he had left behind in 1940; that may have been very oblique code for mental deterioration. Bob Santamaria also offered his advice, saying that the New South Wales Labor party should abandon Evatt. The *Sun-Herald* columnist 'Onlooker' wrote about Evatt's 'painful suspense' and said that Santamaria's 'snapping at the Doc's heels' was 'too much'. In an editorial, the *Sydney Morning Herald* lamented that the high dignity of the office of chief justice was being 'degraded' by the controversy; it was now caught up in 'the hostilities and divisive tendencies latent in the State ALP', which were becoming 'open and explosive'.

Letters to the editor debated Evatt's merits, and queried whether federal Labor was grabbing 'a golden opportunity' to unload their 'bag of trouble' on the New South Wales branch. The state Labor executive, and Trades Hall figures in Sydney were reportedly pressuring Downing to buckle, but he insisted the decision was his as attorney-general; the right was adamant they would not support Evatt, and the whole squalid episode was becoming a replay in miniature of the frictions of the split. For once, Evatt was restrained in public, keeping silent and avoiding throwing petrol on the flames. But he was working the phones, desperately trying to organise his escape. Fred Daly, who disliked Evatt, nevertheless had some sympathy, writing: 'Evatt was dismayed and humiliated by the delay in his appointment. It seemed likely that he would not get the position … behind the scenes he was almost demented and on the phone day and night pressurizing and pleading'. Les Haylen, always an Evatt supporter, also described his distress: 'I saw the tragedy of Evatt trying to persuade the Groupers to persuade the state government to make sure that he got the appointment, because otherwise he would fall into a chasm and never emerge.' Haylen thought the manner of Evatt's removal was 'the shabbiest trick in Labor history'.

This stalemate went on till 10 February, with cabinet deferring a decision and constant media commentary about Evatt's humiliation. 'Whatever may be thought of him and his stormy career, he deserved better of his party and of Australia', wrote a *Sun-Herald* editorial. When it was all over, the *Sydney Morning Herald* muttered that it had been a 'sordid and humiliating wrangle'; Evatt as a politician, the editor thought, had always raised 'a residue of serious doubt', particularly in 'behaviour as ill-judged as … during and after the Petrov proceedings'. Doubtless, the *Herald* thought, many in Labor must now 'feel a certain relief that his undoubted juristic attainments have brought him alternative employment'. Daly was a lot more explicit. When the appointment was announced, he wrote: 'There was a sigh of relief throughout the Parliamentary Labor Party. It was the end of a nightmare'. Evatt's twenty years in the federal parliament had ended with yet another controversy, though this one was hardly of his

DROPPING THE PILOT

This cartoon was published on the day Evatt's appointment to the
Supreme Court was announced. 'Dropping the pilot' was a reference
to the practice of ships being led out of port by a pilot who was then
dropped off in a launch to return to land. Hetherington's sketch
referred to an earlier and very famous cartoon with the same name;
published in England in 1890, the original had depicted the graceful
retirement of the German chancellor, Bismarck, walking calmly down
a series of steps from the ship of state. Hetherington had Evatt being
dropped without any dignity; his feet are entangled in the rope ladder,
with Calwell and Ward trying to cut him loose, while his judicial wig
is about to fall into the sea.

Norman Hetherington, *Bulletin*, 10 February 1960,
© Norman Frederick Hetherington, licensed by Viscopy, 2016

own making. He had been unceremoniously and humiliatingly unloaded.

There was no send-off. Evatt walked out of the parliament without his few remaining supporters even knowing he was leaving. There is fragmentary footage of this, Evatt walking alone down the steps of the parliament and getting into a car. Haylen wrote: 'I shall never forget Evatt walking down the steps of parliament on his last day there, alone, unhonoured and unsung'. In a later interview, he said: 'The tragedy … is that he walked out of that house after his great national service … walked down the marble steps of Parliament House and out into the bright sunlight outside without any of us knowing he was going'.

Despite the surface normality and congratulations at the swearing-in ceremony in the Banco Court in Sydney, Evatt's tenure as chief justice was no refuge. His dementia was soon evident, and distressing to those around him, though it seems to have fluctuated. At times he was confused, or falling asleep, or reading papers upside down or losing his way in the corridors. One of his fellow judges, Wilfred Collins, recalled that sometimes Evatt would not recognise some of the judges, and that he 'forgot where the Banco Court (in which he always sat) was located and used to wander up and down the corridors looking for it'. Collins said Evatt should never have been appointed chief justice: 'It was obviously to get rid of him from parliament'. John Brennan saw Evatt at home during this time and found it 'absolutely devastating' that Evatt at first knew who he was, and then a little later said he did not know him. Mary Alice was understandably reluctant to admit what was happening, claiming he was just tired.

Another of the judges, F.G. Myers, wrote later that Evatt's appointment, given his incapacity, was 'a disgraceful act of political expedience' and 'an act of callous cruelty'. Evatt had been placed 'in a situation where he could only end his days in shame and censure'. Myers disliked Evatt's politics, but found him 'a kindly man' who deserved better from his party, but instead 'what he got was treachery'. Kilgour, Evatt's old school headmaster, had once predicted he would become chief justice of New South Wales, but, Myers now wrote, 'how tragically his prediction was fulfilled'.

The other judges covered for Evatt, helping write his judgements and working around him. Reg Downing, who had eventually given in to the pressure and allowed the appointment, said that Evatt's fellow judges 'realised he'd gone down the hill so far that he had to be helped', and added, 'They were very, very charitable towards him, I thought, all of them.' But the bright young barristers of Sydney were less charitable, ridiculing Evatt. Michael Kirby, who celebrated Evatt's commitment to civil liberties and would himself go on to be a High Court judge, recalled as an articled clerk seeing Evatt 'surrounded by well-groomed young lawyers who mocked this mental giant in his closing months'. For Kirby, he was 'like Lear, disconsolate'.

The end

Hartley Grattan saw Evatt for the last time in early 1960, shortly after he had left politics. He was 'bellyaching' about politics and 'still licking his political wounds', which exasperated Grattan, who said he surely should have known the terms and conditions of political life: 'Why lament them now you are out of politics?' Evatt didn't like that, according to Grattan, and even less did Mary Alice. They then argued; Evatt went on to claim that the US embassy had been spreading 'hostile propaganda' against him, and Grattan, like any good American, was 'appalled and disgusted' at the very idea. He said he would want to see the evidence, and Evatt appealed to Brian Fitzpatrick, who was with them, for his support: 'It's true, isn't it, Brian?' When Fitzpatrick said he would also want to see the evidence, Evatt brooded in silence. Grattan wrote with regret that it was his last encounter with his friend: 'I knew … that I had broken a magic spell that had been sustained for twenty-three years. No subsequent efforts of mine to repair the damage by letter had the slightest tangible effect'.

Evatt was not entirely out of touch yet, and his condition fluctuated, but the combination of his developing dementia with his suspicious nature meant people on the court had to find ways of working around him. Reg Downing said the judges suggested sending Evatt on an overseas tour. Downing knew if he had made the suggestion himself, Evatt would have been 'suspicious that I wanted to get rid of him'. Instead he asked Evatt to nominate the best judge to visit the US and Britain to investigate pre-trial mechanisms to reduce court congestion; Evatt concluded that he – Evatt himself – was the best available. In March 1962, on the way to England with Mary Alice, he suffered a major stroke aboard ship in Perth. They flew back to Sydney, and he was described being 'assisted down the gangway of the plane and walking slowly to a waiting car'. He was reportedly suffering from 'severe hypertension'.

A few weeks later, there were press reports that he was unlikely to return to the bench, and he had been granted six months' sick leave. When the sick leave expired in late October, his retirement was announced. There was no recovery, but he lingered on for three more years, living in Canberra. Colin Moodie, who had worked with Evatt in the Department of External Affairs, lived in a house backing onto that of Rosalind and Peter Carrodus, and later said he would sometimes see Evatt next door 'sitting in the sun, vacant and quite chapfallen'. The Modigliani was sold during this period, reportedly to pay for the costs of nursing care; Mary Alice was still very wealthy and could have sold other assets such as shares, but perhaps she had tired of the austere but beautiful painting.

A letter Evatt received the day after his stroke urged him to devote the necessary time to writing his memoirs: 'You mustn't leave your writing until too late as Billy Hughes did'. But it was already too late. Evatt would leave several books unwritten. Ten years earlier, in the early 1950s, he had been collecting materials on the wartime government under Curtin and apparently intended to write a history, and he had long thought about a biography of Hughes. There had also been talk of a book about his time in politics; Allan Dalziel recalled a few conversations about it shortly after Evatt had joined the Supreme Court. Evatt had suggested Dalziel start drafting it, a huge task from which Dalziel quickly retreated. 'I could see that Dr Evatt was in no way fit to embark upon so big an undertaking … He was losing track of things.' Not long after, Evatt was approached by a publisher in London about an autobiography; they were very keen, and advised that 'the reader should feel by the time he has finished it that he has got to know the author …' But though Mary Alice thought he could write his memoirs, he was long past writing. In any case, with his lack of self-reflexivity, an autobiography would probably have been a detailed defence of all his turbulent life and actions, perhaps more like his vigorous, partisan case in defence of William Bligh than a reflective autobiographical account of all he had lived through.

Paul Hasluck left a word sketch of the last time he saw Evatt. It was shortly after the stroke in 1962, when he visited the Evatts in Mosman:

> We sat in the sitting room and after a while this figure, closely
> followed by a nurse, came in and sat alongside me. I spoke. Mary
> Alice reminded him who it was. He grinned and gave a chuckle
> much like he used to and said: 'Yes, San Francisco. Remember
> what we did to Stettinius? Yes. Paul. You were there. Stettinius' …
> His mind left us and never returned.

***

Evatt died on 2 November 1965, aged seventy-one. There was a state funeral at St John's Anglican Church in Reid, where Rosalind had been married. Among a large crowd of political and diplomatic figures there were also friends; and Menzies and Calwell were both there, as pallbearers. One journalist wrote that Evatt was 'the last of the famous Big Four of the wartime Curtin Government'. The others he meant were Curtin, Jack Beasley and Chifley, who had died in 1945, 1949 and

1951 respectively. Evatt had said to the journalist 'rather oracularly', in 1942, when the strain was fiercest, that they were 'four doomed men'. But Evatt had outlasted them all.

Burgmann had retired; his replacement as the bishop of Canberra and Goulburn, K.J. Clements, delivered an address that referred to Evatt as 'one of the most controversial figures of recent history'. He talked about Evatt's courage in stepping down from the High Court, his contribution as foreign minister in the war, and his aspiration to build 'a world free of war' through the United Nations. Clements went on to Evatt's campaign against attempts to ban the Communist party, and the referendum he fought in 1951. 'It took courage also to fight for individual liberties … Some would say that he was foolhardy and careless of his reputation and his seat. But the act remains one of courage. And there is an element of a certain kind of abandon – lack of regard for himself – as he immersed himself in the cause of personal liberty.'

Frank Chamberlain was there in the church, and recalled: 'Menzies had to suffer the vituperative tongue of the bishop … I sat close by and I saw Menzies had the decency to blush'. Chamberlain assumed it was shame or embarrassment, but Menzies may not have been blushing, but flushing with indignation. Clements, like Burgmann, was sounding like another meddlesome, left-wing priest siding with Evatt in his long struggle with Menzies. Five years later, when Menzies wrote a chapter in his memoirs about the Petrov affair, there was no sign of remorse: he demolished Evatt again, and quoted with relish all the best and cruellest parts of his 1955 speech ridiculing Evatt's obsessions and delusions. There was no suggestion Menzies might have felt any regret about his triumph after their decades-long rivalry.

Many people who knew Evatt saw him as someone living life to the full, robust and forceful and prodigiously energetic. Growing up without a father from the age of seven, he had been moulded by a mother who demanded he meet her high expectations, and he pushed himself and flourished. As a young barrister in the 1920s he had been outstanding, clearly marked out for great things, and profoundly shaped by his success in the practice and modes of legal rationality. He had spent a decade in the relatively sheltered environment of the High Court but had grown increasingly frustrated. Stepping down to return to politics was seen by many as a sacrifice, but he presented it as a duty to serve his country in a time of need and perhaps to redress the loss of his brothers in the previous war. It was the beginning of his two decades at the epicentre of Australian politics, as foreign minister and attorney-general and then as Labor leader. But being in politics put him in the public spotlight and, while he needed and loved recognition for his achievements, the spotlight was also merciless in exposing his failures and flaws. His high self-regard meant he attracted more than the usual measure of ridicule and even hatred; among the many reasons he would have been better to avoid politics was the fact that he was thin-skinned, as the ridicule and hatred often hurt and bewildered him.

He lacked the social skills for political work, and particularly for leadership; Chifley had sensed that. Menzies probably sensed it as well, and adroitly exploited the advantage, particularly as the tempting prospect of a Labor split opened up in front of him. Evatt wanted desperately to succeed in politics, but was unable to translate what he knew – legal rationality – into political acumen and judgement. Grattan thought that ambition was 'the factor that made Bertie run, and that destroyed him'. There is an element of tragedy in that, but it was a measure of his lack of self-knowledge that he appeared not to sense the danger. Or perhaps he did sense it, because in 1946 and 1950 he clearly considered backing out of politics, but was persuaded to continue. Grattan was convinced that it was Mary Alice who pushed him on. If that were true it would add another layer of tragedy: that they clearly loved each other yet she urged him on to his destruction.

But we should not leave it there, finishing with a focus on Evatt's failures. Hartley Grattan wrote that for all his faults and failings, he was 'a remarkable man, a stupendous Australian', and 'a splash of invigorating color on the muddy gray canvas of life'. The things he achieved were and remain important legacies: articulating an independent foreign policy, helping found the United Nations, and arguing the case for civil liberties during the Cold War. He could not have done these things without his fierce sense of patriotism, his enormous drive and his tenacious commitment to legal rationality. Perhaps his mother might finally, after all this and at the end, have been appeased.

Epilogue

The day I visited the Woden cemetery in Canberra, it was overcast and the wind was biting cold. An enormous mob of sulphur-crested cockatoos had taken over the place. Hundreds of fat white birds were strutting about in the grass, sitting chattering in the trees and perching on the gravestones. They set up the raucous, boisterous racket cockatoos love to make. They reminded me of a group of excited, tipsy youngsters taking over a restaurant, shouting and singing.

I wandered about in the cold trying to find Evatt's grave before the gates closed at dusk, and after a while I found it. Evatt was buried in the Anglican section in 1965, and Mary Alice beside him eight years later. Her epitaph describes her as 'a wonderful wife, mother and friend'. But Evatt's headstone is more distinctive and more loaded with meaning. Beneath his dates of birth and death, he is simply described as a 'Son of Australia', and below that is a polished square of dark grey marble etched with the global emblem of the United Nations, and the words '1948–1949, President of the United Nations'.

These were the two dominant, often contending, themes in his life: nationalism and internationalism; profound attachment to his country, and the urgent desire to see an international system governed by the law. Kylie Tennant said that when Mary Alice was asked about her husband's epitaph, she said all his achievements could not fit in and that the presidency of the UN was 'the honour he most valued'. Evatt was actually president of the UN General Assembly, rather than head of the United Nations itself, but perhaps Mary Alice preferred the more important-sounding title. It is significant that this is how she, closer to Evatt than anyone else, wanted him to be remembered: not merely as a patriot, and not as a husband and father, not even as a High Court judge, or a leader of the Labor party, but as a figure with a prominent voice on the world stage.

Tennant wrote in the conclusion to her biography: 'On either side of Evatt lie migrants, one of them Greek, become now part of Australian earth and democratically sharing what there is to share, equal enough'. In her original notes, the wording was slightly different: 'On one side of him lies a Greek and on the other another alien. To him all nations were one'. It seems a fitting image for Evatt's cosmopolitanism – except that it is not true. On one side lies Dorlas Eleanor Archer, and on the other, beyond Mary Alice, are Julie and William Etchells, who could perhaps have been postwar migrants and qualified as 'aliens'. Behind and further down the row there are the graves of a Greek family. But as with the 'President of the UN', the facts have been rearranged to make the story more compelling. Even in his grave, Evatt is being interpreted, recontextualised.

Just as Evatt finished his books not with a conclusion but with a 'judgement', those who write epitaphs get to have a final say – but even a headstone is not truly final. Throughout his life, Evatt was a contentious and polarising figure, demanding, contrary and volatile, exceptionally talented and exceptionally neurotic, interpreted by others in a multitude of ways: as a champion of civil liberties, or the mad wrecker of the Labor party; as a maligned hero, or a dangerous radical. He was almost always at the centre of controversy and while many made their judgements of him, many also puzzled over his complex and contradictory character.

As the light faded, the gang of cockatoos grew louder, more raucous and exuberant, all clamouring to be heard, setting up a distinctly Australian sound. I thought that Evatt would have liked their irreverent, insistent, boisterous voices about him.

The players

This listing is intended to help readers keep track of the large number of characters mentioned in this book; they are included if they appear more than twice, and also had significant influence on or engagement with Evatt.

Anderson, Francis: Sydney University professor of logic and mental philosophy from 1890; profound influence on Evatt's education

Atyeo, Sam: prominent modernist artist in Melbourne in the 1930s; part of the Heide circle; taken up by Evatt as art adviser, court jester and general contact person

Bailey, Kenneth: University of Melbourne law professor from 1927; from 1943 consultant to Evatt as attorney-general; Commonwealth solicitor-general from 1946

Beasley, Jack: federal Labor MP from 1929, aligned with Lang; from 1941 minister for supply and development; high commissioner in London from 1946–1949

Beazley, Kim (senior): WA federal Labor MP from 1945; a critic of Evatt's but not part of the Groupers

Boote, Henry: editor of the *Australian Worker*, 1914–1943, the Australian Workers' Union newspaper in Sydney; trustee of the Mitchell Library

Bourke, Bill: one of the anti-communist Victorian Labor MPs elected in 1949; expelled from the ALP during the split and lost his seat in 1955

Bracken, Brendan: minister of information in Churchill's wartime government; friend and regular correspondent of W.S. Robinson

Brennan, John: Evatt's associate, 1930–1938, when Evatt was on the High
Court; brother of Keith and nephew of Frank, attorney-general in the
Scullin government

Brennan, Keith: Evatt's associate, 1938–1940, when Evatt was on the
High Court; brother of Keith; later worked in the Department of
External Affairs

Bruce, Stanley Melbourne: son of a wealthy Melbourne mercantile
family; Nationalist prime minister, 1923–1929; high commissioner in
London, 1933–1945

Burgmann, Ernest: editor of *Morpeth Review* in the 1930s; bishop of
Goulburn from 1934 (later Goulburn and Canberra); active in left-
wing and peace movement circles

Burke, Tom: federal Labor MP from Western Australia from 1943;
aligned with the Groupers and a strong critic of Evatt's but did not
join the DLP; lost his seat in 1955

Burton, John: employed by the Department of External Affairs but
worked from Evatt's office; secretary of the department, 1947–1949;
active in ALP politics in the 1950s

Cahill, Joe: Labor premier of New South Wales, 1952–1959; very
instrumental in containing the effects of the split in New South Wales

Calwell, Arthur: federal Labor MP from Victoria from 1940; minister of
information, 1943–1945; minister for immigration, 1945–1949; Evatt's
restive deputy from 1951 till 1960

Cameron, Clyde: AWU state secretary in South Australia from 1941, and
ALP state secretary, 1946–1949, then an ALP senator; a key figure
opposed to the Groupers

Carrick, John: general secretary of the New South Wales division of the
Liberal party, 1948–1970

Casey, Richard and Maie: he was an engineer and diplomat, who in 1931
entered federal parliament as a UAP, later Liberal, member; from
1939, Australian minister in Washington, back in parliament from
1949; his wife, Maie, was a friend of Mary Alice, with some common
interests through art

Chamberlain, 'Joe' (Francis Edward): ALP state secretary in Western Australia from 1949; federal vice-president from November 1953, and president from late 1955

Chamberlain, Frank: prominent political journalist for the Murdoch newspapers

Chifley, Ben: federal Labor treasurer, 1941–1949, prime minister, 1945–1949; Labor leader in opposition till his death in 1951

Childe, Vere Gordon: Evatt's friend at university; author of *How Labour Governs*; professor of archaeology at the universities of Edinburgh and then London

Cranborne, Viscount: Marquess of Salisbury; UK secretary of state for the colonies, then dominion affairs, 1942–1945

Cross, Roland: British high commissioner to Australia, 1941–1946

Cullen, William: University of Sydney law lecturer, university chancellor, 1914–1934; chief justice of New South Wales from 1910

Curtin, John: federal Labor leader from 1935; prime minister, 1941–1945

Daly, Fred: federal Labor MP from New South Wales from 1943; a critic of Evatt's, and on the right, but not a Grouper

Dalziel, Allan: Christian Youth activist, Evatt's electoral secretary from 1940; private secretary and electoral secretary until 1960

Dixon, Owen: High Court judge from 1929; Australian minister to Washington from 1942 to 1944; chief justice, 1952–1964

Dougherty, Tom: national general secretary of AWU from 1944; powerbroker in New South Wales Labor politics; until mid-1954 aligned with the Groupers

Downing, Reg: Labor member of the New South Wales upper house from 1940; state minister for justice from 1941 and attorney-general from 1956

Duthie, Gil: Tasmanian federal Labor MP from 1946; strong supporter of Evatt's; member of the federal executive, 1954–1955

Evatt, Clive: Evatt's younger brother; barrister; Labor MP in New South Wales from 1939; expelled from the party in 1956; sat as an independent until losing his seat in 1959

Fadden, Arthur: Country party leader from 1941; briefly prime minister in late 1941; treasurer in Menzies' governments from 1949 to 1958

Ferguson, Jack: member of the Communist party until 1940, then joined the ALP; New South Wales state president, 1947–1952; federal president, 1950–1952; a key ally of Chifley

Forde, Frank: federal Labor MP from Queensland from 1922; deputy prime minister under Curtin and Chifley; briefly acting prime minister after Curtin's death; lost his seat in 1946

Frankfurter, Felix: migrated from Vienna to America in his teens; professor of law at Harvard from 1921; appointed to the United States Supreme Court in 1939

Grattan, Hartley Clifton: American journalist and historian with a keen interest in Australia; friends with Evatt from 1937; wanted to write a biography of Evatt but unfortunately never did

Halifax Lord (Edward Wood, Viscount Halifax): British foreign secretary 1938–1940; supporter of appeasement of Hitler; ambassador to the United States, 1941–1946

Hasluck, Paul: worked closely with Evatt in the Department of External Affairs, 1940–1947; federal Liberal MP from 1949; minister for external affairs, 1964–1969

Haylen, Les: journalist, playwright, and news subeditor at the *Australian Women's Weekly*; close ally and supporter of Evatt's from 1940; federal Labor MP from 1943

Higgins, Henry Bournes: liberal politician in Victoria and then federally; judge of the High Court and of the Court of Conciliation and Arbitration, 1906–1929; his 1907 Harvester judgement established a basic minimum wage

Holt, Edgar: journalist; federal public relations officer of the Liberal party from 1950

Kennelly, Pat: ALP Victorian state secretary, 1947–1949; federal
  ALP secretary 1946–1954; senator from 1953; a Catholic
  opposed to the Groupers

Keon, Stan: the most talented and sharp-tongued of the anti-
  communist Victorian Labor members elected in 1949; expelled
  from the ALP in the split and lost his seat in 1955

Kilgour, Alexander James: headmaster at Fort Street Model School,
  1905–1926

Lang, Jack: New South Wales Labor leader from 1923; premier,
  1925–1927; premier again from 1930 till his dismissal by the
  governor in 1932

Latham, John: Nationalist party leader from 1929; attorney-general
  and minister for external affairs 1932–1934; High Court chief
  justice, 1935–1952

Lovegrove, 'Dinny' (Denis): CPA member till 1933; Victorian ALP
  state secretary 1950–1955; aligned with the Groupers, then
  sided with intervention; federal president, 1953–1954

McConnell, John: general secretary of the Victorian Liberal party
  division, 1945–1971

McKay, Claude: with Frank Packer and Joynton Smith, launched
  Smith's Weekly in 1919; in the 1930s and 1940s was alternately
  editor and managing director

McTiernan, Edward: New South Wales Labor attorney-general
  from 1920–1922 and 1925–1927; appointed to the High Court
  with Evatt, who called him 'eggshell Eddie'

Menzies, Robert: as a Nationalist, moved from the Victorian to the
  federal parliament in 1933; UAP attorney-general, then prime
  minister to 1941; reshaped the conservatives in 1944 as the
  Liberal Party of Australia; prime minister, 1949–1966

Molotov, Vyacheslav: Soviet minister for foreign affairs, 1939–1949
  and 1953–1956; not the inventor of the 'Molotov cocktail' petrol
  bomb, that was a description of his negotiation of the Hitler–
  Stalin pact

Mullens, John: prominent as one of the anti-communist Victorian Labor members elected in 1949; expelled from the ALP in the split and lost his seat in 1955

Ormonde, Jim: journalist; left-wing Catholic opposed to the Movement; instrumental in Sydney moves against their influence; ALP senator from 1958

Palmer, Nettie (Janet Gertrude) and Vance: both writers, critics and significant literary networkers, especially encouraging Australian writers; friends of the Evatts in the late 1930s but the association did not last; Evatt addressed her in letters as 'Mrs Palmer'; she was the niece of H.B. Higgins

Reed, Sunday and John: publishers and art patrons; he was the brother of Cynthia Nolan; from 1935, their house in Heidelberg, 'Heide', became a centre for sponsorship of modern art; active in the Contemporary Arts Society from 1938 and keen to have Evatt's willing patronage as a champion of modern art

Reid, Alan: prominent political journalist, from the 1930s to 1970s, for the Sydney *Sun*, and later for Packer's *Daily Telegraph*; an active member of the Labor party

Robinson, William Sydney: mining businessman and industrialist; close to Curtin and Evatt; accompanied Evatt on his 1942 and 1943 missions to the US and UK

Santamaria, 'Bob' (Bartholomew Augustine): key figure in the development in Melbourne of Catholic Action, then the Catholic Social Studies Movement, dedicated to anti-communist action in the union movement; never a member of the Labor party but a key player in the split

Starke, Hayden: High Court judge, 1920–1950; it was said Starke refused to resign until Evatt was no longer attorney-general and could not decide his successor

Stettinius, Edward: American industrialist; Roosevelt's secretary of state from 1943; US ambassador to the United Nations, 1945–1949

Stout, Victor: secretary of the Victorian Trades Hall Council,
1938–1964; ALP Victorian state president from 1942; initially
close to the Movement, then opposed

Ward, Eddie: federal Labor MP from New South Wales from 1931;
minister for labour and national service, 1941–1949; a former
professional boxer, Evatt likened him to an attack dog on a leash,
and said he was relieved the leash was there

Watt, Andy: prominent barrister with whom Evatt began his legal
career in 1919

Notes

For the sake of brevity, while still providing a guide to my sources, I have largely restricted end notes to direct quotations, identified by the first few words quoted. In those chapters or sections where I have relied heavily on published research, I provide an indication of this in the notes for that chapter. References to published works are abbreviated to author and title, with the full citation in the list of sources. Evatt's own papers at Flinders University are identified by their file names, and references to archives employ the acronyms below. Where files in government documents have very long titles I have truncated them, while providing enough information for others to locate them.

Acronyms used in the notes

AWW   *Australian Women's Weekly*
CP   Peter Crockett papers, State Library of Victoria
EP   Herbert Vere Evatt papers, Flinders University
FDRL   Franklin Delano Roosevelt Library, Hyde Park, New York State
FPLP   Federal Parliamentary Labor Party (Caucus Minutes)
FPRPC Federal Public Relations Planning Committee (Liberal Party of Australia)
GP   Hartley Grattan papers, University of Texas at Austin
LP   John Latham papers, National Library of Australia
NAA   National Archives of Australia
NFSA   National Film and Sound Archives

NLA   National Library of Australia
SMH   *Sydney Morning Herald*
TP   Kylie Tennant papers, National Library of Australia
UKNA   United Kingdom National Archives, Kew
V&NPP Vance and Nettie Palmer papers, National Library of
       Australia

Introduction: The puzzle
Page
3   'The Liberals were roaring': Beazley, *Father of the House,* p. 104.
3   'I will expose' and 'rubbed his hands together': Frank Chamberlain
        interview, NAA, no pagination.
3   'A bit too emotional': Haylen interview, NAA, p. 9, and 'grave urgency':
        Evatt to J. Martin Kastengren, 9 February 1955, EP: 'Petrov Affair:
        Molotoff [sic] letters'.
4   'It was a disaster': Haylen interview, NAA, p. 9; 'more and more erratic':
        Beazley, *Father of the House,* p. 104, and 'had always been prone': Ward,
        A Nation for a Continent, p. 314.
5   The three biographies are: Kylie Tennant, *Evatt: Politics and Justice;*
        Ken Buckley, Barbara Dale and Wayne Reynolds, *Doc Evatt: Patriot,*
        Internationalist, Fighter and Scholar and Peter Crockett, *Evatt: A Life.* The
        more limited studies are Allan Dalziel, *Evatt: The Enigma,* Paul Hasluck,
        Diplomatic Witness: Australian Foreign Affairs, 1941–1947, and Alan
        Renouf, *Let Justice Be Done: The Foreign Policy of Dr H.V. Evatt.*
6   'A wonderfully complex character': Reid interview [Pratt], NLA, p. 53, and
        'no generalisation about Bert Evatt': Keith Brennan interview, CP: box 28,
        p. 3.
7   'The basic and essential genre': MacIntyre, 'The Virtues, the Unity of a
        Human Life …' pp. 246–49.
7–8   'Ambition was both a spur': Hasluck, *Diplomatic Witness,* p. 34; 'He could
        not stop': Hasluck, *The Chance of Politics,* p. 82, and 'No matter how high':
        'Grattan Manuscript Notebook on Dr H.V. Evatt' [1968], p. 48, GP:
        University of Texas at Austin, series iv, 19:17–18. [For brevity, I refer to this
        hereafter as 'Grattan manuscript notebook'.]
9   'Established judicial practice' and 'correct legal protocol': Ward, *A Radical*
        Life, p. 224.
11   'It is as though he did not want': Grattan notes, GP: series iv, 19.17.
12   *Oedipus* or *King Lear*: here I am drawing on Steiner, *The Death of Tragedy.*

Chapter 1: The boy

15   'Mellowed to a quiet and poor respectability': W.A. Wood 'East Maitland Hotels in 1900–06 and Some Incidental Notes', p. 3, (1968), TP: box 34, folder 14; Morpeth family details: Ayres to Crockett, 18 August 1992, CP: 'Education: Maitland PS and HS; Fort St.; folder 1'; 'was enlivened by visits': Wood, 'East Maitland Hotels' and Hunter and Boydell, *Time Gentlemen Please!*

15   History of the Maitland area: Hendy-Pooley, 'History of Maitland'; Hunter and Burge collections, Maitland Public Library, and Brayshaw, *Aborigines of the Hunter Valley.*

16   'A modest weatherboard structure' and following quotations: Interview notes 'W.A. Wood', [undated], TP: box 34, folder 14.

16   Public events in the Bank Hotel: *Maitland Daily Mercury*, 3 September 1894 and 2 February 1897; *SMH*, 10 December 1897 and 22 May 1900.

17   'One of the jolliest' and 'It was about five years ago': *Maitland Mercury and Hunter River General Advertiser*, 28 March 1891.

18   'Heart and kidney disease': John Hamilton Evatt, death certificate, TP: box 37, folder 42.

18   'The Old Boys, the citizenry': Ayres to Crockett, 18 August 1992, CP: 'Education: Maitland PS and HS; Fort St.; folder 1'.

19   'Persons who were not travellers': *Maitland Daily Mercury*, 21 September 1903; St Peter's choir: CP: 'Name file, Evatt, J.S.', and Women's Guild: *Maitland Daily Mercury*, 2 June 1905.

19   'A profoundly religious person' and 'She expected them': Mary Alice Evatt interview, NLA, pp. 1: 2/7 and 3: 1/37.

20   'Recollections of Childhood': 'Essays by H.V. Evatt', 30 May 1910, EP: 'Publications: Miscellaneous'.

21   'Schoolboy's admiration': Reid interview [Crockett], CP: box 28, p. 32.

21   'Never made a thing about it': Haylen interview, NAA, p. 23.

21   'It was an obstruction': *Argus*, 19 and 21 December 1942.

21–22 'Nonchalantly stuck his thumb' and 'Of course the accent': Tennant notes from *The Coal Miner*, March 1966, TP: box 34, folder 15.

24   'No man should be in a Labor ministry': Frank Chamberlain interview, NLA, no pagination.

24–5   'Burning novelist's desire': Tennant to Grattan, 9 June 1968, TP: box 37, folder 40; 'old whiskery characters' and following quotations: Tennant, *Evatt*, pp. 6–7 and 9.

26   'Utterly charming and rested' and following quotations: Haylen interview, NAA, p. 4, and 'won everything' and following quotations: Mary Alice Evatt interview, NAA, p. 9.

27   'When the family came to Sydney': Interview: 'George Evatt, March 23, 1967', TP: box 34, folder 14.

28   St John's church: Betty A. Crosby to Crockett, [indistinct, Nov. or Dec.] 1992, CP: 'Name File: Evatt, J.S.', and Milsons Point: Margaret Park, 'Milsons Point', Dictionary of Sydney, 2008, <www.dictionaryofsydney.org/entry/milsons_point>, viewed 11 August 2012.

28   'Mostly mawkish' and following quotations: 'Essays by H.V. Evatt', 16 May

1910 and 23 August 1909, EP: 'Publications: Miscellaneous'.

29   'Watched the growth' and 'The old building': *SMH*, 30 November 1931,
       and 'an outstanding scholar': Ron Horan to Crockett, 23 May 1991 and
       8 October 1992, CP: 'Personal Correspondence, F–H'.

29   'He loved Fort Street' and following quotations: Mary Alice Evatt
       interview, NLA, pp. 3: 1/37–38; 'though his standards' and 'He wore
       spectacles': Bruce Mitchell, 'Kilgour, Alexander James (1861–1944)',
       Australian Dictionary of Biography, and 'used to write him letters': Mary
       Alice Evatt interview, NAA, p. 5.

30   Prize books are in his collection at Flinders University; dux: *SMH*,
       18 December 1909 and 17 December 1910, and Bridges prize: undated
       and untitled draft, EP: 'Evatt: Biographical'.

30   'He wouldn't be able to go': Mary Alice Evatt interview, NAA, p. 9, and
       Senior Public Examination results, 1912, CP: 'Education University of
       Sydney, folder 2'.

31   'The broad, powerful shoulders': typescript of diary, February 1939,
       V&NPP: series 17, folder 2. Reproduced in Smith (ed.), *Nettie Palmer*, p.
       248, and 'at one time it was touch and go': Evatt to Peter Evatt, undated
       [October 1940], EP: 'Correspondence, Evatt to Peter Evatt'.

Chapter 2: The young Evatt

33   'By far the most brilliant student': leaflet: 'To the Intelligent Electors in
       the Balmain Selection Ballot', [undated but shortly before November
       1924], EP: 'Australian Labor Party: Branch, Balmain'; 'They practically all
       wanted': Mary Alice Evatt interview, NLA, p. 1:2/18, and 'proud to say':
       NSW Parliamentary Debates, vol. 101, 12 August 1925, p. 69.

34   'Deplorable' and following quotations: *The St Andrews College Magazine*,
       December 1912, EP: 'University of Sydney: Miscellaneous'.

35   The university and curriculum: Turney, Bygott and Chippendale, *Australia's
       First*, chapter 8 and Appendices 4 and 6, and 'He said he could get a
       scholarship': Mary Alice Evatt interview, NLA, pp. 1: 1/15–16

35   Evatt's transcript and prizes: CP: 'Education: University of Sydney'.

36   'Minutes of the Rhodes Scholarship Trust of New South Wales', November
       13, 1914, transcription, CP: 'Education: University of Sydney'; 'In the
       Evatt family': Tennant, *Evatt*, p. 23; Elizabeth Evatt, 'The Evatt Family in
       World War 1', 2014, Flinders University Library, and certificate rejecting
       his enlistment: Keith Brennan interview, CP: box 28, pp. 26–27.

37   'The Mater must often': Frank to Evatt, 3 December 1917, EP: 'Evatt,
       Frank', and Evatt's university record: notes from university calendars, CP:
       'Education: University of Sydney'.

37–8   'Old and uncomfortable', 'This was probably' and 'should have been
       adopted': Turney, Bygott and Chippendale, *Australia's First*, pp. 421, 545;
       on the law school, see Star, *Julius Stone*, chapter 3.

39   'Some decent policies' and 'conscription is dead': Evatt to Charlie Bennett,
       2 May 1917, quoted in 'The Evatt Family in World War 1', p. 77.

39–40 Proposing a book 'renouncing bourgeois radicalism': quoted in Irving,
       'On the Work of Labour Governments', p. 83; 'politicalism' and following

quotations: Childe, *How Labour Governs*, p. 71. On Childe, see Green, *Prehistorian*, and essays by Beilharz, Irving and Melleuish, in Gathercole, Irving and Melleuish (eds), *Childe and Australia*.

41   'My husband's very precious favourite brother': Mary Alice Evatt interview, NLA, p. 1/1/7; 'The AIF Project: Raymond Scott Evatt', <www.aif.adfa. edu.au/index.html>, and 'The Evatt Family in World War 1'.

41–2   'I hope Ray is allright': Frank to Evatt, 29 September 1917; Ray 'had advanced with his company': Gus Morgan to Evatt, 25 September 1917; 'If the worst has happened': Frank to Jeanie, 29 September 1917; 'It is so hard to realize': Frank to Jeanie, 7 October 1917; 'a great success': Frank to Jeanie, 2 December 1917, and 'I think we've done': Frank to Evatt, 3 December 1917, all in EP: 'Evatt, Frank', except Gus Morgan to Evatt, in EP: 'Evatt, Ray'.

42   'Always looked to Ray': Frank to Evatt, 3 December 1917; 'a glowing tribute': Frank to Evatt, 27 August 1918; 'usual excellent results': Frank to Jeanie, 26 May 1918; 'certainly mounting the ladder of fame': Frank to Jeanie, 23 July 1918, and 'usual mediocrity': Frank to Evatt, 27 August 1918, all in EP: 'Evatt, Frank'.

43   'Holman failed to realize': Evatt, *Australian Labour Leader*, p. 365, and he 'was tortured' and 'irrationally convinced': Tennant, *Evatt*, p. 23.

44   'November 12, 1918', [signed H.V.E.], *Hermes*, vol. xxiv, no. 3.11.1918, p. 276, and 'he loved the hymns': Mary Alice Evatt interview, NLA, p. 1: 2/7.

45   Prize at Fort Street: *The Fortian*, vol. 27, no. 2, November 1929, p. 9; 'he felt that loss': Keith Brennan interview, pp. 26–27; 'tremendously important' and 'In order to discuss it': John Brennan interview, p. 20, both in CP: box 28, and 'his family was a military family': Reid interview [Crockett], CP: box 28, p. 8.

46   'A small, neat man' and 'the first and only lecture room': Green, *Prehistorian*, p. 10.

46–7   'Discredited' and following quotations on new liberalism, pp. 74–76, and 'the caucus system', 'liberalism should be prepared' and following quotations, pp. 60–63, Evatt, *Liberalism in Australia*.

48   On 'Fusion', see Rickard, *Class and Politics*, and on liberalism between the wars, Beilharz, 'The Young Evatt'.

49   Evatt was not 'keen on this idea': Mary Alice Evatt interview, NLA, p. 3:1/39.

Chapter 3: Love and the law

51   'I don't know how': Baracchi to Mary Alice Evatt, 6 December 1967, EP: 'Correspondence: Miscellaneous, 1960 and after', and 'a tall healthy girl': EP: 'Evatt, Mary Alice: Notebook 1914–1915'.

52–3   Samuel Sheffer's investments, 'List of shares S.F.S. 18/7/29', EP: 'Sheffer, Alice M. (c)'; description of the marriage: *SMH*, 30 November 1920, and minutes aboard ship: EP: 'Evatt: Overseas Trips, 1921'.

53   'A protection against problems': *SMH*, 18 February 1921.

53–4   'For God's sake, get a good book': Mary Alice Evatt interview, NLA, p. 3: 1/2; 'He felt we shouldn't': Mary Alice Evatt interview, NAA, p. 3, and 'I have not had much time': Mary Alice to Evatt, [undated, before November 1920], EP: 'Family Correspondence: MAS Evatt to [H.V.] Evatt'.

54 'We liked fresh air' and 'a good book-case': Mary Alice Evatt interview, NAA, pp. 6–7, and 'He said "have you read every one of those books?"': Mary Alice Evatt interview, NLA, p. 1: 1/20.

55 'This Monday night': Evatt to Mary Alice [undated, October 1921], EP: 'Family Correspondence: Evatt to MAS Evatt', and 'I am sitting on the verandah': Mary Alice to Evatt [undated, late 1921], EP: 'Family Correspondence: MAS Evatt to [H.V.] Evatt'.

56 'Delighted in the surf', 'Our chief purpose' and 'Love and Joy': Evatt to Mary Alice, [undated, early 1922], and 'shake off' their fears: Evatt to Mary Alice, New York [undated, June 1943], EP: 'Family Correspondence: Evatt to MAS Evatt'.

56–7 'You must be busy' and following quotations: Mary Alice to Evatt [undated, shortly before 1 July 1922], EP: 'Family Correspondence: MAS Evatt to [H.V.] Evatt', and Porter: *SMH*, 22 September 1921.

57–8 'Rather absurd not to say': [L.C. Rodd] to Tennant, 12 May 1969, TP: box 37, folder 37, and 'frustrations' and 'his failure': Grattan manuscript notebook, p. 48.

58 'The feeling of transgression' and 'a kind of collusion': Malcolm, *The Silent Woman*, pp. 8, 110.

59 'Are you really going to be cut open tomorrow?' and following quotations: EP: 'Evatt, Mary Alice: Notebook: The Operation'.

59 On Fourness Barrington: *SMH*, 7 April 1922, and Plarr's 'Lives of the Fellows' [Royal College of Surgeons], <livesonline.rcseng.ac.uk>, viewed 2 September 2015.

60–1 Jane Sophia Evatt, death certificate, 5 September 1922, and *SMH*, 6 September 1922; 'Mother does not seem': Evatt to Mary Alice, 7 June 1922; 'Immediately we rang off': Evatt to Mary Alice, 22 June 1922, EP: 'Family Correspondence: Evatt to MAS Evatt', and 'breaking up' and 'She would be perfectly happy': Mary Alice to Evatt [undated, mid-1922], EP: 'Family Correspondence: MAS Evatt to [H.V.] Evatt'.

61 'I've just been telling Ella': Mary Alice to Evatt [undated, between June and September 1922]; 'grow up just half as good': Mary Alice to Evatt [undated, shortly before 1 July 1922]; 'just turned over': Mary Alice to Evatt [undated, mid-1922?], and 'Today is lovely': Mary Alice to Evatt [undated, between June and September 1922], EP: 'Family Correspondence: MAS Evatt to [H.V.] Evatt'.

62 'I missed you last night': Evatt to Mary Alice, [undated, mid-1922?], EP: 'Family Correspondence: Evatt to MAS Evatt'; 'I only feel half myself': Mary Alice to Evatt [undated, between June and September 1922], and 'Today is the perfection of all days': Mary Alice to Evatt [undated, mid-1922?], EP: 'Family Correspondence: MAS Evatt to [H.V.] Evatt', and 'where you and I': Evatt to Mary Alice [undated, October 1921], EP: 'Family Correspondence: Evatt to MAS Evatt'.

64 Transcript of proceedings, EP: 'Legal Material: Walsh and Johnson', and 'great personal effort': W.A. Stanton to Evatt, 16 December 1925, EP:

'Trade Unions: Walsh and Johnson Case'.

65   T.J. Ryan case: *SMH*, 15 August 1919.

66   'The potential scope': Sawer, *Australian Federal Politics and Law, 1901–1929*, p. 217, Menzies, *Central Power in the Australian Commonwealth*, pp. 38–39, and Martin, *Menzies*, vol. 1, pp. 40–42.

66   'Monarch of the Slums': *SMH*, 19 October 1920 and 15 October 1924.

66   'Black list' and description of the royal commission: *SMH*, 27 and 28 October 1921.

67   Appointment as lecturer, 7 December 1923, EP: 'Biographical'.

Chapter 4: Politics and Jack Lang

70   My account of Labor politics draws on Nairn, *The 'Big Fella'*, Freudenberg, *Cause for Power* and McMullin, *The Light on the Hill*.

70–1   'Entered into membership' and following quotations: 'Mosman Branch: Minute book', EP: 'Australian Labor Party: Establishment of Mosman Branch'.

71   'Everyone to whom': Evatt to Mary Alice, 7 June 1922, and 'The world received': Evatt to Mary Alice, [undated, late June 1922], EP: 'Family Correspondence: Evatt to MAS Evatt'; 'O Bert, if the selectors knew': Mary Alice to Evatt [undated, shortly before 1 July 1922], EP: 'Family Correspondence: MAS Evatt to [H.V.] Evatt', and disqualification: *SMH*, 26 June 1922.

72–3   'The big interests detested' and 'were quick to make': McKay, undated interview notes, TP: box 34, folder 17; 'intellectuals were generally regarded': Buckley, Dale and Reynolds, *Doc Evatt*, p. 39; 'sixteen excellent reasons': 'To the Intelligent Electors in the Balmain Selection Ballot', [undated, shortly before November 1924], EP: 'Australian Labor Party: Branch, Balmain', and 'only just blown into the movement': *Labor Daily* quoted in Buckley, Dale and Reynolds, *Doc Evatt*, p. 39.

73   'Firstly, the menus' and 'Should we move?': 6 November 1924, EP: 'Evatt, Mary Alice: Common-place book (1924–5)'.

74–5   'Fresh from his mansion': quoted in Buckley, Dale and Reynolds, *Doc Evatt*, p. 43; 'an investigation' and 'confirmed the views': *SMH*, 18 and 21 April 1925, and 'frivolous and ridiculous': *SMH*, 20 April 1925.

75   'He always held strong views', and following quotations: Mary Alice Evatt interview, NLA, pp. 1: 2/12–16.

76   'Doubled the previous record': *SMH*, 1 June 1925.

76   'A lot to learn': Nairn, *The 'Big Fella'*, pp. 93–95, and 'Nobody really put the red carpet out': quoted in Buckley, Dale and Reynolds, *Doc Evatt*, p. 75.

76   'Rainy and wet' and following quotations: June 22 and 24, 1925, EP: 'Evatt, Mary Alice: Common-place book (1924–5)'.

77–8   Parliament 'memorable': 12 August 1925, p. 69; 'to enable some advocate': 27 August 1925, pp. 433–440, and 'What about your book': 17 September 1925, p. 883, *NSW Parliamentary Debates*, vols 101, 102.

78   'Bert and I lunched': 22 July 1925, 'huge meeting' and 'Bert and I both spoke': 2 and 10 November, 1925, EP: 'Evatt, Mary Alice: Common-place book (1924–5)'.

79   'Rise 6.45 – place white clothes': [undated, mid-1925], EP: 'Evatt, Mary Alice: Common-place book (1924–5)'.

79   'Palatial steamer': *Hobart Mercury*, 6 March 1926; 'glorious lot of flowers': Kingsway exercise book, 'Mary Alice Evatt'; EP: 'Albums', and meeting Curtin: Mary Alice Evatt interview, NLA, pp. 1: 2/8 and 3: 2/29.

80–1 'People who knew him well': Ida Cantwell interview, CP: box 28, pp. 9, 31, 40, *Otranto* committee minute book: EP: 'Overseas trips 1926', and 'With the Test Team at Sea': *Westralian Worker*, 9 March 1926.

81   'Unconditional surrender' and following quotations: 'General Strike, Britain, 1926', EP: 'Overseas trips, 1926'.

82–3 'A very keen struggle' and 'There is nothing to prevent': untitled two-page report, EP: 'Overseas Trips, 1926'; 'bitterly opposed' and 'Australia is not affiliated': *Argus*, 25 June 1926; 'could and should be developed': [*Times*, 24 June 1926], quoted in Buckley, Dale and Reynolds, *Doc Evatt*, pp. 61–62.

83–4 'Enmity' between France and Germany: *Adelaide News*, 4 September 1926, and 'It is a very well known principle': *NSW Parliamentary Debates*, vol. 107, 3 November 1926, p. 789.

84   'Only a matter of time': *Barrier Miner*, 25 September 1926; 'utter chaos' and 'in March the executive split': McMullin, *The Light on the Hill*, p. 146, and 'more and more impossible': Evatt to Mary Alice, [undated, 1927], EP: 'Family Correspondence: Evatt to MAS Evatt'.

84–5 'Reign of terror' and following quotations: 'Balmain Electorate', [undated, after May 1927], EP: 'Australian Labor Party: Branch, Balmain'.

85–6 'The biggest crook': *SMH*, 4 June 1927, and 'wearing the imperial purple' and following quotations: typescript of *Truth* article (5 June), 'The Labor Fight; Dr Evatt Attacks Premier', in EP: 'Lang. J.T.'.

87   'Senior Labor member': two 1927 leaflets: 'Electors of Balmain, Vote Labor thus', and 'Men and Women of Balmain', EP: 'Australian Labor Party: Branch, Balmain'.

88   Evatt's attendance in parliament: *SMH*, 20 December 1927.

89   'Leading constitutional silk': Sawer, *Australian Federal Politics and Law, 1929–1949*, p. 34, and 'I'm on velvet': Douglas interview, NLA, p. 8.

89   'His two staunch medico friends': Clifford Winning, *Cricket Balmania*, [1980] p. 84, 91, CP: 'Personal Correspondence, Winning, C.'.

90   'You are the most sweet': Evatt to Mary Alice, 1 August [1929?], EP: 'Family Correspondence: Evatt to MAS Evatt'.

Chapter 5: The judge

91   Of the many histories of the political crises of the Depression, here I draw on McMullin, *The Light on the Hill*, Nairn, *The 'Big Fella'* and Martin, *Menzies*, vol. 1.

91   'To give Dr Evatt seniority': *SMH*, 29 December 1930. Haylen noted that Evatt insisted on being senior to McTiernan, interview, NAA, p. 16.

92   'Supporters of non-Labor parties' and following quotations: Sawer, *Australian Federalism in the Courts*, pp. 64–65.

92   'An old barbarian': Calwell interview, NLA, p. 28.

93 'Very great ability' and following quotations: Menzies to Evatt, 19 December 1930, EP: 'High Court: Congratulations on Appointment'.

93–4 'Men of the highest legal attainments': *Argus*, 23 December 1930; 'To put it bluntly': *SMH*, 20 December 1930, and 'mellowed experience' and 'the reek of party conflict': *Argus*, 19 December 1930.

94 Description of the High Court swearing-in ceremony: *SMH*, 6 January 1931, *Argus* and *Advertiser,* 7 January 1931.

95 'In accepting this position' and following quotations: Kilgour to Evatt, 22 December 1930, and 'I suddenly had a vision': Boote to Evatt, 22 December 1930, EP: 'High Court: Congratulations on Appointment'.

96 'The moderates in the Party': *West Australian*, 8 January 1931, and 'By its decision today': *SMH*, 24 January 1931.

96 Lang's attempt to abolish the Legislative Council: *SMH*, 17 March 1931, and Evatt's account in *The King and His Dominion Governors*, p. 157.

98–9 *Financial Agreements Enforcement Act* cases: *SMH*, 7, 19, 22 and 23 April 1932.

99 Devanny case: *SMH*, 23 November and 9 December 1932.

100 'A member of the International Society': Zogbaum, *Kisch in Australia*, pp. 5, 56. Zogbaum describes Kisch's work in Germany and the British background; see also Macintyre, *The Reds*, pp. 270–273.

101 'Somewhat mystified', 'considerable excitement' and 'determined ... to uphold its authority': *SMH*, 17 and 19 November 1934, and 'Lead us not into temptation': quoted in Zogbaum, *Kisch in Australia*, p. 97.

102 'Anxious to get away': *SMH*, 6 February 1935.

103 Evatt on New Guinea and Bailey on ILO conventions: *SMH*, 21 August 1933; both on the Commonwealth's external affairs power: *SMH*, 2 December 1935; see also Evatt, 'The British Dominions as Mandatories'.

104 'As an entity separate' and following quotations: *SMH*, 16 July 1935, and 'Protest by Judge' and following quotations: *SMH*, 19 September 1935.

105 'It does one's heart good': Laski to Evatt, 18 January 1934, item 412, and 'All one can do': Cripps to Evatt, 27 October 1936, item 358, EP: 'Correspondence: Miscellaneous', folder 3.

105 'Liberty and the law' and following quotations: Burgmann to Evatt, 19 August 1933, item 403, EP: 'Correspondence: Miscellaneous', folder 3; Peter Hempenstall, 'Burgmann, Ernest Henry (1885–1967)', *Australian Dictionary of Biography*.

106–7 'I rather fancy a dining table': Mary Alice to Evatt, [undated, early 1931]; 'The library is charming': Mary Alice to Evatt, [undated, early February 1931], and 'very modern and charming' and 'You were the best choir boy': Mary Alice to Evatt, [undated, February 1931], EP: 'Correspondence: Evatt Family, Mary Alice to Evatt'.

108 'Keeping pace': *AWW*, 21 October 1933, 'the ornate and the stuffy': *AWW*, 24 March 1934, and 'We are more aware': *SMH*, 24 January 1935.

108 'Outside it is raining': Mary Alice to Evatt, 18 September 1932, EP: 'Correspondence: Evatt Family, Mary Alice to Evatt'.

108–9 'To be most punctual' and following quotations: Evatt to Peter Evatt, 2 March 1936, EP: 'Family Correspondence: Evatt to Peter Evatt', and

'Nothing gives me or Mother' and following quotations: Evatt to Peter Evatt, 30 April [late 1930s?], TP: box 20, folder 7.

109–10   'We want you to succeed': Evatt to Peter Evatt, 18 April 1940 and 'spend any leisure time': Evatt to Peter Evatt, [undated, April 1940], in EP: 'Evatt, Peter – Correspondence'.

110   'He lived out in Mosman': Haylen interview, NAA, p. 1.

110–1   Evatt family wealth: H.S. Harvey, statement: 12 December 1933, EP: 'Accounts (a) to (e)'.

111   Mary Alice's inheritance: 'Sheffer, Alice M. (c)', 'Statement', [undated, 1939?] EP: 'Evatt, Mary Alice: Miscellaneous (a), and 'Deed', 30 March 1939, EP: 'Evatt, Mary Alice: Miscellaneous (b)'.

112   'To help relieve': Balmain Rozelle Relief Fund to Evatt, 16 March 1930, EP: 'Correspondence: Miscellaneous', folder 3, and Balmain Distress Relief Committee, *Sunday Sun*, 1 November 1931, EP: 'Australian Labor Party: Branch, Balmain'.

112   Balmain Cricket Club: Clifford Winning, *Cricket Balmania*, [1980], CP: 'Personal Correspondence, Winning, C.', p. 84, 91.

Chapter 6: The moderns

113   This section on modernism relies on Burke, *The Heart Garden*, McQueen, *The Black Swan of Trespass* and Haese, *Rebels and Precursors*.

113–4   'It was like something going across Russia': Cantwell interview, CP: box 28, pp. 15–16, and 'Not only was it an affront': Haese, *Rebels and Precursors*, p. 21.

114   'In walks this old guy' and following quotations: Terry Ingram, 'Sam Atyeo', *Financial Review*, 31 October 1980, and Atyeo, 'Notes for Kylie Tennant', 22 November 1967, TP: 37, folder 39.

114–5   'Sam was a real playboy' and following quotations: Cantwell interview, CP: box 28, pp. 3, 29, 31.

115   'A sort of free for all': quoted in Burke, *The Heart Garden*, p. 125.

116   'Balanced dynamic symmetry': Mary Alice Evatt, 'The Crowley Fizelle Arts School', p. 314.

116   'He would have preferred' and following quotations: Hinder to Crockett, 15 November 1986, CP: 'Personal Correspondence: F–H'.

116   'Paint me' and 'our future Prime Minister': postcard, [undated], V&NPP: series 28, folder 7.

117   'If only for the sake': Shore to Evatt, 19 December 1935, item 429, EP: 'Correspondence: Miscellaneous', folder 3.

117–8   'Almost as adventurous' and 'the host of obstacles': GP: series iv, 'Research Materials' (19.17–18), Grattan, 'Evatt: An Interim Evaluation: Notes', p. J.

118   'Insubordination against ruling authority' and following quotations: Gay, *Modernism*, pp. 4, 190, 262.

119–20   'I must express my protest': Evatt to Latham, 26 January 1937; 'an important Mitchell Library meeting': notes between Latham and Evatt, 20 April 1936, items 29–31, LP: series 62, 'Papers and Correspondence as Chief Justice'. [The references to Latham's correspondence that follow in this and chapter 8 are all from this series.]

120 'Starke was difficult' and 'absolutely devastating': John Brennan interview, pp. 18–19 and 'Evatt despised Rich' and following quotations: Keith Brennan interview, p. 6, both in CP: box 28, pp. 18–19.

120–1 'The artificial light' and following quotations: Evatt to Latham, [undated, 1936], item 63, LP, and Menzies' 'lordly manner': John Brennan interview, CP: box 28, pp. 10–11.

121 'Compromise in matters of right' and 'then Dixon suddenly alters': Starke to Latham, [undated, just after 23 February 1937], item 103; 'becoming more and more dependent': Starke to Latham, 31 March 1937, item 106a, and 'I feel frightened': Dixon to Latham, 1 June 1937, item 123, LP.

122 Mary Alice to Peter Evatt from London; 28 June 1938, EP: 'Family Correspondence: Evatt to Peter Evatt', and 'a vivid memory of him': O'Reilly to Crockett, 29 April 1985, CP: 'Personal Correspondence, O'Reilly, W.J.'.

122 'I worked hard from nine till five' and following quotations: 'Colourful Glimpses of Life among Art Students', *AWW*, 28 January 1939, pp. 24, 32.

123 'I find my preference for the Moderns' and following quotations: Evatt to Vance Palmer, 6 August 1938, V&NPP: series 1, Correspondence 1/5414.

123 'Black treachery': Evatt to Vance Palmer, 16 January 1939, V&NPP: series 1, Correspondence 1/5487; 'Bert became startlingly convinced': Atyeo, 'Notes for Kylie Tennant', 22 November 1967, TP: box 37, folder 39, and 'not to tell a soul': Atyeo to Tennant, 24 June 1971, TP: box 37, folder 40.

124 'A whole room devoted to Modigliani' and 'beauty of design': 'Colourful Glimpses of Life among Art Students', *AWW*, 28 January 1939, pp. 24, 32.

124 'He is doing well': Evatt to Latham, 12 September 1938, item 214, LP.

124–5 'At Harvard I lectured' and 'I met the President': Evatt to Nini, 2 November [1938], EP: 'Family Correspondence: Miscellaneous'.

125 'Long yarn': Mary Alice to Alice Sheffer, 27 October 1938, EP: 'Family Correspondence: Miscellaneous'; 'I saw the President': Evatt to Frankfurter, [undated, late October 1938], Frankfurter papers, 'General Correspondence, 1878–1965', file: Evatt, Herbert V.

125–6 'New York has really got hold of us' and 'some responsible officer': Evatt to Nini, 2 November [1938] EP: 'Family Correspondence: Miscellaneous'.

126 'Considerable interest' and 'praised the work': *SMH*, 4 November 1938 and 'I hope you will always remember us': Evatt to Grattan, 6 December [1939], GP: folder 3.9.

127 'Even more important': *SMH*, 27 December 1938.

127 'The next appointment': Evatt to Frankfurter [undated, October 1938]; 'unless unified' and 'I mentioned a name': Evatt to Frankfurter, [undated, late October 1938], all in Frankfurter papers, 'General Correspondence, 1878–1965', file: Evatt, Herbert V.

128 'Confidential: For the President alone' and following quotations: Evatt to Roosevelt, 11 November, FDRL: President's personal file: file 5707 'Evatt, Herbert T. [sic]'.

128–9 'Not an easy letter to answer': cover note, 7 December, and 'keen observations': Roosevelt to Evatt, 8 December 1938, FDRL: President's personal file: file 5707 'Evatt, Herbert T. [sic]' and 'Dear "Mr Justice" Frankfurter': Evatt to Frankfurter, 15 January [1939], Frankfurter papers,

American Legal Manuscripts, part iii, 'Correspondence and Related Material', reel 21.

129   'Great art speaks' and 'They have set certain standards': *Argus*, 23 March 1937 and 'Edwardian pomposity': Haese, *Rebels and Precursors*, p. 42.

130   Modigliani: EP: 'Cultural Activities – Art'.

130   'To pollute our gallery' and 'I never liked French art': quoted in Haese, *Rebels and Precursors*, pp. 62, 110.

130–1   'Strict preservation of mediocrity': quoted in Haese, *Rebels and Precursors*, p. 43.

131–2   'Unwarranted assumption': *SMH*, 7 June 1939; 'painting, sculpture and drawing' and following quotations: draft speech [undated], EP: 'Contemporary Art Society'.

132–3   'Hatless' and 'coldly cerebral': *SMH*, 17 August 1939, and 'swept the world' and following quotations: *SMH*, 18 August 1939.

133   'Greetings in the modern manner': EP: 'Contemporary Art Society'.

133–4   'The moderns and primitives' and 'The man leaves you with a sense': typescript for *Fourteen Years*, V&NPP: series 17, folder 2, reproduced in Smith (ed.), *Nettie Palmer*, pp. 247–248.

Chapter 7: The historian as judge

136   'The very coronation' and 'Unless trade unionists': Evatt, *The Tolpuddle Martyrs*, pp. 71–72.

137   'A source of great pride': Kilgour to Evatt, 6 July 1936, EP: 'Correspondence: Miscellaneous, 1941(a)'.

137–8   'It is often impossible to tell' and following quotations: Evatt, *The King and His Dominion Governors*, pp. 117–120, 151.

139   'You derive your authority': Game quoted in Evatt, *The King and His Dominion Governors*, p. 164.

139–40   'Of great constitutional importance' and following quotations: Evatt, *The King and His Dominion Governors*, pp. 165, 170 and 172–74.

141   'Evatt surged into the library': Tennant, *Evatt*, p. 110 and 'He threw himself': draft in TP: box 34, folder 12.

141–2   'The agriculturalists' and 'legal dictatorship': Evatt, *Rum Rebellion*, pp. 121, 128.

142   'The uncompromising sea monster': Ellis, *John Macarthur*, pp. 331–333; 'grossly inaccurate': Ellis, 'Rum Rebellion Reviewed', p. 19 and 'Evatt was blind': Fitzgerald and Hearn, *Bligh, Macarthur and the Rum Rebellion*, p. 125.

142   'A deep sense of respect': Evatt, *Rum Rebellion*, p. 91.

142   'True forum of the little colony' and 'bitter skirmishes': Evatt, *Rum Rebellion*, pp. 121–122.

143–4   'I suppose it would be intolerable', 'art and science', 'The handling of documents' and 'given a competent and honest tribunal': Evatt, *Rum Rebellion*, pp. 13–14, 344.

144   'Holy trinity': Nicolson, 'Taking Epistemology Seriously', p. 2; see also Twining, 'The Rationalist Tradition of Evidence Scholarship'.

144   'The first thing was the facts': Mary Alice Evatt interview, NLA, p. 2:1/39 and 'He felt that in legal decisions' and 'It's difficult, but if you are trained': NAA, pp. 11–12.

145   'Upon this footing', 'I am of opinion' and 'Sooner or later': Evatt, *Rum Rebellion*, pp. 173, 176, 353, and 'Mr Justice Evatt of the High Court': *Sydney Daily Telegraph*, 18 June 1938.

145   Atkinson, *The Europeans in Australia*, vol. 1, chapter 13.

146   'Bligh's fate has been': Evatt, *Rum Rebellion*, p. 88; 'It is not the type of story': Richard Halliday to Keith Brennan, 16 July 1940; 'indeed interesting': Franklyn Underwood to Keith Brennan, 19 July 1940, and 'errors of historical fact': Roger Tillam to Frank Lloyd, 16 July 1940, all in EP: 'Publications: Rum Rebellion: Correspondence'.

147   'Undertaking Will's life' and following quotations: Ada Holman to Evatt, 22 January 1936, EP: 'Publications: Australian Labour Leader (i)' and 'a whole trunkful of papers': Mary Alice Evatt interview, NLA, p. 1: 2/9. [The cache of Holman papers is in EP: 'Publications: Australian Labour Leader'.]

148   'I am sure we ought to': Laski to Evatt, 27 August 1938, item 410, EP: 'Correspondence: Miscellaneous folder 3'; 'awaiting news': Evatt to Grattan, 28 August [1938 – letter is mistakenly dated 1937], GP: folder 3.9, and 'One of the tragedies': Victor Gollancz to Evatt, 12 December 1938, EP: 'Publications: Correspondence'.

148   'There was hardly enough room': Evatt, *Australian Labour Leader*, p. 137.

149   'It looked like two different people' and following quotations: Evatt to Vance Palmer, 2 February [1940], item 1/5694, and 'I can't believe': Vance Palmer to Evatt, 13 December 1939, item 1/5634–6, both in V&NPP: series 1, Correspondence.

150   'Social democratic organizations' and following quotations: Evatt, *Australian Labour Leader*, pp. 3–4, 67, 532.

151   'Deliberately or negligently', 'the authorities in London' and 'The implications of this last criticism': Evatt, *Australian Labour Leader*, pp. 406–407; see also Fitzhardinge, *The Little Digger: 1914–1952*.

152   'Created one another' and following quotations: Niall, *Mannix*, pp. 80–81.

152   'Tens of thousands' and 'rationalist, socialist, anti-clerical': Evatt, *Australian Labour Leader*, pp. 410–411.

153   'Even Low could not resist'; 'gave up almost everything' and 'found himself leading': Evatt, *Australian Labour Leader*, pp. 550, 572.

153–4   'Profound pessimism', 'The Labour Party, starting with a band' and 'be renewed and re-invigorated': Evatt, *Australian Labour Leader*, pp. 572–573.

155   Tennant, *Evatt*, p. 116; 'Simply decided privilege was wrong': GP: series iv, Research materials (19.17–18), Grattan, 'Evatt: An Interim Evaluation: Notes', pp. B–C.

155–6   'Anglo-Saxon, you see' and following quotations: Mary Alice Evatt interview, NAA, pp. 11, 14–15, and Mary Alice 'liked' politics: Grattan manuscript notebook, p. 52.

156   'Talk both witty and real': Nettie Palmer diary, 24 October [1939], V&NPP: series 16.

Chapter 8: The celebrity candidate

157 'More than ever hell bent': Boote diary, 11 June 1940, series 2, MS2070, NLA, Henry Boote papers. [For brevity, in this and following chapters I refer to this as 'Boote diary'.]

158 'Invited to become the Australian Minister': Cohen to Roosevelt, 28 July 1939, FDRL: President's personal file: file 5707, 'Evatt, Herbert T. [sic]'.

158–9 'So that I can place a story' and following quotations: McIlwraith to Evatt, 12 December 1939, item 321, EP: 'Correspondence: Miscellaneous', folder 3.

159 'I cannot imagine how': Evatt to Latham, 13 June 1939, item 188, and 'I was not told': Latham to Evatt, 15 June 1939, item 189, LP.

159–60 'Everybody else was ready': Latham to Evatt, 29 June 1939, item 191; 'I object to its tone': Evatt to Latham, 3 July 1939, [no item number]; 'You make a complete mistake' and following quotations: Latham to Evatt, 5 July 1939, item 195, and 'dirty insinuation' and following quotations: Starke to Latham, 6 May 1940, item 212, LP.

160–1 'Read by clerks': Latham to Evatt, 10 October 1939, item 205; 'It's no use scolding me' and following quotations: Evatt to Latham, 12 October 1939, [no item number]; 'but four judges' and following quotations: Latham to Evatt, 14 October 1939, [marked 'not sent' – no item number], and 'Dear Evatt, I acknowledge': Latham to Evatt, 14 October 1939, item 209, LP.

161–2 'Surveying the lie of the land' and following quotations: Spender, *Politics and a Man*, p. 71. For the political dynamics of this period, my account draws on Crisp, *Chifley*, Day's biographies of Curtin and Chifley, and Martin, *Menzies*, vol. 1.

162 'He is still contemplating leaving' and 'Buckland will make': Boote diary, 6 March 1940.

163 'Pretty upset' and 'go to bloody Balmain': Downing interview, CP: box 28, p. 14, and Macquarie preselection: Crisp, *Ben Chifley*, p. 127.

163 'In constant touch' and 'were not supposed to appear in politics': Boote diary, 3 and 4 May 1940.

164 'Mischievous and disruptive': *The Times*, 21 March 1940 and 'It would appear almost obvious': *The Times*, [no date on clipping, about 28 March 1940], item 1134, LP.

164 'Lead an attack': Boote diary, 10 April 1940, and 'unfortunate and embarrassing position' and following quotations: *SMH*, 4 May 1940.

164 'Too young' and following quotations: McKay, undated interview notes, TP: box 34, folder 17.

164–5 'I hope you'll stand': Piddington to Evatt, 27 August 1940, item 468, EP: 'Correspondence: Miscellaneous', folder 4; 'very, very pleased' and 'To find a great scholar': Buttrose interview, CP: box 28, p. 1, and 'I assume that the project': Dixon to Latham, 24 August 1940, item 232, LP.

165 'Temporarily abandoned', 'He seemed worried' and 'would carefully consider': Boote diary, 8, 24 and 26 August 1940, and 'As to politics': Evatt to Vance Palmer, 27 August [1940], 1/5585, V&NPP: series 1, Correspondence.

166 'Confronts his Honor' and 'should continue to be': *SMH*, Editorial, 28 August 1940.

Notes

166–7	'Some of my friends': *SMH*, 30 August 1940, and 'All I can say' and following quotations: typescript press statement, undated, EP: 'Elections, 1940'.
168	'After ten years': 'Dr H.V. Evatt', *Movietone News*, A0301 (no. 04), 7 September 1940, title no. 88896, NFSA.
168	'All references highly eulogistic': Boote diary, 30 August 1940; 'brought a degree of respectability': Cameron interview, CP: box 28, p. 62; 'won us at least six seats': Calwell interview, NAA, p. 4, and 'For Evatt manifestly': McKay, undated interview notes, TP: box 34, folder 17.
169	'Splendid national gesture': *Newcastle Sun*, 2 September 1940; 'courageous and public-spirited': *SMH*, 30 August 1940, and account of farewell from the High Court: *SMH*, 3 September 1940.
169	'I now make a personal appeal': leaflet, 'Dear Elector of Barton', 19 September 1940, EP: 'Elections, 1940'.
170	Letters to Evatt from Nettie Palmer, 1 September; Starke, 4 September; Margel and Frank Hinder, 30 August; Frank Wraith, 2 September; R.W. Robson, 31 August, and Harold Mathews, 6 September, 1940, EP: 'High Court: Resignation – 1940 (a)'.
170	'On the day you were farewelled': Ormonde to Evatt, 24 September 1940, EP: 'High Court: Resignation – 1940 (a)'.
171	'The splendid step you have taken': Chas. Davidson to Evatt, 30 August 1940, and 'in a voluntary capacity': Haylen to Evatt, 30 August 1940, EP: 'High Court: Resignation – 1940 (a)'.
171–2	'Filled with brightness and color', and following quotations: 'A Breakfast Interview with Dr Evatt', *AWW*, 14 September 1940.
172	'Most regrettable' and 'acting with scant generosity': *SMH*, 31 August 1940, and 'with his grand manner': *Truth*, 1 September 1940.
172–3	'Poor matter and dull delivery' and 'more enthusiasm than discrimination': Boote diary, 4 and 13 September 1940.
173	'We drank gallons of coffee': Haylen, *Twenty Years' Hard Labour*, pp. 69–70, and 'was regarded as inevitable': *SMH*, 23 September 1940.
173–4	'Most ebullient and vocal': Crisp, *Chifley*, p. 131; 'trying to round up votes': Crisp to Tennant, 23 July 1968, TP: box 37, folder 40; 'blowing soap bubbles': *Courier-Mail*, 26 September 1940 and 'Has Evatt so soon forgotten' and following quotations: Boote diary, 24, 26, 28 and 30 September 1940.
174	'Pushing his own barrow', 'would be wise' and 'only wanted to serve': Boote diary, 8 and 11 October 1940, and 'As soon as he came to Canberra': Buttrose interview, CP: box 28, p. 2.
175	'Cost him a place': Crisp to Tennant, 23 July 1968, TP: box 37, folder 40.
175	'At one time it was touch and go' and following quotations: Evatt to Peter Evatt, [undated but late October 1940], EP: 'Evatt, Peter – Correspondence'.
176	'I have good reason to complain' and following quotations: Evatt to Curtin, 24 October 1940, item 462, EP: 'Correspondence: Miscellaneous', folder 4.
177	'Seriously ill', 'will to power' and 'hopeless as a leader': Boote diary, 30 October, 8 November and 6 December 1940.

177   'Benevolent' opposition: *Argus*, 10 February 1941; Day, *Curtin*, and Crisp, *Chifley*, deal with the political calculations restraining Curtin.

177–8   'Like a bee-in-a-bottle' and 'Chifley rarely spoke ill': Crisp to Tennant, 23 July 1968, TP: box 37, folder 40; 'indifference': *Argus*, 23 December 1940; Curtin on the candidate in Swan: Day, *Curtin*, p. 394, and 'old brigade' and 'passionately desirous of office': Boote diary, 23 December 1940 and 20 January 1941.

179–80   'Realism of outlook': *Argus*, 23 April 1941; 'He denied that his statement': Boote diary, 23 April 1941; 'play politics': *Argus*, 26 May 1941, and 'He didn't feel it was playing': Mary Alice Evatt interview, NLA, p. 1/2/28.

180–1   'Closer association' and following quotations [emphasis in original]: Evatt to Menzies, 24 May 1941, EP: 'War, ALP Government, Formation of, 1941', and 'squashed this move': Crisp to Tennant, 23 July 1968, TP: series 4, box 37, folder 40. Martin, *Menzies*, vol. 1, p. 364, discusses Evatt's letter, without comment on Menzies' reaction.

181   'Curtin was prepared' and following quotations: Menzies, *Afternoon Light*, p. 52.

182   'Showdown' and 'your people want': Evatt to Wilson, 11 September 1941, EP: 'War: ALP Government, Formation of, 1941'.

182   'He believed he could be of service': Reid interview, CP: box 28, p. 8.

Chapter 9: The minister

184   'Conciliatory and patient': Sawer, *Australian Federal Politics*, p. 137, and see passim for the legislation; 'I have explained the origin' and following quotations: Evatt, 'Statute of Westminster', 2 October 1942, Evatt, *Foreign Policy of Australia*, pp. 83, 93–94.

185   For a good example of this Labor tradition, see Lee and Waters (eds), *Evatt to Evans*.

185   'All Australia': Boote diary, 2 January 1942; on the debate about a Japanese invasion, Stanley, *Invading Australia*; on whether Australia knew, or should have known, about the 'beat Hitler first' strategy, Day, 'H.V. Evatt and the "Beat Hitler First" Strategy' and Horner, *High Command*, chapter 3.

186   'Seeing Australia very dimly': Grattan manuscript notebook, p. 6, and Casey as an Anglo-Australian: Hudson, *Casey*.

186–7   'One of Evatt's contributions' and following quotations: Grattan manuscript notebook, pp. 1–2 and 6–9.

187   'Strong influence' and following quotations: Co-operation with Dominion Governments, War Cabinet, 21 January 1942, UKNA: CAB 66/21/9, and 'former naval person': Churchill to Roosevelt, 23 March 1942, UKNA: FO 954/4B.

188   'Australia looks to America': Day, *Curtin*, pp. 438–439, and 'The whole incident' and following quotations: Evatt to Frankfurter, 22 February 1942, FDRL: President's secretary's file, box 23, 'Diplomatic Correspondence: Australia: 1939–Aug. 1942'.

189   'A terrific headache' and the flight across the Pacific: Mary Alice Evatt interview, NLA, pp. 2: 1/6–1/10.

189–90   'Great joy': Blainey, *If I Remember Rightly*, p. 185, and Robinson papers, box 5, file 97, 'The Wars'; 'So we proceeded on': Mary Alice Evatt interview, NLA,

p. 2: 1/34, and 'I slept quite soundly': Evatt to Rosalind, 2 April 1942, EP: 'Family Correspondence: Evatt, Rosalind – Correspondence'.

190   'There are vital questions': *Argus*, 16 July 1943. On Lewis, Blainey, *The Steel Master*.

191   'You know how sensitive' and following quotations: Frankfurter to Roosevelt, 30 March 1942, FDRL: president's secretary's file, subject files, box 135, 'Felix Frankfurter'.

191   'I have come to bang on closed doors' and following quotations: Grattan manuscript notebook, p. 10; 'We want the right': *Argus*, 24 March 1942; 'effective machinery': 'Australia's Danger' speech, 28 March 1942, Evatt, *Foreign Policy of Australia*, p. 49; 'the most invigorating visitor': *Argus*, 4 April 1942, and 'Having expected to dislike him': Halifax to Churchill, 23 March 1942, UKNA: FO 954/4B.

192   'Evatt is most eager to play ball': Frankfurter to Roosevelt, 30 March 1942, FDRL: president's secretary's file, subject files, box 135, 'Felix Frankfurter', and 'much impressed': Halifax to Churchill, 29 March 1942, UKNA: FO 954/4B.

192   'Mad on Roosevelt': Ida Cantwell interview, CP: box 28, p. 45, and 'You certainly have taken the Austrylian': Frankfurter to Roosevelt, [date unclear, but April 1942?], FDRL: president's secretary's file, subject files, box 135, 'Felix Frankfurter'.

192–3   'Should be favourably impressed' and following quotations: Hughes to Dominions Office (for Churchill), 30 March 1942, and 'an exceptionally distinguished welcome': Cross to Dominions Office, 27 March 1942, 'Prime Minister's Office: Confidential Correspondence and Papers; Imperial; Dr Evatt's visit to UK', UKNA: PREM 4/50/6.

193   'Sheets of ice' and 'We miss you both': Evatt to Rosalind and Peter, 15 April 1942, EP: 'Evatt, Peter – Correspondence'.

194   'I've been so upset at the changes': Evatt to Mary Alice, [1 May, 1942], EP: 'Correspondence: Evatt Family, Evatt to MAS Evatt'.

194   'The trip across the Atlantic': Evatt to Curtin, 5 May 1942, EP: 'Cables, London, 1938–42'; 'pretty awful' and following quotations: Robinson papers: box 2, file 59, 'Aircraft', and 'looking well and rested': *Argus*, 4 May 1942.

195   'If early reinforcements': War Cabinet 56 (42), 4 May 1942, UKNA: CAB/65/26/17; 'beat Hitler first': *Argus*, 6 May 1942, and 'exhilarating' and 'He was informative': *Argus*, 7 May 1942.

195   'Even temporary occupation' and 'the same allegiance': broadcast 17 May 1942, 'Australia and Britain', Evatt, *Foreign Policy of Australia*, p. 60, and 'made his case': *Argus*, 19 May 1942.

196   Evatt told his sister-in-law the story about Churchill's brandy consumption: 'Recollections of Marjorie Evatt', undated, CP: 'Name File: Evatt, M'.

197   'Immediately after': *West Australian*, 5 March 1943.

197   'Desperately anxious' and following quotations: Evatt to Churchill, 20 May 1942, 'Cabinet Office: Private Collections of Ministers and Officials' Papers, Sir Stafford Cripps, Australia, Correspondence with

Dr Evatt and High Commissioner', UKNA: CAB/127/65.

197–8   Military chiefs' arguments in cabinet and 'symbolic effect': War Cabinet, 21 May 1942, 65th conclusions, minute 1, UKNA: CAB/65/30/13, and 'Evatt's eloquent appeal', 'a great bunch of feathers': Blainey, *If I Remember Rightly*, p. 189.

198   'The work of our mission' and following quotations: Evatt to Curtin, 28 May 1942, EP: 'Cables, London 1938–42'.

198–9   'Tie of brotherhood and kinship' and following quotations: *The Times*, 30 May 1942, Evatt, *Foreign Policy of Australia*, pp. 123, 124, 126. [Note this is mistakenly attributed to 1943.]

199   'Curtin and Churchill between them' and 'the best that money can buy': Evatt to Mary Alice, 30 May [1942], EP: 'Family Correspondence: Evatt to MAS Evatt'; 'the bridal suite' and 'It took the steward and I': W.S. to L.B. Robinson, 1 November 1950, Robinson papers: box 1, file 21, Personal and General, and 'I know now that I was wrong': W.S. Robinson to Minister for Information, [undated, before 26 May 1942], 'Prime Minister's Office: Confidential Correspondence and Papers; Imperial; Dr Evatt's visit to UK', UKNA: PREM 4/50/6.

199–200 'Vital war mission' and following quotations: *Argus*, 22 June 1942, and 'common struggle': 'Declaration by United Nations', FDRL: president's secretary's file, box 168, 'United Nations'.

200   'Appreciated the personal attention' and following quotations: Gowrie to Churchill, 6 July 1942, 'Prime Minister's Office: Confidential Correspondence and Papers; Imperial; Dr Evatt's visit to UK', UKNA: PREM 4/50/6, and 'The trip of Evatt': Frankfurter to Roosevelt, 18 May 1942, FDRL: papers as president, subject files, box 135, 'Felix Frankfurter'.

200–1   'Capitalist press': Boote diary, 29 June 1942; 'the most valorous man in the world': 'Dr Evatt Tells How Victory Can Be Won', *Movietone News*, A0447 (no. 01), 3 July 1942, title no. 89548, NFSA, and 'behind-the-scenes helper' and following quotations: *AWW*, 4 July 1942.

201   'Showed the liveliest' and following quotations: 'The success of the mission', speech 3 September 1942, Evatt, *Foreign Policy of Australia*, pp. 71, 73, 76.

202   'Irreparable injury', and 'unless there was good ground': *Argus*, 7 September 1942 and 'been active in support' and 'no sympathy': *Argus*, 19 December 1942. On the Australia First internments: Munro, *Inky Stephenson*, and on the CPA's shifts during the ban, Macintyre, *The Reds*, chapter 14.

202   'Build up a peace economy': *Argus*, 23 November 1942.

203   'Exploit the element of surprise': *Daily News*, 4 March 1943; 'invincible': *SMH*, 5 March 1943, and 'last year I thought': *SMH*, 8 March 1943.

204   'Saved England and the civilised world' and following quotations: 'Spitfires over Australia', *Cinesound Review*, No. 0568, 12 March 1943, Title no. 83398, NFSA.

205   'Very disgruntled' and 'lack of respect for democracy': Cross to Dominions Office, 3 February 1943, and Curtin to Churchill, 24 February 1943, Prime Minister's Office: Confidential Correspondence and Papers; Imperial; Dr Evatt's visit to UK', UKNA: PREM 4/50/8, and Curtin 'utter fabrication' and 'I am getting a little tired': *Argus*, 1 March 1943.

205–6   'To prosecute the war': 10 April; 'fighting speech': 12 April; 'it is an open secret': 15 April; film screening: 1 May, all in *Argus*, 1943.

206   'Which greatly helped': Evatt to Churchill, 6 May 1943, 'Prime Minister's Office: Confidential Correspondence and Papers; Imperial; Evatt's visit to UK', UKNA: PREM 4/50/8; 'frankly he has pounded us': Marshall to Roosevelt, 25 May 1943, FDRL: president's secretary's file, box 23, 'Diplomatic Correspondence: Australia: Sept. 1942–1944'; 'relieved': Evatt to Churchill, 12 June 1943, Dominions Office and Commonwealth Relations Office: Original Correspondence; WC 75/2, UKNA: DO 35/1462.

206–7   'Please never think' and following quotations [emphasis in original]: Evatt to Mary Alice, [undated, June 1943], EP: 'Family Correspondence: Evatt to MAS Evatt'.

207   'A remarkable man': 6 May 1943, and Somerville comments: 1 June 1943, S.M. Bruce, monthly war files, 1943, NAA: CRS M100.

208   'Keen-eyed, keen-minded' and 'we recall': *Argus*, 16 April 1943; 'analagous to that of Britain' and 'Mr Churchill's allocation': *Argus*, 18 June 1943.

208   'Insultingly rude' and following quotations: S.M. Bruce, monthly war files, 16 June 1943, NAA: CRS M100.

209   'Very long, tiring and dangerous trip' and following quotations: Evatt to Peter and Rosalind Evatt, 25 July [1943], EP: 'Evatt, Peter – Correspondence'.

210   'Overseas triumphs' and 'who could impress himself': *Argus*, 4 August 1943.

210   'Delight' and 'greater offensive action': 'Minister Returns: Dr Evatt Back from Overseas Mission', *Movietone News*, vol. 14, no. 34, 6 August 1943, Title no. 128281, NFSA, and 'a gifted artist' and 'stimulating experience': *AWW*, 21 August 1943.

211   'The advantages of a National Government': *SMH*, 5 August 1943; 'detachment from party extremism': *SMH*, 5 August 1943; Curtin 'mystified': *Cairns Post*, 11 August 1943; 'make his inevitable choice': *Daily Examiner*, 9 August 1943, and 'convert … I would welcome': *Advertiser*, 10 August 1943.

212   'I think you'll find' and following quotations: Reid interview [Pratt], NLA, pp. 29 and 43–44, and 'do nothing to impair his health': *Mail*, 14 August 1943.

212   'Always been a keen advocate' and following quotations: [Evatt to Fadden], 4 February 1943, EP: 'Elections, 1943'. Note this letter is not signed by Evatt, nor explicitly addressed to Fadden; I am interpreting them as writer and recipient on the basis of internal evidence. A copy is also in CP: 'Federal elections, 1940 – 1943, folder 1'.

213   Churchill: 'I feel Evatt is after my job': Grattan manuscript notebook, p. 45, and 'odd streak' and following quotations: *Sunday Mail*, 15 August 1943.

Chapter 10: To San Francisco

214   The 1943 election: Goot, 'Labor's 1943 Landslide' and *Argus*, 10 September 1943.

215   'Crucially important': *Argus*, 30 April 1943, and 'economic collaboration': *Argus*, 2 July 1943.

215   'Attacked it' and following quotations: Hasluck, *Diplomatic Witness*, p. 104.

215–6   'Theory of collective security' and following quotations: 'Australia's war aims: 14 October 1943', Evatt, *Foreign Policy of Australia*, pp. 137, 139–142, 145.

216   'Dictatorial powers': *Argus*, 5 August 1944, and Melbourne Town Hall meeting: *Argus*, 1 August 1944. On the referendum, Sawer, *Australian Federal Politics*, pp. 171–173, and Macintyre, *Australia's Boldest Experiment*, pp. 253–270.

218   'Dr Evatt has never made a secret': *Argus*, 4 December 1944, and editorial: *Argus*, 6 December 1944.

218–9   'Full responsibility' and following quotations: 'Australian–New Zealand Agreement: 21 January 1944', Evatt, *Foreign Policy of Australia*, pp. 154–171; Cranborne: 'unfortunate' and 'so many general questions': 'Australia–New Zealand Agreement of 21st January 1944', War Cabinet, 2 February 1944, UKNA: CAB 66/46/20, and 'in terms of nationhood': Hankinson to Dominions Office, 'Australia–New Zealand Agreement', War Cabinet, 23 March 1944, UKNA: CAB 66/48/19.

219   'Frankly disturbed': secretary of state to American Legation, Canberra, 1 February 1944; 'tell him very frankly' and 'aimed, all too obviously': Department of State, memorandum for the president, 22 April 1944, and 'behaving outrageously': Department of State, memorandum for the president, 31 May 1944, all in FDRL: president's secretary's file, box 23, 'Diplomatic Correspondence: Australia, Sept. 1942–1944'.

220   'Colonial Office despatches' and 'world-wide Colonial responsibilities': 'Correspondence between Lord Cranborne … and Dr H.V. Evatt … on need for consultation with Dominion Governments', Dominions Office and Commonwealth Relations Office: Original Correspondence, UKNA: WR 213/26, DO 35/1899.

220   'Succeeded in the major task': Hasluck, *Diplomatic Witness*, p. 143.

220   'Lost opportunity' and 'It is a miracle': 'Australia and America: March 1945', Evatt, *Australia in World Affairs*, pp. 2, 12.

220–2   'The constitutional machinery' and following quotations: 'World Organization: 8 September 1944', Evatt, *Foreign Policy of Australia*, pp. 209, 211–213, 215.

223   'Realism … inspired by idealism' and 'for the defence of international law': 'Introduction', Evatt, *Foreign Policy of Australia*, p. ix.

223   'Frankly, I envy you' and following quotations: Boyer to Evatt, 13 September 1944, EP: 'Correspondence: Miscellaneous, 1944–5'.

224   Roosevelt's nomination of Stettinius: *Argus*, 16 February 1945; Forde's nomination: *Argus*, 20 February 1945; Forde as 'genial and likeable' and following quotations: high commissioner to Machtig, 12 March 1945, in WR 208/3/3 'International Political Organisation, British Commonwealth Meeting …', Dominions Office and Commonwealth Relations Office: Original Correspondence, UKNA: DO 35/1213.

225   'In a rather awkward position': Wilson interview, CP: box 28, p. 9; 'bullying': notes, CP: name files, box 8, folder 56, 'Wilson, R.', and 'The rebuff was public': Hasluck, *Diplomatic Witness*, p. 154.

225–6 'Like Marco Polo' and following quotations: Haylen interview, NAA, p. 13; 'Evatt, his wife, Atyeo and Burton' and following quotations: Hasluck, *Diplomatic Witness*, pp. 166–167, and 'much more like': Hasluck, 'H.V. Evatt', p. 123.

226 'Why Evatt should regard': Eggleston to Curtin, 3 April 1945, [from NAA: box 61, MP1217], in CP: name file 'EAA–EVA'.

226 'Most of the way we flew' and 'He thought we were losing height': Hasluck, *Diplomatic Witness*, pp. 167–168.

227 Commonwealth as 'the third of the Great Powers': 'W.M. (45) 39TH Conclusions, Minute 1, Confidential Annex, 3 April 1945', War Cabinet, UKNA: CAB 65/52/1.

227–8 'Furious concentration' and following quotations: Hasluck, *Diplomatic Witness*, pp. 171–173.

228 'Unanimous consent' and following quotations: *Argus*, 10 April 1945, and 'effective and acceptable': 'Australia and America: March 1945', Evatt, *Australia in World Affairs*, p. 15.

228 'We should remember': 'Australia and the United Nations Charter: 30 August 1945', p. 60, and 'judicial institutions': 'The Dominions and San Francisco: 9 April 1945', pp. 18–19, both in Evatt, *Australia in World Affairs*.

229 'We must keep our eyes on the ball' and following quotations: *Argus*, 24 April 1945.

229–30 'Working almost ceaselessly' and following quotations: 'Our Editor Reports from San Francisco', *AWW*, 26 May 1945. See Hasluck's detailed description in *Diplomatic Witness*.

230 'Done by Evatt, or under his instructions' and following quotations: Eggleston to Bruce, 9 July 1945, S.M. Bruce, monthly war files, July 1945, NAA, CRS M100, and 'amazing flair' and 'ill-feeling': Cox interview, NLA, pp. 29–31.

230–1 Kaiser ships: Cox interview, NLA, pp. 29–31, and Hasluck, 'Australia and the Formation of the United Nations', p. 161.

232 Evatt on 'sacred trust' and colonies: 'Dr Evatt explains trusteeship proposals at San Francisco', *AWW*, 9 June 1945.

232 'Voluntarily be placed under trusteeship' and following quotations: Cranborne, 'International Aspects of Colonial Policy', War Cabinet, 10 April 1945, UKNA: CAB 66/64/28.

233 'Not only on a voluntary basis': Evatt to Eden, 3 May 1945; 'We could not possibly agree': Cranborne to Evatt, 12 June 1945; 'unfair' and 'her full credit': all in WR 208/255 'Attitude of Dr H.V. Evatt, Australian Minister of External Affairs, to United Kingdom Delegation at the San Francisco Conference', Dominions Office and Commonwealth Relations Office: Original Correspondence, UKNA: DO 35/1883. [For brevity, this large file is in this chapter referred to as 'UKNA: WR 208/255 "Attitude of Dr H.V. Evatt …"']

233–4 'Domestic jurisdiction': Evatt to Eden, 9 May 1945, UKNA: WR 208/255 'Attitude of Dr H.V. Evatt …', and 'scarcely consistent with his general policy': Sawer, 'The United Nations', p. 96.

234 'Rightly or wrongly', 'keep the Russians in the fold' and 'appeared to think':
Cockram to Stephenson, 23 June 1945, UKNA: WR 208/255 'Attitude of
Dr H.V. Evatt …'

234 'Madison Square Garden', 'In Australian labour disputes' and 'a fate that
in the end': *Manchester Guardian*, 22 June, 1945, UKNA: WR 208/255
'Attitude of Dr H.V. Evatt …'

235 'Legal, moral and ethical standards': Sawer, 'The United Nations', p. 95.

235–6 'A closed-door debate' and following quotations: *Argus*, 2 July 1945, and
'At noon the word came': *Manchester Guardian*, 22 June 1945, UKNA: WR
208/255 'Attitude of Dr H V Evatt …'

236 'The greatest fighting man' and account of the final committee meeting:
West Australian, 26 June, *Argus*, 25 and 30 June 1945; and Wilson, notes,
CP: name files, box 8, folder 56, 'Wilson, R'.

236 'The hard-hitting lawyer' and following quotations: *Argus*, 30 June 1945.

238 'Britain's voice' and following quotations: *SMH*, editorial, 28 June
1945, and 'the leader of the opposition': extract from telegram sent by
the United Kingdom delegation, San Francisco to the Foreign Office,
23 June 1945, S.M. Bruce, monthly war files, June 1945, NAA: CRS
M100.

238–9 'I know all Evatt's weaknesses' and 'You must not take it': Eggleston to
Bruce, 9 July 1945, S.M. Bruce, monthly war files, July 1945, NAA: CRS
M100.

240 'Frankly, at San Francisco the attitude taken': Evatt to Frankfurter, 3 July
[1945], Frankfurter papers, 'General Correspondence, 1878–1965', file:
Evatt: Herbert V.

Chapter 11: 'The president of the world'

242 'Marco Polo' and 'because they knew': *Commonwealth Parliamentary
Debates*, HoR, vol. 187, 19 June and 1 July 1946, pp. 1508, 2443, and Frith
cartoon: *SMH*, 2 October 1947.

242 McKenna: notes of Tennant interview: TP; box 4, folder 19.

243 'Pronounced': *Morning Bulletin*, 23 June 1945, and 'no ambitions in that
direction': *Sunday Times*, 24 June and *Argus*, 25 June 1945.

243 'We were having a drink': Buttrose interview, CP: box 28, pp. 20–21;
'regarded as a bit of a joke': Reid interview [Pratt], NLA, p. 74, and 'it must
have been generally known': *Argus*, 24 July 1945.

244 Gallup polls: *Advertiser*, 7 July 1945; 'swinging electors': *SMH*, 16 July
1945; 'Labour would be abandoning': *SMH*, 9 July, and editorial, 10 July
1945; leadership vote: *Courier-Mail* and *Advertiser*, 13 July 1945.

244–5 'Prior bargains': *West Australian*, 17 July 1946, and 'placed in the San
Francisco position': 'The Four Powers and Other Governments at Paris',
24 July 1946, Dominions Office and Commonwealth Relations Office:
Original Correspondence, WR 207/7/28, 'Paris Peace Conference,
Procedure: the Four Powers and other Delegations', UKNA: DO 35/1213.

245–6 'Embarrassed him': *Advertiser*, 30 July and 31 August 1946; 'under the high
gilded ceiling' and 'friendly blue haze': *SMH*, 5 August 1946; 'grim battler
in session' and following quotations: Matheson, *AWW*, 24 August 1946;

Mary Alice at the Louvre: *SMH*, 30 August 1946, and Mary Alice Evatt interview, NLA, p. 3: 1/14.

246 'Minor sensation' and 'to have a part': *Argus*, 31 July 1946; 'to ensure a majority': *News*, 6 August 1946, and 'a clumsy game': *Argus*, 2 August 1946.

246 'Heated exchanges': *SMH*, 5 August 1946, and 'a rather temperamental member': *Newcastle Herald and Miners' Advocate*, 13 August 1946.

247 'We do not want to be handed treaties': *SMH*, 30 August 1946, and 'What do you': *Advertiser*, 17 August 1946.

247 'Close observer' and following quotations: *Sunday Mail*, 11 August 1946; 'in his self-chosen role' and 'Australia's (or Dr Evatt's) single voice': *Courier-Mail*, 27 August 1946, and 'making a great noise': *Daily Advertiser & Courier-Mail*, 17 August 1946.

248 'Rubber stamp': *SMH*, 26 August 1946, and 'the abuse by Russia of the power of the veto' and 'If we do not tie up': *SMH*, 31 August 1946; arrival back: *SMH*, 30 August 1946.

248–9 'Looking as fit': *Truth*, 1 September 1946; 'Chifley didn't want him to': Calwell interview, NLA, p. 18, and 'After early disappointments': Haylen, *Twenty Years' Hard Labour*, p. 69.

249 'Had not intended to take any part' and following quotations: Mary Alice Evatt interview, NLA, p. 2: 2/15 and 3: 1/30, 35.

249 'Had won a high place': *Argus*, 4 September 1946, and 'notoriety at Paris': *Argus*, 5 September 1946.

250 'Complete over-all understanding': Evatt to Chifley, 1 August 1947, EP: 'Cables: Tokyo 1946–9'.

251 On anti-colonial movements: Sawer interview, NLA, p. 37, and 'always unclear': Macmahon Ball to Tennant, 7 January 1969, TP: box 4, folder 22. This section on Indonesian independence draws on George, *Australia and the Indonesian Revolution*, Dorling, *Diplomasi*, Lee, *Australia and Indonesia's Independence* and chapters 19–20 of Buckley, Dale and Reynolds, *Doc Evatt*.

251 Chifley's initiative in taking the Indonesian dispute to the UN: *Courier-Mail*, 22 December 1948, and see George, *Australia and the Indonesian Revolution*, chapter 8.

252 'Firm and constructive' and 'The Nations of the world': Frankfurter to Evatt, 29 October 1947, Frankfurter papers, 'General Correspondence, 1878–1965', file: Evatt: Herbert V. This section on Palestine draws on Mandel, 'A Good International Citizen', and Evatt's later account: 'Australia's Part in the Creation of Israel'.

253 Evatt's support for partition: *West Australian*, 31 March 1948, and EP: Cables, London, 1947–1948; 'As one of the midwives': Frankfurter to Evatt, 10 February 1949, Frankfurter papers, 'General Correspondence, 1878–1965', file: Evatt, Herbert V., and 'You can't walk out on us': Robinson to Evatt, 22 December 1949, EP Robinson, W.S.: 1946–1960.

253–4 'Spared no effort': *Daily Mercury*, 31 August 1948, and *Advertiser*, 20 September 1948. On leaks from Evatt's department and the establishment of ASIO: Horner, *The Spy Catchers*, chapters 13 and 14, and Waters, 'Anglo-Australian Conflict over the Cold War'.

254 'Had already committed': note to secretary of state [dominions], 29 July

1948, Dominions Office and Commonwealth Relations Office, 'Strained relations between the United Kingdom and Australia caused by the un-cooperative attitude of Dr H.V. Evatt, Australian Minister for External Affairs', UKNA: DO 121/55.

254 'On the great Louis Quatorze chair', 'a small apartment' and 'he really believes': *AWW*, 23 October 1948; 'terribly exciting': Rosalind Carrodus interview, NAA, p. 8; also Mary Alice Evatt interview, NLA, p. 2: 2/16.

255 Declaration of Human Rights: Eleanor Roosevelt's papers are in FDRL: Eleanor Roosevelt papers; 'General Correspondence 1945–1952' and 'United Nations Materials'.

255 Evatt's arrival at the general assembly: McMullin, *The Light on the Hill*, p. 245.

255–6 'The enormous number of irons': F. Cumming-Bruce to secretary of state [dominions], 24 November 1948; 'manipulating' the assembly and 'an extreme appeasement policy': F. Cumming-Bruce to secretary of state, 2 December 1948, Dominions Office and Commonwealth Relations Office, 'Strained relations between the United Kingdom and Australia caused by the un-cooperative attitude of Dr H.V. Evatt, Australian Minister for External Affairs', UKNA: DO 121/55.

256 Analysis of the Cold War in the department: Waters, 'The Great Debates'.

259 Banks case: Crisp, *Chifley*, pp. 335–337, and 'tried to persuade him' and 'I gather from our friend': Bracken to Robinson, 4 October 1948, Robinson papers, box 3, file 64, Bracken correspondence.

260 The five Lords of Appeal: *Newcastle Herald and Miners' Advocate*, 26 October 1948 and *SMH*, 11 November 1948, and 'All the fountains': Mary Alice Evatt interview, NLA, p. 3: 1/11.

260 'Instead of blowing me up': *Canberra Times*, 3 November 1965.

261 'Terribly tired' and 'more than just a holiday': Grattan manuscript notebook, pp. 43–44.

261 Chifley telling Evatt to stay in Australia: *SMH*, 7 September 1949.

261 Coal Strike: Deery, ed., *Labour in Conflict*; the CPA's aggressive policy and numerical strength: Davidson, *The Communist Party of Australia*, pp. 83–93, and Ward, *A Nation for a Continent*, p. 296.

262 'The deep nation-wide penetration': Santamaria, *The Price of Freedom*, p. 8.

263 The Movement's clandestine meetings: Ormonde, *The Movement*, and 'The basic principle of counter-organisation': Santamaria, *Santamaria*, p. 82.

264 'A revolutionary situation' and 'Ah, well, Johnny': Record of conversation with J.A. Ferguson, [undated], TP: box 34, folder 19.

264 'Economic war' and 'The community, through the national parliament': *Commonwealth Parliamentary Debates*, HoR, vol. 201, 29 June 1949, p. 1677; Woomera rocket range: Buckley, Dale and Reynolds, *Doc Evatt*, chapter 18.

265 'A criminal offence' and following quotations: *Commonwealth Parliamentary Debates*, HoR, vol. 196, 7 and 30 April 1948, pp. 619, 621–23.

266 'The antithesis of his whole approach': Beazley, *Father of the House*, p. 55, and 'A lot of grass roots': Cameron, *The Confessions*, p. 55.

266 'Link socialism to communism': Hancock, *National and Permanent?*, p. 101.

266 'One of the biggest shocks' and election results: *SMH*, 21 December 1949.

Chapter 12: The Labor leader

267   This and following chapters are indebted to Murray, *The Split*, Fitzgerald, *The Pope's Battalions*, Cameron, *The Confessions*, Duncan, *Crusade or Conspiracy?*, Horner, *The Spy Catchers*, Manne, *The Petrov Affair*, and Henderson, *Santamaria*.

267   'Chifley's faithful lieutenant': Murray, *The Split*, p. 35; Ferguson described his meeting with Evatt in 'Record of Conversation with J.A. Ferguson' [undated], TP: box 34, folder 19.

267–8   'Talking privately': Dalziel, *Evatt the Enigma*, p. 11; 'it would have been far better': Grattan manuscript notebook, p. 52, and 'practically impossible': Mary Alice Evatt interview, NLA, pp. 3:1/39–40.

269   'Paranoid theme': Hofstadter, *The Paranoid Style in American Politics*; 'holding illicit, suppressed feelings': Miller, *Timebends*, p. 341, and 'lurid' and 'threats to the social order': Brett, *Robert Menzies' Forgotten People*, pp. 97–98.

270   'Tough and dedicated sons of the Church': Cameron, *The Confessions*, p. 64.

271   'Communism in Australia': McAllister and Moore (eds), *Party, Strategy and Change*, p. 172.

272   Australian gallup polls, April and June 1950: these are detailed in Murphy, *Imagining the Fifties*, chapter 7.

272–3   'A political measure' and 'It strikes': quoted in Crisp, *Chifley*, pp. 386, 388.

273   'Ruinous for the labour movement' and 'He seemed relieved': 'Record of Conversation with J.A. Ferguson', [undated], TP: box 34, folder 19.

273   Kennelly's report on the federal executive views on the CPA Bill: Kennelly to Chifley, 8 June 1950, EP: 'Chifley Correspondence', folder 37, and 'the safest way': Cameron, *The Confessions*, pp. 73–74.

274   Chifley 'greatly disturbed': 'Joe' Chamberlain interview, NLA, p. 2: 2/18; 'the bitter announcement': Cameron, *The Confessions*, p. 76; 'recriminate, and we shall split': quoted in Crisp, *Chifley*, p. 396, and 'surely the most abject surrender' and the 'great retreat': 'Referendum on Communism', [undated, before or during the 1951 referendum], MS5000 Liberal Party Federal Secretariat, box 1234, folder: 'Communism'.

275   'A lot of pressure': Green to Tennant [undated], TP: box 37, folder 42, and Ferguson's account in 'Record of Conversation with J.A. Ferguson', [undated], TP: box 34, folder 19.

275–6   'Set legal as well as political circles': 'Candid Comment', *Sunday Herald*, 29 October 1950; 'another critical angle': 'In Canberra Today', *Geraldton Guardian*, 4 November 1950; 'By this stage the caucus' and Cameron's description of Chifley: Cameron, *The Confessions*, pp. 76–77, and 'his lack of political acumen': 'In Canberra Today', *Geraldton Guardian*, 4 November 1950.

276   'A small wake going on' and 'Ivan the Terrible': Cox interview, NLA, p. 40.

277   'In sub-arctic weather' and 'Evatt opened his coat': Haylen, *Twenty Years' Hard Labour*, p. 83.

277   Liberal election advertising: *SMH*, 15 April 1951, *Age*, 19 April 1951, and *Courier-Mail*, 24 April 1954.

278   'Associate Dr Evatt with' and 'had every intention': Hancock, *National and Permanent?*, p. 133, and 'great difficulties': McAllister and Moore, *Party, Strategy and Change*, p. 177.

278–9 'Bert is my Deputy': Cameron, *The Confessions*, p. 82; 'I'll wait for a few months': Daly, *From Curtin to Kerr*, p. 105, and Chifley 'under no illusions' and 'As long as I am here': 'Jo' Gullett to Tennant, 11 January 1968, in TP: box 37, folder 39.

279   'Sobbing like a child': Cameron, *The Confessions*, p. 83; 'Evatt was crying': 'Record of Conversation with J.A. Ferguson', [undated], TP: box 34, folder 19; 'an almost small boy reverence': Reid interview [Pratt], NLA, p. 51, and 'His belief was': Haylen, *Twenty Years' Hard Labour*, pp. 47–48.

279   Evatt speech in caucus: FPLP, caucus minutes 20 June 1951, May 1938 to September 1952, MS 6852, box 3. [For brevity, in this and following chapters this referred to as 'FPLP caucus minutes'.]

280–1 'The Caucus had doubts' and 'political incompatibility': 'Record of Conversation with J.A. Ferguson', [undated], TP: box 34, folder 19.

281   This account of the referendum campaign draws on Webb, *Communism and Democracy*.

282   Evatt's itineraries are in EP: 'Communist Party of Australia: Referendum 1951: Correspondence.'

282   'Wiped out or incarcerated': Aarons, *What's Left?*, p. 75, and 'That little reprehensible man': Tennant notes of interview with Ernest Platz [undated], TP: box 34, folder 19.

283   'Voluntary organisations, political parties': Ward, *A Nation for a Continent*, p. 308.

283   'I no more like Australia receiving instructions': *Age*, 15 September 1951, and see Leicester, *Communism and Democracy*, chapter 6.

284   'Many strong personalities' and following quotations: FPRPC minutes, 19–20 July and 13 August 1951, MS5000, Liberal Party Federal Secretariat, box 15, folder: 'P.R. (Staff) Planning Committee, Minutes 1946–1961'. [For brevity in this and following chapters, these files are referred to as 'FPRPC minutes'.]

285   'Fascist in spirit': quoted in Buckley, Dale and Reynolds, *Doc Evatt*, p. 362; 'alarming': Webb, *Communism and Democracy*, pp. 55, 63, and 'wild allegations' Murray, *The Split*, p. 85.

286   'The human rice' and 'the Australian papal': 'Candid Comment', *Sunday Herald*, 1 January 1950.

287   'Just tipped the scales': Cameron, *The Confessions*, p. 82; 'a man talking with utmost sincerity': Haylen, *Twenty Years' Hard Labour*, pp. 83–84, and 'that night Evatt was the supreme lawyer': Haylen interview, NAA, pp. 3–4.

287–93 'It's a tragic thing', and following extensive quotations from Evatt's Bondi referendum speech, 20 September 1951, are transcribed from a recording held in the Flinders University library.

293   The supposed 'Britishness' of Evatt's idea of justice is developed in Bongiorno, 'Herbert Vere Evatt and British Justice'.

295   'Finest hour': Buckley, Dale and Reynolds, *Doc Evatt*, and Kirby, 'H.V. Evatt: Libertarian Warrior'; analysis of the referendum vote:

Webb, *Communism and Democracy*, chapter 12, and Warhurst, 'Catholics, Communism and the Australian Party System'.

295   'It was an educational campaign': FPLP caucus minutes, 26 September 1951; 'the splendid victory': Lovegrove to Evatt, 4 October 1951, and 'political maturity': Evatt to Toohey, 10 October 1951, EP: 'Communist Party of Australia: Referendum 1951: Correspondence'.

Chapter 13: The Petrov affair

297   'Propaganda' and 'development': Holt, 'Political Appreciation' [undated], Menzies papers, NLA, MS4936, series 14, 'Liberal Party', box 414, folder 35; 'Your future looks': Robinson to Evatt, 19 December 1951, and 'When this Parliament has run its course': Robinson to Evatt, 15 December 1952, EP: 'Robinson, W.S.: 1946–60'.

299   Evatt having little choice: Murray, *The Split*, p. 38, and 'to continue to rend' and 'although, as always': Santamaria, *Santamaria*, pp. 110–111.

299   'The Catholic influence' and following quotations: Allee to Evatt [undated], and 'Mr Chifley was acutely aware' and following quotations: Evatt to Allee, 23 July 1952, EP: 'Correspondence: Miscellaneous, A–C'.

301   'The job lying in front of us' and following quotations: 'The Movement of Ideas in Australia' [undated, March 1953], EP: 'Catholic Action and B.A. Santamaria'. That the transcript was circulating by February 1954 is in Duncan, *Crusade or Conspiracy?*

302   'The type of measures' and 'It was all rather disgusting': Santamaria, *Santamaria*, pp. 123–124, and Tennant's notes of interview with B.A. Santamaria, 6 September 1968, TP: box 34, folder 19.

302   'Because the trade unions' and following quotations: 'A Clear and Present Danger', resolution to the Movement's national executive, July 1954, Santamaria, *B.A. Santamaria: Running the Show*, pp. 243–244.

304   'The split in Political Labor's ranks' and following quotations: *FPRPC minutes*, 8–9 September 1952, and 28 September 1953.

304   'We have to get the Groups' and 'two sharply divided': Murray, *The Split*, pp. 42–3 and 199.

305   'Dr Evatt suddenly said': *Argus*, 16 December 1953.

306   'In case the best man', *Sunday Telegraph*, 23 September 1979; Rosalind Carrodus interview, NAA and *Sun-Herald*, 29 November 1953.

306   'It makes me realise': *News*, 18 April 1953, and 'like a cat on hot bricks' and following quotations: Tennant interview with Peter Evatt, typed notes, TP: box 34, folder 15.

307   'Bitter political fight' and 'the political foe': *Mail* (Adelaide), 27 February 1954, and Menzies 'staying in politics': Frank Chamberlain interview, NLA, no pagination.

308   'SENSATION': Duthie diary, 13 April 1954, NLA, MS7076 [for brevity, this is referred to in this and following chapters as 'Duthie diary'], 'dramatic revelations' and following quotations: *Mail* (Adelaide) 17 April 1954, and 'one of the biggest strokes of luck' and following quotations: 'Candid Comment', *Sun-Herald*, 25 April 1954.

309   'The High Cost of Evatt': 'Candid Comment', *Sun-Herald*, 16 May 1954, and *Courier-Mail*, 26 May 1954.

309   'As innocent of financial knowledge', 'I don't know the state of mind' and 'a series of insults': quoted in Murray, *The Split*, p. 152, and 'duel to the death': 'Candid Comment', *Sun-Herald*, 9 and 16 May 1954.

309   Influence of Petrov on the election: Manne, *The Petrov Affair*, especially chapter 8.

310   'LABOR AND RED POLICIES' and other advertisements: *Age*, 17 May 1954 and *Mercury*, 24 and 26 May 1954.

311   'Disunity of Labor helped' and a 'good PR campaign': FPRPC minutes, 16–18 July 1954.

311   'On the boil': Murray, *The Split*, p. 163; 'whispering in the corridors': *Mail* (Adelaide), 7 August, and 'a ruthless struggle for power': 'Candid Comment', *Sun-Herald*, 8 August 1954.

312   'Like a bullfight crowd' and following quotations: *SMH*, 13 August 1954.

312   'Hysteria' and following quotations: *SMH*, 17 August 1954.

313   'Amazed and disgusted': Evatt to O'Sullivan, 4 June 1954, EP: 'Petrov Affair; Correspondence, miscellaneous', and 'the elimination of one H.V. Evatt': Robinson to Evatt, 17 July 1954, Robinson papers, box 3, file 70; Evatt correspondence.

313   ASIO's warnings to Evatt are detailed in Horner, *The Spy Catchers*, chapters 13 and 14.

314   'A complete split' and 'split beyond further camouflage': *SMH* and *Mail* (Adelaide), 14 August 1954.

314   'Evatt at Spy Probe': *Newcastle Sun*, 16 August 1954, and 'an atmosphere' and following quotations: 'Petrov Enquiry: Dr Evatt Appears for Secretariat Members', *Cinesound Review*, no. 1190, 19 August 1954, title no. 28740, NFSA.

314–5 'Consolidate both his supporters' and description of Evatt at the royal commission: *SMH* and *West Australian*, 17 August 1954, and 'finished as a political leader' and 'Caucus still simmers': *Mail*, 28 August 1954.

316   'The Communist Party's greatest asset': quoted in Ormonde, *The Movement*, p. 58; 'it be left to': FPLP caucus minutes, 25 August 1954; and 'We all felt': Downing interview, CP: box 28, p. 7; debate about Evatt's appearance: Duthie diary, 25 August 1954.

316   'Vagueness and irrationality' and 'some sort of persecution': quoted in Murray, *The Split*, p. 165.

316–7 'You cannot dissociate your function' and following quotations: *Illawarra Daily Mercury*, 8 September 1954, and 'I can't help feeling': Bracken to Robinson, 15 September 1954, Robinson papers, box 3, file 64; Bracken correspondence.

317   'Very heated' and 'nasty accusations': Duthie diary, 8 September 1954.

318   'Is Dr Evatt Facing Breakdown?' and 'He seizes almost any opportunity': *News* (Adelaide), 10 September 1954, and 'The Petrov Commission infuriated Evatt': Daly, *From Curtin to Kerr*, p. 141.

318   The files in which Evatt picked over the Petrov case are EP: 'Petrov Affair.'

320   'Latter-day Sherlock Holmes deductions': Dalziel, *Evatt*, p. 94. Subsequent

historians: Manne, *The Petrov Affair*, McKnight, *Australia's Spies and Their Secrets*, Buckley, Dale and Reynolds, *Doc Evatt*, and Crockett, *Evatt* have all spent considerable time on the intricacies of the Petrov defection and subsequent royal commission.

320　'Difficult periods' and 'pretty down': Rosalind Carrodus interview, NAA, pp. 8–9, and 'a very, very strange affair': Mary Alice Evatt interview, NLA, 3: 2/19–20.

321　'Nor make any further': *FPLP caucus minutes*, 22 September 1954; 'Bill Bourke viciously and spitefully': *Duthie diary*, 22 September 1954, and 'as an act of contempt': Cameron, *Confessions*, p. 117.

322　Letters, petitions and testimonials sent to Evatt, including 'interesting people': Rev. Herbert Hayes to Evatt, 8 September 1954, and 'moral courage': W. Lewis to Evatt, 27 August 1954, EP: 'Petrov Affair: Correspondence, Miscellaneous'.

322　'As win you must' and 'go tell Caucus': Clune to Evatt, 27 August 1954, EP: 'Correspondence: Personal A–C'.

Chapter 14: 'The wrecker'

324　Kennelly's attack on 'outside influence': Murray, *The Split*, p. 141.

324　'In and out of [Evatt's] office': Frank Chamberlain interview, NLA, no pagination, and Dougherty's intervention with Evatt: Cameron, *Confessions*, pp. 107–108.

325　'Thinly veiled' and following quotations: Evatt's statement is reproduced in Murray, *The Split*, pp. 179–181.

325–6　'All this time': Cameron, *Confessions*, p. 108, and 'disruptors and disloyalists': Duthie diary, 5 October 1954.

326　'I was wondering how long' and following quotations: Alderman to Evatt, 6 October 1954, EP: 'Australian Labor Party: Industrial Groups, the Movement and the Split: Correspondence'.

326–7　'The bitterness': Cameron, *Confessions*, p. 109; FPLP caucus minutes, 13 October 1954, and 'ninety per cent calm' and following quotations: Duthie diary, 13 October 1954.

327　'The extreme right wing' and following quotations: Evatt to Clarey, 15 October 1954, EP: 'Correspondence: Miscellaneous, 1954'.

328–31　This account of the 20 October meeting draws on FPLP caucus minutes, 20 October 1954; Cameron, *Confessions*, pp. 109–117; Daly, *From Curtin to Kerr*, p. 128, and Duthie diary, 20 October 1954.

331–2　'Very bitter in their attitudes' and following quotations: Joe Chamberlain interview, NLA, p. 2: 2/23, and Weller and Lloyd (eds.), *Federal Executive Minutes*, pp. 581–609.

332–4　'But when you are in a war': Cameron, *Confessions*, p. 142, and 'political recognition', 'enter fields other than those intended' and 'grand strategy': Murray, *The Split*, pp. 199, 223–233.

335　'A bogus break-away Labor Party': Stout to Evatt, 14 April 1955, EP: 'Australian Labor Party: Industrial groups, the Movement and the Split: Correspondence'.

337　'Won an assured place': quoted in Murray, *The Split*, p. 261.

337   'PROVED LEADER OR PROVED WRECKER' and other advertisements, *Age*, 5 and 8 December 1955, and *Advertiser*, 5 December 1955.

337   'Although a great lawyer': Daly, *From Curtin to Kerr*, pp. 105, 153, and 'Had Chifley been leading': Daly interview, CP: box 28, p. 26.

338   'The central figure' and 'extremely disturbed': Murray, *The Split*, pp. 182–183, 355, and 'If Machiavelli were alive today': Reid, *The Bandar Log*, p. 338.

339   'To drive them': Kane, *Exploding the Myths*, p. 153; Evatt 'knew they had worked before': notes of Tennant interview with B.A. Santamaria, 6 September 1968, TP: box 34, folder 19, and 'set out to guarantee': Santamaria, *Santamaria*, pp. 129–130.

339   'This would be much regretted': A.S. Martin to Evatt, 16 April 1958, EP: 'Correspondence: Miscellaneous, M–N'; 'exposure of the plotting': W. Lewis to Evatt, 11 October 1957, EP: 'Correspondence: Miscellaneous, 1957', and 'triumphed over Fascism': V.R. Leslie to Evatt, 29 May 1955, EP: 'Correspondence: Miscellaneous, G–L.'

340   'Never took any notice': 'Record of Conversation with J.A. Ferguson', [undated], TP: box 34, folder 19; 'extremely difficult': F.E. 'Joe' Chamberlain to Tennant, 19 October 1971, TP: box 36, folder 37; 'those who administered the party': Pat Kennelly interview, NAA, p. 3, and 'no great love': Daly, *The Politician Who Laughed*, p. 33.

341   'Everybody was deemed to be equal': Joe Chamberlain interview, NLA, p. 2: 2/29, and 'Bert was a lousy politician': Grattan manuscript notebook, p. 50.

342   'What if' histories: for example, Evans' essays on counterfactual history in *Altered Pasts*.

342   'When Chifley died': Daly interview, CP: box 28, pp. 28–29

Chapter 15: The wreckage

344   'Menzies-Fadden-Santamaria-Fascist cell': quoted in Murray, *The Split*, p. 282, and his chapters 18 and 19 for attempts to then contain the split.

345   Correspondence and appeals to the federal secretariat, NLA, MS4985, boxes 14–16.

346   Lapse of membership: Holt, 'Professor Crisp and the Attempted Anti-Evatt Putsch'; 'a smoke dream': McManus, *The Tumult and the Shouting*, p. 86, and Evatt to Mosman Branch, 31 March 1955, EP: 'Correspondence: Personal, M–N (b)'.

346–7   'On the national and international level' and following quotations: FPRPC minutes, 6 November 1954 and 28–29 June 1955, and see Roskam, 'The Liberal Party's Response to the Split'.

347   Petrov should not be 'dug up': *Argus*, 20 October 1955, and 'All your friends' and following quotations: Fitzpatrick to Evatt, 10 October 1955, EP: 'Fitzpatrick, Brian.'

348   'Political fraud' and following quotations: *Commonwealth Parliamentary Debates*, HoR, vol. 8, 29 September – 27 October 1955, 19 October 1955, pp. 1694–1718; 'great gusts of laughter' and following quotations: Menzies,

The Measure of the Years, pp. 186–187, and 'suffering from strain': *Argus*, 20 October 1955.

348–9   'Two unknown young men' and following quotations: Ward, *A Radical Life*, pp. 223–4.

349   'Handing to the Government on a platter': *Canberra Times*, 21 October 1955; 'one of the most brilliant': Martin, *Menzies*, vol. 2, p. 311; 'I decided that I must dispose': Menzies, *The Measure of the Years*, p. 189, and description of Menzies' reply: *Canberra Times*, 26 October 1955.

350   'Illogicality' and following quotations: *Commonwealth Parliamentary Debates*, HoR, vol. 8, 29 September – 27 October 1955, 25 October 1955, pp. 1858–1875, and 'Evatt Under Delusions': *Argus*, 26 October 1955.

351   'It would be flying in the face': quoted in Martin, *Menzies*, vol. 2, p. 315; Evatt's 'Molotov cocktail': *Raymond Terrace Examiner and Lower Hunter and Port Stephens Advertiser*, 27 October 1955; 'political stupidity': *Canberra Times*, 27 October 1955, and 'like unwilling troops': *Canberra Times*, 29 October 1955.

351   Speech 'strictly vetted': *Central Queensland Herald*, 27 October 1955, and 'virtually gagged': *Argus*, 3 November 1955. Evatt ordering copies of his speech: Government Printing Office to Evatt, 20 November 1956, EP: 'Correspondence: Personal, G–L (a)'.

352   'Broken Labor Party' and following quotations: *Argus*, 16 November 1955; 'worked himself into': *Canberra Times*, 16 November 1955; 'I have no intention to hurt him': *Argus*, 6 December 1955, and 'barrage of interjections' and following quotations: *Argus*, 6 December 1955.

353   'Quite deliberately' and following quotations: Holt, 'Political Appreciation' [undated, late 1955 or early 1956], FPRPC minutes. Subsequent analysis of the DLP and the Catholic vote: Warhurst, 'Catholics, Communism and the Australian Party System'.

354   'Would have been sunk' and 'Our old friend': Bracken to Robinson, 18 January and 20 April 1956, Robinson papers, box 3, file 64; 'Bracken correspondence'.

355   'Still had the Irish attitude': Beazley, *Father of the House*, pp. 103–104; 'defended even by those': McManus, *The Tumult and the Shouting*, p. 74

355   'Although the way has been rough': Katharine Susannah Prichard to Evatt, 11 August 1958, and 'due in part': Leo Bartley to Evatt, 10 November 1958, EP: 'Correspondence: Miscellaneous, 1958'.

356   'Brutalising experience': Haylen interview, NAA, p. 25; 'superb over Suez': Beazley to Tennant, 6 May 1968, TP: box 34, folder 18. On the Suez crisis, see W.J. Hudson, *Blind Loyalty*.

356–7   'Presence' and following quotations: Barrett Reid interview, CP: box 28, pp. 10–12, 32, and 'Bert's talk gave people': Reed to Mary Alice, 9 June 1956, in EP: 'Evatt, Mary Alice: Cultural activities'.

358   'Tragic theme' and following quotations: Evatt, 'Trial of Socrates', pp. 44–48.

358   'Evatt's despair': Green, *Prehistorian*, p. 146, and Evatt to Miss Bishop [*Meanjin*] 29 October 1957, EP: 'Correspondence: Personal, M–N'.

360 'Magnificent', 'magnanimous' and 'blatant confidence trick': *Canberra Times*, 22, 23, 31 October 1958.

360 'The voters wanted' and following quotations: FPRPC minutes, 3, 4 and 5 July 1959.

361 'Insanity' and 'Cunning concealment': Murray, *The Split*, pp. 182–183, and 'made an existing problem' and following quotations: Murray, 'Looking Back on Evatt and the Split', pp. 20, 22, 25.

361–2 'Psychopathology' and following quotations: Campbell, 'Dr H.V. Evatt – Part One: A Question of Sanity', pp. 25–39.

364 Narcissistic and paranoid personality traits: I am drawing here on the American Psychiatric Association, *Diagnostic and Statistical Manual* (fourth edition).

364–5 'An extraordinarily distrustful man': John Brennan interview, p. 7, and 'One is that Bert thought': Keith Brennan interview, both in CP: box 28, p. 20.

367 'My impression': Pringle, 'The Split and Mr Petrov', p. 45.

368–9 'Some people say': Cameron, *The Confessions*, p. 105; 'I noted strangeness': Beazley to Tennant, 6 May 1968, TP: box 34, folder 18; 'the obsession that this was a plot': Daly interview, CP: box 28, p. 22, and 'later discovered to be': Tennant, *Evatt: Politics and Justice*, p. 355.

369 Noad to Crockett, 23 April 1985, CP: 'Personal Correspondence: Noad, K.'; 'demented': Buckley, Dale and Reynolds, *Doc Evatt*, p. 406, and 'a disintegration of the brain cells': Else-Mitchell interview, CP: box 28, p. 18.

369–70 'Agree to your diagnosis': quoted in Buckley, Dale and Reynolds, *Doc Evatt*, p. 405; 'a medical man' and following quotations: Haylen interview, NAA, p. 11, and 'mental condition he had' and following quotations: Rodd to Tennant, 12 May 1969, TP: box 36, folder 37.

Chapter 16: 'Dropping the pilot'

372 'Ashen-faced': *Canberra Times*, 12 November 1958; 'obviously feeling the strain': *Sun-Herald*, 2 September 1959; 'the loss of support': *Canberra Times*, 17 February 1959; 'Behind the Headlines', *The Biz*, 25 February 1959, and 'lost his grip,' 'obvious deterioration' and 'Many Labor men': 'Behind the Headlines', *The Biz*, 8 July 1959.

373 'Within about six months': 'Behind the Headlines', *The Biz*, 8 July 1959; 'soundings had taken place': *Canberra Times*, 22 October 1959, and 'Candid Comment', *Sun-Herald*, 25 October 1959.

373 'Evatt was downhill at this stage': Downing interview, CP: box 28, pp. 8–9.

373–4 'Expected within' and 'certain to accept': *Canberra Times*, 9 December 1959, and 'the guests, including Evatt and Menzies': Martin, *Menzies*, vol. 2, p. 409.

374 'Damagingly controversial' and following quotations: *SMH*, 29 January 1960, 'his capacity': *Canberra Times*, 9 December 1959; 'painful suspense' and 'snapping at the Doc's heels', 'Candid Comment', *Sun-Herald*, 14 February 1960, and 'degraded' and 'the hostilities and divisive tendencies': *SMH*, 3 February 1960.

374–5 'A golden opportunity' and 'bag of trouble': *SMH*, 8 February 1960; 'Evatt was dismayed and humiliated': Daly, *From Curtin to Kerr*, p. 152; 'I saw the

tragedy of Evatt': Haylen interview, NAA, p. 7, and 'the shabbiest trick':
Haylen, *Twenty Years' Hard Labour*, p. 68.

375   'Whatever may be thought of him': *Sun-Herald*, 7 February 1960; 'sordid
and humiliating wrangle' and following quotations: *SMH*, 11 February
1960, and 'There was a sigh of relief': Daly, *From Curtin to Kerr*, p. 152.

377   'I shall never forget': Haylen, *Twenty Years' Hard Labour*, p. 69, and 'the
tragedy … is that he walked out': Haylen interview, NAA, p. 6.

377   'Forgot where the Banco Court' and 'It was obviously': Collins to Crockett,
13 February 1988, CP: box 1: 'Personal Correspondence: Collins. W.H.';
'absolutely devastating': John Brennan interview, CP: box 28, p. 31, and 'a
disgraceful act' and following quotations: Myers to Crockett, 22 January
1987, CP: box 1: 'Personal Correspondence: Myers, F.G.'

378   'Realised he'd gone down the hill': Downing interview, CP: box 28,
p. 17, and 'surrounded by well-groomed young lawyers': Kirby, 'H.V. Evatt:
Libertarian Warrior', p. 17.

378   'Bellyaching' and following quotations: Grattan manuscript notebook,
pp. 29–31.

379   'Suspicious that I wanted': Downing interview, CP: box 28, p. 15, and
'assisted down the gangway' and 'severe hypertension': *Canberra Times*,
13 March 1962.

379   'Sitting in the sun': Moodie, 'Notes on Dr Evatt', [1987], CP: Personal
Correspondence, M.

379–80 'You mustn't leave your writing': H.V. Howe to Evatt, 14 March 1962, EP:
'Correspondence: Miscellaneous, 1960; 'I could see that Dr Evatt': Dalziel,
Evatt the Enigma, p. 164, and 'the reader should feel': W.A.R. Collins to
Evatt, 4 April 1961, EP: 'Evatt: Publications, Correspondence'.

380   'We sat in the sitting room': Hasluck, *Light That Time Has Made*, p. 132.

380–1 'The last of the famous Big Four': 'Candid Comment', *Sun-Herald*,
7 November 1965; 'one of the most controversial' and following quotations
from Clements' speech: *SMH*, 5 November 1965.

381   'Menzies had to suffer': Frank Chamberlain interview, NLA, no pagination.

382   'The factor that made Bertie run', 'a remarkable man' and 'a splash of
invigorating color': Grattan manuscript notebook, pp. 52–54.

Epilogue

384–5 'The honour he most valued': notes 'Wyndham', [undated], TP: box 34,
folder 19, and 'On either side of Evatt': Tennant, *Evatt*, p. 359.

Sources

Archives

Flinders University Library, Adelaide

The Evatt papers are a large collection of seven filing cabinets and nine bays of shelving containing both personal and official correspondence and files. There are some family and private papers and letters, but the largest part of the collection is from 1941, when Evatt became a minister, running through to the end of the 1950s. A great deal of the correspondence is incoming rather than outgoing, as Evatt wrote few letters.

The official files include a large quantity of records and cables from his period as minister for external affairs, which he kept, and which accounts for the relative paucity of Australian Archive official records. Hasluck had warned in *Diplomatic Witness* that the combination of poor departmental record keeping, plus Evatt's tendency to keep papers for himself, meant the official records were patchy. The papers were deposited by Mary Alice in 1970, much to the chagrin of Harold White and Finlay Crisp, who expected the National Library should have them.

In addition to photographs, memorabilia, folders of newspaper clippings and Evatt's collection of books and cartoons, the collection also includes a manuscript prepared by Elizabeth Evatt, 'The Evatt Family in World War 1' (2014), based on family letters, and a recording of Evatt's final speech in the Communist party referendum campaign, broadcast from Bondi on 20 September 1951.

It is worth recording that the Evatt papers also include four 'sub-collections' and that these reflect Evatt's magpie-like tendencies. These are:

- Forty-five folders of Ben Chifley's office correspondence from 1945 to 1951, which Evatt obviously kept when he took over as leader after Chifley's death.
- Some original material related to William Holman, collected while Evatt was writing his biography, including certificates of Holman's official appointments, and correspondence from 1890 to the 1920s, reflecting the formation of the Labor party in New South Wales.
- A series of letters between T.E. Shaw – one of the pseudonyms of Lawrence of Arabia – and Frederick Manning, the Australian-born author of *Her Privates We*. How these came to be in Evatt's possession is a mystery.
- Papers related to Bertha McNamara, the Sydney-based socialist, feminist and

bookshop owner known as 'mother of the labour movement', whose daughters married Henry Lawson and Jack Lang; Evatt knew her and apparently intended to write about her.

National Library of Australia, Canberra
- MS1009: John Latham papers: series 62, papers and correspondence as chief justice.
- MS1174: Vance and Nettie Palmer papers: series 1, 'Correspondence', and series 17, Nettie Palmer's diaries from 1910 to 1961.
- MS2070: Henry Boote papers: series 2, includes Boote's diary from the early 1940s.
- MS4936: Robert Menzies papers: series 2, correspondence.
- MS4985: Australian Labor Party Federal Executive minutes (unpublished after 1955) and correspondence of the Federal Secretariat.
- MS5000: Liberal Party of Australia, Federal Secretariat papers, including the minutes of the Federal Public Relations Planning Committee.
- MS6852: Australian Labor Party Federal Caucus minutes (unpublished after 1949).
- MS7076: Gil Duthie diaries, 1943–1976.
- MS10034: Kylie Tennant papers: series 4, research papers for her biography of Evatt.

National Archives of Australia, Canberra
- A467: Attorney-General's Department, special correspondence.
- A989: Department of External Affairs, correspondence files, 1927–1945.
- A1067: Department of External Affairs, correspondence files, 1942–1953.
- M100: Stanley Melbourne Bruce, monthly war files, September 1939 – August 1945.

University Melbourne archives
- 2001.0070: W.S. Robinson papers: files 11, 21, 29, 32, 61, 64, 70, 97.

State Library of Victoria
- MS13347: Peter Crockett records: archive of papers collected for his biography.

Maitland Public Library
- 'Local Studies' collections by local historians Andrew Burg and Cynthia Hunter.

United Kingdom National Archives, Kew

Government papers from 1941 to 1958; fruitful series were:
*   CAB 65, 66, 129 and 195: cabinet minutes and papers
*   PREM 4: Prime Minister's Office
*   DO 35: Dominions Office
*   FO 954: Foreign Office.

Franklin Delano Roosevelt Library, Hyde Park, New York State

The most fruitful series were:
*   papers as president: president's personal files, president's secretary's file subject files, map room files and official files
*   Harry Hopkins papers: box 132, file 'Australia'
*   Sumner Welles papers: box 161, 'Australia'
*   Eleanor Roosevelt papers: general correspondence and United Nations materials.

Library of Congress (Washington)

*   Papers of Felix Frankfurter, microfilm, 'General Correspondence, 1878–1965'; file: Evatt, Herbert V., 1941–49, box 53, reel 32–33
*   Felix Frankfurter papers, American legal manuscripts from the Harvard Law School Library (duplicate microfilm); part iii, 'Correspondence and Related Material'.

Harry Ransom Humanities Research Center, University of Texas at Austin

*   C. Hartley Grattan papers (circa 1920–1978); correspondence with Evatt is negligible, but series iv, Research materials (at 19.17–18), contains Grattan's notes for an intended, but never written, biography of Evatt. In 1968, he drafted for Kylie Tennant a long manuscript notebook, which he asked her to cite as 'Grattan Manuscript Notebook on Dr H.V. Evatt' and to return to him. In addition, there are also four draft sections called 'Introduction', 'Preface', 'I: What Manner of Man?' and 'Evatt: An Interim Evaluation'. Substantial sections of the Grattan manuscript were reproduced in a paper by Frank B. Poyas, '"A Hazardous Occupation": Dr H.V. Evatt's Twenty-Three Year Friendship with C. Hartley Grattan', presented to 'The Life and Work of Dr H.V. Evatt' conference, at Bond University in July 1990.

Newspapers

Trove, the National Library's prodigious work of digitising newspapers (except *The Age*), facilitates newspaper research up till 1954 and in some cases further. Major publications most often used are the *Sydney Morning Herald*, *Argus*, *Courier-Mail* and *Canberra Times*.

Oral history interviews

An extraordinary number of people have recorded their impressions and opinions about Evatt, or about the history of which he was a part. The selected list below contains those I found most useful.

National Archives of Australia (Sydney)

Series C1580: Interviews about Evatt by John Thompson and Alan Carmichael:
- Kim Beazley (Snr), 1967: 106/8430820
- Arthur Calwell, 1972: 137/8430852
- Clyde Cameron, 1967: 104/8430818 and 112/8430827; and 1972: 142/8430856
- Rosalind Carrodus, 1967: 131/8430846
- Frank Chamberlain, 1972: 139/8430854
- Allan Dalziel, 1967: 124/8430849
- Mary Alice Evatt, 1967: 132/8430847
- Leslie Haylen, 1967: 115/8430830
- Pat Kennelly, 1967: 133/8430848
- Cyril Wyndham, 1972: 140/8430855

National Library of Australia (Canberra)

- Henry Bland, 1975, by Mel Pratt: 738858
- Stanley Melbourne Bruce, 1962–1963, by Cecil Edwards: 87444, TRC187
- Arthur Calwell, 1971, by Mel Pratt: 718385
- Clyde Cameron, 1971–1988, by Mel Pratt: 765378
- Frank Chamberlain, 1972–1973, by Mel Pratt: 2288795, TRC121/39
- Francis (Joe) Chamberlain, 1977, by Joan Ambrose: 1161756, TRC581
- Harold Cox, 1973, by Mel Pratt: 741341
- Irvine Douglas, 1972, by Mel Pratt: 766383
- Elizabeth Evatt, 1979, by Amy McGrath: 4611269
- Mary Alice Evatt, 1973, by Mel Pratt: 2251128, TRC121/41
- John Frith, 1994, by Shirley McKechnie: 1813652
- Peter Heydon, 1970, by Mel Pratt, 2241376
- Alan Reid, 1972–1973, by Mel Pratt: 766843; 1980, by Toby Miller: 558630, TRC734; and 1987, by Daniel Connell: 405843, TRC2172

- Geoffrey Sawer, 1971–1972, by Mel Pratt: 765219; and 1995, by John Farquharson: 2216879
- Alan Watt: 1974, by Bruce Miller: 788329, TRC306; and 1983, by Ian Hamilton: 1592583

Crockett papers, State Library of Victoria

Peter Crockett conducted a large number of interviews for his research; transcripts are in box 28.

- Hazel Bell [undated notes]
- John Brennan, 1986
- Keith Brennan, 1984
- John Burton, 1987
- Charles Buttrose, 1986
- Clyde Cameron, 1984
- Ida Cantwell, 1984
- Fred Daly, 1984
- Reg Downing, 1986
- Rae Else-Mitchell, 1987
- Leslie Melville, 1986
- Tony Mulvihill, 1983
- Alan Reid, 1986
- Barrett Reid, 1986
- Lloyd Ross, 1984
- Russel Ward, 1986
- Roland Wilson, 1985

Newsreels

National Film and Sound Archive, Canberra

- *Movietone News*, A0301 [no. 04], title no. 88896, 'Dr H.V. Evatt' (7 September 1940)
- Cinesound Review, no. 0508, title no. 79892, 'Public Opinion: The Russian Alliance: What Do People Think?' (25 July 1941)
- Movietone News, A0447, [no. 01], title no. 89548, 'Dr Evatt Tells How Victory Can Be Won: Pacific War Council' (3 July 1942)
- Movietone News, A0448 [no. 04], title no. 123627, 'Dr Evatt Speaks' (c. 1942)
- Cinesound Review, no. 0614, title no. 83672, 'Dr Evatt Reports on Mission Abroad' (6 August 1943)
- Movietone News, vol. 14, no. 34, title no. 128281, 'Minister Returns: Dr Evatt Back from Overseas Mission' (6 August 1943)
- Cinesound Review, no. 0568, title no. 83398, 'Spitfires over Australia' (12 March 1943)

Sources

- Universal Newsreel, C1945, title no. 51393, 'New York Honors Dr H.V. Evatt' (c. 1945)
- Cinesound Review, no. 0775, title no. 84050, 'World Affairs: Evatt Speaks for Australia' (6 September 1946)
- Movietone News, vol. 25, no. 38, [A1340–1341], title no. 119277, 'Dr Evatt at Petrov Probe' (19 August 1954)
- Cinesound Review, no. 1190, title no. 28740, 'Petrov Inquiry: Dr Evatt Appears for Secretariat Members' (19 August 1954)
- Movietone News, A1727, A1728, title no. 130065, 'N.S.W Chief Justice: Dr Evatt Resigns as Labor Leader' (18 February 1960)

Bibliography

Works by Evatt

Liberalism in Australia: An Historical Sketch of Australian Politics down to the Year 1915 (Sydney: Law Book Company, 1918).

'The British Dominions as Mandatories', *Proceedings of the Australian and New Zealand Society of International Law*, 1 (1935), 27–54.

'The Jury System in Australia', *Australian Law Journal*, 10: 6 (1936), 49–77.

The King and His Dominion Governors: A Study of the Reserve Powers of the Crown in Great Britain and the Dominions (Melbourne: F.W. Cheshire, 1967 [1936]).

The Tolpuddle Martyrs: Injustice within the law, (Sydney, Sydney University Press, 2009). Originally published as *Injustice within the Law: A Study of the Case of the Dorsetshire Labourers* (Sydney: Law Book Company, 1937).

'The Judiciary and Administrative Law in Australia', *Canadian Bar Review*, 40: 4 (1937), 247–269.

Rum Rebellion: A Study of the Overthrow of Governor Bligh by John Macarthur and the New South Wales Corps (Melbourne: Lloyd O'Neil, 1971 [first pub. 1938]).

'Constitutional Interpretation in Australia', *University of Toronto Law Journal*, 3: 1 (1939), 1–23.

'Control of Labor Relations in the Commonwealth of Australia', *University of Chicago Law Review*, 6: 4 (1939), 529–551.

'Some Legal Aspects of Industrial Arbitration in the Commonwealth of Australia', *Arbitration Journal*, 3: 3 (1939), 356–377.

'The Judges and the Teachers of Public Law', *Harvard Law Review*, 53: 7 (1940), 1145–1163.

Australian Labour Leader: The Story of W.A. Holman and the Labour Movement (Sydney: Angus and Robertson, 1942 [1940]).

'Introduction', *Raffaello Carboni, The Eureka Stockade* (Melbourne: Lloyd O'Neill, 1980 [introduction first published 1942]).

'Post-War Reconstruction: Temporary Alterations of the Constitution: Notes on the Fourteen Powers and the Three Safeguards' (Canberra: Commonwealth Government Printer, 1944).

'The Organisation of the Australian Foreign Service', *Journal of Public Administration*, 7: 1 (1944), 3–9.

Foreign Policy of Australia: Speeches by H.V. Evatt (1941–44) (Sydney: Angus and Robertson, 1945).

Australia in World Affairs (Sydney: Angus and Robertson, 1946).

'Economic Rights in the United Nations Charter', *Annals of the American Academy of Political and Social Science,* January: 243 (1946), 4–5.

'Risks of a Big-Power Peace', *Foreign Affairs,* 24: 2 (1946), 195–209.

The United Nations: An Account of the Formation and Development of the United Nations Organization, Revised from the Oliver Wendell Holmes Lectures Delivered at Harvard University, October 1947 (Melbourne: Oxford University Press, 1948).

'Trial of Socrates: The Mural Sculpture of Tom Bass', *Meanjin,* 16: 1 (1957), 44–48.

'Australia's Part in the Creation of Israel', *Australian Jewish Historical Society Journal,* 5: 4 (1961), 153–170.

Secondary sources

Aarons, Eric, *What's Left?: Memoirs of an Australian Communist* (Ringwood: Penguin, 1993).

Atkin, Elsa and Brett Evans (eds), *Seeing Red: The Communist Party Dissolution Act and Referendum 1951: Lessons for Constitutional Reform* (Sydney: Evatt Foundation, 1992).

Atkinson, Alan, *The Europeans in Australia, vol. 1* (Melbourne: Oxford University Press, 1997).

Beaumont, Joan, Christopher Waters and David Lowe with Garry Woodward, *Ministers, Mandarins and Diplomats: Australian Foreign Policy Making, 1941–1969* (Melbourne: Melbourne University Publishing, 2003).

Beazley, Kim E., *Father of the House: The Memoirs of Kim E. Beazley* (Fremantle: Fremantle Press, 2009).

Beilharz, Peter, 'The Young Evatt: Labor's New Liberal', *Australian Journal of Politics and History,* 39: 2 (1993), 160–170.

—— 'Vere Gordon Childe and Social Theory', in Peter Gathercole, T.H. Irving and Gregory Melleuish (eds), *Childe and Australia: Archaeology, Politics and Ideas* (Brisbane: University of Queensland Press, 1995), 162–182.

Bell, John, 'The Acceptability of Legal Arguments', in Neil MacCormick and Peter Birks (eds), *The Legal Mind: Essays for Tony Honore* (Oxford: Clarendon Press, 1986)

Blainey, Geoffrey (ed.), *If I Remember Rightly: The Memoirs of W.S. Robinson 1876–1963* (Melbourne: F.W. Cheshire, 1967).

—— *The Steel Master: A Life of Essington Lewis* (Melbourne: Melbourne University Press, 1995).

Bongiorno, Frank, 'Commonwealthmen and Republicans: Dr H.V. Evatt, the Monarchy and India', *Australian Journal of Politics and History,* 46: 1 (2000), 33–50.

—— 'H. V. Evatt, Australia and Ireland's Departure from the Commonwealth: A Reassessment', *Irish Historical Studies,* 32: 128 (2001), 537–555.

—— '"British to the Bootstraps?": H.V. Evatt, J.B. Chifley and Australian Policy on Indian Membership of the Commonwealth, 1947–49', *Australian Historical Studies,* 36: 125 (2005), 18–39.

———— 'Herbert Vere Evatt and British Justice: The Communist Party Referendum of 1951', *Australian Historical Studies*, 44: 1 (2013), 54–70.

Boyde, Melissa, 'A Fresh Point of View: The Life and Work of Mary Alice Evatt', exhibition catalogue for *Mary Alice Evatt: 'MAS' 1898–1973* (Bathurst: Bathurst Regional Art Gallery, 2002).

———— 'Making it Accessible: Mary Alice Evatt and Australian Modernist Art', in R. Dixon and V. Kelly (eds), *Impact of the Modern: Vernacular Modernities in Australia 1870s–1960s* (Sydney: Sydney University Press, 2008), 125–136.

Brayshaw, Helen, *Aborigines of the Hunter Valley: A Study of Colonial Records* (Scone and Upper Hunter Historical Society, 1987).

Brennan, Niall, *Dr Mannix* (Adelaide: Rigby, 1964).

Brett, Judith, *Robert Menzies' Forgotten People* (Sydney: Pan Macmillan, 1992).

Buckley, Ken, Barbara Dale and Wayne Reynolds, *Doc Evatt: Patriot, Internationalist, Fighter and Scholar* (Melbourne: Longman Cheshire, 1994).

Burke, Janine, *The Heart Garden: Sunday Reed and Heide* (Sydney: Random House, 2005).

Cameron, Clyde, *The Confessions of Clyde Cameron, 1913–1990: As Told to Daniel Connell* (Sydney: ABC Enterprises, 1990).

Campbell, Andrew, 'Dr H.V. Evatt – Part One: A Question of Sanity', *National Observer: Australia and World Affairs*, 73 (2007), 25–39.

———— 'Dr H.V. Evatt – Part Two: The Question of Loyalty', *National Observer: Australia and World Affairs*, 76 (2008), 33–55.

Childe, Vere Gordon, *How Labour Governs: A Study of Workers' Representation in Australia*, (Melbourne: Melbourne University Press, 1964 [first published London, 1923]).

Constable, Marianne, 'Democratic Citizenship and Civil Political Conversation: What's Law Got to Do with It?', *Mercer Law Review*, 63:3 (2012), 877–889.

Costar, Brian, Peter Love and Paul Strangio (eds), *The Great Labor Schism: A Retrospective* (Melbourne: Scribe, 2005).

Cotton, James, 'Australia in the League of Nations: Role, Debates, Presence', in James Cotton and David Lee (eds), *Australia and the United Nations* (Canberra: Department of Foreign Affairs and Trade, 2012).

Cowan, Zelman, 'Mr Justice H.V. Evatt and the High Court', *Australian Bar Gazette*, 2: 1 (1966), 3–5.

Crisp, L.F., *Ben Chifley: A Political Biography* (Sydney: Angus and Robertson, 1977).

Crockett, Peter, *Evatt: A Life* (Melbourne: Oxford University Press, 1993).

Curthoys, Ann and Joy Damousi (eds), 'Special Issue: Remembering the 1951 Referendum on the Banning of the Communist Party', *Australian Historical Studies*, 44: 1 (2013).

Daly, Fred, *From Curtin to Kerr* (Melbourne: Sun Books, 1977).

———— *The Politician Who Laughed* (Ringwood: Hutchinson, 1982).

Dalziel, Allan, *Evatt: The Enigma* (Sydney: Lansdowne Press, 1967).

Dando-Collins, Stephen, *Captain Bligh's Other Mutiny: The True Story of the Military Coup That Turned Australia into a Two-Year Rebel Republic* (North Sydney: Random House, 2007).

Darwin, John, *Britain and Decolonisation: The Retreat from Empire in the Post-War World* (London: Macmillan, 1988).

Davidson, Alastair, *The Communist Party of Australia: A Short History* (Stanford: Hoover Institution Press, 1969).

Day, David, 'H.V. Evatt and the "Beat Hitler First" Strategy: Scheming Politician or Innocent Abroad?' *Historical Studies*, 22: 89 (1987), 587–603.

—— *Menzies and Churchill at War* (New York: Paragon House, 1988).

—— (ed.), *Brave New World: Dr H.V. Evatt and Australian Foreign Policy, 1941–1949* (St Lucia: University of Queensland Press, 1996).

—— *John Curtin: A Life* (Sydney: Harper Collins, 1999).

—— *Chifley* (Sydney: Harper Collins, 2001).

De Matos, Christine, 'Diplomacy Interrupted?: Macmahon Ball, Evatt and Labor's Policies in Occupied Japan', *The Australian Journal of Politics and History*, 52: 2 (2006), 188–202.

Deery, Phillip (ed.), *Labour in Conflict: The 1949 Coal Strike* (Canberra: Australian Society for the Study of Labour History, 1978).

—— 'Santamaria, the Movement and the Labor Split of 1954–55: A Re-Examination', *Journal of the Australian Catholic Historical Society*, 22 (2001), 47–59.

Dorling, Philip (ed.), *Diplomasi: Australia and Indonesia's Independence: Documents 1947* (Canberra: Australian Government Publishing Service, 1994).

Duffy, Michael, *Man of Honour: John Macarthur – Duellist, Rebel, Founding Father* (Sydney: Macmillan, 2003).

Duncan, Bruce, *Crusade or Conspiracy: Catholics and the Anti-Communist Struggle in Australia* (Sydney: UNSW Press, 2001).

Edmondson, Ray, 'The Last Newsreel', *Cinema Papers*, March/April (1976).

Edwards, Peter, 'Evatt and the Americans', *Historical Studies*, 18: 73 (1979), 546–60.

—— *Prime Ministers and Diplomats: The Making of Australian Foreign Policy, 1901–1949* (Melbourne: Oxford University Press, 1983).

Eggleston, F.W., *Reflections on Australian Foreign Policy* (Melbourne: F.W. Cheshire, 1957).

Ellis, M.H., *John Macarthur* (Sydney: Angus and Robertson, 1955).

—— 'Rum Rebellion Reviewed', *Quadrant*, 2: 1 (1958), 19.

Evans, Richard, *Altered Pasts: Counterfactuals in History* (St Ives: Little Brown, 2014).

Evatt, Mary Alice, 'The Crowley Fizelle Arts School', *Art Gallery of New South Wales Quarterly*, 8: 1 (October 1966), 314–316.

Firth, Marjorie and Arthur Hopkinson, *The Tolpuddle Martyrs* (London: Martin Hopkinson, 1934).

Fitzgerald, Ross, *The Pope's Battalions: Santamaria, Catholicism and the Labor Split* (St Lucia: University of Queensland Press, 2003).

Fitzgerald, Ross and Mark Hearn, *Bligh, Macarthur and the Rum Rebellion* (Kenthurst: Kangaroo Press, 1988).

Fitzhardinge, L.F., *The Little Digger, 1914–1952: William Morris Hughes, a Political Biography, vol. 2* (Sydney: Angus and Robertson, 1979).

Freudenberg, Graham, *Cause for Power: The Official History of the New South Wales Branch of the Australian Labor Party* (Sydney: Pluto Press, 1991).

Galligan, Brian, *Politics of the High Court: A Study of the Judicial Branch of Government in Australia* (St Lucia: University of Queensland Press, 1987).

Gathercole, Peter, T.H. Irving, and Gregory Melleuish (eds), *Childe and Australia:*

Archaeology, Politics and Ideas (Brisbane: University of Queensland Press, 1995).

Gay, Peter, *Modernism: The Lure of Heresy, from Baudelaire to Beckett and Beyond* (New York: W.W. Norton and Company, 2008).

George, Margaret, *Australia and the Indonesian Revolution* (Melbourne: Melbourne University Press, 1980).

Gollan, Robin, *Revolutionaries and Reformists: Communism and the Australian Labour Movement 1920–1950* (Sydney: Allen and Unwin, 1985).

Goot, Murray, 'Labor's 1943 Landslide: Political Market Research, Evatt, and the Public Opinion Polls', *Labour History*, 107 (2014), 149–66.

Green, Sally, *Prehistorian: A Biography of V. Gordon Childe* (Bradford-on-Avon: Moonraker Press, 1981).

Greenwood, Gordon and Norman Harper (eds), *Australia in World Affairs: 1950–1955* (Melbourne: F.W. Cheshire, 1957).

Haese, Richard, *Rebels and Precursors: The Revolutionary Years of Australian Art* (Ringwood: Penguin, 1988).

Hancock, Ian, *National and Permanent? The Federal Organisation of the Liberal Party of Australia: 1944–1965* (Melbourne: Melbourne University Press, 2000).

Harper, Norman and David Sisson, *Australia and the United Nations* (New York: Manhattan Publishing Company, 1959).

Hasluck, Paul, *The Government and the People: 1939–1941* (Canberra: Australian War Memorial, 1952).

—— 'Australia and the Formation of the United Nations', *Journal of the Royal Australian Historical Society*, 40: 3 (1954).

—— *The Government and the People: 1942–1945* (Canberra: Australian War Memorial, 1970).

—— *Diplomatic Witness: Australian Foreign Affairs, 1941–1947* (Melbourne: Melbourne University Press, 1980).

—— 'H.V. Evatt', in Paul Hasluck, *Light That Time Has Made* (Canberra: National Library of Australia, 1995)

—— *The Chance of Politics* (Melbourne: Text Publishing, 1997).

Haylen, Les, *Twenty Years' Hard Labour* (Melbourne: Macmillan, 1969).

Head, Brian and James Walter (eds), *Intellectual Movements and Australian Society* (Melbourne: Oxford University Press, 1988).

Henderson, Gerard, *Mr Santamaria and the Bishops* (Sydney: Hale and Iremonger, 1983).

—— *Menzies' Child: The Liberal Party of Australia 1944–1994* (Sydney: Allen and Unwin, 1994).

—— *Santamaria: A Most Unusual Man* (Melbourne: Miegunyah, Melbourne University Publishing, 2015).

Hendy-Pooley, G., 'A History of Maitland', *Australian Historical Society*, 2: 11–12 (1907–09), 283–298.

Hergenhan, Laurie, *No Casual Traveller: Hartley Grattan and Australia* (Brisbane: University of Queensland Press, 1995).

Hofstadter, Richard, *The Paranoid Style in American Politics* (London: Cape, 1966).

Hogan, Ashley, *Moving in the Open Daylight: Doc Evatt, an Australian at the United Nations* (Sydney: Sydney University Press and Evatt Foundation, 2008).

Holt, Stephen, 'Professor Crisp and the Attempted Anti-Evatt Putsch of April

1955', in Brian Costar, Peter Love and Paul Strangio (eds), *The Great Labor Schism: A Retrospective* (Melbourne: Scribe, 2005)

Horner, David, *High Command: Australia and Allied Strategy, 1939–1945* (Sydney: Allen and Unwin, 1982).

———— *The Spy Catchers: The Official History of ASIO, 1949–1963* (Sydney: Allen and Unwin, 2014).

Hudson, W.J., *Blind Loyalty: Australia and the Suez Crisis, 1956* (Melbourne: Melbourne University Press, 1989).

Hudson, W.J. and H.J.W. Stokes (eds), *Documents on Australian Foreign Policy 1937–49, vol. v, July 1941 – June 1942'* (Canberra: Australian Government Publishing Service, 1982).

Hunter, Cynthia and W. Ranald Boydell, *Time Gentlemen Please! Maitland's Hotels Past and Present* (Maitland City Heritage, 2004, EM/3).

Irving, Terry, 'On the Work of Labour Governments: Vere Gordon Childe's Plans for Volume Two of *How Labour Governs*', in Peter Gathercole, T.H. Irving and Gregory Melleuish (eds), *Childe and Australia: Archaeology, Politics and Ideas* (Brisbane: University Queensland Press, 1995), 82–94.

Judt, Tony, *Postwar: A History of Europe since 1945* (New York: Penguin, 2005).

Kane, Jack, *Exploding the Myths: The Political Memoirs of Jack Kane* (North Ryde: Angus and Robertson, 1989).

Kiernan, V.G., *From Conquest to Collapse: European Empires from 1815–1960* (New York: Pantheon, 1982).

Kirby, Michael, 'H.V. Evatt: Libertarian Warrior', in Elsa Atkin and Brett Evans (eds), *Seeing Red: The Communist Party Dissolution Act and Referendum 1951: Lessons for Constitutional Reform* (Sydney: Evatt Foundation, 1992)

———— 'Sanctuary from the Monsoons: The Artistic Life of Mary Alice Evatt', *Quadrant*, 47: 9 (2003), 48–52.

Lee, David, *Australia and Indonesia's Independence: The Transfer of Sovereignty, Documents 1949* (Canberra: Department of Foreign Affairs and Trade, 1998).

Lee, David and Christopher Waters (eds), *Evatt to Evans: The Labor Tradition in Australian Foreign Policy* (St Leonards: Allen and Unwin, 1997).

Lloyd, Clem and Richard Hall (eds), *Backroom Briefings: John Curtin's War* (Canberra: National Library of Australia, 1997).

Lowe, David, *Menzies and the 'Great World Struggle': Australia's Cold War 1948–1954* (Sydney: UNSW Press, 1999).

———— *Australian Between Empires: The Life of Percy Spender* (London: Pickering and Chatto, 2010).

MacIntyre, Alasdair, 'The Virtues, the Unity of a Human Life and the Concept of a Tradition', in Lewis P. Hinchman and Sandra K. Hinchman (eds), *Memory, Identity, Community: The Idea of Narrative in the Human Sciences* (New York: State University of New York Press, 2001), 241–263.

Macintyre, Stuart, *The Reds: The Communist Party of Australia from Origins to Illegality* (Sydney: Allen and Unwin, 1998).

———— *Australia's Boldest Experiment: War and Reconstruction in the 1940s* (Sydney: NewSouth, 2015).

Malcolm, Janet, *The Silent Woman: Sylvia Plath and Ted Hughes* (Vintage Books: New York, 1995).

Mandel, Daniel, 'A Good International Citizen: H.V. Evatt, Britain, the United Nations and Israel, 1948–49', *Middle Eastern Studies*, 39: 2 (2003), 82–104.

Manne, Robert, *The Petrov Affair: Politics and Espionage* (Sydney: Pergamon, 1987).

Martin, A.W., *Robert Menzies: A Life, vol. 1, '1894–1943'* (Melbourne: Melbourne University Press, 1993).

———— *Robert Menzies: A Life, vol. 2, '1944–1978'* (Melbourne: Melbourne University Press, 1999).

McAllister, Ian and Rhonda Moore (eds), *Party, Strategy and Change: Australian Electoral Speeches since 1946* (Melbourne: Longman Cheshire, 1991).

McCarthy, Helen, *The British People and the League of Nations: Democracy, Citizenship and Internationalism, c. 1918–45* (Manchester: Manchester University Press, 2011).

McKernan, L., 'Newsreels: Form and Function', in R. Howells and R.W. Matson (eds), *Using Visual Evidence* (Maidenhead, Berks.: Open University Press, 2009)

McKnight, David, *Australia's Spies and Their Secrets* (Sydney: Allen and Unwin, 1994).

McManus, Frank, *The Tumult and the Shouting* (Adelaide: Rigby, 1977).

McMullin, Ross, *The Light on the Hill: The Australian Labor Party, 1891–1991* (Melbourne: Oxford University Press, 1991).

McQueen, Humphrey, *The Black Swan of Trespass: The Emergence of Modernist Painting in Australia to 1944* (Sydney: Alternative Publishing Cooperative Ltd., 1979).

Meaney, Neville, 'Australia, the Great Powers and the Coming of the Cold War', *Australian Journal of Politics and History*, 38: 3 (1992), 316–333.

———— 'Dr H.V. Evatt and the United Nations', in James Cotton and David Lee (eds), *Australia and the United Nations* (Canberra: Department of Foreign Affairs and Trade, 2012)

Melleuish, Gregory, 'The Place of Vere Gordon Childe in Australian Intellectual History', in Peter Gathercole, T.H. Irving and Gregory Melleuish (eds), *Childe and Australia: Archaeology, Politics and Ideas* (Brisbane: University of Queensland Press, 1995), 147–161.

Menzies, Robert, *Afternoon Light: Some Memories of Men and Events* (Melbourne: Cassell, 1967).

———— *Central Power in the Australian Commonwealth* (Melbourne: Cassell, 1968).

———— *The Measure of the Years* (Sydney: Cassell, 1970).

Millar, T.B., *Australia's Foreign Policy* (Sydney: Angus and Robertson, 1968).

Miller, Arthur, *Timebends: A Life* (London: Methuen, 1987).

Munro, Craig, *Inky Stephenson: Wild Man of Letters* (Brisbane: University of Queensland Press, 1992).

Murphy, John, *Imagining the Fifties: Private Sentiment and Political Culture in Menzies' Australia* (Sydney: Pluto Press and UNSW Press, 2000).

Murray, Robert, *The Split: Australian Labor in the Fifties* (Melbourne: Cheshire, 1972).

———— 'Looking Back on Evatt and the Split', *Quadrant*, 48: 10 (2004), 20–26.

Myers, Hal, *The Whispering Gallery* (Sydney: Kangaroo Press, 1999).

Nairn, Bede, *The 'Big Fella': Jack Lang and the Australian Labor Party 1891–1949* (Melbourne: Melbourne University Press, 1986).

Niall, Brenda, *Mannix* (Melbourne: Text Publishing, 2015).

Nicolson, Donald, 'Taking Epistemology Seriously: "Truth, Reason and Justice" Revisited', *The International Journal of Evidence and Proof,* 17: 1 (2013), 1–46.

Ormonde, Paul, *The Movement* (Melbourne: Thomas Nelson, 1972).

—— (ed.), *Santamaria: The Politics of Fear* (Richmond: Spectrum, 2000).

Osmond, Warren G., *Frederic Eggleston: An Intellectual in Australian Politics* (Sydney: Allen and Unwin, 1985).

Porter, Robert, *Paul Hasluck: A Political Biography* (Nedlands: University of Western Australia Press, 1993).

Pringle, John, *Australian Accent* (London: Chatto and Windus, 1958).

—— 'The Split and Mr Petrov', *Quadrant,* 15: 1 (1971), 42–47.

Pronay, Nicholas, 'The Newsreels: The Illusion of Actuality', in P. Smith (ed.), *The Historian and Film* (New York: Cambridge University Press, 1976)

Radi, Heather and Peter Spearritt (eds), *Jack Lang* (Sydney: Hale and Iremonger, 1977).

Reeves, Anthony R., 'Judicial Practical Reason: Judges in Morally Imperfect Legal Orders', *Law and Philosophy,* 30: 3 (May 2011), 319–352.

Reid, Alan, *The Bandar Log: A Labor Story of the 1950s* (Ballarat: Connor Court, 2015).

Renouf, Alan, *Let Justice Be Done: The Foreign Policy of Dr H.V. Evatt* (St Lucia: University of Queensland Press, 1983).

Reynolds, Wayne, *H.V. Evatt: The Imperial Connection and the Quest for Australian Security, 1941–1945* (PhD, Newcastle University, 1985).

Rickard, John, *Class and Politics: New South Wales, Victoria and the Early Commonwealth, 1890–1910* (Canberra: Australian National University Press, 1976).

Robertson, Geoffrey, *H.V. Evatt: A Prophet Without Honour in His Own Land* (Sydney: Peripheral Press, 2015).

Roskam, John, 'The Liberal Party's Response to the Split', in Brian Costar, Peter Love and Paul Strangio (eds), *The Great Labor Schism: A Retrospective* (Melbourne: Scribe, 2005), 260–276.

Ross, Lloyd, *John Curtin: A Biography* (Melbourne: Melbourne University Press, 1996 [1977]).

Santamaria, B.A., *The Price of Freedom: The Movement – After Ten Years* (Melbourne: Hawthorn Press, 1966).

—— *Santamaria: A Memoir,* previously published as *Against the Tide* (Melbourne: Oxford University Press, 1997).

—— *B.A. Santamaria: Running the Show: Selected Documents: 1939–1996* (Melbourne: Miegunyah Press in association with the State Library of Victoria, 2008).

Sawer, Geoffrey, *Australian Federal Politics and Law, 1901–1929* (Melbourne: Melbourne University Press, 1956).

—— 'The United Nations', in Gordon Greenwood and Norman Harper (eds), *Australia in World Affairs 1950–55* (Melbourne: Cheshire, 1957)

—— *Australian Federal Politics and Law, 1929–1949* (Melbourne: Melbourne University Press, 1963).

—— *Australian Federalism in the Courts* (Melbourne: Melbourne University Press, 1967).

Sawer, Marian, *The Ethical State? Social Liberalism in Australia* (Melbourne: Melbourne University Press, 2003).

Smith, Vivian (ed.), *Nettie Palmer: Her Private Journal 'Fourteen Years', Poems, Reviews and Literary Essays* (Brisbane: University of Queensland Press, 1988).

Smyth, Russell, 'Judicial Interaction on the Latham Court: A Quantitative Study of Voting Patterns on the High Court 1935–1950', *The Australian Journal of Politics and History*, 47: 3 (2001), 330.

Spender, Percy, *Politics and a Man* (Sydney: Collins, 1972).

Spratt, Elwyn, *Eddie Ward: Firebrand of East Sydney* (Adelaide: Rigby, 1965).

Stanley, Peter, *Invading Australia: Japan and the Battle for Australia, 1942* (Melbourne: Viking, 2008).

Star, Leonie, *Julius Stone: An Intellectual Life* (Melbourne: Oxford University Press, 1992).

Steiner, George, *The Death of Tragedy* (London: Faber and Faber, 1961).

Street, Jessie, *Truth or Repose* (Sydney: Australasian Book Society, 1966).

Tennant, Kylie, *Evatt: Politics and Justice* (Sydney: Angus and Robertson, 1981 [1970]).

——— 'Dr H.V. Evatt: The Man and His Times', *Journal of the Royal Australian Historical Society*, 59: 1 (1973), 52–67.

Trades Union Congress, *The Book of the Martyrs of Tolpuddle, 1834–1934* (London: Trades Union Congress, 1934).

Turney, Clifford, Ursula Bygott and Peter Chippendale, *Australia's First: A History of the University of Sydney, vol. 1, '1850–1939'* (Sydney: University of Sydney and Hale & Iremonger, 1991).

Twining, William, 'The Rationalist Tradition of Evidence Scholarship', and 'Legal Reasoning and Argumentation', in *Rethinking Evidence: Exploratory Essays* (Cambridge: Cambridge University Press, 2006)

Ward, Russel, *A Nation for a Continent: The History of Australia, 1901–1975* (Richmond: Heinemann, 1977).

——— *A Radical Life: The Autobiography of Russel Ward* (South Melbourne: Macmillan, 1988).

Warhurst, John, 'Catholics, Communism and the Australian Party System: A Study of the Menzies Years', *Politics*, 14: 2 (1979).

Waters, Christopher, 'Anglo-Australian Conflict over the Cold War: H.V. Evatt as President of the UN General Assembly, 1948–9', *Journal of Imperial and Commonwealth History*, 22: 2 (1994).

——— *The Empire Fractures: Anglo–Australian Conflict in the 1940s* (Melbourne: Australian Scholarly Publishing, 1995).

——— 'The Great Debates: H.V. Evatt and the Department of External Affairs, 1941–49', in Joan Beaumont, Christopher Waters and David Lowe (eds), *Ministers, Mandarins and Diplomats: Australian Foreign Policy Making, 1941–1969* (Melbourne: Melbourne University Publishing, 2003)

Watt, Alan, *The Evolution of Australian Foreign Policy, 1938–1965* (London: Cambridge University Press, 1968).

——— *Australian Diplomat: Memoirs of Sir Alan Watt* (Sydney: Angus and Robertson, 1972).

Bibliography

Webb, Leicester, *Communism and Democracy in Australia: A Survey of the 1951 Referendum* (Melbourne: Cheshire, 1954).

Weller, Patrick (ed.), *Caucus Minutes, 1901–1949: Minutes of the Meetings of the Federal Parliamentary Labor Party, vol. 3, '1932–1949',* (Melbourne: Melbourne University Press, 1975).

Weller, Patrick and Beverley Lloyd (eds), *Federal Executive Minutes, 1915–1955: Minutes of the Meetings of the Federal Executive of the Australian Labor Party* (Melbourne: Melbourne University Press, 1978.

Whitlam, Nicholas and John Stubbs, *Nest of Traitors: The Petrov Affair* (Milton: The Jacaranda Press, 1974).

Zogbaum, Heidi, *Kisch in Australia: The Untold Story* (Melbourne: Scribe Publications, 2004).

Index

Aarons, Eric 282
Advisory War Council (AWC) 31, 174–6, 179–180, 211
anti-communism 2–3, 151–2, 262–4, 269–72, 299–301, 302–3, 308, 329, 335, 346, 349, 353, 360, 365
anti-Grouper forces 301, 304, 323–6, 330–2
Alderman, Harry 326
America, United States of 52, 123, 127–8, 131, 133, 158–9, 185–91, 206–7, 225, 269, 292, 301, 378
    Australian Minister to 158, 186, 261, 387, 388
    isolationism 125, 178–9, 185–6, 201
    war strategy 185–6, 205
        post-war strategy and policy 218–9, 222, 227, 244, 250–4
Anderson, Francis 35, 45–6, 386
Anglican church 15, 19, 27–8, 44, 107, 305, 380
Aranha, Oswaldo 252
Argus, The (Melbourne) editorial comment on Evatt 94, 218
    endorses 'no' vote in CPA referendum 283
Asia 178, 185, 190, 215–6, 229, 250–1
Askin, Robert 374
Atkinson, Alan 145
Atlantic Charter (1941) 179, 200, 214
Atyeo, Sam 114–5, 122–3, 225, 254, 386
Australian Academy of Art 129–131
Australian Broadcasting Commission 57, 223
Australian Council of Trade Unions (ACTU) ix, 327, 331, 334
Australia First Movement 201–2
Australian Labor Party *see* Labor party
Australian Labor Party (Anti-Communist) 335 *see also* Democratic Labor Party
Australian Labor Party (Official) 345
Australian-New Zealand Agreement 218–9
Australian Security Intelligence Organisation (ASIO) 254, 307, 313, 350
Australian Women's Weekly see *Women's Weekly*
Australian Worker 95, 324, 386
Australian Workers Union (AWU) 95, 262, 271, 298, 324–5, 345, 386
Baddeley, John 85
Bailey, Kenneth 103, 259, 386
Baillieu, W.L. 114, 190
Baldwin, Stanley 81
Balfour Declaration 198–9

Ball, William Macmahon 251
Balmain 33, 72–5, 85, 87, 107, 112
    Cricket Club 17, 87, 89, 112
    Rugby League club 57, 76, 170
Balson, Ralph 132
bank nationalisation 241, 258–60
Baracchi, Guido 51
Barrington, Fourness 59
Barwick, Garfield 258, 260, 276
Bass, Tom 357–8
Bavin, Tom 85, 87
Beasley, Jack 97–8, 162–3, 170, 175, 177, 187, 279, 380, 386
Beazley, Kim snr 3–4, 264–5, 355–6, 368, 386
Bell, George 115, 130
Ben-Gurion, David 253
Berlin blockade 256–7, 260
Bligh, Governor William 27, 140–6, 154
Boote, Henry 95, 157, 162–6, 168, 172, 174, 177–9, 185, 200, 324, 386
Bourdieu, Pierre 68
Bourke, Bill 309, 316, 321, 325, 328, 331, 335, 337, 386
Boyer, Richard 223
Bracken, Brendan 199, 207, 259, 317, 354–5, 386
Brennan, Frank 93
Brennan, John 120–1, 364, 377, 387
Brennan, Keith 6–8, 36, 45, 120, 146, 365, 387
Brett, Judith 269
Britain
    Australian High Commissioner (London) 21, 194, 207–9, 386, 387
    Australian independence from 104, 184, 198
    bipartisan War Cabinet 105, 157, 181, 193, 195, 197–8
    Commonwealth 184, 220, 226–7, 233, 244
    Dominions Office 245, 254
    empire 14, 24, 38, 151–2, 169, 184, 187, 190, 197, 199, 220, 232–3, 238, 247
    High Commissioner (Canberra) 187, 193, 205, 219, 224
    Labour party 105, 157, 159, 312
    Ministry of Information 195, 199, 386
    press reaction to Evatt 195, 198
Bruce, Stanley Melbourne 21, 194, 207–8, 210, 230, 238, 387
Buckland, George 162–3, 174

442

Buckley, Ken 5, 72, 369
Bukowski, Joe 324, 345
Burgmann, Bishop Ernest 105–6, 156, 305, 381, 387
Burke, Tom 270, 274–6, 311, 328, 387
Burton, John 205, 224–6, 247, 256, 283, 346, 349, 387
Buttrose, Charles 165, 174, 243

Cahill, Joe 85, 344, 354, 373, 387
Cain, John snr 332, 335
Cairns, Jim 352
Calwell, Arthur 24, 92, *117*, 168, 249, 277, 279–80, 282, 311, *333*, 324, 373, 380, 387
    Evatt, relations with 24, 281, 327, 340, *376*
Cameron, Clyde 168, 262, 265–6, 270, 273, 274–5, 276, 278–9, 287, 298, 321, 324–5, 328, 330–4, 337–8, 340, 343, 387
Campbell, Andrew 361–2
Canada 137, 184, 191–4, 203, 387
Cantwell, Ida and H.J. 80–1, 113, 115, 192
Carrick, John 284, 346–7, 360, 387
Carrington Coal and Coke Shipping Union 64
Carrodus, Peter 305, 379
Casablanca conference (1943) 205
Casey, Maie 115, 387
Casey, Richard 115, 186, 210, 387
Catholic Action 262, 308 *see also* 'Movement'
Catholic Social Studies Movement *see* 'Movement'
Catholicism 38, 151–2, 279, 283, 300–3
    anti-Catholicism 283, 299, 324–6, 339, 355
    anti-communism 152, 262, 275, 303
    church hierarchy 263–4, 301, 303, 324, 342
    political influence 299, 324
    voters 295, 338, 346, 353, 360
Catholic Worker 301
Chamberlain, Frank 3, 24, 307–8, 311, 314–5, 324, 381, 388
Chamberlain, Joe 274, 304, 331–4, 340–3, 354, 359, 388
Chamberlain, Neville 123, 157
Chifley, Ben 10, 21, 66, 183, 213, 221, 242, 244, 258–61, 264, 266, 272–6, 278–9, 309, 337, 340, 342, 388
    concern about succession 278–9
    relations with Evatt 78, 163, 176–8, 249, 251–2, 276, 279
    invoked by Evatt 286, 290–2, 295, 299–300, 301
child endowment 78, 85
Childe, Vere Gordon 39–40, 45, 49, 54, 70, 150, 153–4, 358, 388
China 191, 200, 227, 229, 262, 269, 282, 299, 302, 334
Christian Socialists 106, 156
Churchill, Winston 47, 105, 157, 159, 181, 188, 205
    Atlantic Charter 178–9, 214
    relations with Evatt 186–8, 192–3, 195–9, 205–6, 209, 213, 227

    promises Spitfires 197–8, 203–4
civil liberties 48, 127, 163, 201–2, 264, 287, 378, 381
Clarey, Percy 327–8
Clark, Manning 25
Cleland, Don 284
Clements, K.J. 381
Clune, Frank 322
coal strike 261, 264–5, 271, 298
Cohen, Ben 129, 158
Cold War 1, 5, 202, 251, 253, 255–8, 262, 266, 268–9, 271, 307, 358,
    Evatt's misjudgements during 342, 349, 365, 371
Cole, George 327–9
Coles, Arthur 182
Collingwood Football Club 170
Collins, Herbie 80–1
Collins, Wilfred 377
Comintern 100, 312
Commonwealth powers 65–6, 99, 103–4
    Evatt's attempts to expand 184, 202–3, 216–8
communism 2, 87, 265, 266, 268–70, 277, 281, 291–2, 302, 310, 346
Communist Party Dissolution Bill / Act 271–2, 321
    definition of 'communist' 272, 289–90, 329–30
    divisions within the ALP 273, 282–3
    constitutional challenge to 274–6
    Evatt's initial position 273
    referendum 9, 86, 278, 280–7, *280*, *285*, 294–5, 299, 308, 323, 337
    CPA role in referendum 281–2, 337
Communist Party of Australia 262, 298, 337
    banning of 86, 99–100, 157, 202, 264–5, 268, 271–2, 274, 276
    control of Miners' Federation 261, 264–5
Conscription (1916–1917) 43, 149, 150–2
    Evatt's apparent support for 38–9
constitutional change *see* Commonwealth powers *and* Westminster, Statute of
Contemporary Art Society 130–1, 356
Cooke, Alistair 234, 236
Coombs, H.C. 'Nugget' 205, 207–8
Country party 174, 181, 211, 216, 265, 271, 305
Cox, Harold 230, 276
Cranborne, Lord 21, 219–20, 230, 232–4, 388
Cripps, Stafford 104–5
Crisp, Finlay 173, 175, 177–8, 181, 260, 346, 426
Crockett, Peter 5, 18, 24, 225, 356, 369
Cross, Sir Ronald 187, 388
Crowley, Grace 115–16, 132
Cullen, William 38, 39, 49–50, 388
Curtin, John 31, 79, 153, 172–6, 181–3, 186, 188–9, 194–6, 198, 203, 205, 219, 242–4, 301, 380, 388
    relations with Evatt 176–9, 187, 210–3, 224–6, 279

Daly, Fred 278, 318, 328, 330, 337, 340, 342, 368, 375, 388

Dalziel, Allan 5, 156, 267, 313–4, 320, 325, 370, 380, 388
Darwin 185, 203–4, 308
Day, David 224
Deakin, Alfred 10, 47–8
decolonisation 215–6, 250–1
Dedman, John 279
Democratic Labor Party (DLP) 2, 344–5, 353, *359*, 359–60
Depression, the 89, 91, 96, 98–9, 106, 112, 213, 220, 258
Devanny, Francis 99
Dixon, Owen 92, 95, 120–1, 165, 276, 388
dominion status 126, 135, 137–8, 184, 198–9, 233–4, 238, 245, 254
Dougherty, Tom 271, 304, 324–5, 340, 388
Douglas, Irvine 89
Downing, Reg 163, 316, 373, 375, 378–9, 388
Drakeford, Arthur 204
Duffy, Frank Gavan 92, 94–6, 98–9, 161
Dumbarton Oaks conference 227, 232, 234
Duncan, Bruce 301
Dunstan, Albert 216
Dutch in Indonesia 185, 216, 251–2
Duthie, Gil 308, 317, 321, 326–8, 330–1, 388

Eden, Anthony 229–30
Eggleston, Frederic 230, 238–9, 241
Ellis, M.H. 142
Else-Mitchell, Rae 369
Engels, Frederich 39, 155
Engineers' Case 65–6
Evatt, Clive (brother) 14, 26, 27, 37, 42, 99, 344, 389
Evatt, Frank (brother) 14, 27–28, 36, 40–43, 45, 51, 171, 236, 250
Evatt, George (brother) 14, 27
Evatt, Herbert Vere
general
  biographies of 5–6
  funeral 380
  Mitchell Library 119, 141, 162, 386
  music 11, 44, 61, 305
  sport 17-19, 21–2, 30–1, 34, 37, 73, 80–1, 87, 89, 112, 122
childhood
  birth 16
  family background 22–3, 45
  father and 'father figures' 20–1, 23, 32, 95, 279, 362, 381
  mother, influence of 19–20, 26, 31–3, 44, 67–8, 109, 171–2, 381
education
  ability and prizes 20, 26, 30–1, 33–7, 42, 49, 144, 155
  Fort Street High School 21, 25–31, 33, 45, 57, 95, 161, 307, 390
  University of Sydney 31–41, 42, 67–8, 291

  academic record 35–7, 67
  editor of *Hermes* 38, 44
  president of Undergraduates Association and University Union 37
  Rhodes scholarship committee 36, 49
  St Andrew's College 31, 34, 39
personal characteristics
  ambition 7–8, 25–6, 174, 176–8, 181–2, 187, 212–3, 239, 243, 258, 322, 364, 382
  as a (neglectful) correspondent 11, 31, 54–7, 60–2, 105, 109–10, 124–5, 193, 299, 326
  assertiveness 186–7, 191, 197, 200, 205, 207, 227–8, 238–9, 247
  eccentricities 1, 259, 277, 362
  fear of flying 54, 189, 194, 225–6, 362
  friendships 6, 18, 39, 51, 57, 58, 80, 89, 105, 112, 114–5, 122, 124, 137, 156, 166, 170, 176, 192, 326, 347, 357–8 364–5, 378, 380
  generosity and charity 112
  humour 146, 199, 236
  impact of death of brothers 41–5, 182, 236–8
  intellectual talent 8, 35, 63–4, 68–9, 155, 227, 365
  lack of self-awareness 10–12, 354, 380
  memory 18, 260, 370
  physical descriptions 31, 49, 52, 114, 133, 168, 187, 201, 210, 356–7, 380
  prudery 115, 197
  self-regard and narcissism 8–9, 171, 362–5, *363*, 371, 382
  suspicion and mistrust 8–9, 160, 306–7, 313, 319–20, 338, 361–5, *366*, 378–9
  treatment of staff 113, 313
  voice 22, 63, 75–6, 210, 286–94, 305
marriage and private life
  adoption of children 57–8, 61–2, 108
  as a father 90, 108–10, 175, 193–4, 209, 305–6
  domestic life 54, 73–5, 79, 90, 106–8, 110–1, 113–4, 171, 320
  influence of Mary Alice 54–5, 71, 78, 107, 156, 189, 201, 206–7, 226, 249, 268, 382
  houses
    Beecroft 90, 106
    Canberra 379
    East St Kilda 110, 113–4
    first flat, Mosman 54
    Grove Street, Balmain 87
    Hay Street, Leichhardt 75
    'Kelmscott', Leura 90, 106, 108, 110–11, 177
    Milton Avenue, Mosman 60, 62
    'Nuuanu', Mosman 52, 62, 74, 106–7, 110–11, 166–7, 171, 225, 325, 380
  library, personal 27, 54, 46, 107, 155
  marriage 11, 51–5, 62, 90
  private papers 11, 54–5
  wealth 52, 110–2, 130, 166, 379
health and decline
  health 31, 175, 212, 261, 368–70, 372, 379

cerebral arteriosclerosis 368–9, 370–1
dementia 370–1, 377, 379
state of mind 317–20, 338, 350, 361–2, 367–8, 371

law
appointed King's Counsel 88
appointed law lecturer 54, 67
constitutional law, commitment to 37, 53, 65–7, 89, 103, 105, 126–7, 136–40, 220–1, 228, 239, 281, 305
early appearances in High Court 64–7, 88–9
legal practice 49–50, 64–7, 88–9
legal reasoning, faith in 9–10, 68–9, 143–6, 221, 239, 294, 322, 382–3
legal reasoning, talent for 9–10, 67–9, 294, 341, 365, 382–3
performance in the law 63–4, 68

High Court
appointment 30, 89, 91–6
associates 6, 45, 49, 120–1, 135, 387
Devanny and Kisch cases 99–102
farewell 169–70
law lectures in America 124–6
Lang challenges 98–9, 139
Latham, relations with 21, 120–21, 124, 159–61
sabbatical leave 122, 148
relations with other judges 119–21, 159–61
restlessness 152, 157, 161–2
rumours of appointment to Washington 156–8, 186

writings
Australian Labour Leader 39–40, 43, 106, 147–54, 165, 168
bias as historian 141–3, 145–6, 380
Hughes, planned biography of 21, 156, 249
Injustice within the law 135–6
juvenile writings 20, 28
Liberalism in Australia 37, 46–9, 73–5, 78, 150
poetry 20, 44, 51
Rum Rebellion 27, 134–5, 140–47, 153–4, 380
'Social and Political Tendencies in Australia' (MA thesis) 37
'The 1917 Strike and the Aftermath' (pamphlet) 67
The King and His Dominion Governors 67, 135–40, 154
writing habits 135

art and cultural life
art, modernism 11, 107–8, 114–9, *117*, 123, 129–33, 356–8
Australian Academy of Art 129–31
Contemporary Art Society 130–1, 356
literary taste 117–8, 260

politics
ALP membership 70–1, 87, 162, 345–6
election campaigns
Balmain 87

Barton 166, 169, 172–3, 211, 214, 248–9, 266, 353
Hunter 359
expulsion and Independent Labor candidate (1927) 87–8
Mosman branch 70–2, 346
NSW Fighting Platform Committee 72
preselection 33, 48, 71–4, 86–7, 162–3, 165
relationship with labour movement 75, 154, 340–1
return to politics (1940) 116, 123, 152, 155–8, 161–5, 168, 171

political relationships
Bruce, relations with 21, 194, 207–8, 210, 238–9
Calwell, relations with 24, 168, 327, 340
Chifley, relations with 10, 21, 66, 78, 163, 176–8, 249, 251–2, 261, 275–6, 278–9
Churchill, relations with 187–8, 187–8, 192–3, 195–9, 200, 205–6, 209, 213, 227
Cranborne, relations with 21, 219–20, 230, 232–4
Curtin, relations with 79–80, 153, 171, 173–81, 198, 201, 205, 210–12, 224–25
Forde, relations with 176, 224–6, 229–31, 236, 243
Lang, relations with 78, 84–7, 138–40, 162–3, 165
Menzies, relations with 3, 10, 12, 25, 65–6, 69, 93–4, 101–2, 120–1, 129–30, 158, 162, 164, 172, 179–80, 216–8, 247, 249, 282, 286–94, 307, 309, 313, 316, 348–352, 374, 380–1
Roosevelt, relations with 125–8, 133, 158, 188, 192, 199, 201, 205, 219

political views
Anderson, influence of 35, 45–6
Childe, influence of 39–40, 45, 49, 54, 70, 150, 153–4, 358
civil liberties 127, 163, 201–2, 264, 287, 358
detachment from Labor traditions 49, 155, 162, 281
lack of interest in Marxism 39, 155
liberalism 10, 25, 39, 45–9, 68–69, 70, 74–5, 92, 148, 154–5, 221, 281, 292
Evatt criticised for endorsing 49, 73–5, 78, 281
Labor as the continuation of 49, 78, 155
patriotism / nationalism 45, 168–9, 182, 186–7, 200, 235, 239, 383
political development 10, 39, 46, 47, 69, 156
secularism 44, 45, 152, 300
socialism 22, 31, 39, 48, 52, 82, 90, 106, 110, 123, 149, 152–53, 155–6, 283
totalitarianism 86, 284–5, 287, 289–91, 292–4, 300, 325

internationalist views
champion of smaller nations 228, *231*, 236
early repudiation of 83
embrace as foreign minister 185, 239

evolving interest in 102–3
internationalism as a 'new province' 221, 234, 239
League of Nations 78, 83, 102–4, 198, 215,
    220–2, 232, 235
liberal internationalism 185, 256
realism in international affairs 239, 258
as Attorney-General
bank nationalisation case 258–9
constitutional change 183–4, 202–3, 216–8, 250
legislative initiatives 183–4
Privy Council appeal 241–2, 258–60
reliance on McKenna 242
as foreign minister
as president of General Assembly 252–6, 261,
    384
Australian-New Zealand agreement 218–9
'beat Hitler first' strategy 186, 195, 198
decolonisation 215–6, 250–1
Department of External Affairs 205, 215, 254,
    256
expansion of 'security zone' 216, 218
international social justice 221–2
Japan, advocates punitive treaty 250
ministerial statements 215, 220
Paris Peace conference 245–7
Preparatory Commission of UN 244
reputation 187, 191–2, 196, 237, 248, 341
San Francisco conference 104, 220, 222–3, 224,
    226–30, 232–6, 238–40, 241–4, 250–1, 294,
    341, 380
Commonwealth delegates' meeting, London
    226–8
travel to America 185–7, 191–2, 199, 205–6,
    225, 241
travel to Britain 79–82, 122, 192–3, 195–6, 198,
    206–9, 226, 241, 244, 253, 260
see also World War Two *and* United Nations
as ALP leader
blamed for the split 281, 300, 323, 325, 335–40,
    336, 342–3, 354–6
Cold War, Evatt's misjudgements during *315*,
    342, 349, 354, 371
Communist Party Act challenge 274–6
considers leaving politics (1946 and 1950) 248–9,
    267–8, 382
deputy leader 174, 250
leadership 12, 173, 244, 278–81, 298–9, 337,
    340–2, 354, 359, 372
leadership challenges 281, 311, 326–31, 354
leadership flaws 337, 340–2, 382
as NSW Chief Justice
appointment fiasco 373–7, *376*
opinions of other judges 377–8
Evatt, Jeanie (Jane Sophia) (mother) 14–6, 27–8,
    36, 37, 43, 60–1, 72
ambition for sons 19–20, 26–7, 29, 32–3, 68,
    109, 306

Evatt, John (brother) 14
Evatt, John Ashmore Hamilton (father) 14, 15,
    16–8, 20
Evatt, Mary Alice
general
appearance 52, 76, 167, 210
artist 114–6, 122–3, 126, 210
art, modernism 107, 113–4, 116, 122, 124, 130,
    245–6, 260, 357
education 53–4
parents 51–2, 111
National Gallery of NSW, trustee 210
reading 54, 55, 90
marriage and private life
adoption of children 57–8, 61–2, 108
domestic life 54, 73–5, 79, 90, 106–8, 110–1,
    113–4, 171, 320
later interview comments about Evatt 18, 19–20,
    26, 29–30, 35, 41, 44, 49, 53–4, 68, 75, 80, 106,
    144, 147, 155–6, 179–80, 188–9, 249, 255, 268,
    286, 320, 368, 384
influence with Evatt 71, 74–6, 79, 107, 156, 201,
    226, 249, 268, 382
journal 73–6, 79
correspondence 51, 55, 60–2, 71
health crisis and infertility 56–60
marriage 11, 51–53, 62, 73, 90
protective of Evatt 320, 369, 377–8, 380, 384–5
wealth 52, 110–2, 130, 166, 379
politics
newsreel appearances 167, 210
political engagement 51–2, 81, 107, 156, 174,
    192, 201, 254, 320
political campaigning 33, 73–6, 78–9, 305
public speaking 210, 230
William Morris 52, 90
Evatt, Peter (son) 31, 57–8, 61, 79, 90, 108–10, 122,
126, 171–2, 175, 193, 209–10, 306
Evatt, Ray (brother) 14, 28, 36, 40–3, 45, 51, 236,
250
Evatt, Rosalind (daughter) 57, 61, 108, 110, 122,
    171, 189, 193, 209–10, 225, 241, 247, 253–4,
    260, 305–6, 320, 379
external affairs
Burton, John 205, 224, 247, 283
constitutional power over 103, 217–8
Department of 215, 254, 256
Hasluck, Paul 215, 426

Fadden, Arthur 181, 211, 212–3, 305, 310, 389
fascism 86, 91, 100, 102, 105, 123, 125, 136, 155–7,
    159, 200, 202, 220, 285, 291, 294, 339
Federated Ironworkers' Association 298
Ferguson, Jack 264, 267–8, 273, 275, 279–80, 283,
    295, 298, 340, 389
Financial Agreement Enforcement Act 97–9, 139
First World War *see* World War One

Fitzgerald, Joe 329
Fitzpatrick, Brian 149, 347–8, 378
Fizelle, Rah 115–6, 132
Forde, Frank 175–6, 224–6, 229–31, 236, 243–4, 249, 389
Frankfurter, Felix 124, 125–9, 133, 188, 199, 240, 252–3, 389
    advises Roosevelt about Evatt 190–2, 200, 286
freedom 46, 105, 127, 133, 202, 284, 288, 299–300, 310, 358 *see also* liberty
Frith, John 258

Gair, Vince 345
Game, Sir Phillip 139–40
Gollancz, Victor 148
Gowrie, Lord 200
Grattan, Hartley Clifton 6–8, 11, 12, 21, 24, 26, 58, 104, 117–8, 126, 148, 155–6, 186–7, 191–2, 195, 213, 242, 261, 267–8, 322, 341, 378, 382, 389
Gray, John Thomas 15, 27
Green, Frank 275
Green, T. H. 10, 46, 47
Griffith, Samuel 92
Gromyko, Andrei 229, 236
Groupers 263–4, 270–4, 280, 295–6, 298–9, 301–2, 304, 307, 311, 323–5, 330–5, 338–9, 340, 344–7, 352, 356, 361, 367, 373 *see also* Movement
Grundeman, Albert 313–4
Gullett, 'Jo' 278
Gwydir by-election 305

Haese, Richard 114, 129
Halifax, Lord 191–2, 206, 230, 233, 234, 238, 389
Hall, Bernard 114
Hancock, Ian 266, 278
Hankinson, Walter 219, 234
Hasluck, Paul 6, 68, 215, 220, 224–8, 230–1, 238, 252, 362, 380, 389, 426
Haylen, Les 3–4, 18, 21, 26, 31, 110, 171, 173, 225, 249, 277, 279, 287, 294, 307, 325, 356, 369–70, 375, 377, 389
Healy, Jim 275
Heffron, Robert 373
Heide 114–5, 130, 356, 391
Heiser, Ron 348
Higgins, Henry Bournes 10, 47–8, 64, 78, 91–2, 126, 133, 154, 169, 221, 389–90
High Court 8–10, 30–1, 38, 45, 64–5, 67, 88–9, 167, 183
    patterns of appointments 92
    political role 96, 98–99, 217–8, 258–9, 274–6, 289
    tensions between judges 119–21, 159–61
    see also Evatt, High Court
Hinder, Frank 116, 132, 170
Holloway, Jack 279
Holman, Ada 147

Holman, William 21, 23, 38–40, 43, 106, 147–54, 165, 168, 339
Holocaust 250, 252
Holt, Edgar 284, 297, 352–3, 389
Holt, Harold 164
Hopkins, Harry 192
How Labour Governs 39–40, 150, 153–4, 358
Hughes, Billy 21, 23, 38–9, 48, 53, 92, 147–153, 156, 173, 190, 211–3, 247, 339, 355, 379
    advises Churchill about Evatt 192–3
Hull, Cordell 219
Hunter River Steam Navigation Company 14–5, 27

India 14, 227, 229, 251, 254
Indonesia 185, 216, 251–2, 257
Industrial Groups *see* Groupers
industrial strikes 21, 51, 66–7, 77, 81, 261, 264–6, 271, 298
international conventions 82–3, 103–4, 217
International Court of Justice (world court) 221, 228, 234–5
International Labour Organization 80, 82–3, 103–4
Isaacs, Isaac 10, 64, 91–2, 94, 169
Israel 245, 252–53, 255–6, 372

Jackson, Alice 229–30
Japan 123, 125, 185–6, 188–90, 195, 197–8, 202–4, 205, 208, 210, 215, 229, 241, 243, 244, 248, 250
Jewish Council to Combat Fascism and Anti-Semitism 282
'Joshua-Keon group' 335–6

Kaiser Victory ships 230–1
Kane, Jack 338–9, 346
Kennelly, Pat 271, 273, 280, 302, 304, 323–4, 331–4, 340–4, 354, 390
Keon, Stan 3, 270, 283, 302, 321, 328–32, 335, 343, 348, 352, 390
Kisch, Egon 100–2
Kilgour, Alexander James 26, 29–30, 95, 136–7, 377, 390
Kirby, Michael 378
Knox, Adrian 64, 92
Korean war 269

Labor Daily 67, 73, 78
Labor Leagues *see* Political Labor Leagues
Labor party viii–xi
    branches
        Canberra 345–6
        New South Wales 84, 97, 147–8, 162–3, 263–4, 267, 271, 273, 283–4, 298, 304, 324, 334, 340, 342–5, 354, 373–5
        Queensland 273, 283–4, 298, 304, 324, 334, 345
        South Australia 283–4, 273, 298, 343
        Tasmania 273, 283–4, 326, 334
        Victoria 270, 273, 283–4, 298, 304, 323, 325,

331–2, 334–5, 342–3, 345, 353
Western Australia 273–4, 283–4, 298, 334
conferences 173, 304, 323–4, 332, 334
divisions over banning the Communist party
    273, 282–3
federal executive 162, 165, 267, 273–4, 283,
    295–6, 299, 323, 325, 326–7, 331–32, 342, 351
federal parliamentary executive (shadow cabinet)
    316, 327
origins, loyalty and the pledge 22–5, 40, 47, 75,
    148, 150
split (1916) 38–9, 149, 150–3, 212, 355
split (1931) 97–8, 119, 212, 317, 355
split (1955) 12, 152, 268, 272, 299–300, 303–4,
    314, 323–5, 333, 334–40, 336, 342–6, 352–6,
    359, 375
Lang, Jack 76–8, 84–7, 90, 96–9, 138–40, 162–3,
    184, 186, 344–5, 390
'Lang Labor' 97, 162, 165, 175
Laski, Harold 104–5, 148
Latham, John 21, 83, 119–22, 124, 159–61, 164–6,
    259, 276, 390
Lenin 85–6, 272, 289
Lewis, Essington 190
Liberal party 217, 264–6, 271, 297, 352, 360, 374
    election advertisements 277, 309–10, 337
    federal secretariat 274, 278, 284, 297, 303, 310,
        346–7, 360
liberalism 10, 25, 39, 45–9, 68–9, 70, 74–5, 78, 92,
    148, 154–5, 221, 281, 292,
liberty 46–7, 105, 118, 132–33, 142, 202, 268, 273,
    284, 287, 355, 358, 381
Lie, Trygve 256
Lockwood, Rupert 313, 317
Lovegrove, Dinny 263, 332, 343, 390
Lyons, Joseph 97, 98, 100, 102, 119, 158, 212–3, 355

Macarthur, John 140, 142–3, 145, 154
MacArthur, General Douglas 185, 188, 198, 201,
    250
MacDonald, J.S. 130
Maitland 15–25, 61
    Bank Hotel 16, 27, 28
    East Maitland 15, 17, 22, 61
    'Evatt High School' 18
    Hunter River Hotel 15
Makin, Norman 175, 244, 261, 279
mandates (trusteeship) 102–4, 227, 229, 232–3, 238,
    250, 252–3
Mannix, Archbishop Daniel 151–2, 263, 296,
    301–2, 360
Marshall, General George 206
Martin, Allan 349
Martin, Clarrie 267
Matheson, Anne 245
Marx, Karl 39, 148, 155, 272, 289
Masaryk, Jan 247

McCarthyism 269, 313, 322, 358
    see also anti-communism
McConnell, John 284, 304, 346, 390
McEwen, John 242
McGirr, Jim 267
McIlwraith, Frank 158
McKay, Claude 66, 72, 164, 168, 390
McKell, William 163
McKenna, Nick 242
McManus, Frank 332, 346, 355
McMullin, Ross ix, 84
McTiernan, Edward 76–7, 85, 91–6, 98, 119–20,
    139, 259, 276, 390
means test policy 308–10, 325, 338
Melbourne
    art scene 114–6, 129–31, 356–8
    High Court sittings 94, 108, 113, 120
Menzies, Robert 117, 359, 390
    anti-communism 151, 157, 202, 265–6, 268,
        270–4, 276–8, 284, 296, 307, 310, 313, 337, 365
    as UAP Attorney-General 100, 120–1
    comparisons with Evatt 10, 25, 69, 286, 304, 337
    critical of Evatt's foreign policy 247, 249
    Communist Party referendum 281–2, 286–7, 295
    cultivates Lyons 97
    engineers' case 65–6
    Evatt offers to collaborate 180–1
    on Australian Academy of Art 115, 119, 129–30
    on Evatt's High Court appointment 93–4
    on Evatt's resignation from High Court 164, 172
    proposes a national government with Labor
        173–4, 177, 179, 181
    opposes attempts to expand Commonwealth
        powers 216–8
    Petrov defection and Royal Commission 308,
        310, 313, 347
    reflects on Evatt's state of mind 312, 349–52, 361
    response to Evatt's Molotov speech 3, 12,
        349–52
    rivalry with Evatt 12, 120–1, 307, 309, 349–52,
        374, 381, 382
migration policy see White Australia policy
Miller, Douglas 369
Milsons Point 27–8, 45, 107
Miners' Federation 261, 265, 298
Mitchell Library 119, 141, 162, 386
Modigliani, Amadeo 11, 122, 124, 130, 132–3, 379
modernism 11, 107–8, 114–5, 117–8, 129–33, 155,
    356–8
Molotov, Vyacheslav 201, 229, 236, 245–46, 390
    Evatt's Molotov letter speech 1–4, 7, 9, 348–52,
        367–8
Moodie, Colin 379
Morpeth Review 105, 387
'Movement', the 263, 300–303, 325, 342, 353, 391,
    392
    see also Groupers

Index

Movement Against War and Fascism 100
Mullens, John 270, 328–9, 331, 335, 343, 348, 391
Murdoch, Keith 130, 388
Murray, Robert 299, 311, 334, 338, 361
Mussolini, Benito 85–6, 285
Mutch, Tom 84–5, 87–8
Myers, S.G. 377–8
Myerson, Emanuel 66

Nairn, Bede 76
'national government' proposals 157, 161, 165,
    173–4, 177–181, 211–3
National Gallery Art School 114
national security regulations 202
Nationalist party 38, 48, 70, 77, 82, 85, 87, 97, 119,
    149, 150, 328, 355, 387
Nazis 101, 118, 123, 157, 158, 178, 265, 283, 285,
    312
New Caledonia 216
New Guinea 185, 206, 216
    Australian mandate over 102–4, 232
New Hebrides (Vanuatu) 216
New South Wales
    Groupers 271, 298, 304
    Labor cabinet (1959–60) 373–4
    Labor Leagues 23, 70, 148
    Labor party 38, 40, 148, 150, 162, 243, 264, 273,
        282–3, 354
    parliament 8, 33, 38, 70, 74–8, 83, 86–8, 148
    Supreme Court 12, 96, 267, 369, 371, 373–5,
        376, 377–80
    Trades and Labor Council ix, 74, 174, 375
newsreels 167–8, 200–1, 203–4, 210, 314
News Weekly 283, 296, 299, 317, 325, 329
New Zealand 126, 180, 191, 195, 218–9, 224, 227,
    232, 238
Niall, Brenda 152
Niemöller, Pastor Martin 288, 291
Noad, Kenneth 369

Ockerby, V.L. 304
O'Reilly, Bill 122
Ormonde, Jim 170, 300–1, 324–5, 391
O'Sullivan, Fergan 313–14, 317–18, 322
O'Sullivan, T.J. 74
Owen, Justice W. 316–17

Pacific, south-west 218–9, 250
Packer, Clyde 66
Page, Earle 186, 211
Palestine 252–3, 255–6
Palmer, Nettie 31, 116, 119, 133, 156, 161, 170, 391
Palmer, Vance 123, 149, 155, 161, 165, 391
Paris 122–3, 254, 259, 341
Paris Peace conference 241, 244–6, 249
Pearl Harbor 189
Pearson, Drew 235

Petrov
    Documents 2, 312–7, 348, 351–2
    Evatt's handling of 2–3, 9, 297, 307, 312–8, *319*,
        322, 325, 338, 347, 348, 351, 361, *366*, 367–8,
        374–5, 381
    Evdokia 307–8
    royal commission *see* royal commission on
        espionage
    Vladimir, defection of 2, 25, 25, 268, 307, 310–12
Phillips, Gilbert 369
Picasso 11, 122
Piddington, A.B. 92, 101–2, 164
Platz, Ernest 282
Political Labor Leagues (NSW) 33, 70–1, 148
Porter, Hubert 57, 89
postwar reconstruction 202, 205, 216, 222, 249–50
Premiers' Plan 97, 107, 317
Preston-Stanley, Millicent 77
Prichard, Katherine Susannah 355
Pringle, John Douglas 367
Privy Council 79, 81–2, 98–9
    bank nationalisation case 241–2, 258–60
progressive liberalism *see* liberalism
Protestantism 38, 300, 303, 338–9, 346
    see also sectarianism

Queensland 65, 92, 97, 139–40, 273, 283–4, 295,
    298, 324, 334, 345–6, 353, 360

radio broadcasts (by Evatt) 195
    Bondi speech 281–2, 286–94
    Molotov letter speech 4, 348–9
railway strike, NSW (1917) 51, 66–7, 77, 275
Railways Union 264, 275
Rainaud's restaurant 77, 165
Reed, Cynthia (Nolan) 114, 391
Reed, John 114–5, 130, 133, 356–7, 391
Reed, Sunday 114, 122, 130, 133, 356, 391
referenda
    communist party *see Communist Party Dissolution*
        Bill / Act referendum
    expanded powers (1944) 203, 216–8
    social services (1946) 217, 250
Reichstag fire 312, 330, 348
Reid, Alan 6, 21, 45, 182, 211–2, 243, 279, 325,
    338, 391
Reid, Barrett 356–7
reserve powers of the crown 67, 135–7, 140, 154
Rich, George 38, 64, 92, 120, 276
Robinson, W.S. 189–90, 194–5, 197–9, 205, 207,
    209, 253, 259, 297, 313, 317, 354, 391
Roosevelt, Eleanor
    meeting with Mary Alice 210
    Universal Declaration of Human Rights
    255
Roosevelt, Franklin Delano
    advised about Evatt 191, 200, 206, 219

and Churchill 179, 186–8, 205, 214
death 242
relations with Evatt 125–8, 133, 158, 188, 192,
    199, 201, 205, 219
royal commission on espionage
Evatt's appearance before 1–2, 306–7, 310–8,
    315, 319, 321–2, 329, 362, 367
final report 1–2, 347–8, 350–1
rugby league 31, 34, 57, 73
Russia see Soviet Union
Ryan, T.J. 65

San Francisco conference 104, 220, 222–3, 224,
    226–30, 232–6, 238–40, 241–4, 250–1, 294,
    341, 380
Santamaria B.A. 152, 262–3, 271, 283, 299–303,
    324–5, 329, 339–40, 342, 374, 391
Sawer, Geoffrey 66, 89, 92, 184, 234–5, 251, 260
Schmella, Jack 334, 345, 354
Scullin, James 93, 95–8, 176–7
Seamen's Union 64
Second World War see World War Two
sectarianism 151–2, 300, 303, 324–6, 338–9, 374
    see also Catholicism and Protestantism
Shaw, George Bernard 90
Shedden, Frederick 224
Sheffer, Nini 90, 124–6
Sheffer, Samuel Fuller and Alice (Mary Alice's
    parents) 52, 111
Shore, Arnold 115–7
Short, Laurie 263, 298
Singapore, fall of (1942) 185, 195
Sleath, Howard 346
Slim, Sir William 374
Smith, A.V. 190
Smith, Sir Joynton 66
Smith's Weekly 66, 71–2, 79, 158, 164, 390
Solomon Islands 216
Somerville, Admiral 207
South Africa 137, 184, 227, 229
South Australia 264, 273, 283–4, 295, 298, 343
Soviet Union 85–6, 100, 178, 200–1, 222, 227, 229,
    234, 244, 246, 253, 256–7, 262, 268–9, 299,
    348, 391
Soviet intelligence 1–3, 254, 297, 307, 313, 322
Spanish Civil War 105
Spender, Percy 161–2, 265
Stalin 2, 86, 157, 159, 178, 202, 246, 268–9, 285
Starke, Hayden 92, 100–1, 120–1, 160–61, 170,
    258, 276, 391–2
Stephenson, P.R. 201–2
Stettinius, Edward 224, 235–6, 380, 391
Stone, Julius 291
Stout, Victor 263, 331–2, 335, 392
Strachey, John 104
St John the Baptist Anglican Church, Milsons Point
    28, 45, 107

St John's Anglican Church, Canberra 305, 380
St Peter's Anglican Church, East Maitland 19
Street, Jesse and Kenneth 83, 373
Suez crisis 356
Sydney Cricket Ground, trustee 17
Sydney Morning Herald editorial comment on Evatt
    94, 166, 173, 211, 238, 244, 312, 374–5

Tasmania 106, 273, 277, 283–4, 295, 298, 304, 326, 334
Tennant, Kylie 4–6, 18, 21–2, 24–5, 27, 36, 43, 57,
    80, 141, 154, 368, 384
Theodore, Ted 97, 139
Tillam, Roger 146
Truman, Harry S. 228, 292
Truth (Sydney) 85, 172

unions see Australian Workers' Union, Carrington
    Coal and Coke Shipping Union, coal strike,
    industrial strikes, Federated Ironworkers
    Association, Miners' Federation, Railways
    Union, Seamen's Union and Waterside Workers'
    Federation
United Australia Party (UAP) 97–8, 119, 156, 158,
    161, 163, 174, 176, 179, 211, 214
United Nations
    as democratic alliance in the war 199–200
    Australian ratification of charter 183, 228
    Berlin blockade 256–7
    British approach to 232, 233, 253
    Committee of Good Offices (Indonesia) 251
    eclipsed by Cold War 255–8
    Evatt as president of General Assembly 250–6,
        261, 384
    General Assembly 221, 228, 235–6, 241, 259
    International Court of Justice 221, 228, 234–5
    Israel and Palestine 252–3
    San Francisco conference 104, 220, 222–3, 224,
        226–30, 232–6, 238–40, 241–4, 250–1, 294,
        341, 380
    Security Council 221, 227–28, 248, 251, 256
    small nations 222, 227, 232, 235–6, 239, 246
    mandates and trusteeships 227, 229–30, 253
    Universal Declaration of Human Rights 255
    UNESCO (Educational, Scientific and Cultural
        Organization) 222, 235
    veto power 227, 228, 234–6, 239, 248, 256–8
University of California 224–5, 228
University of Melbourne 103, 358, 386
University of Queensland 140
University of Sydney 30–32, 33–39, 49, 67–8, 291,
    386, 388
Ure Smith, Sydney 129–30

'Venona' intelligence 254
Versailles, Treaty of 104, 190, 247
Victoria
    ALP branch 270, 273, 283–4, 298, 304, 323, 325,

Index

331–2, 334–5, 342–3, 345, 353
Cain government 332, 335
Catholics in 295, 353
Communist Party referendum result 295
DLP vote in 353, 355–6
'Movement' and 'Groupers' 262–4, 270–1, 295,
    298, 301, 304, 325–6, 332, 334–5, 342–3
Trades Hall Council 263, 331–2
Vietnam 178, 185, 250, 307
Vlaminck, Maurice de 11, 130
Vyshinsky, Andrey 246

wage arbitration 46–7, 126, 155, 221
Wake, Nancy 266
Walsh, Tom 64
Ward, Eddie 226, 277, 280, 317, 329–30, 354, 372,
    392
Ward, Russel 4, 9, 283, 348–9
Waterside Workers' Federation 274–5, 298
Watt, Andy 50, 64, 66–7, 88, 101, 392
Wentworth, William 312
Western Australia 82, 173, 178, 273–4, 283–4, 295,
    298, 311, 334, 360
Westminster, Statute of 126, 183–4, 217
White Australia policy 53, 82–3, 101, 222, 233
Whitlam, Gough 23, 139, 281, 352
Wilson, Alex 182

Wilson, Roland 224–5, 236
widows' pensions 78, 85
Windeyer, Victor 316, 318
Women's Weekly 108, 110, 122, 124, 171, 201, 210,
    229–30, 245, 254–55
Wood, Alan 15, 16
Woomera, SA 264
World Migration conference, London 81
World War One 14, 34, 37–9, 102, 151, 190, 247
    Evatt rejected as volunteer 36
    impact of death of brothers 41–5, 61, 182,
        236–8
World War Two 21, 54, 83, 157–9, 167, 169, 173,
    178–80, 183–6, 188, 197–9, 202–3, 205
    anticipation of 100, 105, 122–3, 125, 148, 155–6,
        190
    British War Cabinet 157, 181, 193, 195, 197
    Pacific theatre 178, 185, 186, 192, 199, 205–6
    Pacific War Council 191–2, 201
    post-war order 183, 202, 206, 208, 214–6,
        218–21, 222–3, 229, 232–3
    total war 190, 200, 202
    see also Advisory War Council *and* Pacific War
        Council
workers' compensation 65, 77, 85, 88, 104

Zinovieff letter 312, 317, 330